HUMAN ORIGINS AND THE IMAGE OF GOD

Human Origins and the Image of God

Essays in Honor of
J. WENTZEL VAN HUYSSTEEN

Edited by
Christopher Lilley and Daniel J. Pedersen

WILLIAM B. EERDMANS PUBLISHING COMPANY
GRAND RAPIDS, MICHIGAN

Wm. B. Eerdmans Publishing Co.
4035 Park East Court SE, Grand Rapids, MI 49546
www.eerdmans.com

© 2017 Christopher Lilley and Daniel J. Pedersen
All rights reserved

Hardcover edition 2017
Paperback edition 2021

ISBN 978-0-8028-7996-7

Library of Congress Cataloging-in-Publication Data

Names: Van Huyssteen, J. Wentzel (Jacobus Wentzel), 1942- honouree. |
   Lilley, Christopher, 1988- editor.
Title: Human origins and the image of God : essays in honor of J. Wentzel van Huyssteen /
   edited by Christopher Lilley and Daniel J. Pedersen.
Description: Grand Rapids : Eerdmans Publishing Co., 2017. | Includes bibliographical
   references and index.
Identifiers: LCCN 2016047031 | ISBN 9780802879967 (pbk. : alk. paper)
Subjects: LCSH: Theological anthropology—Christianity. | Human evolution—
   Religious aspects—Christianity. | Image of God.
Classification: LCC BT701.3 .H863 2017 | DDC 233—dc23
   LC record available at https://lccn.loc.gov/2016047031

In memory of Daniël van Huyssteen

Contents

Foreword x
M. CRAIG BARNES

Preface xii
CHRISTOPHER LILLEY AND DANIEL J. PEDERSEN

Introduction 1
J. Wentzel van Huyssteen and Interdisciplinary Theology
NIELS HENRIK GREGERSEN

Part 1: Natural Scientists

1. The Acquisition of Human Uniqueness 25
   How We Got from There to Here, and How We Did It So Fast
   IAN TATTERSALL

2. Religion as a Technology of Entanglement 43
   Dealing with the Beyond of Entanglements
   IAN HODDER

3. *Imago Dei* and Animal Domestication   64
   Cognitive-Evolutionary Perspectives on Human Uniqueness and the Imago Dei
   JUSTIN L. BARRETT AND TYLER S. GREENWAY

4. The Emergence of Religion   82
   What Evolution, the Human Niche, and Imagination Can Tell Us
   AGUSTÍN FUENTES

5. The Religious Sense   95
   Human Uniqueness, Human Evolution, and the Origins of Symbolism and Culture
   RICHARD POTTS

PART 2: PHILOSOPHERS AND HISTORIANS

6. Persons and Humans   113
   The Dignity and Distinctiveness of the Human Person
   KEITH WARD

7. Axiological Sensitivity   132
   Its Origins, Dynamic Structures, and Significance for Theological Anthropology
   WESLEY J. WILDMAN

8. Human Evolution   156
   Some Tough Questions for the Christian
   MICHAEL RUSE

9. Science, Technology, and Aesthetics   174
   The Manifestation of Adaptive Cognitive Fluidity in Humans
   JOHN HEDLEY BROOKE

Part 3: Theologians

10. Moral Origins and Evolutionary Ethics — 201
    Navigating the Maze in Conversation with J. Wentzel van Huyssteen
    CELIA DEANE-DRUMMOND

11. What Makes Theology Theology? — 225
    Conviction, Communicability, and Comprehensibility
    MICHAEL WELKER

12. Are We Alone? And Does It Matter? — 236
    The Narrative of Human Particularity
    DAVID FERGUSSON

13. Postfoundationalism and the Ethic of Responsibility — 250
    Duet or Duel?
    D. ETIENNE DE VILLIERS

14. Living with Strangers? — 273
    On Constructing Ethical Discourses
    DIRK J. SMIT

    Contributors — 314

    Index of Authors — 317

    Index of Subjects — 320

Foreword

Unlike the professors who have written these profound essays in honor of Professor J. Wentzel van Huyssteen, I'm not a scholar of theology and science. I'm the president of the seminary from which he recently retired, in spite of my pleading. And I'm his friend. I know him well. As I read the essays I kept thinking, "Yes, that sounds like Wentzel."

When readers see the dedication page of a book, they tend to skip past it, thinking it's something personal and has nothing to do with them. But this one's different. This book of extraordinary, state-of-the-art insights is dedicated to Professor van Huyssteen's deceased adult son Daniël.

I was there after Wentzel learned that Daniël got up in the middle of the night, went to the bed of his crying child, laid down to comfort him, and died. After that, the darkness piled up for Wentzel, his wife Hester, and their other children. But there was always something that made the grief almost bearable for him, something that protected him from sliding into nihilism, and something that goes to the core of his life's work in theology.

Wentzel is a private and quiet man, like most brilliant scholars, but when he talks about Daniël it's with so much deep longing that the tears return to my eyes. Hester and he knock themselves out to travel frequently from South Africa, where they retired, to get to California in order to spend precious time with their son's widow and her children. Any glimpse of Daniël in the faces of his children makes the long journey seem short. Missing Daniël, the yearning, and the relentless grief have pressed his theology for all of its worth.

Because he is an integrated man, Dr. van Huyssteen's theology is never just theoretical. It's his way of understanding human life, and the bedrock essence of it, that he gently offers to others. As one of the essayists suggests, he is "meaning obsessed" and sees this as core to the human soul, which is what many of these essays try to understand.

Daniël's death made it clear to Dr. van Huyssteen that human life is not only about its unique attributes, relationships, and capacities, but also its limitations and fragility. Evolution, no matter how seriously the scholars take it, has never figured out a remedy for fragility. And how do we find enough meaning to that?

So my caution is not to read these essays as just another collection of intellectual papers, but to see them as observations on the lifetime work of a scholar whose theology was there when he needed it to guide him through the deepest waters of life. No one expects to bury a child, but the theology of those who've been to that cross and still have life has great credibility.

These essays on the work of Dr. Wentzel van Huyssteen help us understand what it is about human life that makes it unique, and therefore a fragile beauty.

M. Craig Barnes
President
Princeton Theological Seminary

Preface

What, if anything, makes humans unique—perhaps even made in the image of God? How is human uniqueness informed by our evolutionary history? And how do our answers to these questions tell us more about what it means to be human?

In this volume some of the finest natural scientists, philosophers, and theologians from around the world answer these questions with essays on human uniqueness and human origins. Their answers are diverse: it is their quality that they share in common, not their ideas. Some disagree in nuance or detail, some in emphasis. Others disagree more completely, either in substance or in method. All reflect the best findings and arguments available in the interdisciplinary conversation today seeking to connect the evolutionary history of human origins to human uniqueness.

While human origins, human uniqueness, and the image of God are perennial topics, few works genuinely represent the insights of natural scientists, philosophers, and theologians in equal measure. This volume does. The division of this volume reflects these authors' distinct fields of origin. But, in a sign of interdisciplinary vigor, many authors pass beyond the traditional territories of their discipline in their essays. The breadth of claims reflects the enormity of the topic and a deep appreciation from very different scholars, and even from very different fields, for the insights others have to offer.

This spirit of engagement and appreciation is due, in large part, to the work of Wentzel van Huyssteen, who, through friendship and example, has brought these scholars in conversation with one another. This work is in celebration of his remarkable career.

Preface

If it is rare even for a distinguished scholar to be honored with a collection of essays devoted to him or her, then to be honored with two such collections is almost unheard of. In the case of Wentzel van Huyssteen, however, this is exactly the honor he is being accorded on the occasion of his retirement, in celebration of his work in theology and science at Princeton Theological Seminary.

It was not hard to justify according such an honor to van Huyssteen. Wentzel was the first person appointed to the first chair devoted solely to theology and science in the world. He was the first, and only, professor from Princeton Seminary ever to be invited to give the prestigious Gifford Lectures. His book based on those lectures, *Alone in the World? Human Uniqueness in Science and Theology*, has now been translated into several languages and has been published in more than one edition. In his more than two decades as the James I. McCord Professor of Theology and Science, hundreds of future pastors, preachers, social workers, civic activists, and academics have taken his classes. All told, he is one of the most influential thinkers on theology and science in theological education; and he is, without a doubt, the most important theologian from Princeton Theological Seminary to write on the subject since Charles Hodge, almost one hundred and fifty years ago.

This volume celebrates van Huyssteen's extraordinary career with essays themed around the most recent phase of his work: questions of human uniqueness and human origins. For a complete overview of his career, readers are invited to read Niels Gregersen's essay. In short, in the last decade van Huyssteen turned to concrete historical questions of human origins, not only out of genuine interest in the subject, but also as a test site for the ideas about interdisciplinary work and rationality he developed over the twenty years prior.

The nexus of human origins and human uniqueness was a natural choice. Both human uniqueness and human origins have been, and remain, central theological *loci*, topics to which theologians return century after century. Van Huyssteen, too, found himself drawn there. At the same time, questions of human origins—and, by extension, human uniqueness—are central questions in paleoanthropology and its cognate disciplines. As the findings of these fields grow, so does public interest. What have long been central questions for theologians have now become important for scientists and their reading public. Two very different fields of study now find themselves asking, "How exactly did human beings originate?" and "What, if anything, makes humans unique?"

Van Huyssteen, perceiving that the time was ripe, entered into the heart of this conversation with *Alone in the World?* In that work he advances the plausible, yet controversial, claim that humans are distinguished from other animals, and even our closest hominid cousins, by the possession of a religious disposition: an inclination to search for, and a capacity to perceive, ultimate reality. This disposition is not something supernatural, even if its object is. Rather, the human religious disposition appears to be a universal human trait—albeit, one that is manifest only in its concrete, culturally specific, instances—based around humans' embodied powers of language, symbol, morality, and ecstasy. On van Huyssteen's view, this is a wholly natural result of Darwinian evolution. If we are in the image of God, evolution is an iconographer.

Not surprisingly, van Huyssteen's views have invited challenge from all sides. But it is exactly this kind of active, friendly, yet serious dispute that, to van Huyssteen, makes interdisciplinary work like this meaningful, important, enjoyable, and, ultimately, rational. And despite widespread debate and disagreement, van Huyssteen has brought new information, new options, and new questions to the different fields wrestling with human origins and human uniqueness. *Alone in the World?* does not represent the last word, but instead the beginning of a new and vibrant conversation between sometimes estranged fields of study on these perennial questions.

The contributors to this volume are not only excellent scholars, but van Huyssteen's friends and colleagues. It is as much a testament to his scholarship as to his character that he has surrounded himself with so many excellent scholars who are willing to contribute to the celebration of his work. We would like to thank each one of them.

We would also like to thank *Theology Today* for permission to reprint several essays originally published in a special issue in Wentzel's honor, which began as papers given in celebration of Wentzel's work at Princeton Theological Seminary. Without the help of Gordon Mikoski and the generosity of *Theology Today* this volume would not be possible.

CHRISTOPHER LILLEY *and*
DANIEL J. PEDERSEN

Introduction

J. Wentzel van Huyssteen and Interdisciplinary Theology

NIELS HENRIK GREGERSEN

The aim of this chapter is to trace central lineages in J. Wentzel van Huyssteen's academic and spiritual journey in interdisciplinary theology. I'm not the first to do so. Van Huyssteen's oeuvre has already been discussed in a number of special journal issues, and even in a doctoral dissertation.[1] In the festschrift in honor of his sixty-fifth birthday, Kenneth A. Reynhout offers a comprehensive presentation of van Huyssteen's work, probably the best to date. Reynhout distinguishes between a first phase, "Critical Realism as rationality model for theology" (1970-89), a second phase on "the interdisciplinary shaping of rationality in a postmodern context" (1990-99), and a third phase on "the evolutionary origins of rationality and human uniqueness" (2009-present).[2]

---

1. Including *Zygon: Journal of Religion and Science* 32, no. 4 (1997) and 43, no. 2 (2008); *American Journal of Theology and Philosophy* 28, no. 3 (2007); and *Toronto Journal of Theology* 26, no. 2 (2010). See also G. M. H. Loubser, *A Public Theologian: A Critical Study of J. Wentzel van Huyssteen's Postfoundationalist Facilitation of Interdisciplinarity* (PhD diss., Stellenbosch University, 2012), accessible at http://hdl.handle.net/10019.1/20169.

2. Kenneth A. Reynhout, "The Evolution of van Huyssteen's Model of Rationality," in *The Evolution of Rationality: Interdisciplinary Essays in Honor of J. Wentzel van Huyssteen*, ed. F. Leron Shults (Grand Rapids: Eerdmans, 2006), 1-18. In the same volume, I offered my account of the development of van Huyssteen's work, especially in the first and second phases, "What Theology Might Learn (and Not Learn) from Evolutionary Psychology: A Postfoundationalist Theologian in Conversation with Pascal Boyer," 306-26, esp. 307-11. Some observations from this article are expanded below.

This chapter was originally published in *Theology Today* 72, no. 2 (July 2015) and is reprinted by kind permission.

In what follows, my focus will be less on van Huyssteen's chronological development and more on the different locations and intellectual venues for his interdisciplinary theology. Van Huyssteen has indeed undertaken a remarkable journey in his life and career. His homeland was and remains South Africa. As is evident from his "Introduction" to *Essays in Postfoundationalist Theology* (the first book he published after he moved to Princeton), he is acutely aware of the role of geography and place, not least with respect to the half-globe distance between Port Elizabeth and Princeton.[3] There is a difference between lecturing, say, at the Highlands Institute for American Religious and Philosophical Thought (since 2012, Institute for American Religious and Philosophical Thought) and at Princeton Theological Seminary. And again it is different to lecture in Canada and Korea, on the European Continent and in the United Kingdom. Nonetheless, van Huyssteen's program and style of reasoning is remarkably consistent from beginning to end, focused on elaborating an interdisciplinary view of human rationality and theology, in particular for the field of science and religion.

The Home Venue: South Africa

Let me begin with van Huyssteen's own beginnings in his South African context. There is here much of which I only know by hearsay, such as his time as minister in the Dutch Reformed Church (1971–72), followed by his appointment as professor and head of the Department of Religious Studies at the University of Port Elizabeth (1972–91). His early engagement with body phenomenology can be found in his M.A. thesis on *Truth and Relativism in the Thought of Maurice Merleau-Ponty* (1966). This indicates an influence from an interactionist phenomenology in his early education, which in fact reappears in his later work, for example, in his 2006 article "When Our Bodies Do the Thinking, Theology and Science Converge," where the "patterns of our daily experience" are seen as the inevitable entry point for interdisciplinary thinking.[4] No wonder, therefore, that Merleau-Ponty's work comes up again in the Gifford Lectures, and in van Huyssteen's later interaction with Maxine Sheets-Johnstone's phenomenology of body movement.[5]

---

3. J. Wentzel van Huyssteen, "Introduction," in *Essays in Postfoundationalist Theology* (Grand Rapids: Eerdmans, 1997), 1–8 (1).

4. J. Wentzel van Huyssteen, "When Our Bodies Do the Thinking, Theology and Science Converge," *American Journal of Theology and Philosophy* 27, nos. 2–3 (September 2006): 127–53 (153). See also below with reference to the Gifford Lectures.

5. J. Wentzel van Huyssteen, "Should Theology Take Evolutionary Ethics Seriously? A

In his intellectual baggage from South Africa the role of hermeneutics is perspicuous, as evidenced in the Powell Lectures that he delivered at the University of South Africa in 1987. Here he argues that biblical authority should not be appealed to as a discussion stopper, but rather be seen as a primary resource for how Christians come to terms with reality. The focus is on what he calls "the *quality* of the biblical text," including its continuous "referential power" for Christians using the biblical text as a "*way* to God."[6] The Bible is read from a hermeneutical reader-response perspective, informed by the work of James Barr and Paul Ricoeur. As a systematic theologian van Huyssteen is thus interested in

> the reader's actions involved in responding to the biblical text. This text (1) evokes religious experience, (2) implies ontological commitment, and (3) provides, through the metaphorical nature of the central concepts of biblical language, a striking continuity of reference in the history of Christian thought.[7]

By ascribing to a reader-response perspective (as early as 1987), van Huyssteen argues against a biblical literalism while also guarding himself against the opposite danger that the Bible is read at the mercy of a pure relativism: "The role of the reader can, however, never be pressed in such a way as to imply an infinite relativism on the part of the text or its authority."[8] The text has a reality of its own, one may say, which is then used to illuminate the world in front of us.[9]

In his early lectures on biblical hermeneutics, van Huyssteen is already

---

Conversation with Hannah Arendt and Maxine Sheets-Johnstone," *Nederduitse Gereformeerde Teologiese Tydskrif* 54, nos. 3–4 (2013): 275–85.

6. J. Wentzel van Huyssteen, "The Realism of the Text: A Perspective on Biblical Authority," in *Essays in Postfoundationalist Theology* (Grand Rapids: Eerdmans, 1997), 124–61 (158–60); italics in original. Later, in his Gifford Lectures, he speaks of the biblical texts as having a "gravitational force" or "pull," a power of attraction mediated by the reception history; see *Alone in the World? Human Uniqueness in Science and Theology* (Grand Rapids: Eerdmans, 2006), 115: "a canon, as a complex but identifiable core identity, and as embodying a rich galaxy of meanings, thus has gravitational force, or a gravitational pull that is the result of the way its own internal structure relates to and is construed in the always plural history of its interpretative relations."

7. Van Huyssteen, "The Realism of the Text," 151.

8. Van Huyssteen, "The Realism of the Text," 148.

9. As phrased by Paul Ricoeur: "To interpret is to explicate the type of being-in-the-world unfolded in front of the text"; see "The Hermeneutical Function of Distantiation," in *Hermeneutics and the Human Sciences: Essays on Language, Action, and Interpretation*, ed. John B. Thompson (Cambridge: Cambridge University Press, 1981), 131–44 (141).

referring to science-religion discussions. The natural sciences should not necessarily "be regarded as *the* paradigm for what constitutes reliable knowledge."[10] The future program of postfoundationalism was here in the making, though still couched mainly in the framework of a critical realism. But also later, when the postfoundationalist view was in place, as in the John Albert Hall Lectures given at the University of Victoria, Canada, published as *Duet or Duel? Theology and Science in the Postmodern World* in 1998, van Huyssteen emphasized the "semantic surplus" of theology in relation to science, thus arguing that

> the theological redescription of the world, therefore, can never be merely a mirroring of the world of science. It is always, rather, a complementary view in which the very special epistemological focus, distinct experiential dimension and heuristic apparatus of theological reflection creatively illuminate not only the world of science, but also the wider world around it.[11]

From one perspective, our scientific understanding of the world is capable of both constraining and expanding views of reality offered by theology, but on the other hand, theology has many other epistemic resources by addressing aspects of reality in which the natural sciences have no particular interest. Accordingly, theology is not to be described as a causal explanation in conflict with scientific explanations, but rather as a complementary interaction with reality. One thing is *causal explanation*; another thing is *semantic explanation*, that is, hermeneutical explication. Indeed, there remains a hermeneutical basis for all theological reasoning, though the questions of ontological truth-claims can't be replaced by the reading of classic texts of tradition: "All systematic theology may be said to be basically interpretative or hermeneutical, but then hermeneutical in a sense that concerns not only meaning but also the question of truth."[12] Certainly, van Huyssteen does not want to succumb to the "pan-linguistic folly" of some current strands of hermeneutical philosophy and deconstructive postmodernism.[13]

---

10. Van Huyssteen, "The Realism of the Text," 127; italics in original.

11. J. Wentzel van Huyssteen, *Duet or Duel? Theology and Science in the Postmodern World* (London: SCM, 1998), 161; cf. 126.

12. J. Wentzel van Huyssteen, *Theology and the Justification of Faith: Constructing Theories in Systematic Theology*, trans. H. F. Snijders (Grand Rapids: Eerdmans, 1989; Dutch ed., 1986), 171.

13. J. Wentzel van Huyssteen, "Response to Critics," *American Journal of Theology and Philosophy* 28, no. 3 (2007): 409–32 (431–32).

Introduction

Between Amsterdam and Munich

The doctoral dissertation on *Rationality and Faith in the Thought of Wolfhart Pannenberg* (Dutch, 1970) was based on studies at the Free University of Amsterdam (1966–70), and a longer stay at Ludwig Maximilian University of Munich during 1969. The topic was here not the rationality of theology per se, but the relation between rationality and faith. Whenever van Huyssteen speaks about epistemology, there is always an undercurrent of first-order religious commitments involved. One would not do justice to van Huyssteen's program in saying that we have faith commitments as a first-order phenomenon, then systematic theology as a second-order reflection on religious experience, and then epistemology as a third-level reflection, staying aloof, as it were, from first-order commitments. Rather, from beginning to end, van Huyssteen's program for a postfoundationalist epistemology emphasizes "the high degree of personal commitment in religious and theological theorizing."[14] While not shying away from taking an intellectual stance to faith commitments as part of a philosophical self-reflection, van Huyssteen underlines that we are never decontextualized human beings. Human beings are human persons, and human persons are both embodied and socially embedded. Therefore, it is finally not propositions that are rational or irrational, but human persons are rational, insofar as they give reasons for their stance in communication with others.

This personal orientation comes fully to the fore in van Huyssteen's critical questions to Wolfhart Pannenberg. In many ways, van Huyssteen's later *Theology and the Justification of Faith* from 1989 is an updated work in line with Pannenberg's *Wissenschaftstheorie und Theologie* from 1973. Here van Huyssteen won his street credits in science and religion by working through distinctive developments of contemporary philosophy of science—from the Vienna School through Karl Popper and Imre Lakatos to Thomas Kuhn and Larry Laudan. In contrast to Pannenberg, however, van Huyssteen also focused on the question of the role of metaphors in theological language, when presenting his version of a critical realism within theology.

Accordingly, there are some particular signatures to van Huyssteen's critical interaction with Pannenberg. First, whereas Pannenberg speaks about theology as a hypothesis of God capable of covering all relevant data, van Huyssteen translates Pannenberg as implying that a theology has proved itself, "if it has succeeded in maximally solving and meaningfully integrating problematic data and mankind's experiences of reality."[15] This emphasis on

---

14. Van Huyssteen, "Introduction," in *Essays in Postfoundationalist Theology*, 6.
15. Van Huyssteen, *Theology and the Justification of Faith*, 95.

problem-solving and experiential meaning can, with hindsight, be seen as a more pragmatic orientation of van Huyssteen's work. A few years later, van Huyssteen is translating Pannenberg's emphasis on theological propositions and "statements" into "convictions."[16] He notes,

> At this stage we may begin to pose a central critical question to Pannenberg: *How does he justify his view of the role of the theologian's personal religious commitment in the process of theorizing in theology, and his definition of truth and objectivity in theology and science?*[17]

This question, if I understand it correctly, is not merely an amendment to Pannenberg's program of theology, but a question about its foundations. Whereas for Pannenberg the idea of God—as a statement about something—is kept "distinct from the person who makes that statement,"[18] van Huyssteen's order goes the other way around, from personal convictions to theological statements. This is not an innocent reversal of order since van Huyssteen eventually questions the distinction between "the context of discovery" and "the context of justification" so central to Popper's (and Lakatos's) philosophy of science. Accordingly, he asks "whether personal faith—which operates in 'the context of discovery'—can really be separated from the theoretical context of justification. Why not consciously allow for the accounting of this subjective element from the outset in one's method?"[19] In other words, the level of the *explanans* and the level of the *explanandum* can't be cleanly separated. Religious interpretation is always self-involving, whereby the explainer himself or herself becomes part of what is to be explained. Human beings are, to use the phrase of Charles Taylor, "self-interpreting animals."[20]

---

16. J. Wentzel van Huyssteen, "Truth and Commitment in Theology and Science: A Critical Appraisal of Wolfhart Pannenberg's Perspective" (1989), in *Essays in Postfoundationalist Theology*, 53–72 (59).

17. Van Huyssteen, "Truth and Commitment," 58; italics in original.

18. J. Wentzel van Huyssteen, "Systematic Theology and Philosophy of Science: The Need for Methodological and Theoretical Clarity in Theology" (1981), in *Essays in Postfoundationalist Theology*, 105–23 (119).

19. Van Huyssteen, "Systematic Theology," 122.

20. Charles Taylor, "Self-interpreting Animals," in *Philosophical Papers*, vol. 1, *Human Agency and Language* (Cambridge: Cambridge University Press, 1985), 45–76.

Critical Realism

When writing *Theology and the Justification of Faith*, van Huyssteen hardly had at hand a fully satisfying model for dealing with the role of the personal commitments and social embedment in theology. What he had at his disposal was a "critical-realist perspective,"[21] by which he situated himself in the Anglo-American discussion on science and religion. Against the trend of postliberal theology, as found in George Lindbeck's work, van Huyssteen insists that religious experience is and remains an indispensable background for theology, not replaceable by a Wittgensteinian emphasis on the cultural-linguistic performances within the church. As a matter of fact, "people grapple with religious experience also outside established denominations, and therefore the theologian is functioning contextually also by defining and attempting to solve valid problems outside existing churches."[22] First, the reality depiction of second-order theological statements presupposes the claims of first-order religious commitments: "At the basis of the reasons for using this term [critical realism] is the *conviction* that what we are provisionally conceptualizing in theology really exists."[23] Second, van Huyssteen makes clear that theological statements rest on a fluid network of religious metaphors and models, which are not fully translatable into theoretical statements but rather have an *explorative* nature: "we are not simply describing realities that are equally accessible by other means. Language does not merely represent or reflect reality; it also constitutes reality. In this sense metaphoric language opens up to us, both creatively and exploratively, the reality of which we speak, since what we see as reality is to a large extent creatively and exploratively determined by the metaphoric potential of the language in which reality is depicted."[24] Third, van Huyssteen is keenly aware that the feature of a "convergent realism" in some of the mature sciences (e.g., geology reaching still better approximations to the movements of tectonic plates) is "virtually impossible" in theology; with

---

21. Taylor, "Self-interpreting Animals," 125–77.
22. Taylor, "Self-interpreting Animals," 166.
23. Van Huyssteen, *Theology and the Justification of Faith*, 155; italics mine. Van Huyssteen's early position is presented in condensed form in "Experience and Explanation: The Justification of Cognitive Claims in Theology" (1988), in *Essays in Postfoundationalist Theology*, 162–79. The author points out that he is only willing to argue "for a qualified and weak form of critical realism" (167), in so far as the referential claims are derived from "basic assumption and good reasons," without the reasons being conclusive and without the claim of a progressively convergent realism. See also my article, "Critical Realism and Other Realisms," in *Fifty Years in Science and Theology: Ian G. Barbour and His Legacy*, ed. Robert J. Russell (Aldershot: Ashgate, 2004), 77–96.
24. Van Huyssteen, *Theology and the Justification of Faith*, 137–38.

Ernan McMullin he worries about a too direct move from scientific realism to a critical realism in theology: "I think that anyone considering the possibilities of scientific realism for theology should be extremely wary of an uncritical, superficial transferring of the realism of science to the domain of religious belief, and to theology as the reflection on the claims of this belief."[25]

Here again, the hermeneutical character of van Huyssteen's argument comes to the fore. Theology only refers to divine reality in the context of linguistic networks that open up possibilities of human engagement with divinity. Accordingly, theological models and metaphors are *redescribing* the world(s) of nature as already (partly) described and (partly) explained by the sciences.[26] This hermeneutical orientation may also explain why van Huyssteen never followed otherwise popular attempts to apply Lakatos's model of rationality to the justification of religious truth-claims.[27] The realism, in other words, is not between words and things (as if they were two quite different areas), but applies to *structures*—in theology to the *relations* between God and humanity/world, as apprehended by religious interpreters. Here indeed there is a similarity to the basic realist claim that also "the scientist is in a creative way discovering the *structures* of the world."[28]

This critical realism was seriously transformed in the wake of van Huyssteen's later pragmatist orientation. Seen from the postfoundational perspective, realism "does not represent a discovered fact or a justified position, but rather the methodological presupposition of our praxis of inquiry."[29] The

---

25. Van Huyssteen, *Theology and the Justification of Faith*, 150 and 155. See also Fabio Gironi, "The Theological Hijacking of Realism: Critical Realism in 'Science and Religion,'" *Journal of Critical Realism* 11, no. 1 (2012): 40–75. Gironi wrongly presupposes that when theologians such as van Huyssteen refer to the reality of God, they slip in "a Reality at the top (or at the base) of the order of being, well beyond both the human and the natural ontological stratum" (48–49). If God is the infinite or encompassing Reality, there is no such natural-supernatural dichotomy.

26. The concept of "redescription" only comes up occasionally in *Theology and the Justification of Faith* (e.g., 157), but attains a central role in van Huyssteen, *Duet or Duel?* 125–28 and 160–64. Van Huyssteen kindly refers to my insistence that the role of offering causal explanations and the task of giving semantic explanation should not be conflated. The term "redescription," by the way, has its provenance in Donald Davidson's concept of "radical interpretation," where no formal translation schemes exist.

27. See van Huyssteen's criticism of Nancey Murphy's bold work in her *Theology in an Age of Scientific Reasoning* (Ithaca, NY: Cornell University Press, 1990), in "Is the Postmodernist Always a Postfoundationalist? Nancey Murphy's Lakatosian Model for Theology," *Theology Today* 50, no. 3 (1993): 373–86, reprinted in *Essays in Postfoundationalist Theology*, 73–90.

28. Van Huyssteen, *Theology and the Justification of Faith*, 151 (with reference to Ernan McMullin).

29. See his "Postfoundationalism in Theology and Science," in *Rethinking Theology and*

realism is thus a *presupposition* undergirding the multiple interactions of the believer with worldly realities, when speaking of the encompassing reality of God. Since there is no strict dichotomy between the "natural" and the "supernatural," no reductionist choice should be made between scientific and theological descriptions of reality.[30]

Princeton: A New Habitat for Interdisciplinary Theology

Princeton became and remains the second home for J. Wentzel and Hester van Huyssteen. Preceded by a fellowship at the Center of Theological Inquiry in 1990, van Huyssteen came to Princeton Theological Seminary January 1, 1992, as the inaugural holder of the James I. McCord professorship in theology and science. Here at Princeton he found a fertile collegial work space that allowed him to teach science and religion courses continuously, to put the books he wanted to work with in the curricula, and to discuss them intensely with the excellent students at the seminary. Always work with the best and newest literature in the field became his working motto, as also revealed in his many interactions with contemporary scientists and philosophers. Any reader is therefore well educated through van Huyssteen's essays, resulting from the sometimes-hectic lecture program of the new Princetonian. In fact, Princeton Theological Seminary not only served as a home base, but also as an open door to the outside world—not only to the American Academy of Religion and the Highlands Institute, but also to the creative triangle between Princeton, Scotland, and Seoul, and to many Canadian and European audiences.

Already the inaugural lecture for the James I. McCord chair, "Theology and Science: The Quest for a New Apologetics," revealed many of the topics to be developed in the coming years. "The question how theology and science should relate to one another is, of course, neither a theological nor a scientific issue. It is, rather, an *epistemological* issue, that is, an issue about how two very different claims to knowledge are to be related."[31] With Philip Clayton, van Huyssteen pointed out the "contextualist shift" in the contemporary philoso-

---

Science: Six Models for the Current Dialogue, ed. Niels Henrik Gregersen and J. Wentzel van Huyssteen (Grand Rapids: Eerdmans, 1998), 13–50 (39). Or as put in Nicholas Rescher's terms: "*realism is a position to which we are constrained not by the push of evidence, but by the pull of purpose*" (50; italics in original).

30. J. Wentzel van Huyssteen, "Pluralism and Interdisciplinarity: In Search of Theology's Public Voice," *American Journal of Theology and Philosophy* 22, no. 1 (January 2001): 65–87 (78).

31. J. Wentzel van Huyssteen, "Theology and Science: The Quest for a New Apologetics" (1993), in *Essays in Postfoundationalist Theology*, 215–37 (221).

phy of the natural sciences, where the search for explanation and intelligibility is "relativized and becomes an element within the broader hermeneutical task of science."[32] Also, the distinction between personal, communal, and transcommunal explanations comes up in the inaugural lecture, the latter offering new ways of articulating the theological tradition of apologetics and natural theology in a contemporary context.[33] Even the phrase "the shaping of rationality" is announced, later to become the title of van Huyssteen's main work in epistemology, *The Shaping of Rationality* (1999).

The program of a postfoundationalist theology earlier announced was refined and presented in a fuller scale in *The Shaping of Rationality: Toward Interdisciplinarity in Theology and Science*. As rightly observed by Josh Reeves, van Huyssteen here uses both a negative and a positive strategy in defining the space for postfoundationalism.[34] The negative strategy is to show that both foundationalism and nonfoundationalism fail—the first by discouraging conversation by reference to the safe haven of scientific evidence, the latter by referring to the safe haven of establishing holistic webs of beliefs, such as in narrative theology. The positive strategy is to show that postfoundationalism steers a middle course by offering the best from the worlds of modernity and postmodernity. For example, accept science for what it is, the best bet we have for understanding the structure of the universe and evolution of life and humanity. But also, acknowledge that rationality remains person- and situation-relative, always undergirded by a flexible use of commonsense deliberations, reaping from many resources of human experience.

In *The Shaping of Rationality*, van Huyssteen reemphasized the earlier hermeneutical orientation, while giving hermeneutical interpretation a pragmatist twist. The hermeneutical orientation was retained insofar as he continues to underline the pre-theoretical character of rationality while pointing to the formative role of traditions as "boundaries of our habitations."[35] Traditions are inescapable as our epistemic starting points—they are the boundaries from which we address the world. But traditions are not inevitably our final destination—we can both extend our traditions by entering into transcommunal

---

32. Van Huyssteen, "Theology and Science," 232.
33. Van Huyssteen, "Theology and Science," 232 and 234.
34. Josh Reeves, "Problems for Postfoundationalists: Evaluating J. Wentzel van Huyssteen's Interdisciplinary Theory of Rationality," *The Journal of Religion* 93, no. 2 (2013): 131–50.
35. See J. Wentzel van Huyssteen, *The Shaping of Rationality: Toward Interdisciplinarity in Theology and Science* (Grand Rapids: Eerdmans, 1999), 252–59, where he (following Delwin Brown, *Boundaries of Our Habitations: Tradition and Theological Construction* [New York: State University of New York Press, 1994]) discusses how rational self-reflection is shaped by traditions without being tied up with unnegotiable truth-claims.

dialogues and also take leave of traditions, even if we continue to be marked by them.³⁶

The new pragmatist orientation implies that rationality no longer resides first and foremost in the capacity to open up interpretative horizons, but in the capacity of rational agents to form responsible judgments and seek optimal understandings, given the specific context and the specific problems to be solved. Human rationality is indeed humane.

There are several philosophical inspirations behind this shift of orientation in van Huyssteen's work.³⁷ The first name to be mentioned is probably Nicholas Rescher, from whom van Huyssteen learned to speak of the *dimensions of rationality*. Alongside the cognitive dimension we have the evaluative and the pragmatic dimensions, which correspond to the human pursuit of values and appropriate action. With Rescher, van Huyssteen regards science as the prime case for the cognitive pursuit of truth, while insisting that scientific rationality is just one subset of rationality at work.³⁸ Accordingly, philosophers and theologians must learn to acquire what Rescher calls a "dissensus tolerance" between the different forms of reasoning, each proper for different and distinctive purposes.³⁹ Finally from Rescher comes the view that any "theoretical cycle" of argumentation is always accompanied by an "applicative cycle" of real-life implementation, which finally determines the fertility of our leading ideas, hence deciding about their feasibility.⁴⁰

Another source of inspiration is Harold Brown's theory of rationality, which led van Huyssteen to see the concept of rational beliefs to be *derivative* to the reasoning of agents, who are making the rational estimates about truth, values, and adequate behavior.⁴¹ Rationality is not only a general capacity, but also an "epistemic skill" to be learned, in analogy to physical skills.

Finally, Calvin Schrag had used the term "transversal rationality" to de-

---

36. See further van Huyssteen, "When Our Bodies Do the Thinking," 141–46, esp. 143.

37. Again, this pragmatic orientation is anticipated in van Huyssteen's early reception of Larry Laudan's work in *Theology and the Justification of Faith*, 172–90.

38. Van Huyssteen, *Essays in Postfoundationalist Theology*, 246–47; *The Shaping of Rationality*, 128–29 and 162: "I think the selection of science as our clearest example of the *cognitive/theoretical dimension* of rationality at work is indeed justified. What is not justified, however, is any claim for the superiority of scientific rationality, and any attempt to extend uncritically the nature of a strictly scientific rationality to the rationality of religious or any other reflection." Cf. Nicholas Rescher, *Rationality* (Oxford: Clarendon, 1988).

39. Van Huyssteen, "When Our Bodies Do the Thinking," 150.

40. Nicholas Rescher, *A System of Pragmatic Idealism*, vol. 1, *Human Knowledge in Idealistic Perspective* (Princeton: Princeton University Press, 1992), 175.

41. Van Huyssteen, *Essays in Postfoundationalist Theology*, 247–54; *The Shaping of Rationality*, 142–50. Cf. Harold Brown, *Rationality* (London: Routledge, 1990).

scribe the fact that rationality is not domain-specific but emerges in the intersection, crossing-over, or interweaving of forms of rational discernment in different areas of life—from the sciences to religion and everyday practices.[42] In a sense, this open-ended transversality replaces the modernist concept of unrestricted universality.[43]

Interestingly, the concept of transversality itself goes back to Jean-Paul Sartre's concept of the intersection of intentionalities, by which past experiences are retained in ever new intentional acts of the I. What would have happened if van Huyssteen had written out the phenomenological insights undergirding his epistemological reflections? Anyway, the comprehensive view of rationality that van Huyssteen develops from beginning to end accentuates that rational agents are always embedded in communicative contexts, in which agents have to account for their views while taking issue with the best candidates on the market of rational ideas, and having to apply these ideas in real-life contexts. On the one hand, there exists no solitary epistemological subject à la Kant (but only contextually situated individuals). On the other hand, rational procedures guide our behavior, even where we have no foundational starting points available. Our steps forward can't be controlled by following rules set up prior to our walking.

In consequence, the dialogue between science and religion shows different aspects of contact: (1) There are *shared resources of rationality* between theology and the sciences (e.g., logic and the search for order and intelligibility). (2) There are *overlapping elements of rationality* (such as the role of models and metaphors in theorizing, and our realist instincts guiding our search for truth). (3) We have very *distinctive forms of rationality* that cannot easily be transferred from one discipline to another. Mathematical equations in science, for example, have no counterpart in theological rationality, whereas the search for meaning, value, and existential relevance in theology has no immediate analogue in the proper sciences (though, perhaps, in popular science).[44]

---

42. Van Huyssteen, *The Shaping of Rationality*, 132–39. Cf. Calvin O. Schrag, *The Resources of Rationality: A Response to the Postmodern Challenge* (Bloomington: Indiana University Press, 1992), and especially, "Transversal Rationality," in *The Question of Hermeneutics*, ed. T. J. Stapleton (Amsterdam: Kluwer, 1994).

43. Van Huyssteen, "When Our Bodies Do the Thinking," 137; cf. 140: "transversality ultimately replaces universality."

44. Van Huyssteen, *Duet or Duel?* 160–66.

Was van Huyssteen Ever a Postmodernist?

While distancing himself from the relativistic versions of postmodernism, there should be no doubt that during the 1990s van Huyssteen felt postmodernism as a liberation from the imprisonment under too abstract notions of rationality. "In a postfoundationalist epistemology the modernist distinction between 'objective' empirical (read: scientific) reasons and more 'subjective' ethical, religious, or aesthetic reasons is revealed as nonsensical."[45] Accordingly, he was seen by many (perhaps even by himself at that time?) as a postmodernist thinker. I must admit that I sometimes asked myself at that time, Are the cognitive contents of theology, and the empirical elements of scientific reasoning taken sufficiently seriously in the wake of van Huyssteen's pragmatist turn and postmodern leanings? So, in the fall of 1996, when we together wrote the introduction to our coedited book, *Rethinking Theology and Science*, we agreed on using the term "cognitive pluralism" as a description of the postmodern situation rather than seeing postmodernism as a normative concept in contrast to modernism.

Those fearing in those days that van Huyssteen was about to go down the slope of postmodernism should be aware that for him the discourse of postmodernity remains in contact with modernity, just as the discourses of modernity remain within the web of postmodern discourse.[46] Uncompromisingly stated, "postmodern thought is undoubtedly part of the modern and not modern thought coming to an end."[47] For van Huyssteen there is a "to-and-fro movement" between modernity and postmodernism, not a unilateral road leading from modernity to postmodernity. Indeed, as we will now see, there is even a strong sense of a premodernity living in us and being with us in the form of phylogenetically acquired forms of cognition.

The Venue of Evolutionary Epistemology

In *Duet or Duel?* (1998), the issue of epistemology was now also approached from an evolutionary perspective. With evolutionary epistemology, van

---

45. Van Huyssteen, *The Shaping of Rationality*, 150.
46. J. Wentzel van Huyssteen, "Is There a Postmodern Challenge in Theology and Science?" (1997), in *Essays in Postfoundationalist Theology*, 266-79 (279). See also *Duet or Duel?* 25-26.
47. J. Wentzel van Huyssteen, "Should We Be Trying So Hard to Be Postmodern? A Response to Drees, Haught, and Yeager," *Zygon: Journal of Religion and Science* 32, no. 1 (March 1997): 567-84 (582).

Huyssteen pointed to the common biological roots of human rationality. These roots may explain, at least in part, the "universal traits" of human reasoning:

> Evolutionary epistemology thus reveals the process of evolution as a belief-gaining process, a process that in humans, too, is shaped preconsciously. All our beliefs, and I would argue, also our religious beliefs, thus have evolutionary origins and were established by mechanisms working reliably in the world of our ancestors. This still does not mean, however, that the theory of evolution by natural selection can offer an adequate explanation for beliefs that far transcend their biological origins. But this again underlines the fact that cognition is a general characteristic of all living beings, and that human rationality, therefore, can only be fully understood if its biological roots are understood.[48]

So, while evolutionary epistemology certainly can explain the general trajectories of human reasoning, it can't explain the particular routes of philosophical and religious traditions and the particular ways of knowing and arguing within these traditions. For the same reason, particular forms of belief, such as Christology and Trinitarian belief, or Zen Buddhism, can't be said to be validated by evolution, even though some of their basic assumptions follow general trajectories honed by evolution.

Van Huyssteen takes a very similar position in regard to the idea of evolutionary ethics. The fact that morality is rooted in our biological makeup as social embodied primates does not mean that particular moral codes can be derived from evolution: "From the evolutionary genesis of our moral awareness we cannot derive moral codes for right or wrong. Accepting that our moral awareness has evolved also means accepting that our moral codes may not be fixed forever as unchangeable entities."[49] Van Huyssteen thus follows the same kind of reasoning regarding the evolutionary roots of religion and ethics. Just as there is no reason to distrust empathy as a guideline for ethics, there is no a priori reason to distrust the sense of the divine in religion, though we can't claim that particular ethical or religious systems are simply true by being biologically rooted. Rather, biological evolution facilitates a cultural space for evaluating truth-claims and ethical judgment.

If *The Shaping of Rationality* could be read as an epistemological withdrawal from more substantial interactions between science and theology, *Duet or Duel?* evidenced that this was far from the author's intention. And soon the

---

48. Van Huyssteen, *Duet or Duel?* 151–52.
49. Van Huyssteen, "Should Theology Take Evolutionary Ethics Seriously?" 282.

Introduction

transversal concept of "interdisciplinarity" laid out in *The Shaping of Rationality* was to be applied to the discussion of human origins and human nature. Put in Rescher's terms, the "theoretical cycle" of postfoundationalist epistemology was to be exercised on material problems in a large-scale "applicative cycle" involving paleoanthropology and theological anthropology.

The Venue of Paleoanthropology

I am here, of course, referring to van Huyssteen's 2004 Gifford Lectures at Edinburgh University, *Are We Alone? Science and Theology on Human Uniqueness*, later published under a slightly changed title.[50] (What the old pharaohs aimed to achieve by mummification—immortality—van Huyssteen achieved by publication.)

Alone in the World? discusses the species specificity of humanity in close conversation with leading paleoanthropologists and archaeologists, and in more critical interaction with evolutionary cognitive theories of religion. How to speak of humans as created in the image and likeness of God in this context? I guess I am correct in saying that van Huyssteen's book is the only comprehensive book dealing with this subject matter from a theologically informed perspective. He was indeed alone in creating a fertile space for an interaction between paleoanthropology and theological anthropology.

The point of *Alone in the World?* is exactly to show how "transversal lines of argument between evolutionary epistemology and paleoanthropology converge and intersect on the fact that the very first modern humans were distinct in the evolution of their symbolic, cognitive fluid minds."[51] It is this "cognitive fluidity" (a term coined by Steven Mithen) that leads to the creative symbolic behavior witnessed in cave art and in the emergence of religious awareness.

With evolutionary epistemology, van Huyssteen understands human species as a particular form of an information-processing system: "Not only has evolution produced cognitive phenomena, but evolution itself can be as a cognition process or, more precisely, a cognition process."[52] We are thus still carrying with us earlier instincts (e.g., fear of snakes) in a phylogenetic memory that is not in principle different from the hissing of kittens at dogs.[53] Moreover, this phylogenetic memory must have some adaptive value, also for

---

50. Van Huyssteen, *Alone in the World?*
51. Van Huyssteen, *Alone in the World?* 212.
52. Van Huyssteen, *Alone in the World?* 87.
53. Van Huyssteen, *Alone in the World?* 84.

early humans. Even if not totally correct, such species-wide knowledge has proven to be overall reliable by facilitating appropriate forms of orientation vis-à-vis the environment. Evolutionary epistemologists such as Franz Wuketits admit that human cognition also entails a drive for metaphysical explanation, including notions of another world and life after death.[54] But curiously enough, Wuketits finds this religious awareness to be fully unreliable, and without any importance for the future development of the human race. Here van Huyssteen raises two questions to Wuketits:

> Why should we, so suddenly and only on this point, distrust the phylogenetic memories of our direct ancestors, and why should the emergence of religious consciousness be explained only in terms of specific life-conditions in prehistoric times? Might there not be something about being human, something about the human condition itself, that could offer us a slightly different perspective on the enduring need for religious faith?[55]

Van Huyssteen is fully aware that evolutionary epistemology can't be used to bolster the correctness of particular religious views, just as it can't serve as a proof for the reality of God.[56] But he insists that the space opened by religious awareness, for reasons of consistency, should be treated fully on par with other outcomes of evolutionarily evolved cognition, also by evolutionary epistemologists. As a matter of fact, the questioning of the material limitations of human existence seems to be species-specific to humanity.

Moreover, central to evolutionary epistemology is its interactionist orientation.[57] The adaptations of early humans to their environments gave rise to an intra-organismic development, not least evidenced in the development of the prefrontal cortex and in the particular array of human *uses* of our flexible brains. But the process also goes the other way around: the shaping of rationality through adaptive evolution is accompanied by the constructive shaping of the environment by human communities, building up external niches for human communities in a gradual move from natural habitats to sociocultural homes, including religious traditions.

---

54. Van Huyssteen, *Alone in the World?* 94.
55. Van Huyssteen, *Alone in the World?* 218.
56. Van Huyssteen, *Alone in the World?* 102-9.
57. Toward the end of *Alone in the World?* (276), van Huyssteen quotes Maurice Merleau-Ponty's "phenomenology of the flesh": "I cannot understand the function of the living body except by enacting it myself, and except in so far as I am a body which rises towards the world" (Maurice Merleau-Ponty, *Phenomenology of Perception*, trans. Donald A. Landes [London: Routledge and Kegan Paul, 1962; French ed., 1945]), 75.

I cannot but note that van Huyssteen's program here seems closely akin to later work done at Harvard University on the idea of *deep history*, in which also the traditional divide between historical time and prehistory evaporates.[58] Both Daniel Lord Smail and van Huyssteen understand human personhood and community formation from an interactionist perspective that focuses on human agency as embodied in its relationships to ecological environments, constantly remolded by human intervention, and guided by the use of symbolic thought unique to the human species. As a result, we may not be so vastly different from our forebears. As van Huyssteen notes, the Cro-Magnons of the Upper Paleolithic were, in a sense, "us."[59]

From a methodological perspective, this interactionist view of biological and cultural evolution differs from the fixed-view understanding of the human mind that one finds in the works of some proponents of the evolutionary cognitive theory of religion. Pascal Boyer, for example, presupposes that the human mind works as a semiautomatic machine, restlessly generating foreseeable outputs in reaction to minimal inputs. Concepts of God, for example, are generated by a "Hyperactive Agency Detection Device" (HADD), which comes up spontaneously when humans are confronted with fear. According to Steven Mithen, by contrast, our minds are evolved through a general intelligence that was later specialized, until it reached the level of cognitive fluidity: the symbolic threshold. In this view we are embodied beings with flexible minds, capable of exercising a broad array of self-reflective capacities. Art, morality, and religion are thus to be seen as typical expressions of the human mind. Accordingly, human symbolic behavior can't be divided into early modern constructs of a natural "agency detection device" versus a "hyperactive" one. Similarly, ritual behaviors can't be categorized into too clear-cut distinctions between what is useful, or adaptive, in a mundane sense, and what is more than useful, such as play and religious imagination. While van Huyssteen agrees with evolutionary psychology that there is a "naturalness" to religious imagination, he insists that naturalness is not the same as pre-reflective automaticity. There is no reason to believe that the religious mentality of early humans was devoid of self-reflection.[60] Religious imagination is thus a "natural" propensity, using the same neuronal structures and the same cognitive fluidity as in tool construction, in the planning of a hunt, in the moral ordering of social sys-

---

58. Daniel Lord Smail, *On Deep History and the Brain* (Berkeley: University of California Press, 2006); *Deep History: The Architecture of Past and Present*, ed. Andrew Shyrock and Daniel Lord Smail (Berkeley: University of California Press, 2011).

59. Van Huyssteen, *Alone in the World?* 218.

60. Van Huyssteen, *Alone in the World?* 261–70.

tems, or in the production of art and deliberate burial sites, showing the vital importance of religious imagination for Neolithic communities.[61]

Of special interest to van Huyssteen's project is what Ian Tattersall has called the "cultural exploration" from 60,000 to 30,000 years ago. Here we find new expressions of art and other expressions of a symbolic awareness that seem to go beyond the realm of the visible. Van Huyssteen is well aware that archaeological findings and paleoanthropological material are open to interpretation. Any paleoanthropologist needs to muse on the meanings of the findings, and to make inferences to the best explanation of the available data. Could we have flutes without ritualized dancing? Could we have cave paintings without a symbolic meaning that goes beyond mere referential meaning? Could we have burial sites with the heads placed toward the east without having belief in afterlife? The vote of van Huyssteen to these questions is a resounding no. And do perhaps some cave paintings indicate shamanism as an early form of religion, but other sites not? Could we have a symbolic mind prior to the formation of the laryngeal tract, the precondition for complex oral speech? The vote of van Huyssteen to these questions is an emphatic yes. From here he goes on to raise a larger set of new research questions: What role might the body language of bipedal walk have had prior to oral language, for sexual exposure, for example? And were our ancestors just imagining the invisible in linguistic forms? Couldn't a religious meaning be carried by a deliberate ordering of material structures, as evidenced in Çatalhöyük, where the bodies of the deceased were buried inside the houses, excavated after some time, dismembered, using the sculls as pillars for new houses, while ornamenting other sculls and body remnants? Moreover, are we a species that has discovered God as "praying animals" (Robert W. Jenson), not just by being a species speaking about "the beyond," but a species experiencing being addressed by God? Similarly, what is the relation between early religion and the morality of living together in groups, with rules for food sharing, kinshipping, and burial sites?[62]

Questions such as these feature centrally in *Alone in the World?* as well as in the subsequent discussions thereof. Van Huyssteen is the first to admit the unknowns.[63] But it is consistent with his own program that such questions can

---

61. On burial sites, see J. Wentzel van Huyssteen's reflection on Ian Hodder's studies on the understanding of individual selfhood and transgenerational transcendence in the Lower Neolithic society of Çatalhöyük (Turkey), "The Historical Self: Memory and Religion at Çatalhöyük," in *Religion at Work in a Neolithic Society: Vital Matters*, ed. Ian Hodder (Cambridge: Cambridge University Press, 2014), 109-33 (114-21).

62. Questions of social hierarchy, food-sharing, sexual intercourse, and the possibility of including non-kin in "kinshipping" are central to the program of "deep history."

63. See, in particular, van Huyssteen, "Response to My Critics."

Introduction

only be dealt with in an academically responsible manner, if one is willing to participate in long-term conversations with the best experts in the field—even though they sometimes disagree. Some argue for a more gradualist approach, others for a more discontinuous development. As argued by van Huyssteen, the distinction between gradualism and discontinuity can't be kept up rigidly.[64] There are both a continuity between humans and higher apes, and a discontinuity in the sense that oral speech and symbolic language (and the fluid mind undergirding it) are found only in the surviving human lineage that happens to entail agential and self-reflective persons not quite unlike us. We are, in brief, "alone in the world" in a twofold sense: from a paleoanthropological view, we are alone by being the last remnant of the hominids on planet Earth; from a theological perspective we are alone by "being invited into a personal relationship with God."[65]

A Trans-generational Concept of the *imago Dei*

What in the end is important for van Huyssteen's theological project when reinterpreting the biblical symbol of the *imago Dei* is an understanding of human beings as embodied persons endowed with a symbolic awareness.[66] Van Huyssteen makes a tour de force through the interpretation history of the concept of the *imago*. Here he is particularly drawn to the view of John Calvin, who stated that it may be particularly appropriate to say that humanity is created in the image of God in respect of the human soul but that the image extends also to other aspects of human existence—"there was no part even of the body in which some rays of glory did not shine."[67] Similarly he's tracking the record of twentieth-century interpretations of the *imago* interpreted in terms of substantive capacities, functional roles, and relational structures, pausing (with his typical sense of humor) to note that Karl Barth once remarked that laughter and smoking also belong to the *proprium* of being created in the im-

---

64. Van Huyssteen, *Alone in the World?* 199–203.
65. Van Huyssteen, *Alone in the World?* 121.
66. As for the evolution of personhood, see J. Wentzel van Huyssteen, "When Were We Persons? Why Hominid Evolution Holds the Key to Embodied Personhood," *Neue Zeitschrift für Systematische Theologie* 52, no. 4 (2010): 329–49. On *imago Dei* and Christology, see "What Makes Us Human? The Interdisciplinary Challenge to Theological Anthropology and Christology," *Toronto Journal of Theology* 26, no. 2 (Fall 2010): 143–60.
67. John Calvin, *Institutes of the Christian Religion* (1559), I.15, quoted in van Huyssteen, *Alone in the World?* 111 and 131.

age and likeness of God.[68] Yet in the end van Huyssteen sides with Pannenberg in his eschatological interpretation of the *imago* (finally a Lutheran sneaks in!). The point is here that Pannenberg's wider eschatological perspective is able to integrate the substantive, functional, and relational aspects of the *imago*. Not that the *imago* is only a matter of a future realization, but the *imago* is a task waiting to be realized for any human being. The capacity for being humane is a *gift* of creation, endowed to the human species, and yet it is a *destiny* in front of us.[69]

According to Christian anthropology, the full humanity and the true image of God is fully realized in Jesus Christ (Col. 1:15; Heb. 2:6-9). Even though van Huyssteen is critical of too eager dogmatic attempts at showing that the *imago* is only understandable from a Trinitarian perspective (as if being a Christian was a matter of having a particular Christian *gnosis*), he does indeed present a picture of what it means to be a human person, which, in my view, can best be interpreted as related to an economic understanding of the Father, Son, and Holy Spirit, integrating creation, Christology, and the future fulfillment. The symbolic awareness of humans thus allows us to be in discourse with God (both as speaking and as listening), and to be connected to one another in caring relationships, also to our "sister species." In this understanding, the final basis for speaking of a human likeness to God does not lie merely in our *possession* of some intellectual capacities, but in specific *uses* of these abilities.[70] Thus understood, speaking of the *imago Dei* can't be a descriptive affair only. It must also take the form of a directive speech, orienting our ways of thinking and informing our modes of action.[71]

Conclusion

Allow me at the end to compare the outcomes of van Huyssteen's theological itinerary with another Gifford Lecturer, Bruno Latour, who gave the lectures in Edinburgh in 2013. In *We Have Never Been Modern*,[72] Latour argued that

---

68. Karl Barth, *Church Dogmatics* III/2 (Edinburgh: T&T Clark, 1960), 82-83: "What a pity that none of these apologists considers it worthy of mention that man is apparently the only being accustomed to laugh and smoke!"; quoted in van Huyssteen, *Alone in the World?* 136.

69. Van Huyssteen, *Alone in the World?* 139-44.

70. Van Huyssteen, *Alone in the World?* 38 and 159-62.

71. See van Huyssteen, *Alone in the World?* 161.

72. Bruno Latour, *We Have Never Been Modern*, trans. Catherine Porter (Cambridge, MA: Harvard University Press, 1993; French ed., 1991).

we never really managed to believe in the modern idea of a dichotomy of the natural versus the cultural, nor in the early modern idea of a full separation of God and world. In the vein of van Huyssteen, we could add that if God *is*, God can't be fenced into the domain of the supernatural as opposed to the natural but must be the encompassing reality, the source and matrix of all our natural endowments and cultural strivings. Now, if van Huyssteen's postfoundationalist epistemology is basically correct, we have never been purely postmodern, either. Moreover, if his thesis in *Alone in the World?* stands (as I believe it will do), we have never been purely premodern, either. Also, our ancestors had small spaces of a "modern" control of their environments, as they also had aspects of a "postmodern" awareness of fluidity, a sense of the possible. They are "us," and we "them." *Alone in the world* we may be as a species, but humans have always been living and laughing *together*, as they have also been weeping, mourning, and hoping *together*.

PART 1 Natural Scientists

1 The Acquisition of Human Uniqueness

How We Got from There to Here, and How We Did It So Fast

IAN TATTERSALL

As borne out by the rich diversity within the covers of this celebratory volume, not to mention J. Wentzel van Huyssteen's distinguished career, to be interested in human origins is to be interested in many different things. Even from a biologist's insular point of view, there are innumerable ways—both structural and cognitive—in which we human beings are distinct from even our closest relatives in nature. As a result, a huge diversity of phenomena have to be explained if we wish to understand how we became the extraordinary creatures we are. Perhaps most obviously, we walk upright in a way unmatched in the rest of nature, our capacious heads precariously balanced atop vertical spines. Our dental apparatus is tiny, housed within shrunken jaws that are tucked beneath our skulls, rather than projecting in front of them. Our hands are capable of manipulating objects with extraordinary precision and delicacy, while our feet have lost virtually all grasping ability. Perhaps most important of all, our minds process information in an entirely unprecedented fashion. Uniquely—and crucially—we mentally deconstruct our internal and external worlds into a vocabulary of intellectual symbols that we can recombine to derive new notions of reality.

In all of these ways, and in many more besides, we are clearly distinguished from even our closest living primate relatives, the great apes. Yet it is equally evident from our bodily and molecular structures that we are descended from an ancestor that was basically a run-of-the-mill primate displaying none of these peculiarities. What is more, in evolutionary terms that ancestor existed very recently indeed. So how did we get from there to here, and how did we do it so fast?

The easy answer to the first question, and the one still favored by many paleoanthropologists, is that our lineage was gradually modified by natural selection from an essentially ape-like condition toward the modern human one, as ancient hominids abandoned the ancestral forests in favor of life in more open environments: initially woodlands and bushlands, and ultimately largely treeless savannas. As the hominid body became adapted to bipedal walking on the ground, the hominids found themselves in more complex ecological and social situations to which they adapted by growing smarter via the development of larger brains. These metabolically expensive luxuries were paid for by dietary and ecological changes involving the occupation of open habitats, in which animal fats and proteins were increasingly consumed: new resources that were processed using technologies as diverse as the manufacture of sharp stone cutting tools, and the domestication of fire.

There is much that is still of substance in this scenario. Yet there can be no doubt that it is very far from the whole story; and there are aspects of it that are just plain wrong. For one thing, as the known human fossil record grows it becomes increasingly evident that the actual events of human evolution were much more complex than the notion of gradual fine-tuning implies. Back in the mid-twentieth century, many imagined that human phylogeny had simply involved the modification of a single transforming hominid lineage that was shaped consistently, over a vast span of time, by natural selection. And given a limited fossil record, together with the undisputable fact that *Homo sapiens* is the lone hominid in the world today, this certainly seemed a permissible deduction at the time. Yet, we now know that our lonely state is a remarkable (if eloquent) exception in the history of our hominid family (or hominin subfamily; for present purposes, the difference is purely notional), and that several different kinds of hominid typically shared the African continent—and later the entire Old World (see Figure 1.1)—over the entire seven million years or so since our family originated. Evidently the story of human evolution, far from having been a linear struggle from primitiveness to perfection, via the preferential reproduction of the fittest, has involved vigorous natural experimentation with variations on the basic hominid theme. New species constantly appeared on the scene, competed with others on the ecological stage, and in most cases ultimately disappeared into extinction. What's more, we also know now that this complex scenario unfolded in the context of extreme climatic instability, as environments changed dramatically and sometimes on very short time schedules.

The Acquisition of Human Uniqueness

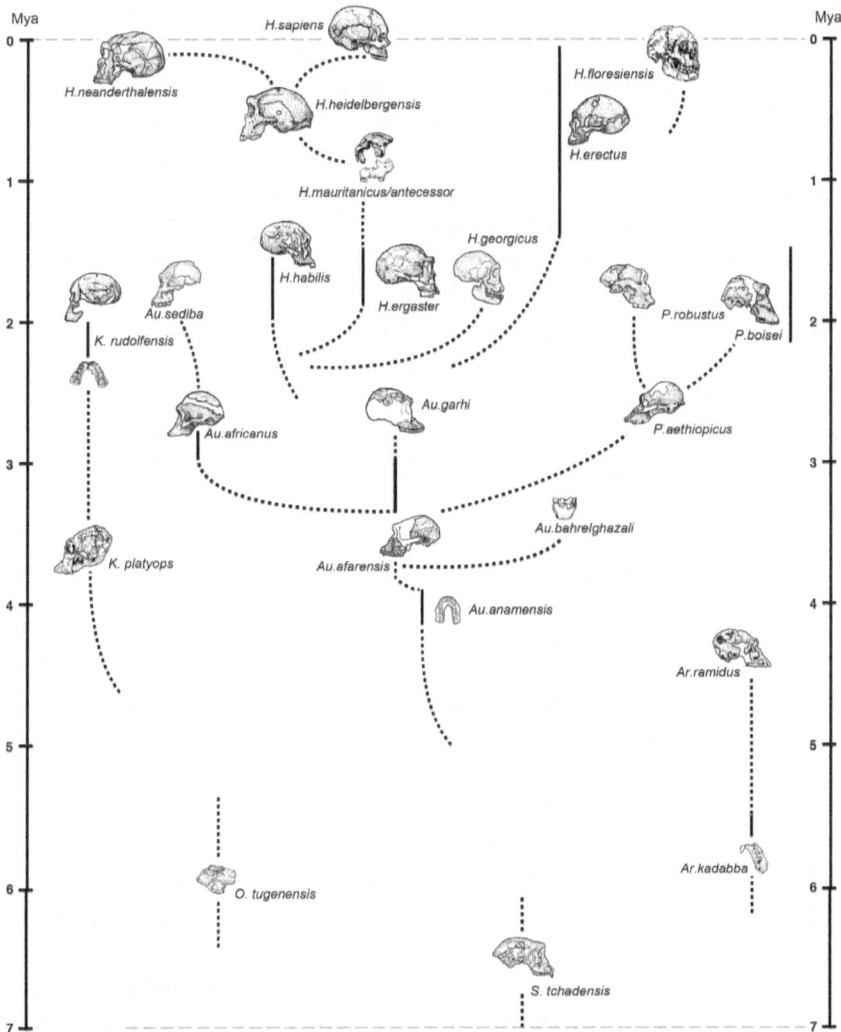

Figure 1.1. Highly tentative and genealogical tree of the hominid family, showing multiple lineages and the pronounced tendency for several different hominid species to coexist at any one time. Drawn by Jennifer Steffey; © Ian Tattersall.

Bipedality

The basic adaptive shift that ultimately resulted in the emergence of modern humankind involved the hominid ancestor's adoption of bipedal locomotion on the ground. In descriptive terms, that ancestor was still an "ape," whose primary habitat was the forest canopy. Facultatively, all modern great apes are capable of limited bipedality; but all are essentially quadrupeds: when there is any serious locomotion to be done on the ground, they move on all fours. As a result, that move to terrestrial bipedality on the part of the ancestral hominid not only underwrote everything that was to come in human evolution, but also involved a serious departure from any form of hominoid locomotion that we can observe today. Unsurprisingly, the magnitude of the locomotor shift involved, combined with its ramifying consequences, has made its causes a major focus of debate among paleoanthropologists. Charles Darwin started the ball rolling with these words:

> If it be an advantage to man to stand firmly on his feet and to have his arms free, of which there can be no doubt from his pre-eminent success in the battle of life, then I can see no reason why it should not have been advantageous to the progenitors of man to have become more erect or bipedal. They would thus have been better able to have defended themselves with stones or clubs, or to have attacked their prey, or otherwise obtained food. (Darwin 1871, 136–37)

Darwin's clearly implicit assumption, derived from his belief that human beings were most closely related to the quadrupedal African apes, was that the descent to terra firma came first, to be followed by the adoption of an orthograde posture. Almost all of his successors have shared this supposition that the ancestral hominid initially came to the ground (whether "pushed" by the disappearance of its forest habitat, or—more likely, given recent paleoecological findings—"pulled" by the attraction of the new resources available terrestrially), and only then worked out how best to accommodate to this radically new milieu.

As a result, virtually every story concocted to explain why hominids adopted upright posture has embedded this assumption. Among scenarios of this kind are the proposals that bipedality enabled the carrying of food by early hominids in their pursuit of scavenging (Hewes 1961); that it facilitated male display and the provisioning of females in the service of monogamy (Lovejoy 1981); that it aided in threat displays (Jablonski and Chaplin 1993); that it allowed vulnerable hominids to see over long grasses and spot predators farther away (Dart 1959); that it permitted more energy-efficient movement on the ground (Rodman and McHenry 1980); that it allowed woodland hominids to feed more effectively on low-hanging fruit (Hunt 1996); and that it minimized the absorption of solar heat, and maximized the dissipation of body heat in the open savanna (Wheeler 1984). This pretty much covers the waterfront, save for such oddities as the "aquatic ape" hypothesis (Morgan 1982).

Yet, as Robinson (1972) pointed out, there is unlikely to have been one single reason why bipedality proved such a successful strategy—locomotor or otherwise—for the early hominids. After all, once you have become a biped all of the multifarious advantages of moving this way—and the equally numerous disadvantages, among them a potentially disastrous slowness of movement—are yours. In standing upright, you have not browsed off a menu of potential benefits; you have purchased a complete package. But can we thereby conclude simply that terrestrial bipedality was adopted by early hominids because it was advantageous as the sum of its parts, rather than because it incorporated a particular key factor?

The answer here is both yes and no. In retrospect, bipedality certainly offered hominids a highly successful ecological strategy. But that cannot be the whole story, for it does nothing to explain why the hominid ancestor became a biped in the first place. What's more, there is no evident way in which any basically quadrupedal canopy-dweller—even one far less anatomically specialized than a chimpanzee—would ever have become an upright biped on the ground for no better reason than that this odd locomotor pattern might have offered some future advantage. In other words, none of the traditional "terrestriality first, then upright posture" explanations for bipedality is sufficient. Ultimately, there can be only one reason why an arboreal hominoid descending to the ground would ever have moved bipedally there: it already held its trunk upright when moving and resting in the trees. Necessarily a form that specialized in manual suspension in the forest canopy, a hominid ancestor with this physical disposition would simply have felt most comfortable when standing and moving erect on the terrestrial substrate. That is clearly the reason why today's highly arboreal lemurs of the genus *Propithecus* in Madagascar, and the equally arboreal lesser apes of the genus *Hylobates* in eastern Asia, adopt an upright posture on the ground—albeit each for a very different reason, and each in its own distinctly non-hominid-like fashion. What is more, several Late Miocene fossil hominoids of the broadly 13 to 7 myr (million-year) period, among them *Pierolapithecus* (Moya-Sola et al. 2004) and *Oreopithecus* (Köhler and Moya-Sola 1997), are interpreted as highly orthograde arborealists, and show some anatomical features that are otherwise associated only with bipeds. The demonstrable existence of Late Miocene hominoids of this kind not only makes it all the more unsurprising that a hominoid experimenting with life on the ground should have adopted a bipedal stance, but invites speculation that the same thing might have occurred in multiple hominoid lineages, as the African forests gradually yielded to more open formations over the past 9 myr or so (Feakins et al. 2014). What is more, it provides a possible explanation for the rather eclectic assortment of forms that have been described as hominids in the 7 to 4 myr period (see Gibbons 2006).

Currently, terrestrial bipedality is definitively documented only with the appearance in Kenya, at about 4.2 myr ago, of the earliest "australopith," *Australopithecus anamensis*. The most fully documented exemplar of the australopith group is the slightly later eastern African species *A. afarensis*, of which the best-known representative is the famous 3.2 myr-old skeleton nicknamed "Lucy." Members of this species had broad pelvises and lower limbs that were clearly constructed for bipedality on the ground; but with relatively small bodies (females stood about three and a half feet tall, males a bit more), longish arms, narrow shoulders, and long, curved extremities, they were clearly also agile climbers (Susman, Stern, and Jungers 1984). *Australopithecus afarensis* roamed through a remarkable spectrum of environments, ranging from dense forest to open savanna (Behrensmeyer and Reed 2013); and, while members of this species were at home on the ground, they evidently still depended heavily on the trees for both sustenance and shelter. The initial hominid descent to the ground was thus incomplete (albeit highly successful, if the relative anatomical stability seen in the period between about 4 and 2 myr is any indicator), in the sense that complete commitment to terrestrial environments still lay well in the future.

Brain-Size Expansion and Toolmaking Thought

Modern human body proportions appeared only about 2 myr ago, with the emergence of the first tall, striding members of the genus *Homo*. But the first stone tools had already been manufactured half a million years earlier, apparently invented by hominids of the archaic kind. Those tools were crude: merely sharp flakes struck from a stone core. Nonetheless, they were highly effective; and they continued to be made well after the first *Homo* turned up, inaugurating a durable pattern of innovation whereby the appearance of new hominids never coincided with the introduction of new technologies. What is more, change itself was not typically gradual, in either the biological or technological realms. Both species and technologies tended to appear suddenly, and then to linger; a pattern that persisted at least up to the appearance of *Homo sapiens*, after which the picture changed dramatically.

Even the vaunted tendency toward increasing hominid brain size with time was not a simple matter. To put this in perspective, shortly after 2 myr ago, fossils begin to show up that indicate the achievement by that time of essentially modern body size and proportions. The definitive fossil in this context is the amazingly complete "Nariokotome Boy" skeleton from northern Kenya (Walker and Leakey 1993), dating to around 1.6 myr ago. How much taller this adolescent, a representative of the species *Homo ergaster*, would have become if he had survived to maturity is disputed; but he would certainly have been taller than the average human today, and he was slenderly built, with long legs that show a commitment to living out on the open savanna, far from the shelter of trees. Significantly, the Boy's brain was larger than that of any australopith, announcing that the trend toward increase in the average size of hominid brains had begun. But it is important to remember that, over this period of brain expansion, several different species of hominid were typically around at any one time. This suggests that the increase was at least as likely due to the preferential ecological success of larger-brained species, as it was to the reproductive success of individuals within evolving species. What is more, brain-size expansion and the presumably greater cognitive complexity associated with it clearly occurred independently in several different lineages within the genus *Homo*, suggesting that the overall trend to bigger brains capitalized on a generalized potential of the genus, rather than on any quality unique to *Homo sapiens* and its particular forebears.

Large brains do not come for free: the brain is a metabolically expensive organ that in *Homo sapiens* consumes between 20 and 25 percent of all energy taken in, despite accounting for a mere 2 percent of body weight. Clearly, the expansion of the hominid brain must have been underwritten by a more energetically rewarding diet than the vegetation-based regime typical of other hominoids. This higher-quality diet was most plausibly furnished by animal fats and proteins; and obtaining these resources implies a transition beyond purely opportunistic scavenging, to active hunting. It has further been speculated (Wrangham 2009) that both detoxifying and extracting adequate energy from animal foods (and in the latter case vegetal ones too) would have necessitated the use of fire (the control of which would also have provided a measure of safety out on the predator-infested savanna). This is a theoretically compelling argument; but currently physical evidence for fire control only goes back about a million years (Berna et al. 2012), and it is only at around 400,000 years (kyr) ago that hearths become a regular feature in archaeological sites.

Hominids had left Africa for the first time by 1.8 myr ago, as documented at the remarkable Caucasian site of Dmanisi that has yielded the remains of several archaic hominids. These fossils are quite diverse, and have been very variously interpreted as to species (see review by Tattersall 2014a). With brains not much bigger than those of australopiths, and a stone tool kit no more sophisticated than that of the very earliest stone toolmakers, the Dmanisi hominids probably owed their new-found mobility to their more-or-less modern body proportions (Lordkipanidze et al. 2007), though their stature was rather small, certainly compared to that of the Nariokotome Boy. Not long after the Dmanisi hominids lived, the first *Homo erectus* appeared in island southeast Asia (Swisher et al. 1994), though the first hominid fossil (attributed to a species of *Homo*) turns up in Europe only at about 1.2 myr ago (Carbonell et al. 2008).

Throughout the million years or more following Dmanisi times, the general evolutionary pattern among hominids appears to have been one of local diversification; and it is not until about 600 kyr ago, in both Africa and Europe, that we find evidence of the first cosmopolitan hominid species, *Homo heidelbergensis*. Known from as far afield as China, *H. heidelbergensis* possessed a brain that was within the (very large) size range of that of *Homo sapiens*, although it was significantly below the modern average. Within its timespan, several important technological innovations occurred, among them the deliberate construction of free-standing shelters, the hafting of stone tools, the first documented making of throwing spears with sharpened tips, and the production of an entirely new kind of stone tool (see below and overviews by Klein 2009; Tattersall 2012).

The first major innovation in stone toolmaking technique subsequent to the introduction of deliberately manufactured implements at 2.6 myr had occurred with the introduction, again in Africa, of the teardrop-shaped "handaxe" at about 1.6 myr (there is one early outlier at 1.78 myr: Lepre et al. 2011). The handaxe and its variants were the first implements fashioned to a standardized shape "template" that evidently existed in the mind of the toolmaker before work started; and in concept it contrasts completely with the early sharp flakes that were not made to a predetermined form, but instead merely provided a sharp cutting edge. With the advent of the handaxe we clearly see evidence of a conceptual leap of some kind, although what this meant in terms of the toolmakers' broader apprehension of the world is not obvious. An equally important conceptual advance was made during the time of *Homo heidelbergensis*, with the introduction of "prepared core" stone tools. These were made by shaping a stone nucleus, via multiple blows from a stone or bone hammer, until a final strike would detach a more or less preformed tool. This implement possessed a continuous cutting edge around its periphery, and sometimes several such tools would be detached in sequence and finished according to their intended purpose.

Beginning with the first prepared-core tools at under 300 kyr ago, we see another evident increase in the complexity of toolmaking thought. But, once again, we are unable to tie this new phenomenon in with any specific cognitive state on the part of the toolmaker. Indeed, it is worth observing parenthetically that subjectively understanding any kind of thought process so similar to, but also so significantly unlike our own, may well be beyond our powers of imagination. Significantly, though, however intuitively smart *Homo heidelbergensis* may have been, we have no convincing evidence that symbolic thinking lay behind any of its material productions (or those of any of its predecessors). All such manufactures, however sophisticated, are strictly functional. There is, in other words, nothing particularly convincing in the archaeological record to suggest that members of *Homo heidelbergensis* were manipulating mental symbols, even in a rudimentary manner—if indeed that is possible.

The same is broadly true of the species *Homo neanderthalensis*, which appeared in Europe and adjacent Asia after about 200 kyr ago, having last shared an ancestry with *Homo sapiens* substantially before the half-million-year point. Prior to their extinction some 30 kyr ago (preceded by some minor gene exchange with *Homo sapiens*: Green et al. 2010), the Neanderthals created a rich and extensive record of their activities. This record testifies to their considerable resilience and resourcefulness, in the face of sometimes very rigorous climatic conditions. Yet these large-brained hominids (Neanderthal brains were as voluminous as those of contemporaneous *Homo sapiens*, and larger on average than ours today) left us with little evidence that they mentally manipulated information as we do. Despite the recent discovery on the floor of a cave in Gibraltar (Rodriguez-Vidal et al. 2014) of an engraved geometric design that had been covered by Neanderthal occupation debris, there is very little in the Neanderthal record to indicate a form of intelligence that, sophisticated as it may have been, was *qualitatively* different from that of their predecessors. Certainly, symbolic behaviors were not a routine part of their repertoire. What is more, there is a great deal to suggest that the Neanderthals possessed a highly focused and coldly practical attitude to life: one that contrasts strikingly with the curious combination of imagination, spirituality, and (ir)rationality that characterizes the behaviors of all *Homo sapiens* populations today (see discussion by Tattersall 2012).

Interestingly, while *Homo sapiens* appeared in Africa about 200 to 160 kyr ago as a recognizable anatomical entity (McDougall, Brown, and Fleagle 2005; White et al. 2003), its earliest fossil members are still found in archaic archaeological contexts (see Klein 2009). Indeed, we have little reason to think that these most ancient *Homo sapiens* were thinking or behaving significantly differently from, say, the Neanderthals. As far as we can tell, then, the transition to symbolic thought from prior, more intuitive, cognitive modes did not occur coincident with the emergence of anatomically modern *Homo sapiens*. Nonetheless, the acquisition of modern morphology was in itself a major event, involving numerous skeletal changes in all areas of the body. Most likely, these ramifying effects were the result of a change in gene regulation that was small in terms of DNA structure, but that had cascading and ramifying developmental effects. Those effects were almost certainly not confined to the skeletal system—which is what we have preserved in the fossil record—but may well also have impacted the development of soft-tissue complexes such as the brain. In this light, changes that took place at or before speciation may have furnished the prerequisites for the later adoption of symbolic cognitive processes.

Symbolic Thought

The first convincing evidence we have of the working of symbolic minds comes from African Middle Stone Age sites of the period following about 100 kyr ago. Initial stirrings of the new cognitive mode are found in marine gastropod shells pierced for stringing (and sometimes colored with ochre), and hence presumably used in bodily ornamentation (Bouzouggar et al. 2007; Henshilwood et al. 2004; Vanhaeren et al. 2006; d'Errico et al. 2009). In historically documented societies such ornamentation is—or was—invariably symbolic of social status, cohort membership, political importance, and other such factors. But even if personal adornment is considered a little indirect as an indicator of symbolic thought patterns, we do not have to wait long for more explicit evidence of symbolic activity. The world's earliest overtly symbolic objects are a couple of smoothed ochre plaques, found in 77-kyr levels at the site of Blombos Cave, in South Africa (Henshilwood et al. 2002), and engraved with a geometric motif. Since the plaques are slightly separated stratigraphically, yet bear basically the same decoration, it would appear that this design was not the result of idle doodling, but carried a message that remained stable over time—a conclusion reinforced by approximate repetitions at the slightly later Diepkloof Cave, several hundreds of kilometers away (Texier et al. 2010). Significantly, at about the same time, at Pinnacle Point, a coastal cave complex not far to the east of Blombos, a complex fire-based technology was developed to convert a common but poor toolmaking material (silcrete) into a much better one (Brown et al. 2009). This has subsequently also been demonstrated at Blombos (Mourre et al. 2010). Arguably alone among known Paleolithic technologies, this multistage process was so complex as to have necessitated symbolic reasoning on the part of its practitioners.

Clearly, something cognitively significant was happening among early *Homo sapiens* in Middle Stone Age Africa in the period following about 100 kyr ago. And we see this perhaps most dramatically reflected in a revolutionary transformation of the pattern of human behavioral innovation. Previously, major behavioral novelties had been both sporadic and rare. Technological stability over huge stretches of time was the norm—even as climates and environments oscillated wildly. Now, however, change itself was evidently the rule. The African archaeological record is sparse in the period just before the first behaviorally modern *Homo sapiens* first left Africa at about 60 kyr ago (Templeton 2005). But once *Homo sapiens* began rapidly to spread across the Old World (and to replace other *Homo* species that retained older cognitive patterns—apparently with the odd exchange of genes here and there) evidence of new ways of doing things and of viewing the world comes thick and fast.

Most dramatic of such manifestations was the flowering of sophisticated artistic activity in Europe following about 40 kyr ago; but there are intimations of similar developments in Australia and southern Asia at around the same time or maybe even earlier (see Klein 2009). And significantly, at the end of the last Ice Age some 12 kyr ago, the hominid response was not retrenchment, as it had been so many times before. Earlier, significant climate change had the effect of extirpating local hominid populations, or of spurring those populations to bend old tools to new uses. But now, for the first time, humans responded with a revolutionary change in lifeway. This involved the adoption of sedentary lifestyles and the domestication of plants and animals, involving by far the most radical change in the human relationship to nature that ever occurred—and one that necessitated the invention of multiple new technologies by the newly creative *Homo sapiens*. Once settled life was established, of course, towns and cities were not far behind. And, with the invention of writing at around 5 kyr ago, the rest literally became history: a story obviously far too complex and eventful to be summarized here, but one that has culminated in the active expectation of rapid and constant change that governs our lives today.

Language

So what happened? Just what was it that took place, around 100 kyr ago in Africa, to start the anatomically strange new species *Homo sapiens* behaving in this equally strange and unprecedented new way—for symbolic thought, albeit superimposed on some very ancient and still-active neural systems, is not simply an improvement on what went before it, but instead represents an entirely new way of processing information? Given that the neural underpinnings for this new cognitive style were necessarily already in place—as they had almost certainly been since the acquisition, 100 kyr earlier, of the new skeletal morphology—we have to look for a *cultural* stimulus for this fateful change.

The identity of this stimulus has been debated loud and long; but by far the most plausible candidate is the invention of language. Language, after all, is the ultimate symbolic activity, depending as it does on the creation of a vocabulary of vocal symbols to represent the world, and on the reshuffling of those symbols—according to rules—to create new ones. In this sense, language is virtually synonymous with modern thought; and it is certainly difficult or impossible for us to conceive of our own thought processes in the absence of language—or vice versa. What is more, we know that systematically constructed languages can be spontaneously invented (Kegl, Senghas, and Coppola 1999); and it is relatively easy to envisage at least in principle how, in some tiny isolate of early *Homo sapiens*, buffeted by the climatic vagaries of Late Pleistocene Africa, an innovative practice of naming objects might rapidly have given rise to a structured language. That structure then fed back into the way in which the brain processed the information embedded in the vocal signals.

The wiring of the brain is extremely responsive to experience, especially at young ages, inviting the conjecture that this fateful innovation was made by a group of children at play. The new behavior would then have readily spread upward though the hierarchy of the biologically pre-adapted society to which the children belonged—and eventually beyond, to the entire functionally predisposed species.

Much of this is, as I've said, pure conjecture. But while complex vocal communication doubtless has a long history among hominids, there is little in the archaeological record, or indeed, in language itself (Bolhuis et al. 2014), to suggest that language as it is familiar to us today necessarily evolved gradually, or had deep evolutionary roots in the human lineage. Of course, many have considered language so complex that it could not have just popped into existence. And certainly, there can be little doubt that the language faculty is superimposed on complex pre-existing forms of vocal and other communication. Put these factors together, and it might seem natural enough to conclude that anything as complicated and multidimensional as language must have been fine-tuned by evolution over a vast period of time. But two things need to be borne in mind here. First of all, especially under Ice Age conditions, natural selection is unlikely to be a consistent driver of change over long periods of time (see Tattersall 2012). And second, the final acquisition of language and symbolic thought in humans was indeed unquestionably based on a long series of neural innovations that were made over several hundred millions of years of vertebrate evolution. For reasons that had nothing to do with the end result, these many accreting innovations finally underpinned a structure that, with the adventitious addition of a single "keystone" innovation at the origin of *Homo sapiens*, was pre-adapted to thought. Nothing at any stage in this long succession of acquisitions could have occurred without everything that had gone before; but nothing that materialized along the way happened in anticipation of the final outcome. Currently, nobody knows for sure what the keystone neural innovation was, though theories abound (see DeSalle and Tattersall 2012); but we ourselves are proof that it was acquired. There is nothing in our long history to predict that a linguistic, symbolic creature would ever have emerged from it; but here we are.

Whatever it may be neurologically that makes us *different*, if anything you might call a "soul" was ever breathed into the human species, this event surely occurred at the moment when the human brain began to process information symbolically. Symbolic reasoning of the kind implicit in language allowed human beings to escape, for the first time, from the confines of immediate reality, and to imagine worlds and causes beyond the seen and the heard. There can be no doubt that Neanderthals and other archaic hominids were cognitively sophisticated beings, possessing the ability to react in highly subtle ways to everything happening in the world around them. They may even have possessed inchoate feelings about things beyond that world, and they almost certainly possessed at least a rudimentary aesthetic sense. But there is little to suggest that the Neanderthals created new worlds in their minds: that they had the ability to imagine, in detail, things they could not see, or feel. They lived in the world that nature presented to them; and they did not seek to change it, despite possessing all the bodily resources that modern humans ultimately employed to implement such change. In contrast, modern humans rapidly took over the world, and then began vigorously to change it, precisely because they processed information about it in a fundamentally different and unprecedented way.

Material Culture

It was not just the transition from non-symbolic to symbolic cognition that took place so fast. Physically, human beings have come a very long way in a remarkably short space of time, to such a degree that we are a lot more different from our ancestors of two million years ago than any other modern mammal is. The question is obvious: what, exactly, was going on in the lineage that gave rise to modern humans to accelerate evolution so unusually?

Almost certainly, our possession of material culture is somehow implicated in this process. Up to now, the putative role of culture in stimulating human evolution has largely been the province of evolutionary psychologists, who have favored a process of "gene-culture co-evolution." Here evolutionary change among hominids is seen as reflecting the steady operation of natural selection on successive generations of individuals, with a powerful positive feedback between innovations in the biological and cultural spheres (Tooby and Cosmides 1989). Smarter and more adroit members of the population would always have had the reproductive edge; and, in this view, the inherent interplay between genes and culture would have virtually obliged human predecessors to become more intelligent and behaviorally complex, predisposing them in the process to rapid evolutionary change.

But a little thought suggests that there must have been more to it than this (Tattersall 2014b). One problem with the assumption that the pressures of natural selection were consistent over long periods of time is that, as we have seen, our genus *Homo* evolved during a period of notoriously unstable environments. The more we learn about the climatic conditions of the Ice Ages, during which the polar ice caps fluctuated enormously in extent, taking the various ecological zones along with them, the more we realize just how unstable the ancient "environments of adaptation" in fact were. In any one place, resident hominids would typically have found themselves having to react to abruptly changing conditions, in which putative selection pressures would have seesawed wildly.

Clearly, we have to look elsewhere than to internal lineage dynamics to explain rapid change among Ice Age hominids. Yet, basically the same elements implicated in the gene-culture scenario—environmental pressures and material culture—may in fact have been in play. To understand how these factors may have interacted to produce evolutionary change, we first have to recognize that if any substantial innovation—whether genetic or cultural—is to be incorporated into a population, the effective size of that population needs to be small. Large, dense populations simply have too much inertia to be nudged consistently in any direction. Small populations, on the other hand, routinely incorporate novelties: a process that is, indeed, the very basis of evolutionary diversification.

Today our sedentary human population is vast, and it is continuously distributed across all habitable areas of the globe. In Ice Age times, in contrast, hominids were mobile hunters and gatherers, living off nature's bounty and thinly spread across African and Eurasian continents. What's more, tiny local populations were constantly buffeted by climatic changes that severely affected local resource availability, often rendering particular places hostile to hominids, or even uninhabitable by them. These conditions provide the ideal background to evolutionary change; but it remains true that many other mammal lineages went through the same vagaries without accumulating the vast change evident among the hominids.

This is where culture enters the picture. Hominid material culture involves not only stone tool use, but also a whole range of other technologies such as clothing, shelter-building, and the control of fire. All of these allow their possessors to exploit the environment more efficiently, and to transcend the purely physiological limitations that constrain populations lacking them. As a result, once incorporated into the hominid repertoire, material culture evidently permitted our Ice Age predecessors to substantially broaden their ecological niches. In good times, technology would have enabled hominid populations to expand demographically beyond normal limits, and to occupy marginal regions that would have been unavailable to them otherwise.

But the protective value of culture would have been finite. When climatic conditions deteriorated, as they periodically did, culture would have proved an incomplete buffer against the hostile elements. As a result, many populations would both have declined in size and have become fragmented. The resulting small isolates would have provided perfect conditions both for speciation and for the fixation of genetic and cultural novelties—in other words, for evolutionary innovation. And when conditions improved once more, the altered populations would have expanded, coming into contact with others that were spreading similarly.

If speciation had taken place during periods of isolation, competition and selective elimination would have ensued. Conversely, if speciation was incomplete or absent, any genetic novelties would have been incorporated into the merged populations. Either way, change would have resulted. Given that in the unsettled conditions of the Ice Ages there would have been multiple repetitions of these processes in quick succession, the scene was set for fast evolution, ultimately leveraged by our possession of material culture.

It is substantially less exalting to see ourselves as the product of a rapid sequence of random external events than as a process of ongoing refinement over the eons. After all, it makes the eventual emergence of our remarkable species seem entirely adventitious. But, given the nature of the product, it is surely more realistic. It doesn't take much introspection to realize that, for all of its remarkable cognitive and physical qualities, *Homo sapiens* is hugely unperfected—a subject on which countless volumes have been written by evolutionary psychologists, theologians, novelists, and others. This outcome makes much more sense if *Homo sapiens* was *not* honed by natural selection. The process that lay behind the emergence of our "darkly wise and rudely great" species was a much more untidy one, and its implications for our own view of ourselves are profound. For, if we were not fine-tuned by evolution to be creatures of a specific kind, then we do indeed have free will. We *can* make choices about what we do, unencumbered by the crushing weight of biology and adaptation. The corollary, of course, is that we also have to accept responsibility for those choices.

References

Behrensmeyer, K., and K. Reed. 2013. Reconstructing the habitats of *Australopithecus*: paleoenviroments, site taphonomy and faunas. In *The Paleobiology of* Australopithecus, edited by K. E. Reed, J. G. Fleagle, and R. E. F. Leakey, 41–59. Dordrecht: Springer.

Berna, F., and 6 others. 2012. Microstratigraphic evidence of in situ fire in the Acheulean strata of Wonderwerk Cave, Northern Cape Province, South Africa. *Proceedings of the National Academy of Sciences USA* 109:E1215–E1220.

Bolhuis, J. J., I. Tattersall, N. Chomsky, and R. C. Berwick. 2014. How could language have evolved? *PLoS Biology* 12(8).

Bouzouggar, A. N., and 14 others. 2007. 82,000-year-old shell beads from North Africa and implications for the origins of modern human behavior. *Proceedings of the National Academy of Sciences USA* 104:9964–69.

Brown, K. S., and 8 others. 2009. Fire as an engineering tool of early modern humans. *Science* 325:859–62.

Carbonell, E., and 29 others. 2008. The first hominin of Europe. *Nature* 452:465–69.

Dart, R. A. 1959. *Adventures with the Missing Link*. New York: Harper Brothers.

Darwin, C. 1871. *The Descent of Man and Selection in Relation to Sex*. New York: Appleton.

d'Errico, F., and 8 others. 2009. Additional evidence on the use of personal ornaments in the Middle Paleolithic of North Africa. *Proceedings of the National Academy of Sciences USA* 106:16051–56.

DeSalle, R., and I. Tattersall. 2012. *The Brain: Big Bangs, Behaviors, and Beliefs*. New Haven: Yale University Press.

Feakins, S. J., and 5 others. 2014. Northeast African vegetation change over 12 m.y. *Geology* 41:295–98.

Gibbons, A. 2006. *The First Human: The Race to Discover Our Earliest Ancestors*. New York: Doubleday.

Green, R. E., and 56 others. 2010. A draft sequence of the Neanderthal genome. *Science* 238:710–22.

Henshilwood, C. F. d'Errico, M. Vanhaeren, K. van Niekerk, and Z. Jacobs. 2004. Middle Stone Age shell beads from South Africa. *Science* 304:404.

Henshilwood, C. S., and 10 others. 2002. Emergence of modern human behavior: Middle Stone Age engravings from South Africa. *Science* 295:1278–80.

Hewes, G. 1961. Food transport and the origin of hominid bipedalism. *American Anthropologist* 63:687–710.

Hunt, K. D. 1996. The postural feeding hypothesis: an ecological model for the origin of bipedalism. *South African Journal of Science* 9:77–90.

Jablonski, N. G., and G. Chaplin. 1993. Origin of habitual terrestrial bipedalism in the ancestor of the Hominidae. *Journal of Human Evolution* 24:259–80.

Kegl, J., A. Senghas, and M. Coppola. 1999. Creation through contact: sign language emergence and sign language change in Nicaragua. In *Comparative Grammatical Change: The Intersection of Language Acquisition, Creole Genesis and Diachronic Syntax*, edited by M. deGraaf, 197–237. Cambridge, MA: MIT.

Klein, R. G. 2009. *The Human Career*. 3rd ed. Chicago: University of Chicago Press.

Köhler, M., and S. Moya-Sola. 1997. Ape-like or hominid-like? The positional behavior of *Oreopithecus bambolii* reconsidered. *Proceedings of the National Academy of Sciences USA* 94:11747–50.

Lepre, C. J., and 8 others. 2011. An earlier origin for the Acheulian. *Nature* 477:82–85.

Lordkipanidze, D., and 17 others. 2007. Postcranial evidence of early *Homo* from Dmanisi, Georgia. *Nature* 449:305–10.

Lovejoy, C. O. 1981. The origin of man. *Science* 211:344–50.

McDougall, I., F. H. Brown, and J. G. Fleagle. 2005. Stratigraphic placement and age of modern humans from Kibish, Ethiopia. *Nature* 433:733–36.

Morgan, E. 1982. *The Aquatic Ape*. London: Stein & Day.

Mourre, V., P. Villa, and C. S. Henshilwood. 2010. Early use of pressure flaking on lithic artifacts at Blombos Cave, South Africa. *Science* 330:659–62.

Moya-Sola, S., M. Köhler, D. M. Alba, I. Casanovas-Vilar, and J. Galindo. 2004. *Pierolapithecus catalaunicus*, a new Middle Miocene great ape from Spain. *Science* 306:1339–44.

Robinson, J. T. 1972. *Early Hominid Posture and Locomotion*. Chicago: University of Chicago Press.

Rodman, P. S., and H. M. McHenry. 1980. Bioenergetics and the origin of hominid bipedalism. *American Journal of Physical Anthropology* 52:103–6.

Rodriguez-Vidal, R., and 16 others. 2014. A rock engraving made by Neanderthals in Gibraltar. *Proceedings of the National Academy of Sciences USA* 111(37):13301–6.

Susman, R. L., J. T. Stern, and W. L. Jungers. 1984. Arboreality and bipedality in the Hadar hominids. *Folia Primatologia* 43:283–306.

Swisher C. C., III, and 5 others. 1994. Age of the earliest known hominids in Java, Indonesia. *Science* 263:1118–21.

Tattersall, I. 2012. *Masters of the Planet: The Search for Our Human Origins.* New York: Palgrave Macmillan.

Tattersall, I. 2014a. *Homo ergaster* and its contemporaries. In *Handbook of Paleoanthropology*, vol. 3, edited by W. Henke and I. Tattersall. 2nd ed. Heidelberg: Springer.

Tattersall, I. 2014b. If I had a hammer. *Scientific American* 311(3):54–59.

Templeton, A. 2005. Haplotype trees and modern human origins. *Yearbook of Physical Anthropology* 48:33–59.

Texier, P. J., and 11 others. 2010. A Howiesons Poort tradition of engraving ostrich eggshell containers dated to 60,000 years ago at Diepkloof Rock Shelter, South Africa. *Proceedings of the National Academy of Sciences USA* 107:6180–85.

Tooby, J., and L. Cosmides. 1989. Evolutionary psychology and the generation of culture, part I: theoretical considerations. *Ethology and Sociobiology* 10:29–49.

Vanhaeren, M., and 5 others. 2006. Middle Paleolithic shell beads in Israel and Algeria. *Science* 312:1785–88.

Walker, A., and R. E. F. Leakey, eds. 1993. *The Nariokotome* Homo erectus *skeleton.* Cambridge, MA: Harvard University Press.

White, T. D., and 6 others. 2003. Pleistocene *Homo sapiens* from Middle Awash, Ethiopia. *Nature* 423:742–47.

Wheeler, P. E. 1984. The evolution of bipedality and loss of functional body hair in hominids. *Journal of Human Evolution* 13:91–98.

Wrangham, R. 2010. *Catching Fire: How Cooking Made Us Human.* New York: Basic Books.

2 Religion as a Technology of Entanglement

Dealing with the Beyond of Entanglements

IAN HODDER

J. Wentzel van Huyssteen came to the archaeological site of Çatalhöyük in central Turkey over six years as part of two interdisciplinary projects funded by the Templeton Foundation. He was part of groups of scholars that interacted with the excavators and scientists working at Çatalhöyük in order to get to know the site and its data and to contribute to an understanding of religious ritual and symbolism in early farming societies. With one of the groups of scholars, van Huyssteen also visited Göbekli Tepe in southeast Turkey. The resulting chapters that he contributed (van Huyssteen 2010, 2014) explored many salient aspects of the information from the two sites, and he argued that religion at Çatalhöyük should not be seen as a separate sphere divorced from mundane aspects of daily life. More generally, he argued for religion as an emergent property of complex human systems. He has written about the Paleolithic and the evolutionary origins of religion (2006) and in this chapter I aim to contribute to this wider debate from a perspective that owes much to his work and the links he drew to complex systems.

Van Huyssteen and I have both experienced losses of family members very close to us over recent years, and I am grateful to him for the support he gave me. At that time of tragic loss I found myself doing things that seem very irrational. For example, as a nonbeliever, I found myself praying to a supernatural being and lighting a candle in front of an image of a man on a cross in a church. And I have found myself doing similar things at other times of inexplicable, tragic loss. For other people, of course, these are not irrational acts. They were irrational to me but I did them because, despite myself, they provided me with solace and helped me to deal with events that seemed beyond understanding.

Experiencing the deaths of people who had reached a full age or had long suffered, I felt less in need of supernatural solace. Such deaths seemed easier to deal with, much more so than the death of a child. For a long time I tried to rationalize the death and to make sense of it through seeking causes. But all the "rational explanations" in the world seemed unable to assuage my grief. In the end the enormity of what had happened was beyond what I could make sense of intellectually. I needed something more—the solace of something bigger than the known world. I needed to do something in relation to this bigger world—to pray, light a candle, go into a church. Somehow that helped me to get a handle on things. I know that in other cultures and in other contexts I would have felt differently and done different things. I know that what I did was attuned to a specific upbringing. But somehow doing something to deal with what had happened seemed important. I seemed to need to deal with the ineffable by doing things that were beyond my understanding.

In the spirit of Renato Rosaldo's (1984) reconsideration of head-hunting after experiencing grief and rage at the untimely death of his wife, I want to suggest an account of religion that is influenced by my personal experience. I wish to suggest that religion originates in the human impulse to fix things. This notion comes more directly from my attempts to build a theory of entanglement (Hodder 2012). According to this view, humans and things are entangled with each other in numerous ways. Entanglement is the sum of human dependence on things, thing dependence on humans, thing dependence on other things, and human dependence on other humans. Within the central notion of dependence there are both reliance and constraint or dependency. Entanglements between humans and things afford agency, but they also entrap into specific pathways. Entanglement can thus also be defined as the product of a dialectical relationship between dependence and dependency. Put another way, humans and things get caught up in each other and push and pull each other in specific directions. Thus entanglement differs from current notions of networks in that there is a "stickiness" or constraining "caught-upness" (Latour 2005; Knappett 2011). It also differs from many phenomenological approaches where the focus is on "dwelling" rather than being "caught-up" (Heidegger 1973; Ingold 2000; Tilley 1994).

In entanglements there is always need for fixing because of the instability of things and the complexity of interactions. While many contemporary approaches to material culture point to the stabilizing effects of material culture, entanglement draws attention to the ways in which at different time scales things are unstable—they have a material vitality or vibrance (see also Bennett 2009). Things and human-thing relations are always changing so that humans get drawn into fixing things and finding solutions. There is the impulse to do something, find practical solutions to problems, whether it be to solve the problem of mud wall collapse by making sandier bricks, or to solve the problem of inequality by social redistribution.

A distinctive aspect of entanglements (and of many complex systems) is that they involve long, complex, and intersecting chains of dependence that are very unbounded, especially as societies increase in size and in the scale of interactions. It thus becomes very difficult to find solutions to problems as they arise. Causality seems remote and uncontrollable, difficult to understand, difficult to grasp. Fixing things becomes very difficult because the chains of dependency are very long and distant or obscure. In some areas of life the problems we encounter matter a lot to us, although the specific matters that concern us most vary historically. In dealing with problems that matter such as untimely death, illness, misfortune, or suffering, we feel compelled to do something, to fix things. But often the solutions are unclear and beyond immediate understanding. Our impulse is to find a practical solution, and so we bring to bear the full range of practical and intellectual knowledge available at the time in order to do something. In the case of complex entanglements that extend beyond immediate fixing, we get drawn into dealing with the beyond. With the hindsight of Western rationalism and scientific understanding, many of the solutions that we find appear peculiar and irrational. It is thus that we have erected distinctions between the secular and the sacred, the mundane and the religious, the everyday and the beyond or transcendental. But the fixes that are found are logical extensions of existing knowledge and practices.

Thus the religious can be seen as resulting from an impulse to do something in order to fix or deal with deep concerns faced by humans. The specific nature of what causes deep concern and how it is dealt with vary. Modes of religiosity vary (Whitehouse 2004). Many different specific techniques have been used—from music, to dance, to trance, from rare moments of high drama and intensity to sober reading of doctrinal texts. Each society makes use of its own stocks of knowledge and practice in order to find fixes and to do something in practice to deal with problems that matter. But the underlying commonality is that things happen that matter deeply and yet causality is distant, complex, unclear. The solutions that are sought have to deal with this "beyondness," using techniques that themselves extend into the beyond.

The hypothesis that religion is about doing something in order to deal with specific historical and complex problems came about as a result of numerous instances at Çatalhöyük where what had been interpreted as religious rituals actually seemed to be ways of dealing with matters of import that had no easy immediate solution. One example was the placing of wild bull horns around the northeastern platform in the house called Building 77. The bull horns mark off the platform area that was dedicated to human burial. A large number of people were buried beneath this platform and around it. Many have argued that Çatalhöyük was an example of a house society in which the passing down of rights, ritual knowledge, and heirlooms played a central role (Bloch 2010). Indeed, the term "history house" has been coined to describe buildings like Building 77 that contained many burials and installations like bull horns, and were rebuilt in the same spot many times (Hodder and Pels 2010). It seems reasonable to argue that in such a society, transactions with the human dead would have been important, and we do see much effort invested in burial, retrieval of skulls, and memory construction through the circulation and deposition of human skulls. In such a context, death of house members would have been of deep concern although the causes of death, especially the frequent deaths of young children and young adults, would have been difficult to grasp. In such a context, using the power of wild bulls to do something in relation to the dead would have been a reasonable attempt at fixing things. We know from the use of wild bulls in feasting and in the arts that they held a special social and symbolic role at Çatalhöyük. The large aurochsen would have been impressive and powerful creatures, difficult to down. But their power could be appropriated to protect or otherwise act in relation to the dead. Bloch (2010) has argued that the bulls reanimated the house after death at Çatalhöyük.

Much of the geometric wall painting at Çatalhöyük seems focused around burial platforms. There seem to have been a number of things that could be done in order to deal with the human dead, including putting large numbers of colored beads in graves with young children. All these actions can be seen as symbolic or religious, but they can also be seen as practical solutions to deal with matters of social and emotional import that are difficult to make sense of. We now know, as a result of contemporary medical science, some of the entanglements that reduce high infant mortality, but at Çatalhöyük a range of knowledge was developed that linked death to specific actions, including placing bull horns or decorating the platforms and walls around graves.

A further example at Çatalhöyük is the treatment of the human skeleton. After burial beneath the floors of houses, some skulls were removed from the graves and kept and circulated, sometimes painted or plastered to reproduce human facial features. Here there seem to be the goals of keeping the ancestors alive in some sense and of treating them as social beings even after death. In this way the social relations based on these individuals could be sustained. The problem of the continuation of the "house" after the death of significant individuals is "fixed" by keeping that person alive, at least until the relevant social relations dissipate. Again, the keeping of human skulls may seem like an irrational, symbolic, or religious act, but it can also be seen as a practical solution to deal with socially and emotionally difficult issues of continuity and rights. Extending the life of individuals through keeping and circulating their skulls can be seen as a logical extension of existing social practices into the difficult and unknown beyond of the dead.

Humans get entrapped in specific ways of being as a result of human-thing entanglements, and ways have to be found of dealing with this entrapment. As a result, many religions offer salvation, agents (perhaps in the forms of skulls or gods), solace, support for the weak, identity, or community. We could argue, as is often done, that religion performs the function of creating social solidarity at Çatalhöyük. This ignores the fact that religion is also often the cause of conflict and division, and it does not explain why nonsocial means have to be found to enhance solidarity. The human skulls circulated at Çatalhöyük derive from the problem of potential conflict if house continuity is not maintained. The entanglement view is that humans get caught up in things, and this leads to the need for specific solutions and fixes. Social solidarity may have been one of the effects of skull retrieval and circulation at Çatalhöyük. But at the same time, many people (and their bodies after death) were excluded from skull circulation and from membership of dominant buildings in which special skulls were kept. Skull circulation may have been an extension of human practices into the beyond of death, perhaps even denying death, but it did not necessarily lead to social solidarity.

An important part of the "caught-upness" of entanglement derives from spatiotemporal positioning. Entanglements can be seen as made up of cross-cutting operational chains. These chains include the operational sequences (behavioral chain, *chaîne opératoire*) of making things, of the lives of things. They also include the sequences of technologies and styles as new things and ideas are introduced, taken up, and die out; they include the rise and fall of empires and religions. They include the annual cycles of crops, the longer-term cycles of animal growth and tree growth, and the even longer-term cycles of deforestation or global warming. And in all these cross-cutting chains there are the lives of humans that have their own rhythms of opening up and closing down of opportunities—times when it has become too late to have a child, too late to build a house, too late to produce enough to invest in one's children. Most of us are in the wrong place at the wrong time, either through accidents of birth or of where we happened to be when opportunities arose. Human lives are experienced as very constrained and determined. Religion can be seen as playing a role in making sense of, accepting, or coming to terms with, or rationalizing this entrapment. Those at Çatalhöyük who did not have access to decorated and circulated human skulls could at least decorate the burial platforms in their houses; those that did not have access to wild bulls could use wild sheep horns instead (as in Building 52, where a bench with bull horns replaced an earlier smaller bench with wild sheep horns). The "religious" practices allow something to be done about exclusion and marginalization.

Toward Religion as a Fixing of Entanglements That Matter

The notion that religion is about practical engagement with the world rather than about abstract intellectual beliefs has now been widely established. For Asad (1982), the separation of religion from power is a product of a unique post-Reformation history in Europe. He argues that there cannot be a universal definition of religion because it is always historically embedded and reconstructed. "Religious symbols—whether one thinks of them in terms of communication or of cognition, of guiding action or of expressing emotion—cannot be understood independently of their historical relations with nonreligious symbols or of their articulations in and of social life, in which work and power are always crucial" (Asad 1982, 129). For Meyer (2012, 11), too, "the study of religion is haunted by a Protestant legacy and bias that needs to be deconstructed." "It is key to approach religion as a mundane, practical and material affair—as *present in* and *making* a world" (Meyer 2012, 20). Boyer (2001, 314) argues that religion is practical—dealing with problems as they come up. It is not just contemplative. A good example discussed by Boyer is that much religious practice surrounding death is about what to do practically with the body. Super and Turley (2006, 428) argue that "religions seldom retreat into the spiritual realm and ignore the world around them. This might be the case in a few hermetic and monastic traditions, but it does not represent the mainstream of religious history."

Religion is very varied and any universal characteristics have been difficult to identify. Many have argued that one universal aspect is that religions deal with problems and provide solutions. In his book *God Is Not One*, Prothero (2011) points to the diversity of religions, a point with which many anthropologists and historians would today agree. But Prothero nevertheless admits that "what the world's religions share is not so much a finish line as a starting point. And where they begin is with this simple observation: something is wrong with the world. In the Hopi language, the word Koyaanisqatsi tells us that life is out of balance" (36). For Prothero, all religions identify a main problem, a solution or goal, and techniques for achieving those goals. But religions differ in what they see as having gone wrong and in what they see as solutions. Thus Christians see sin as the problem, while Buddhists see suffering (Prothero

2011, 37). For Christians the solution or goal is salvation, for Buddhists it is nirvana. For Christians the techniques for achieving these goals are faith and good works, and for Buddhists meditation. For Confucius, chaos was the main human problem, order the solution, using the techniques of ethics, ritual, and education (Prothero 2011, 291–301). As Burke (2004, 2) puts it, "each of the major religions has a message about the human condition; each points to something that it views as fundamentally wrong and unsatisfactory about our ordinary existence; each offers a diagnosis of the cause of that unsatisfactoriness and points to a possible remedy."

Super and Turley (2006, 22–23) argue that "we all suffer and most religions have much to offer as a way of coping with suffering." Bellah (Bellah and Tipton 2006) follows the work of Lienhardt on the Dinka to argue that religion in small-scale societies helps humans to deal with suffering and the conditions of existence. In ancient or dynastic Egypt, religion provided an elaborate set of technologies for dealing with death, including writing letters to the dead (Meskell 2004, 82), but equally there were rituals of birth and other life stages. In Egypt "the variety of religious and divinatory practices can be seen as integrating a variety of approaches to comprehending and coping with problems of normal existence" (Baines 1987, 94). "Because so many infants and mothers died, the gods were not simply beneficent in birth, which was an occasion of potential tension, affliction, and divine caprice as much as, or more than, others" (95).

Boyer (2001, 34–36) points out that in many cultures people are not worried about explaining misfortune in general (there is not a general angst about existence), but only in explaining particular misfortunes. He also notes (52) that religion often produces more fear or anguish than it resolves, for example, about death or illness. However, religious ritual often involves a movement through trauma and violence to some form of resolution (as discussed at length in Hodder 2010). For Boyer (2001, 58) "it is probably true that religious concepts gain their great salience and emotional load in the human psyche because they are connected to thoughts about various life-threatening circumstances." It is not that there is a general angst about death, but that religion builds on the human response to fear and danger. Thus, overall, there is widespread agreement that religion deals with or is linked to the identification and resolution of problems or dangers or misfortune or suffering.

The causes of suffering, misfortune, or inopportune death are often difficult to define. Entanglement theory, like network approaches, points to the fundamental connectedness of things. What we do or make goes well beyond us. Latour argues that "in all our activities, what we fabricate goes beyond us" (2010, 22–23; see also Meyer 2012, 21). As in all complex systems it is difficult to follow all the threads of things and their interconnections. And things and situations and relations keep changing. Things have vitality, as argued by Bennett (2009). Even apparently stable things like stone churches in England are in a state of flux and need continual attention in order to keep them upright and functional (Edensor 2011). Misfortune can easily occur as things and relationships shift; things are unruly (Hodder 2012). For all of us there is a real beyond, connected to us, but difficult to define or make sense of. This real beyond is linked to us, contributing to entanglement but in ineffable ways.

It has become commonplace to argue that religion can be linked to the beyond, the transcendent. Indeed, this assumption gained considerable purchase in the discussions of religion at Çatalhöyük (see Hodder 2010; Van Huyssteen 2014). If theologians and anthropologists could not agree on a definition of religion, they came closest when defining religion in terms of the beyond. In such discussions the beyond is often seen as constructed. Meyer (2012), for example, describes the material techniques through which we fabricate the sense of a presence of something beyond. Bellah (Bellah and Tipton 2006) argues that the idea of the transcendent, with salvation or enlightenment as the goal, emerged only in historic-era religions, linked to a shift from two-class systems in archaic periods to the four-class systems of historic to modern societies. There is of course a longer tradition of explaining religion as a constructed response to the human predicament. Freud argued that religion is an illusion created by deep psychological needs. Feuerbach, Marx, and Engels described religions as constructed ideologies in the interests of dominant groups.

The entanglement view takes a different tack in that it sees humans as caught up in entanglements that extend into a real beyond. Religion is a pragmatic attempt to make sense of and intervene in that beyond. Certainly bull-horn pedestals are made, churches are built, candles are lit. These are all fabrications. But they are fabrications in the form of technologies that do something to fix or deal with problems that extend off into the distant and apparently arbitrary. Certainly too, these technologies can be appropriated by those in power in order to increase and stabilize dominance. But in origin, such strategies of power are based on a bona fide struggle to deal with difficult problems that matter.

Recent work on materiality highlights the ways in which material objects have agency, often described as a secondary agency imputed by humans to things (Gell 1998). Others (Bennett 2009) have argued for a primary agency in the sense that things are unstable and have impact. When a wall collapses or is on the verge of collapse it draws in the social in very active ways—an individual or social group has to respond to fix the wall. Whether in some sense we can talk of walls having intentionality is beyond the scope of this chapter. But if we at least accept that things have primary agency in the sense of being impactful, and if we accept that things are enchained into remote spatial and temporal scales, then it must be the case that there is a real agency in the beyond that affects us but that we have little purchase on through direct everyday means. So it is not that we impute agency in the beyond or supernatural as a device. Rather, we need to find ways of dealing with real agencies in the beyond. These agencies cause death (we still have little understanding of what causes aging), misfortune (often the result of complex conjunctures of which we have limited understanding including storms, earthquakes, and tsunamis), illness (even today many illnesses are difficult to predict), suffering (the causes of inequality and violence are often deeply entangled in complex systems). And so we develop technologies to deal with these intractable problems—technologies that we have come to define as religion.

The techniques used to fix the beyond often derive from the particular historical circumstances in which people find themselves. In the case of the bull horns around the burial platform in Building 77 at Çatalhöyük, the use of bulls to protect or animate grows out of a particular entanglement between humans and bulls at this site. Wild bulls were still a source of meat in the early levels at the site (domesticated cattle were introduced in the upper levels), and at that time they were preferentially used in feasting events. Wild aurochsen were impressively large animals, so that those killing them and providing feasts must have gained considerable prestige. The paintings from the site show scenes in which numerous individuals surround, tease, and interact with wild bulls. Given the social importance of wild bulls at Çatalhöyük, it is not surprising that they were used so frequently in houses in relation to burial and in relation to rituals of house abandonment and foundation. Given the experience and knowledge of huge aurochs bulls it made perfect sense to appropriate their power in relation to the animation of the house.

As another example of the extension of practical knowledge into areas of the beyond at Çatalhöyük, all house interiors were plastered in a fine white marl. Floors, walls, benches, platforms, and bull heads were all plastered in the same material. Plastering was also extended as a technology to deal with the beyond, as in the example of the plastering of human skulls. Other examples of the extension of existing technologies to deal with the beyond include the use of agricultural symbolism in early agricultural societies in ritual contexts. For example, the soil beneath burial mounds was ritually plowed before mound construction in early agricultural societies in Europe (Bradley 1998). In the so-called Axial Age historical religions, the writing of words or scriptures, texts, and doctrines extended the existing use of bureaucratic technologies. In the modern world, science itself can be seen a technology of religion. In

1930 Einstein wrote that "in this materialistic age of ours the serious scientific workers are the only profoundly religious people" (cited in Bradley 1998, 12) in that they seek "the grandeur of reason incarnate in existence" (cited in Bradley 1998, 37). Our rational techniques, our enlightened reason provide a technology to probe and discover religion.

This technological approach to religion might appear to differ from accounts grounded in cognitive evolution. For example, Guthrie (2014) argues that religion is linked to the evolution of cognitive tendencies to see agency in the world, often in our own image. We have an evolutionary tendency to see animacy in things, and in particular we anthropomorphize. For example, at Çatalhöyük the house was born, had a life, and then died and was buried. In a related vein, Boyer (2001) describes religious forces as counterintuitive agents that we are drawn to because they are both familiar and unfamiliar. We believe that these agents can help us deal with misfortune because we have social minds and so we are predisposed to think that misfortune is social—is caused by someone. But it is not clear that the bull horns around the burial platform in Building 77 need involve either of these claims by Guthrie and Boyer. The bull horns can be seen as powerful in their own right without any anthropomorphism involved, and the agency of the horns can derive directly from the bull, without any social causality imputed. Rather, we can say that finding solutions to entanglements can make use of a very wide range of cognitive processes, including anthropomorphism, or tending to seek social agents, but the religious impulse does not seem restricted to these techniques. Certainly, religious activities are often both familiar and unfamiliar as Boyer argues. But in my view this is not because of cognitive needs to memorize or to be drawn in. Rather, the familiar-unfamiliar mix results from using known technologies and knowledge, and extending or reinventing them to deal with that which is beyond. Cognitive predispositions of the sort defined by Guthrie and Boyer may well exist, but they are only brought into play in relation to religion in so far as they afford technologies to deal with the ineffable, the transcendent.

The Materiality of Religion Increases Entanglements

It is one of the prime arguments of this chapter that religion is a technology that involves a doing. Even in the case of meditation or monastic contemplation, something is done. Even in the case of doctrinal, text-based religions, there is a reading or listening. Religion, as noted above, is not just about belief, but is a practical intervention in the world. As a result, materiality is a key component of religious practice. "As practices and materials are indispensable for religion's existence in the world as a social, cultural and political phenomenon, they need our utmost theoretical and empirical attention" (Meyer 2012, 23).

Meyer (2012, 23) provides an example from the Ewe from Ghana and Togo:

> According to Ewe cosmology, in principle all gods—*trõwo* or *vodu*—by necessity require some material vessel in order to be present and enact their power, and humans can access, and partake in, this power through certain religious acts. These acts begin with the actual carving or moulding of a figure, its subsequent animation through spitting alcohol and saliva, its regular maintenance through sacrifices and feeding, its worship through repeated incantations, body movements, and so on. Here, human action was indispensable for the gods to be present and act on people.

There are numerous examples of external powers and agencies being made present in religious practices. The Orthodox or Catholic icon itself becomes a being that is kissed, carried around, prayed to. Saints and prophets were made present in the form of circulated body parts. The body and blood of Christ are made present (in different ways) in Catholic and Protestant churches. Why does the religious have to be made material to be experienced? I argue this is precisely because religious practice is about "getting a hold on" the beyond, the divine. One gets a hold on the divine partly by making it human and anthropomorphic. As noted above, the practice of seeing human agency in things is found in all areas of life, but it is also used as a technology to intervene in the beyond. More generally, manipulating things allows the practitioner a sense of agency in relation to the beyond, it allows a connection to be made and interventions to occur. Material things are central to religion because they allow us to participate in the divine and to use religion as a technology to manage the beyond of the world in which we live.

This thorough dependence of humans on things in the religious realm creates further entanglement and dependency. At Çatalhöyük the bull horns used around the platform in Building 77 of course came from the slaughter of an aurochs. Much of the ritual practices that dominated domestic life in the early part of the sequence of occupation at the site depended on gaining access to wild bulls. Indeed, this heavy ritual dependence on wild bulls may have been a factor leading to the late adoption of domestic cattle at the site (as argued by Arbuckle 2013). Humans entered into a dependency relationship with wild cattle in that they had to work harder to amass the numbers of wild bulls needed for a variety of rituals. In addition, social and economic relations all became caught up in wild bulls. These relations were threatened by the appearance of domestic cattle, which undermined many of the existing social and ritual relations (Der, personal communication).

We are used to conceiving of religious institutions as laden with material trappings. As religious institutions grew, vast economic wealth often became attached to them. Land was acquired, buildings constructed, alliances made with political movements. Today the material investments and entanglements of churches and religious movements have global reach, including the sourcing of religious paraphernalia, the missionizing of distant populations, the control of media, and the sustenance of online congregations. In all these ways, religion contributes to entanglement, and it contributes significantly to entrapment, the sense of "being stuck" within particular traditions and practices.

The Long Term

One of the distinctive characteristics of religions and religious movements is that they have the ability to endure over long time periods. This was as true in deep prehistory as it is today. Hodder and Meskell (2011) have discussed the long duration of specific ritual practices in the Neolithic of the Middle East and Anatolia by drawing attention to the remarkable similarities in iconography between Çatalhöyük and the site of Göbekli Tepe two thousand years earlier. In both cases there is a focus on dangerous wild animals, and in both there are depictions of headless bodies associated with birds. Vulture depictions are found widely across the Middle East. Sustained by myth or ritual practice, these continuities are remarkable. In more recent millennia we have become embedded in long-term religions and religious traditions, many of which extend back two to three thousand years.

Why when so many other technologies and cultural practices are replaced and die out, do these religious traditions continue? In the entanglement perspective, things endure over the long term if they are central to many strands in the entanglement networks. Because religion is about things that matter, about ultimate questions, it becomes embedded in many areas of life. As Bellah (Bellah and Tipton 2006, 18) states, "religion is the key to culture." It becomes closely linked to identity. It becomes embroiled in politics and law, in right ways of acting. According to Weber (Weber and Parsons 1998), it is entangled with economics. If we were to draw a tanglegram (Hodder 2012) that showed all the dependences and dependencies of religion and religious institutions, most areas of life would be drawn in. This high centrality of religion means that while religions may adapt and transform as entanglements change, there is a strong tendency toward continuity.

Other technologies that endure over the long term are often entangled in multiple domains. For example, when pottery was initially introduced at Çatalhöyük about 7000 BCE, it was used as a container. At this early stage, pottery could have died out without major disruption to overall entanglements. But it quickly came to be used for other purposes as its various affordances were exploited. First it became used for cooking, and later for storage and display. Pottery was to have a long history over millennia at least partly because it was caught up in many entanglements. Much could be said of the wheel, initially used for carts and linked to the domestication of cattle as draught animals, later linked to horses and warfare in chariots, much later to wheeled motorized vehicles, trains, planes, and all the time linked to other activities such as potting (the potter's wheel), gears, clocks, machines, and engines. In these cases, technologies endure over the long term because they are central and dispersed through multiple hubs in entanglements.

Specific religions that endure appear to have similar characteristics. In the case of the Middle East Neolithic, special imagery using bulls lasts through multiple phases but often in different forms. At Çatalhöyük, for example, early bull representations involved installing bull heads and horns into houses. In the later levels, perhaps associated with a shift from imagistic to doctrinal religious modalities (Whitehouse and Hodder 2010), wild bulls are commonly shown in narrative scenes in wall paintings. Later bull imagery is found on pottery rather than on wall paintings, and seems more connected with mobile artifacts that can be moved around. As social and economic change occurs at Çatalhöyük, so the bull symbolism is reinterpreted. Historically all major religions have seen change and reinterpretation as societies have transformed over centuries and millennia.

Religion may have a particular association with the long term because it deals with fundamental issues that matter. Humans are thus very invested in the religious practices and beliefs and are likely to tinker and transform them rather than see them overturned. This is a good example of path dependency, where it becomes too "costly" to turn back or deviate significantly, although here the "costliness" relates to deeply held convictions and embodied practices. It may also be the case that the very beyondness of religion allows reinterpretation and reuse. We have seen that religion is about the remote reaches of entanglements and it tries to find ways of fixing things in those distant spheres that nevertheless affect us in the here and now. It is very striking how often religions provide a fixed point that is distant, elsewhere, transcendent. So many religions refer back to distant times, prophets, events, and books. At Çatalhöyük religious practices involve past ancestors, wild and difficult animals. Much of the special deposition and "magical" practices involve objects that have been obtained at great distances such as obsidian from the mountains of Cappadocia or crystals and speleothems from far-away caves. These objects provide fixed points in the unknown. They provide a way of handling and holding on to and so affecting the beyond. But precisely because these are distant points it becomes possible to interpret current events in their terms. The fixed points remain, but because they are distant, reinterpretation is endlessly possible. Because they are ultimate, reinterpretation is important, and because they are transcendent, reinterpretation is possible. In this dual way, religion is often associated with the long term.

Another interpretation of the long-term duration of religion is that it derives from the play of structures of power and domination. Religion has always been involved in struggle. For example, early Christianity provided a way of dealing with (a technology for) being on the margins of the Roman Empire, trapped and marginalized in a large-scale imperial system. Islam emerged on the margins of the Byzantine Empire. Prothero (2011, 291) argues that Confucianism emerged in the midst of "a particularly chaotic period in Chinese history." Religion as a technology provided solutions to these problems. But precisely because it was successful in these ways, it became appropriated by elites in order to establish new forms and extents of power. Elites enlisted religion in order to impose and extend power and to underpin violence and intervention. Asad (1982) argues that "it was not the mind that moved spontaneously to religious truth, but power that created the conditions for experiencing that truth."

Religion, Entrapment, and Path Dependency

It is perhaps because religion is a way of dealing with ultimate questions that really matter that it can so effectively be used as a way of excluding, marking off, dominating—that it is so linked to power and to intransigent conflict, resurfacing over millennia in new ways and forms. It seems likely that Çatalhöyük was a very unpleasant society to live in—excluding those that did not fit in and forcing women and the young to conform. Religion helped to produce and reproduce these inequalities and entrapments. The burial of ancestors, the presencing of bulls, the whole range of symbolism at the site are embedded in domestic houses that show much habitual repetition of daily practices as well as separations between old and young (Hodder and Cessford 2004). There is a high degree of routinized conformity, and in one case a physical different individual was buried in the midden outside the house (Hodder 2006). The society was divided socially on the basis of age, and older people were likely to have

Religion as a Technology of Entanglement

embedded their power in their ability to deal with the beyond through the technologies of bull installations and the manipulation of human skeletal parts.

Religion has had a long relationship with power and violence, and the political dimensions of religion are today most clearly expressed in religious fundamentalism. We all live today with the image of individuals shouting "Allahu Akbar" as they fly a passenger plane into the Twin Towers, or blowing themselves up in a crowded marketplace across the globe. In the context of global entanglements in which people feel powerless in the face of interventions by the United States and the West, religion becomes a component in a struggle that returns to fundamentals in the face of absolute power. All fundamentalists, whether Islamic, Christian, Jewish, or whatever, use religion as a technology to react to the entrapments of global and state powers. Based on a survey of Christian, Muslim, Jewish, Hindu, and Buddhist fundamentalists, Haynes (2003, 326) argues that "contemporary fundamentalism is rooted in the failed promise of modernity, reactive against perceived unwelcome manifestations of modernization." Religious fundamentalism reacts against modernity, secularization, and state or global political and military control. The specific sources of disaffection vary. For many Muslims the main issues are poverty, declining faith in promises of development (Haynes 2003, 330), and imperial intrusion. Some Christian fundamentalists identify the problem as high levels of amorality in the United States. Some Jewish fundamentalist groups in Israel have an unwillingness to negotiate with Palestinians over what they see as holy land.

There is, then, much evidence that religion is politically engaged in the contemporary world, and a heralded global secularization has failed to materialize. Humans today seem to need religion as a technology as much as ever. But why does politics need religion? There have of course long been discussions of the relationships between religion and the world, or between the church and the state and civil society (Therborn 1994). Weber (1978) saw three types of relationships between secular and ecclesiastical power, and Medhurst (1981) and Mitra (1991) have developed related schemes. For many, including Mitra and Haynes, religion provides the moral basis for political action. But the entanglement view is more that politics deals with fixing problems, and the key problems are extremely difficult to fix. Those problems that concern poverty, suffering, global intervention, or moral behavior involve complex intersecting chains and circuits that extend off into remote spatial and temporal scales. In all this distant uncertainty, religion provides fixed points, some closure to the complex entanglements, something to hold on to as political arguments are made and new directions sought for.

The centrality of religion in entanglements and the fact that it deals with fundamental issues, with things that matter to us, produce a central role for religion in power and conflict. These entanglements with power themselves create greater entrapment so that historically humans get caught in particular pathways. The notion of path dependency (Mahoney 2000) is more normally applied to economic and social and cultural continuities, but it seems particularly appropriate to religion. So much gets invested in the entanglements of religion that it becomes difficult to disentangle and unravel. Long-term continuities are the result. It becomes difficult to change tack or to retrace steps because religion is so central to multiple hubs in entanglement and because it deals with fundamental issues and ultimate questions. But for these same reasons it affords rich grounds for the play of power. Religion provides power with ultimate justification and allows elites to claim an ability to manage and fix ultimate and transcendent issues. By the same token, religion allows dominated groups to act back, for example, by returning to fundamentals and forging new paths, even if in doing so they reproduce continuities.

Conclusions

Much of our work at Çatalhöyük has been to "normalize" the site and its elaborate symbolism and rituals. In earlier accounts the site had seemed exotic, weird, strange (Mellaart 1967; Mithen 2004). What we have gradually done is make it seem quite practical, sensible, and normal, so much so that one can say, "If I had been there I would have done the same thing." The entanglement view of religion turns it into a practical technology of doing that makes sense within a particular frame of knowledge. This practical technology deals with real problems that extend into the beyond within complex, unbounded entanglements. The term "religious" can be used when we try to fix things that are of ultimate significance but that extend beyond our immediate abilities to find solutions. We therefore resort to using the full breadth of human embodied knowledge and intellectual ingenuity available at the historical moment in which we are caught up, in order to deal with and manage the beyond, with all its uncertainties.

In his classic account *Zande of Sudan*, Evans-Pritchard (1937) went beyond cataloguing strange beliefs and showed how sensible the Zande religion was in the context of Zande knowledge and the problems that were being faced (see also Boyer 2001, 35). One day a granary collapsed onto some people sheltering beneath it from the sun. The inhabitants of the village explained the event in terms of witchcraft. Evans-Pritchard pointed out to the Zande that the granary probably collapsed because the house was infested with termites. The villagers responded by agreeing that the termites had undermined the granary structure, but they asked why the roof collapsed at a particular time when people were beneath it, rather than before or after. It was only witchcraft that could explain this particular conjuncture, this particular timing. So, here we see that "religion" describes a situation in which it is difficult to make sense of complex, entangled interactions. The solutions that are found (that witchcraft was involved) are perfectly rational within a specific frame of knowledge. Cause has to be found and it is provided by witchcraft; and indeed rational Western humans may find it equally difficult to explain conjunctures emergent within complex systems. We may indeed, like Einstein, invoke a god when we are faced with the enormous complexity of large systems, beautiful in their order, but uncertain in their emergent properties.

Uncertainty derives from the complexity of interactions within the entangled threads that extend outward all around us, threads that are heterogeneous mixes of the cultural and the biological, the social and the environmental, human and nonhuman. These threads stretch into the beyond but they still affect us. When the effects matter deeply to us, as in the case of the untimely death of a child, we are forced to deal with the beyond. We do what we do in all areas of life, we try to fix things. Religion describes the varied technologies that attempt to fix things in the beyond, using familiar techniques, but extending them to deal with the beyond. In this chapter I have argued that religion is both a response to, and a major contributor to, entanglement. The entanglement with religion is productive but also pernicious. The existence of an ultimate fixed point provides security and a response to suffering, but it also embeds us in ways of being that, because they are bound to the ultimate, entrap us in domination and exclusion. While such a conclusion is contradicted by religious and spiritual movements that promote tolerance, openness, and multiple faiths (such as the Sufism of Jalal ad-Din Rumi, buried in Konya just down the road from Çatalhöyük), the tendency has been for the entanglements of religion to be associated with a long history of intolerance and violence. The impulse to staunch the flows of entanglements by providing fixed points seems to lead too frequently to power, domination, and entrapment.

Discussion

Apart from the personal experiences described toward the beginning of this chapter, the initial motivation for dealing with the topic of entanglement and religion derived from a difficulty that I had encountered in developing methods for the study of networks of dependence and dependency between humans and things. It quickly became clear that defining the edges or boundaries to entanglements was next to impossible. Entanglements that dealt with clay use at Çatalhöyük seemed to blend into other entanglements that themselves were entangled with yet further sets of interactions. Entanglements did not seem to have bounds. Wherever one defined a boundary or limit in order to produce a diagram of entanglements, there was a beyond that could not be mapped but that nevertheless had an impact on whatever was occurring within the limit. Given the presence of this effective beyond of entanglements, it seemed of interest that most of the work on religion that we had undertaken at Çatalhöyük had defined religion in terms of the beyond. I wanted to ask the question whether religion might be a way of dealing with the beyond of entanglements, and to ask the question whether the two types of beyond might be linked.

But is my claim that religion is indeed a technology for dealing with the beyond of entanglements simply a version of the Enlightenment view that religion only has a role where rational science ends? Is it only where we cannot understand or control entanglement using rational means that religion has purchase? To some degree my answer to these questions is yes, although only if rationality is understood as relational and diverse. But even in everyday actions that have a matter-of-fact rationality there is uncertainty. At Çatalhöyük people responded to the collapse of walls by making sandier bricks or by shoring up the walls with buttresses or by doubling the walls so that they could support each other. These eminently sensible solutions worked, but they could not deal with the uncertainty of which walls might collapse next, or which walls might erode first. So in addition to practical solutions they also protected the walls by placing human skulls at the base of posts or conducting feasts at the foundation of houses. These "religious" responses, in addition to the "practical" everyday solutions, were needed to protect the walls, and my argument is that they were needed in order to deal with the indeterminacy or with entangled processes that were beyond contemporary understanding. Today, science has come further in understanding the complexity of things and their interactions. However much rational science extends into the world, there remain much uncertainty and lack of control in our daily lives. Where this matters deeply to us there thus remains a role for religion.

And science certainly has failed to deliver an end to inequality and suffering. In recent centuries the scale of inequalities has increased and solutions seem ever more complex as empires and globalization have extended their reach. Solutions to suffering seem intractable and global institutions seem gridlocked in their attempts to direct social and economic change. There do not seem to be simple solutions to the problems that a rational modernity has produced. The causes of and solutions to poverty, suffering, and disease seem remote and unmanageable. It is thus not surprising, given the argument in this chapter, that secularization has declined globally while religious practices, including religious fundamentalism, are on the rise. It is they that offer ways of dealing with problems that matter to people, and provide tools for disentangling from modernity.

Acknowledgment: I am very grateful to Birgit Meyer for critical comments on an earlier draft of this essay.

References

Arbuckle, B. S. 2013. The late adoption of cattle and pig husbandry in Neolithic central Turkey. *Journal of Archaeological Science* 40(4):1805–15.
Asad, T. 1982. The construction of religion as an anthropological category. In *Genealogies of Religion; Discipline and Reasons of Power in Christianity and Islam*, 27–54. Baltimore: Johns Hopkins University Press.
Baines, J. 1987. Practical religion and piety. *Journal of Egyptian Archaeology* 73:79–98.
Bellah, R. N., and S. M. Tipton. 2006. *The Robert Bellah Reader*. Durham, NC: Duke University Press.
Bennett, J. 2009. *Vibrant Matter: A Political Ecology of Things*. Durham, NC: Duke University Press.
Bloch, M. 2010. Is there religion at Çatalhöyük . . . or are there just houses? In *Religion in the Emergence of Civilization: Çatalhöyük as a Case Study*, edited by I. Hodder, 146–62. Cambridge: Cambridge University Press.
Boyer, P. 2001. *Religion Explained*. New York: Basic Books.
Bradley, R. 1998. *The Significance of Monuments: On the Shaping of Human Experience in Neolithic and Bronze Age Europe*. London: Routledge.
Burke, P. T. 2004. *The Major Religions*. 2nd ed. Oxford: Blackwell.
Edensor, T. 2011. Entangled agencies, material networks and repair in a building assemblage: the mutable stone of St Ann's Church, Manchester. *Transactions of the Institute of British Geographers* NS 36:238–52.
Evans-Pritchard, E. E. 1937. *Witchcraft, Oracles and Magic amongst the Azande*. Oxford: Clarendon.
Gell, A. 1998. *Art and Agency*. Oxford: Clarendon.
Guthrie, S. E. 2014. Religion as anthropomorphism at Çatalhöyük. In *Religion at Work in a Neolithic Society: Vital Matters*, edited by I. Hodder, 86–108. Cambridge: Cambridge University Press.
Haynes, J. 2003. Religious fundamentalism and politics. In *Major World Re-*

ligions: From Their Origins to the Present, edited by L. Ridgeon. London: Routledge.
Heidegger, M. 1973. *Being and Time*. Oxford: Blackwell.
Hodder, I. 2006. *The Leopard's Tale: Revealing the Mysteries of Çatalhöyük*. London: Thames and Hudson.
Hodder, I., ed. 2010. *Religion in the Emergence of Civilization: Çatalhöyük as a Case Study*. Cambridge: Cambridge University Press.
Hodder, I. 2012. *Entangled*. Cambridge: Cambridge University Press.
Hodder, I., and C. Cessford. 2004. Daily practice and social memory at Çatalhöyük. *American Antiquity*: 17–40.
Hodder, I., and L. Meskell. 2011. A "curious and sometimes a trifle macabre artistry": some aspects of symbolism in Neolithic Turkey. *Current Anthropology* 52(2):1–29.
Hodder, I., and P. Pels. 2010. History houses: a new interpretation of architectural elaboration at Çatalhöyük. In *Religion in the Emergence of Civilization: Çatalhöyük as a Case Study*, edited by I. Hodder, 163–86. Cambridge: Cambridge University Press.
Ingold, T. 2000. *The Perception of the Environment: Essays on Livelihood, Dwelling and Skill*. New York: Psychology Press.
Knappett, Carl. 2011. *Thinking through Material Culture: An Interdisciplinary Perspective*. Philadelphia: University of Pennsylvania Press.
Latour, B. 2005. *Reassembling the Social: An Introduction to Actor-Network-Theory*. Oxford: Oxford University Press.
Latour, B. 2010. *On the Modern Cult of the Factish Gods (Science and Cultural Theory)*. Durham, NC: Duke University Press.
Mahoney, J. 2000. Path dependence in historical sociology. *Theory and Society* 29:507–48.
Medhurst, K. 1981. Religion and politics: a typology. *Scottish Journal of Religious Studies* 2(2):115–34.
Mellaart, J. 1967. *Çatal Hüyük: A Neolithic Town in Anatolia*. London: Thames and Hudson.
Meskell, L. 2004. *Object Worlds in Ancient Egypt: Material Biographies Past and Present*. London: Berg.
Meyer, B. 2012. *Mediation and the Genesis of Presence: Towards a Material Approach to Religion*. Utrecht: University of Utrecht Press.
Mithen, S. 2004. *After the Ice: A Global Human History, 20,000–5000 BC*. Cambridge, MA: Harvard University Press.
Mitra, S. K. 1991. Desecularising the state: religion and politics in India after Independence. *Comparative Studies in Society and History* 33(4):755–77.
Prothero, S. 2011. *God Is Not One*. New York: HarperCollins.

Rosaldo, Renato 1984. *Grief and a Headhunter's Rage: Death, Mourning, and Burial*. Malden, MA: Blackwell.
Super, J. C., and B. K. Turley. 2006. *Religion in World History*. London: Routledge.
Therborn, G. 1994. Another way to taking religion seriously: comment of Francis G. Castles. *European Journal of Political Research* 26(1):103–10.
Tilley, C. 1994. *A Phenomenology of Landscape: Places, Paths and Monuments*. London: Berg.
Van Huyssteen, J. W. 2006. *Alone in the World? Human Uniqueness in Science and Theology*. Grand Rapids: Eerdmans.
Van Huyssteen, J. W. 2010. Coding *the nonvisible*: epistemic limitations and understanding symbolic behavior at Çatalhöyük. In *Religion in the Emergence of Civilization*, edited by I. Hodder, 99–121. Cambridge: Cambridge University Press.
Van Huyssteen, J. W. 2014. The historical self: memory and religion at Çatalhöyük. In *Religion at Work in a Neolithic Society: Vital Matters*, edited by I. Hodder, 109–33. Cambridge: Cambridge University Press.
Weber, M. 1978. *Economy and Society*. Berkeley: University of California Press.
Weber, M., and T. Parsons. 1998. *The Protestant Ethic and the Spirit of Capitalism*. Los Angeles: Roxbury.
Whitehouse, H. 2004. *Modes of Religiosity: A Cognitive Theory of Religious Transmission*. Lanham, MD: Altamira.
Whitehouse, H., and I. Hodder. 2010. Modes of religiosity at Çatalhöyük. In *Religion in the Emergence of Civilization: Çatalhöyük as a Case Study*, edited by I. Hodder, 122–45. Cambridge: Cambridge University Press.

3 *Imago Dei* and Animal Domestication

Cognitive-Evolutionary Perspectives on Human Uniqueness and the Imago Dei

JUSTIN L. BARRETT AND TYLER S. GREENWAY

I (Barrett) first met J. Wentzel van Huyssteen in Beijing in the summer of 2008. I had recently reviewed his book *Alone in the World?* (2006) somewhat critically, and was a bit startled to find myself face to face with him at the Forbidden City. Instead of hoping that he had not, and would not, read my review, I decided to come clean and mention it. To my surprise, he almost immediately asked me, in all sincerity, "What did I get wrong?" I was disarmed by his intellectual humility. We had a delightful discussion, and my interest in the evolution and theology of human uniqueness that his book had sparked in me was fanned into a small flame. At that time I did not know that he and I would meet again each of the following two summers as participants in a project led by archaeologist Ian Hodder concerning the religious expression of people living seven thousand to nine thousand years ago at a site known as Çatalhöyük.

Çatalhöyük is notable for representing a transition in cultural evolution. This transition is evidenced by the beginnings of plant and animal domestication in what is modern-day Turkey. Interestingly, Çatalhöyük is also famous for its remarkable evidence of what appear to be domestic shrines and other religious practices. Perhaps the co-occurrence of these two different findings is insignificant, but the physical evidence at Çatalhöyük does raise an interesting question directly related to the evolution and theology of human uniqueness: what is the relationship between the domestication of animals and religious expression—both of which are capacities unique to the human species? If early evidence of both domestication and religious expression coincides, perhaps these two remarkable human behaviors are linked. We take up this topic in this chapter.

Specifically, drawing on insights from cognitive and evolutionary psychology, we propose that animal domestication in particular may have been a critical point in human religious evolution, and may even be central to an understanding of the role humans play as beings created in the image of God, or *imago Dei*, as articulated in Genesis. Indeed, Genesis 1 recalls the uniqueness of humanity, created, male and female, in God's image, and the special charge given to them, to rule over all the animals that populate the Earth. Perhaps the physical evidence found at Çatalhöyük exemplifies a connection between humans being uniquely created in the image of God and humans being tasked as stewards over the birds and beasts.

Before arguing for the *imago Dei* being closely related to animal domestication, we first consider another hypothesis that I (Barrett) have argued for previously: that the evolution of what we term "higher-order theory of mind," or HO-ToM for short, is a critical component of what it means to be *imago Dei*. We place these two hypotheses side by side not because we are convinced that either one is clearly superior to the other in terms of available scientific evidence or theological considerations—indeed, we regard them as potentially complementary—but because they jointly illustrate the productivity in bringing cognitive and evolutionary perspectives on religion together with theology, a science-theology synthesis that van Huyssteen has modeled in his career.

These two hypotheses concerning *imago Dei* each constitute a reply to those who might argue that scientific evidence dismisses the idea that humans, unique among extant species, may claim to be created in the image of God. These individuals might argue that if *Homo sapiens* are descended from other species that were not *imago Dei* through a series of tiny, incremental steps, then it is reasonable to suppose that the modern human population overlaps importantly with earlier species on any number of dimensions that one may want to identify with the *imago Dei*. Rationality? Likely some adult *Homo habilis* or perhaps even australopithecines, for instance, possessed a stronger claim to rationality than contemporary human infants. The same appears likely for nearly any particular capacity one may want to identify with *imago Dei*: many existing humans, such as children or other individuals with limited cognitive capabilities, likely have that particular capacity in a lesser degree than members of a pre-human population. Because of our continuity with other species, it appears that for any given trait, there is no set of beings possessing that trait that includes all human beings and no other animals. Development and disability almost guarantee that at least one human does not possess any particular trait or capacity unique to the human population (i.e., that no other animals have). Moreover, findings from paleontology suggest that some contemporary *Homo sapiens* have different ancestors—all share ancestors from Africa, but some also have Neanderthal and Denisovan ancestors (Venema 2011). At first blush, then, it may appear that evolutionary psychology dooms the idea of *imago Dei*—the lines between species are simply too blurred. We argue by demonstration that, on the contrary, cognitive-evolutionary accounts provide fresh perspectives for understanding human uniqueness and *imago Dei*.

Higher-Order Theory of Mind and *Imago Dei*

In this section we briefly present a case for HO-ToM as a cognitive capacity that distinguishes humans from nonhumans, and, in particular, qualitatively distinguishes humans as capable of being designated *imago Dei*.[1] Barrett and Jarvinen (2015) argued that many of the traits or capacities that have historically been identified with *imago Dei* are all facilitated by HO-ToM. That is, even without choosing one particular capacity (e.g., rationality, moral accountability, I-Thou relationality) as constituting the *imago Dei*, we have strong reason to think that possessing a HO-ToM as part of their nature makes modern humans unique. Here we only present the contribution of HO-ToM to personal relationships with God and others. We regard this relational interpretation of *imago Dei* as among the strongest interpretations and certainly one that appears to be attracting the attention of contemporary theologians. Further, the connection between HO-ToM and relationality is more easily defensible than between HO-ToM and other traits that may be candidates for *imago Dei*.

This argument depends on two critical philosophical moves. First, it maintains that one cannot reduce *imago Dei* to simple divine fiat. One way others have tried to avoid the problem of identifying a single trait or capacity that all humans have but no other animals do is to locate that trait not in the human expression of traits but in God's action. For instance, God could decide to love each human and only humans in a particular way. That divine decision, then, is what could be meant by saying that humans are created in God's image. In rejecting this solution, Barrett and Jarvinen write:

> To avoid locating the image and likeness of God within nonuniversal human capacities ... some have been tempted to transfer the decisive quality to the love of God.... But among all the animals, why humans? Unless God's decision is entirely arbitrary and God could just have easily designated banana slugs as *imago Dei*, such a question inevitably transfers the locus

---

1. For a more complete presentation, see Barrett and Jarvinen, 2015.

back to humans, leaving us chronicling a list of capacities such as those we have previously discussed. (2015, 168)

That is, to protect God from acting arbitrarily, it seems that some reference to particular distinctive human traits may be necessary. What kind of animal is worthy of God's special love that makes them *imago Dei*? What property or trait(s) must this animal possess? These questions deserve answers.

Even though some trait or traits that mark off human uniqueness may be required to sort out the *imago Dei*, the divine fiat strategy highlights that having some distinctive trait(s) may be necessary but not sufficient for being *imago Dei*. That is, we can imagine that during the process of evolution, ancestors of contemporary humans began to show traits that made them capable of some special designation, but that God refrained from designating them *imago Dei* until some later point. For instance, God could have waited to declare our ancestors *imago Dei* until a point in history when all subsequent humans would have some particular trait(s) as part of their potential. Likewise, God could have waited until some particular point in history when humans were somehow ready to have a special relationship or status before God. Our insistence that some distinctive feature or features made humans capable of being designated God's imagers does not entail that as soon as the first animal evinced that trait, that animal was God's imager.

The second philosophical move critical to giving HO-ToM a special place in understanding *imago Dei* is to locate the requisite property or trait(s) in the animal's "nature" and not in its necessary exhibition of that nature. "Nature" here is meant in a particular sense that should not be confused with a species' biology or genetic code. Rather, following Wolterstorff (2008), Barrett and Jarvinen reference a blueprint or design in the mind of God for a particular species. They write:

> We understand him [Wolterstorff] to be suggesting that there is something like a grand design for what humans should be in fully realized form, a design not necessarily present at all stages of development or in all humans, but what humans should be in an ideal form. All human beings have the same human nature, whether it is malformed or in the process of development. (2015, 166)

By virtue of having *human nature*, whether actualized in each and every human being at all times, humans become God's imagers. Barrett and Jarvinen continue: "In a way analogous to a plan, blueprint, or ideal, humans all possess such a nature, and it is by virtue of this nature—which is always potentially realizable, at least from God's perspective—that they are God's special love objects" (2015, 168).

These two philosophical commitments combine to support the proposition that humans can be understood as *imago Dei* by virtue of an idealized nature that is by God's design,[2] but that this nature must possess certain properties that, when properly manifested or actualized, make for an animal appropriate to God's special designation as *imago Dei*. The process of incremental evolution by natural selection may still be seen as the means by which this human nature developed over time, and defenders of *imago Dei* may still feel the burden of having to identify those aspects of human nature that make humans worthy to be designated *imago Dei* by God. What the *imago Dei* defenders need not do, however, is find a trait that *all* humans possess.

It does remain for the *imago Dei* defender to find a trait that only humans manifest, and, ideally, one that humans under normal conditions manifest. After all, it would be surprising for God to designate all humans *imago Dei* when the majority of humans do not manifest any interesting difference from nonhuman animals. It may be that only humans rhythmically beat drums, and perhaps God is fond of percussion and so designated humans *imago Dei*, but drum beating does not have the ubiquity in human experience, day in and day out, that sets it up as a promising candidate on which to hang *imago Dei*. HO-ToM, however, looks much more promising.

Though Barrett and Jarvinen argue for placing HO-ToM in a central place, they do not claim that having HO-ToM as part of human nature *is* the *imago Dei*. Rather, they argue that the strongest candidates for this aspect of human nature require HO-ToM. Further, they suggest that it may have been the case that all of the bricks needed to build *imago Dei* were in place and then HO-ToM's appearance was the mortar that enabled them to be put together. Or, HO-ToM was the spark that set the existing fuel ablaze. How so?

In cognitive science and developmental psychology "theory of mind" (ToM) is jargon referring to the typical way in which one attributes mental states to others and thinks about the interrelations and roles of those mental states in directing action. For instance, to understand that LeRon is gesturing with his empty glass because he wants Wentzel to pass the Scotch requires that we attribute to LeRon a specific desire and recognize that he intends to change Wentzel's mental states (beliefs about LeRon's desires) so that Wentzel's subsequent actions will satisfy LeRon's desire to drink Scotch. This series

---

2. We assume that God could have chosen to create a world through which evolution led to an animal with our character. Thus, we are not denying either God's design or evolution in this chapter.

of attributions and representations is the work of the cognitive subsystem referred to as ToM.

ToM is not an all-or-nothing cognitive subsystem. ToM has a developmental course in the early years of a human life and appears to have an evolutionary developmental progression as well. The most basic ToM is probably attributing states such as desires (the hummingbird wants nectar from the flower) or percepts (the squirrel sees the dog) to another being (accurately or not) and recognizing that these play some role in shaping actions; for instance, that desires will motivate actions in pursuit of the desired object. More sophisticated ToM, sometimes called belief-desire psychology, involves attributing beliefs—representational states that need not map on to the real world—and recognizing the role of beliefs in shaping actions, whether or not the beliefs are true beliefs. That is, what is often regarded as proper ToM in humans is the ability to recognize that beliefs shape action whether or not they are true. Beliefs are representations, and so this mature ToM is sometimes called a representational theory of mind. The litmus test for this ToM has long been "passing" variants of a false-belief task,[3] which require someone to recognize that beliefs may be false representational states and not merely reflections of the way we understand things to be.

Another way to analyze different variants of theory of mind is in terms of "orders of intentionality." First-order intentionality is to simply attribute some specific mental states to another. "Wentzel wants to return to South Africa" is an attribution of a particular mental state (the desire to return to South Africa). Second-order intentionality is to form a thought about the thought as in: "Wentzel thinks that returning to South Africa via ship is the least costly way to get there, but he is mistaken." Adding that reflection (e.g., that the belief is mistaken) is what makes the intentionality second order. Of course, this recursion can go on and on. Beliefs can be about beliefs about beliefs and so forth. Passing false-belief tasks (correctly and knowingly attributing a false belief to another) requires second-order intentionality, and so this ToM may be regarded as higher-order theory of mind, or HO-ToM. It is a real possibility that no other extant species on Earth possess HO-ToM of the second order, let alone higher orders that humans find themselves using with some regularity.[4] "Drew believes (but is wrong) that Paul thinks that Ian desires that Harvey stops desiring to boat on the Thames" may stretch a normal adult HO-ToM

---

3. For examples, see Perner (1991); Wimmer and Perner (1983).

4. We recognize that whether chimpanzees, bonobos, and elephants have second-order theory of mind is contested. We find the evidence ambiguous at best. We are unaware of any compelling evidence that any species today apart from humans engage in third-order or higher-order intentionality.

a bit, but probably will not break it. A typical three-year-old human and an adult chimpanzee, however, do not have theory of mind capacities capable of this type of thinking.

With this description of what HO-ToM is, we may now articulate its importance to various accounts of *imago Dei*. Suppose one is attracted to the idea that the critical capacity that humans possess such that God selected them to be *imago Dei* is the ability to engage in personal loving relationships. Many contemporary theologians share an attraction to relationality as a key characteristic of *imago Dei*. For instance, R. LeRon Shults has described how relationality has emerged as a focus across disciplines, including philosophy, theology, psychology, and even physics (2003). Many have grounded this relational emphasis within Trinitarian perspectives. For instance, Jack Balswick, Pamela King, and Kevin Reimer (2005, 38) follow Karl Barth in regarding *imago Dei* to be a relational concept. They advocate that as the Trinitarian God necessarily combines both uniqueness of persons and unity of the Godhead, so too humans are created to be unique individuals united with God and with others, akin to the I-Thou relationships championed by Barth and Martin Buber.

Arguably, this type of I-Thou relationality is made possible by HO-ToM. HO-ToM makes it possible for me to realize that you may have beliefs about my desires, or for me to understand that you and I both desire the same thing even if we are acting in different ways. The upshot of having HO-ToM is an entirely new type of social interaction, and indeed, its evolution is regarded as being encouraged precisely because of its contribution to interpersonal group living (Dunbar 2007). For example, if Wentzel, a possessor of HO-ToM, is living within a community of people with HO-ToM, he can be consciously aware of other individuals' thoughts, desires, and feelings and also aware that others are aware of his own personal thoughts, desires, and feelings just as he is aware of theirs. This awareness of thoughts, desires, and feelings is more than simple knowledge of behavioral dispositions. Recognition of a particular person as angry and prone to violent outbursts is useful, but complex social relationships require more than identification of these types of behavioral dispositions. Animals with HO-ToM would be able to know (or at least suspect they know) when another knows what they are thinking or feeling. Not only would an individual be able to know that the other has an internal life, but also that this internal life could be concerned about still other individuals, and further that this internal life could be shared and communicated. An individual possessor of HO-ToM could be consciously aware that others have unique thoughts including desires and beliefs, and also aware that some of those unique thoughts, desires, and beliefs could be shared. Arguably, HO-ToM makes I-Thou relationships possible, both with other humans and with God. Thus, if God chooses to engage humans in a special loving relationship marked as *imago Dei* because of their relational capacity, then as HO-ToM is a directly relevant enabler of such a capacity, it indirectly enables humans to be *imago Dei*.

If HO-ToM creates the possibility of individual, personal relationships with another human that includes knowledge of shared (or divergent) beliefs, desires, and attitudes, then HO-ToM also makes a personal relationship of this sort with God possible. Further, HO-ToM would make it possible for more than one person to both know they have a relationship with the same God. For me to know that you know that we both love God, I need HO-ToM. For me to know that God desires for me to change my attitudes toward my neighbor requires HO-ToM. HO-ToM, then, appears to be a necessary quality to have a personal relationship with God. If so, and the potential for a personal relationship with God marks off *imago Dei*, then HO-ToM may be a, or even *the*, key capacity.

Barrett and Jarvinen (2015) suggest that the capacity to consciously reflect on and form beliefs about beliefs, desires, and other mental states also importantly expands moral culpability. If one could not form these representations of one's own desires, for instance, one could not evaluate them in terms of moral content. The metarepresentational possibilities of HO-ToM appear to make possible evaluating potential future actions of self or others in terms of their consequences and justifiability.

One possible way to reconcile incremental human evolution with the notion that humans are *imago Dei*, then, is the following. The immediate ancestors of humans had many of the same traits that humans have but lacked HO-ToM. HO-ToM evolved in a gradual, incremental fashion, building on less sophisticated theory of mind. The result was a species able to enjoy a more complex type of sociality than any previous species. This more complex sociality included being able to cooperate in more complex ways because of the ability to understand the intentions of others and even the intentions of others to change one's own thoughts. This capacity changes and improves the ability to learn from others, thereby producing more rapid cultural transmission and innovation. HO-ToM's evolution simultaneously enabled this species to relate to God personally and not merely as a powerful force. Personally relating to God led to what might be termed "religion." Further, this species was able to morally evaluate potential and past actions, thereby further changing their sociality. In sum, one incremental change in our ancestors' cognition may have spawned a very different type of creature that had many of the traits that theologians have associated with *imago Dei*.

JUSTIN L. BARRETT AND TYLER S. GREENWAY

Imago Dei and Animal Domestication

The relationality of humans may be the current focus of much theologizing concerning human uniqueness and *imago Dei*, but a more traditional view of the *imago Dei* importantly considers the role of humans as God's stewards or managers of the created world. Concerning the *imago Dei*, Herman Bavinck writes, "What this [the *imago Dei*] means is not fully stated, but it does include human dominion over all of the created world in conformity to God's will" (Bavinck 2011). Scripture supports this position, stating that indeed humans are to "rule" over God's creation (Gen. 1:26; Psalm 8) in some sense. This role as God's representative rulers over creation distinguishes humanity from other animals and from angels.[5]

So, what if Barrett and Jarvinen (2015) are mistaken in thinking that higher-order theory of mind is the key driver of human uniqueness in relation to the *imago Dei*? Perhaps its evolution represents one big necessary but not sufficient step in the emergence of human uniqueness and *imago Dei*, like bipedalism or lower-order theory of mind before it. In this section we offer a different and, perhaps, more radical account of *imago Dei* by focusing on a dominion account of *imago Dei*. Though "dominion" in the biblical sense undoubtedly involves numerous psychological capacities, many of which may be unique to humans, perhaps the clearest evolutionary marker of dominion is domestication of animals. Whereas interactions between species are common, the relationship the human species creates with other species is unique. Humans eat plants and animals, much like other species, and have symbiotic relationships with other organisms (consider the *E. coli* in our intestines) as other species do, but humans also work with, breed, and care for plants and animals in ways only hinted at in other species. We love other individual animals, name them, and extend to them moral worth. Could it be that the Genesis treatment of humans being created *imago Dei* was reflecting the dawn of a species marked by its ability to tame and domesticate other species?

Contemporary sentiments regarding human abuses of the environment may steer us away from a full-bodied view of "dominion" or human lordship

---

5. Interestingly, angels are often regarded as rational, moral creatures capable of personal relationships. If angels are not *imago Dei*, then different capacities or responsibilities are needed to explain why humans are something that angels are not. Being a native part of this world, from the dust of the Earth, may be something that distinguishes humans from angels and thereby making them appropriate as God's deputies on Earth. If one takes a relational view of *imago Dei* it seems that either one also needs to deny angels' ability to enjoy I-Thou relationality, or grant that they, too, are *imago Dei*.

over the created world, but the author of Genesis did not seem to have these same concerns. The Revised Standard Version translates Genesis 1:28 thusly:

> And God blessed them, and God said to them, "Be fruitful and multiply, and fill the earth and subdue it; and have dominion over the fish of the sea and over the birds of the air and over every living thing that moves upon the earth."

The theme of God's creative action imposing order on disorder appears to be passed on to his designated image bearers, his stewards or representatives on the Earth. Humans are to impose order (subdue) and rule (have dominion). Why were humans selected for this role? What traits did they possess that made them candidates?

The breadth and gravity of the responsibility to benevolently exercise dominion appears to require a number of capacities that only humans possess. In focusing on what may be required to "subdue" and impose order on the Earth, we are clearly dealing with an unusual animal that uses more than might or brute force to execute its will. The ability to cooperate and coordinate activities, including division of labor, and probably create and use tools would be required to "subdue the Earth." Coordination of activities requires some kind of signaling or communication at least, if not fully developed language. To represent God responsibly, some kind of comprehension of God's will and ability to put it into action is required. Surely some kind of theory of mind—to understand the thoughts of God in some respect—is required.

To care for creation for an extended period of time, the requisite animal must have the capacity to plan and foresee potential problems in the future. In a simple world, it may be that planning is unnecessary for dominion, instinctively caring for creation as different needs arise. Because the world is complex and changing, however, some form of planning and foresight is necessary. The human ability to examine potential futures is made possible by metarepresentation—forming thoughts about thoughts—as this ability allows the individual to represent other possible realities. Metarepresentation is an activity of the HO-ToM system. Making plans and enacting these plans, however, requires a number of additional capacities. Social psychology often divides planning behavior into two categories: setting goals and implementing goals (Maddux and Tangney 2010). Setting goals requires assessment of feasibility and desirability, while implementing goals requires initiative, perseverance, and regulation of resources (Maddux and Tangney 2010). All of these capacities seem necessary for care of creation when future planning is required and all of them are present within the human species.

Additionally, humans must also have the capacity to *care* for creation in order to responsibly exercise dominion. Jonathan Haidt has outlined five moral foundations that guide human decision-making, and one of them, the harm-care foundation, is likely quite helpful for encouraging caring behavior toward other humans, but also for extending care to other species (Haidt and Joseph, 2004). Care for other species and for the rest of creation also requires a certain amount of self-control and the ability to delay gratification. Without these abilities, humanity may wreak havoc on ecosystems in order to pursue their own gain or obtain immediate rewards, and in the process humanity might make Earth an unsustainable place to live. Such restraint is evident in the human species, and, interestingly, even two- and three-year-old humans seem to possess some capacity for self-control and delaying gratification (Gunzenhauser and von Suchodoletz 2014; Mittal et al. 2013).

Many of the previously mentioned capacities are not unique to the human species (e.g., ability to care for others, even non-conspecifics, some degree of self-control, some communication) and a number of them may be (e.g., metarepresentation). Most important, however, is the unique combination of these capacities, as the removal of any one of these capacities would likely involve a diminished ability to exercise dominion. The desire to care without a developed theory of mind may begin to look very egocentric, the ability to care without self-control may never amount to significant help or aid, and planning without perseverance would likely become nothing more than a thought exercise. The fact that a number of capacities are necessary for dominion is significant. Traditionally, arguments focusing on the *imago Dei* attempt to identify a single capacity that separates humanity from other animals. A focus on dominion as a significant part of the *imago Dei*, however, requires a number of capacities that work together.

Domestication

The cluster of capacities sketched above have been present in humans for a long time, likely more than 100,000 years, and possibly more than 200,000. Have humans been *imago Dei* for that long? Perhaps, but maybe the Genesis account points to a much more recent occurrence: the domestication of animals. Human impact on various animals has been deep biologically and behaviorally, leading to new species selectively bred for certain traits that are useful or beneficial for humans. In exchange, these animals are protected by humans from other predators and their survival and reproduction are often enhanced. Consider, for instance, the global presence of domesticated dogs

Imago Dei *and Animal Domestication*

versus the much more restricted range of wolves. Likewise, aurochs are extinct but their domesticated offspring, cattle, are found on every continent except Antarctica. Junglefowl have spread from Asia to the entire world as domesticated chickens. As the original ancient readers of the Genesis creation account were an agricultural people surrounded by domesticated plants and animals, the dawn of domestication would have spoken to them as a critical marking off of a different sort of creation. But is animal domestication evidence of a species capable of "dominion" and, thus, *imago Dei*?

Domestication must first be distinguished from a number of similar behaviors. Some definitions of domestication remain rather broad by focusing on a general interaction and mutual development between species (Power 2012); however, other definitions, including ours, specify that domestication requires the selection for particular traits or characteristics that are needed or preferred by another species resulting in changes of the domesticated species (Larson et al. 2014; Price and Bar-Yosef 2011). Price and Bar-Yosef (2011) note important differences between management, cultivation, domestication, farming, and agriculture. According to their definition, domestication is unique in its result of "morphological or genetic changes in plant and animal species" (Price and Bar-Yosef 2011). The domestication of plants and animals seems to have played a large part in the human species' ability to maintain a sedentary lifestyle, although there is some evidence of sedentism that preceded domestication (Renfrew 2008).

Evidence of the emergence of domestication seems to vary somewhat across the globe. Evidence for the domestication of plants in Southwest Asia has been found dating back to 11,500 BP (before present, scale starting January 1, 1950), but evidence of the domestication of plants in eastern North America only dates back to 5000 BP (Price and Bar-Yosef 2011). Larson et al. (2014) note that this period (12,000–11,000 years ago) was a time of transition into the Present Interglacial Period. Larson et al. (2014) also note that agriculture seems to have developed independently across a large part of the globe, and Price and Bar-Yosef (2011, 171) note that "the almost simultaneous development of agriculture in so many different places is not simple coincidence." Many competing explanations for this convergence exist. The earliest evidence for any domestication is for the dog, at 13,000–17,000 years ago (Zeder et al. 2006), and so we use the dog as our primary illustration in our analysis below.

In taming and domesticating animals (as well as plants), we have clear evidence not just of the capacities for "subduing" and exercising "dominion" but the actual use of those capacities to create a largely harmonious relationship between humans and animals. If human lordship over the Earth is to image God's, then it should be characterized by authority and control, but also being at ease with each other, comfortable. The lords should be caring and unafraid of those in their care. The subjects should rest easy in the care of the lords, and turn to them for care. Domestication is the clearest indication of this quality of relationship between humans and the rest of creation. Consider a right relationship between a dog and its master. The dog recognizes the authority of the master and serves the master, but the master likewise cares for the needs of the dog. Both benefit from the relationship.

Indeed, the manifold ways in which domestication of animals and plants changed the human experience are well documented. Domestication certainly enabled access to new types of food sources and spread sedentism. Without domestication, sedentism (perhaps semi-permanent sedentism) was limited to food-rich areas. As sedentism was more firmly established as a lifestyle for the human species, a number of other advances also emerged. Renfrew (2008) notes that sedentism encouraged the creation of more permanent fixtures such as heavy grinding tools and ovens. As different permanent fixtures began to emerge and as surplus became more readily available, inequality would have become more apparent as well, encouraging further formation of hierarchy. Tools and surplus coupled with the existence of domesticated animals would have raised issues of personal property and inheritance as well. Further, defensive structures to protect these items would also become necessary (Renfrew 2008). Thus, domestication seems to bear with it significant changes in lifestyle for the humans that first began to exercise this ability.

Further, domestication likely changed humans in ways pregnant with theological significance. The process is reciprocal: humans and certain animals have importantly changed selection pressures on each other such that genetic changes have taken place. A textbook example is how adult lactose tolerance has emerged in a large minority of the world's population over the past ten thousand years due to domesticating dairy animals, but we are more interested here in the ways in which living and caring for animals may have enriched human cognitive development in a way that provided new resources for humans to love God and love others more effectively. We admit that these connections are largely speculative, but hope that sharing them will encourage scholarship on this topic, both theoretical and empirical.

To begin the domestication process of the dog, someone likely had the inkling that these wolves that hung around humans might be useful to humans. Once domestication was under way, dogs (or other animals and plants) became living illustrations of the point that certain living things in the human environment are there *for* a reason (related to human service). That is, it would not be a mistake to say that the dog is here for a reason, a purpose. The dog is a designed animal—interestingly noted in popular culture by the term "designer dog" referring to new breeds such as goldendoodles (a golden retriever–poodle mix) designed for very particular traits (a friendly disposition from golden retrievers and non-shedding, hypoallergenic hair from poodles).

Deborah Kelemen and other cognitive developmental psychologists have produced considerable evidence that humans have strong natural propensities to find design and purpose in things and events in the world (Banerjee and Bloom 2014a, 2014b; Kelemen 1999a, 1999b; Kelemen and DiYanni 2005; Kelemen and Rosset 2009). Exactly why humans have this propensity to attribute purpose or design to natural things is contested, but it is quite possible that the presence of domesticated plants and animals in our environments is a contributing factor. It is no mistake to think a dog, a sheep, or a chicken is "designed" for a purpose. Perhaps this realization encourages us to reason more broadly that plants, animals, and other natural things are designed.

Cognitive scientists of religion have argued that this conceptual tendency to think teleologically about the natural world easily encourages thinking about a designing superhuman creator (Barrett 2012; Bering 2011). If correct, and if domestication has encouraged such thinking, then from a theological perspective, domestication produced a form of general revelation of God's role as creator. As humans have designed dogs for purposes, so God has designed humans and the rest of the world for purposes. Just as a dog has traits that exist for purposes beyond itself, humans may have traits that exist for purposes beyond themselves.

It may be, too, that thinking about the natural world in terms of its design and what it was "intended for" could have accelerated the domestication of other crops and animals as well as the use of natural things to create new tools and technologies. That is, domestication could have created an environment that changed human thought toward greater design-based reasoning, which in turn, led to more technological evolution.

Further, living closely with animals may facilitate theory of mind development—particularly perspective-taking, that is, recognizing the possibility that others perceive and know different things. Children living on farms may learn from a young age that cows can hear and smell better than humans. Did the domestication of animals help scaffold more sophisticated theory of mind development?

Living closely with animals may also facilitate empathy. As humans consider the perspectives of other types of beings, and are forced to care for them, they may become better at considering the perspectives of other humans and sharing their emotions. Because some animals, particularly dogs, mimic some of the cues for being part of the family, living with them may encourage us to extend to nonhumans greater moral worth than we might otherwise. Living closely with animals may then broaden the moral circle.

Living closely with animals may also draw attention to the dichotomy between creatures and creator. This interaction with other species may remind humans that they too are animals and that they are also creatures formed by a creator. Likewise, living closely with animals may encourage humans to remember their responsibilities and obligations that transcend the self or kin, and fundamentally disrupt purely gene-centered motives. If an individual is tasked to watch over a herd of sheep, the individual may be frequently reminded that these sheep are dependent on him or her and that he or she has a responsibility to these animals.

Further Implications

What, then, are the implications of this understanding of *imago Dei* if dominion is central to bearing the image of God and domestication is a central marker of dominion? We may begin by first noting that this hypothesis responds to questions about human uniqueness and the human capacity to be considered uniquely *imago Dei*. While other animals certainly care for their young and some even care for some type of home, no other animals care for the Earth (or are even capable of caring for the Earth) to the extent of humans. While some human ancestors may have even been capable of exercising some dominion-like behaviors, the unique combination of capacities outlined above makes modern humans uniquely capable of exercising meaningful dominion. Dominion over the Earth, then, may clearly mark humans as unique among extant species.

It should also be noted that a hypothesis focusing on dominion and domestication is importantly different from a hypothesis focusing on HO-ToM. While both may respond to questions about human uniqueness, a hypothesis focused on HO-ToM is arguably more singularly attending to a particular cognitive capacity that then enables a number of different behaviors. A hypothesis focused on dominion or domestication, however, attends to a particular group of behaviors—caring for and ruling over creation—which require a variety of cognitive capacities as outlined above. One of the strengths of this hypothesis, then, is that instead of associating the *imago Dei* with a singular cognitive capacity that may then be more easily diminished through various psychological disorders, the *imago Dei* is associated with a role or group of behaviors, dominion and more specifically domestication, that are enabled by a variety of cognitive capacities. Using this hypothesis to understand the *imago Dei*, it seems that the capacity to exercise one's image-bearing qualities is less easily diminished. If one of the cognitive capacities enabling dominion is damaged, dominion may still be enabled by the other capacities. Instead of holding up the *imago Dei* quality through a single cognitive support, HO-ToM, this hypothesis argues that several cognitive supports enable it.

A dominion hypothesis also implies that different individuals may exercise their image-bearing qualities differently. Some individuals may specifically exercise dominion over the Earth by planning for the welfare of some aspect of creation; other individuals may specifically exercise dominion over the Earth by learning more about how creation is best cared for. Because different capacities are required for dominion, different capacities can be emphasized and particular individuals can specialize in certain dominion-focused fields.

Using this hypothesis, we may also wonder what the consequences are for those who are less able to exercise dominion over creation. Those individuals who live in urban environments may have fewer opportunities to care for nature or exercise domesticating behaviors. If dominion and domestication are central behaviors of the *imago Dei*, there may be consequences for those who are unable to practice these behaviors as readily. Perhaps ToM may develop differently or the moral circles of these individuals are more narrowly defined. These questions are ripe for further study.

Conclusion

These two hypotheses from an evolutionary psychological perspective have been presented as two possible responses to the argument that incremental evolution dismisses notions of human uniqueness and the *imago Dei*. The human capacity to exercise dominion and domesticate other species is unique to our species and also aligns itself well with the account of humanity's creation in Genesis. This account may further act as a complement to a hypothesis focusing on HO-ToM and the relational abilities HO-ToM enables. Far from eliminating the possibility of humans (and only humans) being sensibly said to be created in God's image, evolutionary perspectives provide an opportunity to re-examine human uniqueness and the image of God fruitfully.

References

Balswick, J. O., P. E. King, and K. S. Reimer. 2005. *The Reciprocating Self: Human Development in Theological Perspective*. Downers Grove, IL: IVP Academic.

Banerjee, K., and P. Bloom. 2014a. "Everything happens for a reason": children's beliefs about purpose in life events. *Child Development* 86:503–18.

Banerjee, K., and P. Bloom. 2014b. Why did this happen to me? Religious believers' and non-believers' teleological reasoning about life events. *Cognition* 133:277–303.

Barrett, J. L. 2012. *Born Believers: The Science of Children's Religious Belief.* New York: Free Press.

Barrett, J. L., and M. J. Jarvinen. 2015. Cognitive evolution, human uniqueness, and the *imago Dei*. In *The Emergence of Personhood: A Quantum Leap?* edited by M. Jeeves. Grand Rapids: Eerdmans.

Bavinck, H. 2011. *Reformed Dogmatics: Abridged in One Volume.* Ed. J. Bolt. Grand Rapids: Baker Academic.

Bering, J. M. 2011. *The Belief Instinct: The Psychology of Souls, Destiny, and the Meaning of Life.* New York: Norton.

Dunbar, R. 2007. The social brain hypothesis and its relevance to social psychology. In *Evolution and the Social Mind*, edited by J. P. Forgas, M. G. Haselton, and W. von Hippel, 21–33. New York: Psychology Press.

Gunzenhauser, C., and A. von Suchodoletz. 2014. Preschoolers' use of suppression influences subsequent self-control but does not interfere with verbal memory. *Learning and Individual Differences* 32:219–24.

Haidt, J., and C. Joseph. 2004. Intuitive ethics: how innately prepared intuitions generate culturally variable virtues. *Daedalus* 133(4):55–66.

Kelemen, D. 1999a. The scope of teleological thinking in preschool children. *Cognition* 70:241–72.

Kelemen, D. 1999b. Why are rocks pointy? Children's preference for teleological explanations of the natural world. *Developmental Psychology* 35:1440–53.

Kelemen, D., and C. DiYanni. 2005. Intuitions about origins: purpose and intelligent design in children's reasoning about nature. *Journal of Cognition and Development* 6:3–31.

Kelemen, D., and E. Rosset. 2009. The human function compunction: teleological explanation in adults. *Cognition* 111:138–43.

Larson, G., D. R. Piperno, R. G. Allaby, M. D. Purugganan, L. Andersson, M. Arroyo-Kalin, . . . D. Q. Fuller. 2014. Current perspectives and the future of domestication studies. *Proceedings of the National Academy of Sciences* 111(17):6139–46.

Maddux, J. E., and J. P. Tangney. 2010. *Social Psychological Foundations of Clinical Psychology.* New York: Guilford.

Mittal, R., B. S. Russell, P. A. Britner, and P. K. Peake. 2013. Delay of gratification in two- and three-year-olds: associations with attachment, personality, and temperament. *Journal of Child and Family Studies* 22(4):479–89.

Perner, J. 1991. *Understanding the Representational Mind.* Cambridge, MA: MIT.
Power, E. R. 2012. Domestication and the dog: embodying home. *Area* 44(3):371–78.
Price, T. D., and O. Bar-Yosef. 2011. The origins of agriculture: new data, new ideas: an introduction to supplement 4. *Current Anthropology* 52(S4):S163–S174.
Renfrew, C. 2008. *Prehistory: The Making of the Human Mind.* London: Phoenix.
Shults, F. L. 2003. *Reforming Theological Anthropology: After the Philosophical Turn to Relationality.* Grand Rapids: Eerdmans.
Van Huyssteen, J. W. 2006. *Alone in the World? Human Uniqueness in Science and Theology.* Grand Rapids: Eerdmans.
Venema, D. 2011, September 23. Neanderthals, Denisovans and human speciation. Retrieved from http://biologos.org/blog/understanding-evolution-neanderthals-denisovans-and-human-speciation.
Wimmer, H., and J. Perner. 1983. Beliefs about beliefs: representation and constraining function of wrong beliefs in young children's understanding of deception. *Cognition* 13:103–28.
Wolterstorff, N. 2008. *Justice: Rights and Wrongs.* Princeton: Princeton University Press.
Zeder, M. A., E. Emshwiller, B. D. Smith, and D. G. Bradley. 2006. Documenting domestication: the intersection of genetics and archaeology. *TRENDS in Genetics* 22:139–55.

4   The Emergence of Religion

*What Evolution, the Human Niche,
and Imagination Can Tell Us*

AGUSTÍN FUENTES

While there is no doubt that J. Wentzel van Huyssteen has had a substantive and even transformative impact on theology, that is not the topic of this chapter. I am not a theologian and do not have any illusions that I could speak coherently or meaningfully on the subject. However, there is another cluster of academics who have also been positively and meaningfully impacted by the insight and generous scholarly engagement of van Huyssteen, and this is an impact that may be unknown to many theologians. This other cluster is that of anthropologists, particularly those of us interested in the human past both materially and cognitively. For many of us the lens that van Huyssteen applies when attempting to understand, and articulate, the human propensity to make meaning of the world, to make space into place, and to see all around us as more than the material of which it is made, is an appealing and innovative one. Most anthropologists are not explicitly humanists, nor are we theologians, and most are not adherents to a particular faith practice, but there is something in what van Huyssteen offers that enables us social scientists to gain from, and join in, a mutually enriching intellectual journey.

This view is exemplified by a quote from van Huyssteen that asks anthropologists not to insert themselves into a theological worldview but rather to be enriched by it and join together as partners in the quest for understanding:[1]

---

1. I should note here that I am equally indebted to the theologian and scientist Celia

---

This chapter was originally published in *Theology Today* 72, no. 2 (July 2015) and is reprinted by kind permission. Research related to this publication was made possible through the support of a grant from the John Templeton Foundation.

"humans are, first of all, embodied beings, and as such what we do, think, and feel is conditioned by the materiality of our embodiment ... there is a 'naturalness' to religious imagination and the human quest for meaning."[2] This quote has implications in a particular theological context and perspective, but it is equally enticing and meaningful to an anthropologist; many of our goals overlap, especially when it comes to seeking understanding of the ubiquitous human tendency to believe, to imagine, and to hope.

Until recently, I had little interest in the broad and often contentious field that is commonly labeled the "evolution of religion." However, I am interested in human evolution, particularly the evolution of complex sociality and what, if anything, we might be able to glean from the archaeological and fossil records about human nature(s). Given this interest and my increasing interface with the available data I am unable to deny the reality that imagination, ritual, and some form of metaphysical engagement with the world are inextricably entangled with our having become human beings.[3] I do not have a choice—in order to have a fuller understanding of human evolution anthropologists must have a deeper understanding of why and how we have imagination, faith, and hope, and channel these through suites of rituals, a process and experience that many would call religion.

I am not seeking the "evolution of religion" as if religion was some "thing" or "trait" that can evolve as does a femur or an immune system response to pathogen attack. Rather, I am increasingly interested in collaborations that can get us closer to better questions and more interesting answers as to what makes us human, and faith and belief are a core part of that. I can thank van Huyssteen and his generous intellectual contributions for assisting me in moving along this trajectory.[4]

Deane-Drummond for providing the same kind of context and the explicit practice of such experience that has arisen from our collaborative research projects on this very subject. See C. Deane-Drummond and A. Fuentes, "Human Being and Becoming: Situating Theological Anthropology in Interspecies Relationships in an Evolutionary Context," *Philosophy, Theology and the Sciences* 1, no. 3 (2014): 251–75, for example.

2. J. Wentzel van Huyssteen, *Alone in the World? Human Uniqueness in Science and Theology* (Grand Rapids: Eerdmans, 2006), 312.

3. Here "imagination" reflects the ability to cognitively derive meaning and construct scenarios, ideas, and perceptions that can involve representations or manipulations of material items, social experiences, sensory experiences, and information passed on to an individual by others, but in these cognitive constructions neither spatial nor temporal nor experiential contact with the aforementioned facets of the items used needs to happen (or to have happened).

4. I also am heavily indebted to my time at the Center for Theological Inquiry, at Princeton, during the Inquiry on Evolution and Human Nature, and to all of my colleagues there for expanding my intellectual engagement in this arena.

Many researchers have proposed that the origin of religion and religious belief is adaptations generated via natural (or cultural) selection to help humans organize large groups and facilitate cooperation.[5] Others argue that religious belief is a by-product of our cognitive complexity and that being self-aware, having theory of mind, produces cognitive mechanisms that promote supernatural agency detection (i.e., the creation of mental impressions that there are supernatural agents). However, there are also those who suggest that it is more complicated than that.[6] There are multiple locations to find reviews of these arguments so I will not summarize them here. However, I do suggest that the evolutionary answers to the question of the origin of, and capability to have, religious belief might not lie wholly in religious beliefs or structures themselves, but rather are, at least partially, manifest in the way in which humans successfully negotiated the world during the terminal portion of the Pleistocene (the past 300,000 to 400,000 years).[7] I argue, following the thread developed by van Huyssteen and others, that a necessary prelude to having religion is the emergence of a human imagination and the embodiment of a quest for meaning as part and parcel of the distinctive human niche that has facilitated our flourishing as a species.

Elsewhere I have argued that what Claude Lévi-Strauss called the "untamed thought" is at the base of being human and can be seen developing in the imagination and the infusion of meaning into the world by the genus *Homo* in the Late Pleistocene. It is this capacity (tendency?) that underlies, precedes, or forms a basis for our current ability to develop a metaphysical orientation to the world, which in turn facilitates the emergence of structured religious beliefs. The anthropologist Robert Bloch has argued that we can see this transformation in our lineage as the move from a group of beings who engage in transactional sociality (as do most animals), even if in a very complex manner (as do many primates), to the kind of beings that add a suite of transcendental relationships to their mode of social interactions. In other words,

---

5. D. D. P. Johnson and J. M. Bering, "Hand of God, Mind of Man: Punishment and Cognition in the Evolution of Cooperation," *Evolutionary Psychology* 4 (2006): 219–33; A. Norenzayan, *Big Gods: How Religion Transformed Cooperation and Conflict* (Princeton: Princeton University Press, 2013).

6. A. Barnard, *Genesis of Symbolic Thought* (Cambridge: Cambridge University, 2012); van Huyssteen, *Alone in the World?*

7. R. Sosis, "The Adaptationist-Byproduct Debate on the Evolution of Religion: Five Misunderstandings of the Adaptationist Program," *Journal of Cognition and Culture* 9 (2009): 315–32; Agustín Fuentes, "Human Evolution, Niche Complexity, and the Emergence of a Distinctively Human Imagination," *Time and Mind* 7, no. 3 (2014): 241–57.

we are simultaneously transactional and transcendental beings.[8] This human reality results in a landscape of meaning and an associated imagination that act as a system that facilitates an array of other symbolic and meaning-laden aspects of human behavior and experience that are core components of our current ways of being in the world.[9]

In the study of the evolution of human beings we need to go beyond explaining our bodies and ecologies and develop a theoretical approach that can describe an effective toolkit for an evolving system that moves from transactional to transactional plus transcendent. We need to develop a model of what facilitated a community of beings to move from the production of simple stone tools two million years ago to increasingly complex tools and widening geographic spread one million years ago, to the use and control of fire, to complex hunting and rudimentary language, to art and complex multi-community social networks, to agriculture and towns, to the megacities, global religions, and world economies of today. An explanation of this process that does not include a robust imagination and a landscape of perceptual reality wherein everything, material or not, is infused with multifaceted meaning is wholly incomplete. It is the human ability to deploy multiple and distinctive modes of responses (both transactional and transcendent) to evolutionary pressures and their concomitant influence on evolutionary landscapes that facilitates the emergence of the aptly named "sapiens" by approximately 200,000 to 100,000 years ago—thus the way we construct the narrative of this evolution is central to our ability to understand it.

A Contemporary Narrative and a Role for Imagination

Our basic understanding, today in the twenty-first-century, of how biological evolution works can be summarized as follows. Mutation introduces genetic variation that in interaction with epigenetic and developmental processes produces biological variation in organisms, which may be passed from generation to generation. Natural selection shapes biological variation in response to specific constraints and pressures in the environment (*sensu lato*), but dynamic

8. Maurice Bloch, "Why Religion Is Nothing Special but Is Central," *Philosophical Transactions of the Royal Society B* 12 (2008): 2055–61.

9. Here the base term "symbol" implies an artifact, idea, or perception that arises from interactions of many elements (materials, bodies, brains, senses, perceptions, experiences, other beings, etc.), but also that none of these elements has in itself the specific property that is reflected in the symbolic experience: it emerges from the interrelationships of these components and the human capacity for imagination.

organism-environment interaction can result in niche construction that changes the patterns, foci, and intensity of natural selection and creates ecological inheritance.[10] But there is more to evolutionary processes than just the biology.

There is substantial support that niche construction, the process by which organisms simultaneously shape and are shaped by their ecologies, plays a key role in human evolutionary processes via our ability to substantially modify our surroundings through behavioral means.[11] Niche construction results in the building and destroying of niches by organisms and the mutually mutable and synergistic interactions between organisms and their environments.[12] Niche construction creates feedback within the evolutionary dynamic, with organisms engaged in niche construction modifying the evolutionary pressures acting on them, on their descendants, and on unrelated populations sharing the same landscape. Niche construction reflects a synthesis of ecological, biological, and social processes rather than treating them as discrete spheres.

Cultural processes provide a particularly robust method of niche construction.[13] Take the examples provided by O'Brien and Laland: evolution of dairying by Neolithic groups in Europe and Africa and the rise of the "sickle-cell allele" among certain agricultural groups in West Africa.[14] O'Brien and Laland illustrate the concept of niche construction (and gene-culture coevolution) by describing the shifting behavioral actions, cultural perceptions, and ecological conditions that mutually interacted to produce genetic and physiological changes, which themselves resulted in further modification to behavior, physiology, and ecologies of particular human populations. Cultural

---

10. Natural selection is what most lay concepts of evolution center on: it is the differential representation of biological variants from generation to generation shaped by restrictions and affordances in the environment. In addition to being influenced by selection, genetic variation is also shaped by the processes of gene flow and genetic drift. See also Kevin N. Laland et al., "Does Evolutionary Theory Need a Rethink? Yes, Urgently," *Nature* 514 (2014): 161–64.

11. F. John Odling-Smee, Kevin N. Laland, and Marcus Feldman, *Niche Construction: The Neglected Process in Evolution*, Monographs in Population Biology 37 (Princeton: Princeton University Press, 2003).

12. I am using the term "niche" in the contemporary ecological and evolutionary view: it is the dynamic N-dimensional space in which an organism exists—the totality of the biotic and abiotic factors that make up an organism's main context for the evolutionary dynamic (the interaction between organisms and evolutionary forces); see David B. Wake, Elizabeth A. Hadly, and David D. Ackerly, "Biogeography, Changing Climates, and Niche Evolution," *Proceedings of the National Academy of Sciences* 106, S2 (2009): 19631–36; and G. E. Hutchinson, "Concluding Remarks," *Cold Spring Harbor Symposium on Quantitative Biology* 22 (1957): 415–27.

13. Jeremy Kendal, "Cultural Niche Construction and Human Learning Environments: Investigating Sociocultural Perspectives," *Biological Theory* 6, no. 3 (2012): 241–50.

14. Michael O'Brien and Kevin N. Laland, "Genes, Culture and Agriculture: An Example of Human Niche Construction," *Current Anthropology* 53, no. 4 (2012): 434–70.

patterns and behavioral actions and perceptions can impact genetic and other biological patterns and the process of natural selection, which in turn can affect developmental outcomes, which can then feed back into cultural patterns and behavioral actions.[15] In human evolution, biological, cultural, and ecological systems are entangled and not separate processes—thus perception and ideas, and the actions emerging from them, can be evolutionarily relevant.

Jablonka and Lamb demonstrate that evolutionarily relevant information is transferred from one generation to the next by many interacting inheritance systems (genetic, epigenetic, behavioral, and symbolic).[16] Genetic inheritance is the passing on of gametes (primarily DNA). Epigenetic inheritance, the inheritance of molecular or structural elements outside DNA, is found in all organisms. This gives rise to phenotypic variations that do not stem from variations in DNA but are transmitted to subsequent generations of cells or organisms. Behavioral inheritance is the transmission, across generations, of behavioral patterns and specific behavioral actions, and is found in many organisms; and symbolic inheritance, the cross-generational acquisition of symbolic concepts and ideologies, is found only in humans and can have pronounced effects on behavioral patterns.

Combinations of behavioral and symbolic patterns are very common in human societies, for example, rituals and social institutions, and can have significant impacts at both the individual and group levels. As such, much evolutionarily relevant variation in humans (and in some other animals) can be seen as constructed, in the sense that what is inherited and what final forms that inheritance takes depend on various filtering and editing processes (at biological and social levels) that occur before and during transmission. Humans play a particularly active role in their own evolutionary processes.

Particularly relevant to this pattern is the recent theoretical and practical work in biology that demonstrates that plasticity in development and phenotypic reactivity is widespread in organisms, with humans in particular displaying considerable phenotypic plasticity in response to evolutionary pressures (morphologically, physiologically, and especially behaviorally), both today and likely across our evolutionary history.[17] From at least 200,000 to

---

15. Richard Boyd, Peter J. Richerson, and Joseph Henrich, "The Cultural Niche: Why Social Learning Is Essential for Human Adaptation," *Proceedings of the National Academy of Sciences* 108, no. 2 (2011): 10918–25.

16. Eva Jablonka and Marion Lamb, *Evolution in Four Dimensions: Genetic, Epigenetic, Behavioral, and Symbolic Variation in the History of Life* (Cambridge, MA: MIT, 2014).

17. Mary Jane West-Eberhard, *Developmental Plasticity and Evolution* (New York: Oxford University Press, 2003). The "phenotype" is the observable and measurable outcomes of biological and social process—for example, height, weight, skull form, muscle density, indi-

300,000 years prior to the first appearance of modern *Homo sapiens sapiens* (ca. 200,000 years ago) there is increasing evidence that this phenotypic plasticity is accompanied, and even superseded, by substantial cognitive flexibility in response to ecological and social challenges.[18] It is argued that it is this behavioral-cognitive plasticity combined with increasingly essential modes of social cooperation and coordination that enabled humans to develop our modern capacity for extensive shared intentionality, metacoordination, and language. Indeed, this capacity and proclivity for cultural complexity is increasingly invoked as a key to evolutionary explanations of human behavior.

In this modern understanding of evolutionary processes the concept that there are basically two material variables in human evolution, the outside (environment) and the inside (genes), is incorrect.[19] Our systems of evolution, development, and inheritance are not purely physical and the boundaries between our genes, epigenetic systems, bodies, ecologies, psychologies, societies, and histories are fluid and dynamic. Perception, meaning, and experience are as central in our evolutionary processes as are nutrients, hormones, and bone density—and all of these elements can interact. How we see the world—or better put, how we imagine the world to be—matters in our evolutionary histories and futures.

The Human *Umwelt*

Contemporary evolutionary theory cannot be wholly classified as an effort in material reductionism, and the whole of human evolutionary experience is not reduced to genes, reproductive fitness, or material explanations. Evolutionary narratives alone will not get us a full explanation of why we are the way we are, but they can get us a range of fascinating insights about mechanisms and processes that integrate our bodies, actions, perceptions, and manipulations of the world and that might get us further along in understanding what it means to be human and to imagine ourselves as such. This is why interaction between anthropology and theology (and other "ologies") can provide a potentially more robust narrative when envisioning the human niche, our *Umwelt*.[20]

---

vidual behavior, patterns of response to specific stimuli, etc. Leslie Aiello and Susan C. Anton, "Human Biology and the Origin of *Homo*," *Current Anthropology* 53, no. 6 (2012): 269–77.

18. Susan C. Anton, Richard Potts, and Leslie C. Aiello, "Evolution of Early Homo: An Integrated Biological Perspective," *Science* 345, no. 6192 (2014).

19. Laland et al., "Does Evolutionary Theory Need a Rethink?" 161–64.

20. Our perceptual life-world as per Jacob von Uexküll, *A Foray into the Worlds of Animals and Humans* (Minneapolis: University of Minnesota Press, 2010; orig. ed., 1934).

The Emergence of Religion

To lay a baseline for dialogue across disciplines in regards to evolutionary patterns and processes in the human lineage, especially in regards to reconstructing the pathways toward a human imagination, even a human metaphysics and the emergence of religious systems, we need to begin with a truly integrated approach to human evolution: we must integrate the cognitive, social, and material, and blur the boundaries between the individual, the group, and a larger regional population.[21] Such a perspective recognizes the mutual mutability of individual actors, social networks, and local ecologies and seeks to incorporate the material with the cognitive as central aspects in a niche-construction process in human evolution.

Evolutionary processes produce both continuities and discontinuities in forms and lineages. Despite the recent emphasis on highlighting the continuities between humans and other forms of life, it is increasingly evident that we need to focus on the discontinuities relative to our peripheral hominin ancestors and other closely related primates to understand evolutionarily relevant aspects of humanity.[22] Despite the strong, and important, commonalities we share with the other organisms, our experience and perception of the world, our *Umwelt*, is distinct in salient ways. Therefore, we need to find the best manner to explain why our genus (and not other hominin genera) succeeded and behaves as it does. Specifically, we need to home in on what evolutionary context and patterns facilitated the emergence of *Homo sapiens sapiens*. This inquiry resides in a locus of shared interest across the social sciences and humanities: the quest to understand and describe human nature—and I assert it involves a core role for the human imagination.

Over the past two million years members of the genus *Homo* underwent significant morphological changes and enhanced behavioral complexity. Most researchers agree that the human niche, our way of making it in the world, consists of extreme cooperation in complex social relationships, in childrearing, in foraging, in information-sharing, and in the development of a symbolic, extended, and shared memory wherein people, places, items, and relationships became imbued with meaning beyond their immediate sensory and temporal contexts.[23] A primary characteristic of this niche is an obligate interdepen-

---

21. A. Fuentes, "Integrative Anthropology and the Human Niche: Toward a Contemporary Approach to Human Evolution," *American Anthropologist* 117, no. 2 (2015).

22. Hominins are all those species and genera on the line that split with the African apes (ca. eight million to ten million years ago) to which humans belong, and of which humans are the last remaining member. Jon Marks, "The Biological Myth of Human Evolution," *Contemporary Social Science* 7, no. 2 (2012): 139–57.

23. Kim Sterelny, *The Evolved Apprentice: How Evolution Made Humans Unique* (Cambridge, MA: MIT, 2012); Andrew Whiten and David Erdal, "The Human Socio-cognitive Niche

dence where being in community with one another is fundamental to successfully becoming, and being, human.

Many humanists, including philosophers and theologians, regard the tendency to be in community as a central locus in investigations of the human. Their perspectives shape the intellectual landscape and influence both academic and public perceptions of what it means to be human. Such a perspective is enhanced if we more seriously connect human evolutionary studies and niche-construction theory to the concept of community as central in the human *Umwelt*.

Human experience of the world, our *Umwelt*, both constructs and is constructed by the interface between our social and ecological lives. To reach a node of increased and effective interdisciplinary entanglement in this arena we need to realize that we are in a data- and theory-rich milieu in the study of human evolution and that there may be numerous insights from diverse perspectives related to our biosocial histories. A generous evolutionary anthropology in dialogue with other disciplines, including theology, can add substantially to our potential for understanding the processes, patterns, and implications of becoming and being human.[24]

Community as the Human Niche

Manipulation of plants and animals, developing tools and machines, construction of dwellings and alteration of landscapes, religious, legal, and familial institutions all affect the contexts and options available to humans in regards to the interactions with evolutionary processes: these structure and channel the strategies of human actors.

Thinking about human evolution, Foley and Gamble refer to the human community as the basic building block for human society. They define the human community as a group with shared dialects, kin bonds, symbolic beliefs,

---

and Its Evolutionary Origins," *Philosophical Transactions of the Royal Society B* 367 (2012): 2119–29; A. Fuentes, "Human Evolution, Niche Complexity, and the Emergence of a Distinctively Human Imagination," *Time and Mind* 7, no. 3 (2014): 241–57.

24. Celia Deane-Drummond, *The Wisdom of the Liminal: Evolution and Other Animals in Human Becoming* (Grand Rapids: Eerdmans, 2014); Jan-Olav Henriksen, *Life, Love and Hope: God and Human Experience* (Grand Rapids: Eerdmans, 2014); Markus Meuhling, *Resonances: Neurobiology, Evolution and Theology Evolutionary Niche Construction, the Ecological Brain and Relational-Narrative Theology* (Göttingen: Vandenhoeck & Ruprecht, 2014); van Huyssteen, *Alone in the World?*; Malcolm Jeeves, ed., *Rethinking Human Nature: A Multidisciplinary Approach* (Grand Rapids: Eerdmans, 2011).

and political organization, and with members having the capacity to maintain these common elements in the absence of close spatial proximity and with long periods where there is no contact.²⁵ This definition resonates with the perspectives of those disciplines that seek to investigate humans via their own lives, histories, and perceptions as it defines the social and the cultural as the basic context in which humans exist. In developing a stronger anthropology (*sensu lato*) of human evolution we can extend beyond the morphological and demographic, beyond descriptions of fossils, material remains, and reconstructed ecologies, and envision the community as a dynamic niche and the focal arena for evolutionary processes in humans (morphological, developmental, behavioral, and cognitive).

The biological anthropologists Susan Anton and Josh Snodgrass recently proposed a model wherein the origin of the genus *Homo*, and our subsequent evolution, is characterized by a "positive feedback loop that drove life history evolution and cultural change."²⁶ This is an iterative process where over the course of hundreds of millennia increasing cognition, dietary quality, and cooperative behavior resulted in lowered extrinsic mortality risk and was connected to changes in brain size, body composition, life history parameters, and behavioral-communicative complexity (what most now call culture). I argue that connecting their proposal with niche-construction approaches in the context of contemporary evolutionary theory enables us to develop more fully the concept of a community niche.

The community niche is the spatial and social niche that includes the social partners and ecologies with which an individual interacts. It is a group with shared kinship (writ large) and histories and the primary source of shared knowledge, security, and development across the lifespan for its members. The community has fluid boundaries but members share cognitive, social, and ecological bonds even in the absence of close spatial proximity. It is within the context of this community niche that members of the genus *Homo* interfaced, interacted with, modified, and were modified by social and ecological worlds during the course of our evolution.

This is a constructed niche that reflects extant, modified, and altered ecological and social interfaces and the concomitant variation in evolutionary pressures that feed back on the organisms within it. Multiple types of actions can affect the feedback process, but of most interest to this discussion is the

25. Richard Foley and Clive Gamble, "The Ecology of Social Transitions in Human Evolution," *Philosophical Transactions of the Royal Society B: Biological Sciences* 364, no. 1533 (2009): 3267-79.

26. Susan C. Anton and Josh Snodgrass, "Origin and Evolution of Genus Homo: New Perspectives," *Current Anthropology* 53, no. 6 (2012): 479-96.

possibility that social behavior spurred by symbolic and perceptual stimuli can play a significant role in the shaping of the niche and is in turn also shaped by the niche. These patterns are about the interaction between social bonds, cognition, communication, and perception and their role in how earlier humans engaged the world and how that engagement fed back into changing bodies, minds, and societies. Conceptualizing human evolution this way provides an intellectual setting for the possibility of connectivity between anthropologists and certain views on human community and human possibility in some theological models of image-bearing and human becoming.[27]

But Where Is the Religion?

Following J. Wentzel van Huyssteen and many others, I argue that a substantive component of our evolutionary success is due to our being a semiotic species: the use of symbol and the development of an imagination in our perceptions of, and dealing with, the world acts as a major factor in human evolutionary histories.[28] The ways in which symbols are generated, perceived, and utilized can be relevant in structuring our perceptions and behavior such that the "material" world is never without semiotic markings, and this can influence our behavior and our perceptions of what challenges and assistances the world around us offers.

Humans have an imagination that is part of our perceptual and interactive reality and it is a substantive aspect of lived experience—thus it is evolutionarily relevant. The human perception of the landscape is always somewhat contingent on socio-cognitive interpretation and the individual and group variability in experience of any given human community. Thus, evolutionary relevant actions can be influenced by variable semiotic "realities" deriving from the range of experiential and perceptual possibilities influenced, and created, by our imagination.

At some point in the past 400,000 years, language and hyper-complex coordination, alongside full-blown shared intentionality, became expressed in human populations and acted to "lock in" the imaginative "more than material

---

27. Celia Deane-Drummond, "God's Image and Likeness in Humans and Other Animals: Performativity, Soul-making and Graced Nature," *Zygon* 47, no. 4 (2012): 934–48.

28. Terrence Deacon, *The Symbolic Species* (London: Penguin, 1997); M. Donald, "Précis of the Origins of the Modern Mind: Three Stages of the Evolution of Culture and Cognition," *Behavioral and Brain Sciences* 16, no. 4 (1993): 737–91; Barbara J. King, "Primates and Religions: A Biological Anthropologist's Response to J. Wentzel van Huyssteen's *Alone in the World*," *Zygon* 43, no. 2 (2008): 451–66.

word" as our permanent perceptual state (*Umwelt*), laying the groundwork for the possibility that metaphysical perspectives could emerge as part of the human experience.

While for most (all?) animals, and many of our earlier hominin relatives, indexical and iconic signs permeate the world (and the transactional nature of social relationships), as humans we add to this world a symbolic landscape. For us, the emergent properties of symbolic representation enable a system wherein imagination, and hope, and the symbols associated with them, can maintain stability and meaning even in the absence of their objects of reference.[29] A key to understanding human consciousness, and the potential for metaphysical and eventually religious thought, is to recognize that our symbolic mode of existence is emergent: our way of being arises from the interactions of many elements (bodies, brains, senses, perceptions, experiences, other beings, etc.), but none of these has in itself the specific property of symbolic experience—it emerges from the interrelationships of these components. We as individuals and as communities share fully in the navigation, and creation, of the indexical and iconic semiotic landscape.

It is my intuition that in order to better understand the ubiquitous importance and deep reality of religious experience for *Homo sapiens sapiens* we need the integrated approach to thinking about the functioning of the human community that I have laid out here, and we need to apply this concept to the examination of the latter part of the Pleistocene—for that is where we will find the first material evidence of imagination that sets the stage for the possibilities of religious experience.[30]

I am not arguing that the origin of religion fulfilled a specific trajectory of the human lineage or for any particular adaptive function of religiosity (i.e., that "religion" is what enabled us to be what we are today). Rather, I think that in an evolutionary context neither religion nor religiosity can appear full blown; the deep history of the religious experience is not to be found in religion at all. It is the search for the kinds of structures, behaviors, cognitive processes, even revelatory experiences (however a given discipline may define this term) that might enhance our understandings of the initial appearances of religious experience, belief, ritual, and their associated institutions in human beings.

I am suggesting that anthropologists and theologians might be able to

---

29. The iconic sign resembles or imitates its signified object and the indexical sign might not resemble its signified object, but it is not arbitrarily assigned and is directly connected in some way to the object. The relationship between what the indexical sign stands for—what it means—might have to be learned. Deacon, *The Symbolic Species*.

30. But I cannot say if that is when imagination arose in our lineage.

have our cake and eat it too. If having an imagination is a central part of the human niche, and this imagination is a basal element necessary for the development of a metaphysical perception of the world, one could see how both adaptive and revelatory perspectives could employ this pattern as part of their understanding of the human. In an adaptive context this way of viewing the human niche lays a groundwork for the development of the functional structures (cognitive and behavioral) that those arguing for religion as a functional adaptation propose. Alternatively, one could see resonance between this niche and the possibility of "ensoulment" or some form of revelatory experience that coincides with the kind of perspectives proposed by theologians and scientists seeking to connect faith and the divine with the patterns in human evolution.

It is highly likely that there is a naturalness to a human imagination that facilitates engagement with, and being in, the world in ways that are distinct from those in other animals, even closely related hominins. If this is the case, it provides a small, and hopefully fruitful, addition to the toolkit of inquiry for both anthropologists and theologians (and others) interested in reconstructing the path to humanity and the possible roles that imagination, belief, and even religion have played and continue to play.

5 The Religious Sense

Human Uniqueness, Human Evolution, and the Origins of Symbolism and Culture

RICHARD POTTS

Conversations across disciplines, central to the theology and scholarly contributions of J. Wentzel van Huyssteen, are essential to our collective yearning to understand the place of humans as evolved and religious beings in the cosmos. While van Huyssteen rightly places emphasis on the interdisciplinarity that underpins truly productive conversations on this topic, the more recent term "transdisciplinarity" refers to the effort where disciplines not only intersect but also truly transform the questions, insights, and scholarly endeavors of one another. I take van Huyssteen's contributions to be deeply transdisciplinary, by which I mean that the aim and impact of his questions and ideas do not merely entwine theology with multiple fields of the sciences and humanities; they are inextricable, fusing them together. It is a source of both humility and inspiration for me, as a paleoanthropologist, that van Huyssteen's enormous intellectual undertakings, especially his efforts to elucidate the place of human beings in the world, have shined a strong light on the scientific discoveries and explanations of human evolution as essential to progress on theological

---

I am forever grateful for the opportunity to get to know J. Wentzel van Huyssteen, and deeply appreciate his sincere passion for scientific investigations of human origins and his interest in my own work. Van Huyssteen served the Human Origins Initiative of the Smithsonian Institution as a member of our Broader Social Impacts Committee, which is dedicated to public understandings of evolution in relation to religious reflection and diverse faith communities. I thank Daniel Pedersen for his invitation and encouragement to contribute this chapter. My appreciation also goes to Catherine Denial for help in tallying answers to the public surveys, and to Jennifer Clark for her expertise in producing the figure. Support from the Peter Buck Fund for Human Origins Research (Smithsonian) helped in producing this chapter.

concerns. It seems appropriate to try my best, therefore, to express how at least this paleoanthropologist's thinking is transformed by van Huyssteen's thesis regarding human uniqueness.

In line with his thesis, the theme of this chapter is that the development of the religious sense in *Homo sapiens* has depended on the evolutionary origin of certain unique aspects of human symbolic behavior, symbolically mediated group identity, and cultural capacities, including the conditional proclivities toward creativity, innovation, and cumulative culture. I wish to describe here the latest archaeological clues concerning these complicated aspects of human origins, and to explore their implications for explaining the process of the origin of our species and how this roiling natural process may relate to theological concerns.

By religious sense, I refer not to specific qualities of any particular religion but rather to belief in a spiritual relationship that evokes transcendence and a sacred attitude of awe toward the cosmos as it is comprehended by an individual or people. While such a generalized approach will, I suspect, seem superficial and perhaps naive to theologians focused on the implications for specifically Christian theology, my sole excuse is my starting point: as an anthropologist, I am eager to explore human uniqueness by first becoming aware of the universals enshrined in our shared humanity. The study of human evolution seeks to uncover a universal narrative prior to the multiple histories that have diversified the human experience. In other words, the emphasis on spiritual relationship and what it evokes seems to me sufficiently wide-ranging to cross the astonishing diversity of religious expressions and beliefs among humans past and present. If we are truly interested in human uniqueness, it better apply to all of us.

Besides my discussions with van Huyssteen, my main understanding of his theological work, so wonderfully brimming with scientific research on human origins, is through his prodigious book *Alone in the World? Human Uniqueness in Science and Theology*.[1] From the outset I must express humility as to whether the observations in this chapter might enlighten theological arguments regarding human uniqueness and our place in the universe. I fully embrace, and try to exemplify in my work, the type of transdisciplinarity that underlies van Huyssteen's contributions, yet proceed here largely unfamiliar (except from reading his book) with the rich scholarly implications, critiques, and inspirations drawn by theologians and philosophers as they consider our evolved origin. *Alone in the World?* heartens me nonetheless to venture into

---

1. J. Wentzel van Huyssteen, *Alone in the World? Human Uniqueness in Science and Theology* (Grand Rapids: Eerdmans, 2006).

new terrain if only because van Huyssteen's book verifies, in stepping boldly beyond my intellectual discipline, I am not alone.

What Does It Mean to Be Human?

My attempt here is not to answer this question, or even to offer a particularly astute analysis of it. The purpose of this section is simply to examine what people think about when answering this question. Beginning in 2010, the Smithsonian Institution in Washington, DC, gave birth to the Human Origins Initiative at the US National Museum of Natural History, an initiative with the theme "what does it mean to be human?" In addition to the decades-long research we have undertaken in the Rift Valley of East Africa and various parts of Asia, the centerpiece of this initiative is a permanent exhibit on human evolution. The exhibit invites visitors to explore the fossils and artifacts bearing on the scientific discovery of human origins. In this setting, we invite everyone to tell us their thoughts on what it means to be human. The initiative's website asks the same question, and tens of thousands of answers can be viewed at http://humanorigins.si.edu/about/involvement/being-human.

It seems that people enjoy this question. Common examples include: We appreciate beauty. To believe in right versus wrong. We write poetry and equations. To create and talk incessantly about it. Imagine the impossible. Laughter. To weep for the loss of a loved one. Understand our connection to other living creatures. We sing, dance, compose music. We remember our grandparents.

Responses from people in more than 220 countries can be organized into several broad categories that encompass anatomy (human physical makeup and genetics); behavior (including technology and the arts); sociality (social relationships); religion (including morality, spiritual sense); cognition (including language, awareness, and imagination); emotions; and ecology (including diet and interactions with the surroundings). These categories overlap, and some answers can integrate ideas across more than one domain.

In an analysis of 774 responses by visitors to the exhibition in Washington, DC, during eight days in 2010, we divvied up the answers into five categories. Cognition was the leading category, comprising 26 percent of the answers. The uniqueness of human language, awareness, reasoning, and intelligence was foremost on people's minds. Of course, because humans can ponder and label their own internal mental tasks, one can imagine that the act of urging people to *think* about this question prompted "cognition" as a common reply. Human emotions came in next at 23 percent. Feelings of love, humor, and empathy were recurrent themes in this realm, suggesting that the emotional ties so central to our yearnings and social relations deeply inspire what people think is unique to the human experience.

In this first round of analysis, social relationships and behavior were treated as a single category, and it included religion, beliefs, and thoughts about how we treat one another. This broad category was reflected in 22 percent of responses. Finally, 11 percent and 8 percent of the replies focused on human physical form and ecology. Given that the question was posed in a setting where people very likely expected to learn about human evolution, it is perhaps surprising that less than one-fifth of the answers were in the categories most strongly informed by the fossil and archaeological evidence (think here about thumbs, walking upright, control of fire, hunting, and effects on other organisms). Yet people carry with them everywhere their personal ideas forged by experiences and values that lie beyond what is most readily addressed by scientific research.

Pertinent to this chapter is a substantially larger collection of 1,819 answers obtained in June–July 2014 as visitors to Washington, DC, posted their thoughts on a board outside the Smithsonian's Natural History Museum but adjacent to a temporary exhibit on human evolution. Distinguishing between behavior, sociality, and religion led us to use seven categories in this new tally. Once again, cognition (29 percent of replies) and emotions (26 percent) dominated what people thought when answering "What does it mean to be human?" Anatomy and ecology (both around 5 percent) were of substantially lesser interest. In the revised division of categories, two of them—religion/spirituality/morality and sociality—both registered at 14 percent, while arts, technology, and other aspects of behavior came to mind in only 8 percent of the responses.

This account of what people think about when asked *what it means to be human*, of course, cannot stand as a scholarly treatment. It does carry a clear message, though, one that is intended and hoped for when the public considers a question of personal meaning and perceptions of human uniqueness. Initial frames of reference have little to do with fossils, phylogeny, and physical form, which are central to most attempts to communicate human evolution. Evident again in this larger survey, most people think about human uniqueness in terms not readily addressed by science, and certainly not in any complete or nearly complete sense by scientific methods and discoveries. Even to scientists, this result should not be very surprising.

Thus, what exactly can the study of paleoanthropology contribute to the most prevalent perceptions and ponderings about what makes us distinctively human? How is it possible that finds excavated from dark underground recesses can enlighten the most prominent aspects of humanity that people care about? Let me start with but two examples.

The Religious Sense

At first glance, it might seem uninspiring yet one beautiful example derives from the mundane study of fossil teeth. Techniques are now available for reliably counting the microscopic layers of enamel deposited each day as teeth grow inside the jaws. This daily layering of tooth enamel is found across all primates and other mammals, also in people—and therefore it applies to our fossil ancestors. Counting these daily layers of enamel, researchers can determine the actual number of days—and thus the rate—at which our teeth and, by extension, our bodies grow. Humans today are characterized by an extraordinarily prolonged period of growing up. This fact of our prolonged maturation, experienced by every person, necessitates the immense energies and care of parents and other caretakers in order for any person to live beyond infancy or childhood. Prolonged life history is associated with the elongated timing of growing a large brain and the many years it takes for each individual to fully exemplify the hyper-social and culturally shaped species that we are. When those miniscule layers of enamel are counted in the fossilized teeth of our ancestors, the surprising result is that this fundamental shift in human maturation, nurturing, and cultural capacity did not occur at the outset of human evolutionary history 6 million years ago, or at the origin of our genus *Homo* nearly 3 million years ago. Only within the past 1 million years, and apparently near the origin of our species 200,000 years ago, did this transformation of greatly prolonged maturation with its profound social implications take place. In other words, we can say when along our evolutionary journey that this quintessential part of our humanness evolved; in the scheme of things, it was a relatively recent development.

My second example is best told as a story. Three days apart in 2010, I gave a tour of the Smithsonian's Hall of Human Origins to a small congregation of self-identified evangelical Christians, and then the same tour to the famed biologist and self-identified atheist Richard Dawkins and the trustees of his private foundation. In the exhibition we feature fossils of two elderly individuals, both of them male, one who lived more than 1.75 million years ago, the other about 65,000 years ago—and both had debilitating conditions clearly evident in their skeletons. The first individual had toothless jaws for the final several years of his life, evidenced by the diminishment of bone along the upper and lower jaws where his teeth had once been in his early years. In the second individual, a healed indentation of the braincase confirmed a blow to the head at a young age that had caused severe brain trauma, resulting in a severely withered opposite side of the body throughout much of this individual's life. In other words, in both cases, these two individuals required an intensive and enduring level of nurturing by the social group, for many years, which ensured a sufficient realization of needs and comfort for these individuals to survive.

Now, it became apparent that the evangelicals were cautious yet quite open as to whether the findings of science might support their beliefs in the moral status of humanity. Upon seeing the two fossils, and largely ignoring their old geological age, the agreement reached by their group was, "This surely is the beginning of morality and the family." The group led by Dawkins sought in these same fossils support for a naturalistic understanding of the world. Their response was, "These fossils indeed show when human morality and family first evolved." The parallels were obviously amusing to me, each group unaware of the commonality. Equally striking is how the fragments of our deep ancestry can indeed speak to our shared curiosity in what it means to be human.

Origins of Symbolism and Culture

Van Huyssteen's study of paleoanthropological findings has led to his immense appreciation for how archaeology and paleontology can inform meaningful reflections on the nature of our humanity. His writings have focused on the remarkable prehistoric cave paintings of Europe, so evocative of the symbolic way of life and the essence of society and religion we intimately experience and express. The fluorescence of cave art in Europe, beginning around 40,000 years ago, in other words several thousand years after *Homo sapiens* arrived in the region, has favored the idea of a "creative explosion" and a "cultural revolution"—a formative period in becoming human, including the dawn of consciousness, imagination, purpose, and religious awareness.

There is, however, an older story disclosed recently by archaeologists working in Africa of a longer development in the symbolic capacity and social awareness of our ancestors prior to the origin of *Homo sapiens*. The revolution in symbolic behavior and consciousness implied by the "creative explosion" has now been countered by evidence of a more prolonged, slower accumulation of behavioral, cognitive, and social innovations in Africa beginning at least 300,000 years before the efflorescence of European cave art. The "revolution that wasn't"—a phrase coined by Drs. Sally McBrearty and Alison Brooks in a now-classic article[2]—refers to this emergence of behavioral modernity in Africa starting before the earliest known existence of our species.

The African Middle Stone Age (MSA) comprises the suite of behaviors that followed the long-enduring Acheulean handaxe technology. Characterized by the production of large cutting tools, the Acheulean persisted for nearly

---

2. S. McBrearty and A. S. Brooks, "The Revolution That Wasn't: A New interpretation of the Origin of Modern Human Behavior," *Journal of Human Evolution* 39 (2000): 453–563.

The Religious Sense

1.4 million years, having arisen in Africa some 1.76 million years ago. The transition from the recurrence of handaxe technology to the creativity of human innovation in the Middle Stone Age couldn't be more striking. The oldest evidence of the MSA includes a smaller, more diverse, and mobile toolkit than devised by Acheulean toolmakers. In my team's digs at the site of Olorgesailie, located in the Rift Valley of southern Kenya, the last of the Acheulean occurred about 500,000 years ago and was gone for good in this region by the time of the oldest known MSA around 320,000 years ago. Innovations included the skilled production of blades, delicate and diverse scrapers, and other small tools. The well-planned preparation of stone cores enabled the production of flakes of predetermined size and shape with a single blow. Through the careful mental chess of preparing cores, small triangular points were knapped that formed the sharp stone ends of the oldest known projectile weapons, most likely throwing spears or darts. The world has never been the same since.

In these same archaeological digs, we also see a notable shift in the use of stone material—and, along with it, evidence of the origin of social networking. During the era of Acheulean handaxes, 98 percent of the stone used in making tools in the southern Kenya Rift was obtained from outcrops no more than 5 kilometers away. Acheulean tools were made by small nomadic groups who chipped away at stones along the route of travel. By contrast, in the oldest MSA, more than 50 percent of the stone used in making tools came from distant sources, especially rare and valuable black obsidian, which was transported en masse, as large blocks, from rock sources at least 24 to 80 kilometers away. The fact that such masses of rocks were introduced from such long distances without being chipped to bare bits provides the signal archaeologists look for in recognizing trade. A commodity of shared value was used in an exchange between distant groups.

The implication is astonishing. By this time, around 320,000 years ago and prior to the origin of *Homo sapiens*, early MSA groups were apparently aware of one another over impressive distances. They could hold in their minds the idea of a valued but not-readily-visible entity—in this instance, a type of stone not present in the local surroundings. This sense of value was evidently shared with other early people who lived beyond the immediate vicinity. How did they do it? How did they develop this shared value, communicate with one another, and retain it in their culture?

An intriguing hint comes from another type of object also found in our digs at the Olorgesailie site: *coloring material*, lumps of black and orange-red pigments concentrated at the archaeological sites where these early humans gathered. The use of pigments is often viewed as the dawning of human symbolic ability: just think of the depths of meaning people give to color—in flags, uniforms, skin, and art—as part of the symbolic universes we build and as a means of creating group and personal identity. Color, for better or for worse, is a fundamental means by which human cultural lives and distinctions are symbolically defined. In these early instances, we do not know what those predecessors were coloring. We see no art or splashes of color on rocky walls, which are absent in these open-air sites. Materials bearing the pigment have apparently decayed. The symbolic nature of these particular pigments remains a beautiful mystery of archaeological research.

Nonetheless, the combination of technological innovation, long-distance awareness, the delayed use and exchange of a valued type of stone, and the attraction to coloring materials all suggests that a major breakthrough had been attained in communicating symbolically via spoken language and social networking across distant groups. The MSA forebears of our species knew of one another over a vastly expanded terrain, implying an enlarged social universe, the mental construction of alliances bound by symbolic linkages, and a consciousness far broader than that of their Acheulean predecessors.

This older emergence of symbolism, culture, and consciousness prior to the origin of *Homo sapiens* does not minimize the amazement and regional significance of the creative explosion in Europe nearly 200,000 years later. At this juncture, however, the sequence of events alerts us to the fact that social, demographic, and other specific contextual factors were at work in the Upper Paleolithic of Europe, indicating that human history had arrived. The current body of evidence demonstrates, by contrast, that all human beings across the continents share a unified heritage of symbolic cultural capability, the result of an older evolutionary foundation that arose where our species arose—in Africa.

For many decades we have thus interpreted things backward, reversing the temporal relationship between the origin of our species and the emergence of certain behaviors that define our modern selves. We have long considered the origin of *Homo sapiens* as Act 1, followed much later by Act 2, the origin of symbolic behavior and consciousness. We paleoanthropologists, in hindsight, lacked a sound explanation as to how the immediate forebears of *Homo sapiens* began their initial divergence from an even earlier ancestor. Now we can entertain the reasonable hypothesis that the behavioral and cognitive shift in our earliest Middle Stone Age ancestors provided that first fateful push, laying down the first roots of our species' existence more than 100,000 years before our kind actually appeared on scene.

The Adaptable Species

The emergence of the Middle Stone Age—the suite of behaviors that provided the context for the origin of *Homo sapiens*—is quintessentially a story of adaptability. From its advent to its end when Late Stone Age technologies developed in Africa around 60,000 years ago, the entire MSA is situated within an era of strong climate variability that lasted more than 300,000 years. Environmental instability came about during a particularly lengthy period when Earth's orbit around the sun was elongated, a condition known as high orbital eccentricity, associated with strong variability in East African rainfall.[3] Thus we may envision how the novel practices of the MSA emerged due to the advantages they conferred on the predecessors of *Homo sapiens* in accommodating to environmental uncertainty. Almost all organisms evolve in a manner that adapts each species to somewhat limited conditions of survival and a narrow range of habitats. In the origin of our species, however, adaptability was the benchmark of survival, favoring the flexibility of the new lifeways of the MSA and a growing attachment to a symbolically enriched, cultural way of life.

Although innovations arose slowly, their increasing pace (Figure 5.1) tended to widen the adaptive options of the MSA ancestors of *Homo sapiens*. Wider social networks and complex symbolic activity indicated by the things they made (or gathered, in the case of pigments) represented the dawning of complex thinking, imagining, reasoning, storytelling, and planning for contingencies. These capabilities as inferred by archaeologists meant a substantial improvement in the cognitive, social, technological, and ecological agility of MSA peoples, helping them to adapt to an era of unpredictable surroundings.

The evolution of adaptability in our hominin ancestors—in fact, in any organism—was a process of *decoupling* from the constraints of any single or narrow range of environments.[4] As our species first evolved, critically important dimensions of human life were put in place: enlargement of mental and behavioral flexibility, expanded connectivity across social groups, and the growth of adaptive options, thus setting the stage for groups of people to diversify into distinct cultures and to adjust with greater facility to a changing world. In a very real sense, the decoupling of our existence from any single ancestral condition of life, inherent in the very origin of *Homo sapiens*, freed

---

3. R. Potts and J. T. Faith, "Alternating High and Low Climate Variability: The Context of Natural Selection and Speciation in Plio-Pleistocene Hominin Evolution," *Journal of Human Evolution* 87 (2015): 5–20. R. Potts, "Hominin Evolution in Settings of Strong Environmental Variability," *Quaternary Science Reviews* 73 (2013): 1–13.

4. R. Levins, *Evolution in Changing Environments* (Princeton: Princeton University Press, 1968).

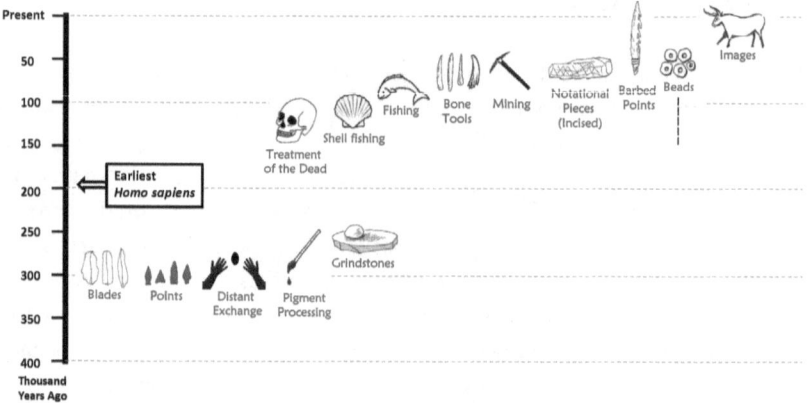

Figure 5.1. A timeline of developments near the origin of *Homo sapiens* as part of the suite of novel behaviors known as the African Middle Stone Age. The top line of the label beneath each visual icon represents the approximate timing of each development. The timeline provides evidence of an evolved capacity for innovation, wider social networks, and complex symbolic activity, thinking, and planning. That these qualities emerged during a period of strong environmental fluctuation in Africa suggests that these developments improved the ability of our species and immediate predecessors to thrive in the face of new environments and social landscapes. (Figure based on McBrearty and Brooks, "The Revolution That Wasn't")

our species from previous mental and social boundaries. This evolved adaptability led humans to constantly revise their overt behaviors, internal beliefs, and cultural norms in amazingly intricate recipes as our species spread around the globe. It became nearly impossible to deny the cognitive and cultural impulse to differentiate and diversify, perhaps most dramatically exemplified by the hundreds of distinct languages and cultural divisions found on Papua New Guinea alone. Our Middle Stone Age ancestors evolved the roots of humanity's diverse cultural responses to "what does it mean to be human?" now displayed by the extraordinary array of cultures worldwide.

A Purpose in the World?

Among the greatest challenges posed by the human evolutionary narrative is the demise of entire species, long-enduring predecessors so nearly like us as to belong with certainty to the story of human origins. Extinction is the counterpart to adaptability, loss the complement to evolutionary change. Over the past several million years, high rates of extinction have occurred in most groups of vertebrates, and this is true in the hominins. Out of a minimum of eighteen different species of evolutionary ancestors and cousins, only one lineage—our species—now exists. All the other ways of life of earlier hominins have gone extinct, even though each species possessed at least some of the unique hallmarks of human life.

During the era of human evolution, planet Earth has had no enduring, stable baseline. Every paleoenvironmental record studied over the past forty years has two signals—the overall trend and the amplitude of variability. Until about two decades ago, every student of human origins considered the variability as mere noise in the all-important trend toward a cooler, drier Earth. The development of savanna grasslands in Africa and Ice Age conditions in northern latitudes were thought to provide the context in which natural selection honed the major milestones in our evolutionary journey. The progress of climate change, the development of a particular ancestral habitat, was considered the signal that elicited the development of uniquely human adaptations. Yet many dozens of environmental records also show evidence of dramatic shifts between wet and arid, between cool and warm. Instability and uncertainty have now become the main theme in the environmental story of human origins.

Our fundamentally human way of life has thus, over time, depended on an ability to cushion the unpredictable, manage the immediate surroundings, and survive novelty. As a result, the overarching narrative of human evolution has changed. It has changed from a story of how the human lineage came to have dominion over some original environment to a story of evolving adaptability, a question of overcoming the ever-changing challenges to human survival. The old story of human inevitability that dominated nineteenth- and twentieth-century evolutionary thinking has now been overthrown by the theme of adaptability, with extinction of our closest evolutionary cousins as a gloomy dissonance.

We discover in these investigations that *Homo sapiens* is the only remaining species of a once-diverse evolutionary clade. This phrase "only remaining species"—resounding the title *Alone in the World?*—requires us to realize that extinction, the demise of past incarnations of humanness and their ways of life, is as much a part of our origin as the success of this lone species. In fact, study of the genetic variation across living populations worldwide suggests that *Homo sapiens* itself may well have hovered near the line of extinction. Despite all the outward diversity in human appearances today, the gene pool of our species exhibits a remarkably low amount of variation. This finding has led geneticists to infer that the reproductive population of our species during a long period of time until roughly 70,000 years ago was remarkably small, on the order of 7,000 to 10,000 adults, or might even have crashed abruptly to a size of no more than 600 to 2,000 adults. In evolutionary terms, we almost didn't make it.

According to one common train of thought, such findings imply that science necessarily obstructs an understanding of the purpose of our existence. As outlined in the previous section, however, we are evolved as meaning-making beings. We are explorers of the symbolic cosmos, conscious of things we have not seen, aware of people we have never met yet who are nonetheless included in the scope of our compassion and empathy. These are solid realities of our humanity, not delusions. Our instinct for symbolic creation; our reasoned talent for recognizing invisible forces in the universe, from gravity to God; consciousness of our own internal mentality and of time-space externalities distant from our own physical limits: all of these do have a discoverable, empirical basis in the long evolutionary history of our species. In the opinion of this paleoanthropologist, the evolved origin of these distinct hallmarks of human life does not and cannot demean our humanity or its meaningfulness.

The question here comes down to whether our definition of purpose requires that humankind be divorced from the processes of nature, whether purpose demands a sacred divide between ourselves and other living forms, and between life and inorganic substance. According to the discoveries of science, these all comprise a unity, a spectrum that falsifies the separation but not the uniqueness. If indeed humanity's uniqueness resides in having emerged, over time, as a meaning-making being, these evolutionary continuities become integral to our purpose in the world. Yes, like the movement of continents, the production of lightning, the effects of gravity, and the spread of microbes, evolutionary processes are not inherently purposeful. Yet these fundamental principles of geology, meteorology, physics, and biology—including their mindless impact on humanity—have no implications about meaning and purpose in the universe or in how human beings relate to it. The uniquely human union of highly complex cognition, sociality, symbolic behavior, restlessness, imagination, and curiosity, all of which can be understood as having evolved, is integral to the foundation on which the only complex meaning-making being has come to exist in Earth's history. This fact of human origins does not necessarily impart special status, certainly no right to hubris in the light of the pervasiveness of extinction and the potential for life elsewhere in the universe. Nonetheless, understanding human beings as creators of meaning and purpose in relation to the cosmos constructs a thoroughly active place for us that could become consonant with understandings of creation in Christianity, in all the Abrahamic traditions, and in other realms of reason, faith, and worship.

I suggest that the greatest challenges posed by the narrative of human evolution are as follows:

The Religious Sense

Extinction
Common ancestry
Natural selection
Existence as survival

Let's examine briefly why these matters present such overwhelming difficulties for many people.

First, if it is true that our evolutionary story included the demise of other lineages, and if it is true that our own species itself once verged on extinction, the idea of the inevitability of humans in the cosmos may well be weakened if not nullified. Second, common ancestry leaves us without an independent origin, situating us as an animal, in conflict with enduring beliefs and values in Western society. Next, natural selection provides a well-reasoned and empirically verified means of explaining origin by a material process. Of course, how else could it be studied and its validity as empirically well tested as other areas of science? Yet origin via a material process is so often interpreted as demeaning to a religious understanding of our place in the world. Finally, the idea that humans exist as the result of adaptation and survival does little to assuage the apprehensions and obstacles implied by other aspects of our evolutionary origin. All of these challenges revolve around long-standing doctrines of meaning and purpose in the world.

Let me further suggest a list of the most promising aspects of the evolutionary process that can potentially strengthen our sense of meaning and purpose in the world. This list is as follows:

Extinction
Common ancestry
Natural selection
Existence as survival

Obviously, the two lists—obstacles and opportunities—are the same. Let me clarify and, in so doing, I believe I am entering the broad and fruitful domain created by van Huyssteen's theological contributions. First, the prevalence of extinction is as daunting as death itself, and it shines a light on the fragility of life. In this fact, evolutionary history demonstrates this fragile quality and highlights the preciousness of life in a theological context. The fragility inherent to evolution illuminates the nature of contingencies, including the origin of our own species, which make a critical difference in the history of life on Earth. Second, although we may lack a separate, special origin as the result of common ancestry, the point is that we are intimately related to all other organisms. This connectedness among living creatures, past and present, is a defining aspect of evolution, and it implies that evolution is a process that creates kinship rather than independence. In everyday life and theological considerations, compassion requires connection. Kinship, whether it is symbolically defined or scientifically measurable, powers the greatest depths of intuited and realized connection—a parallel to how biologists understand the tie between kinship and cooperation. Here may well be a commonality that bridges evolutionary thinking and the exploration of purpose within the realm of theology.

Next on the list is natural selection, which is the core natural process (though certainly not the only one) of evolutionary change. Natural selection is not only about persistence and success. It is also where biologists since Darwin discern and contemplate suffering, so apparent in the natural world, including human life. I have long wondered whether selection might offer a foundation for understanding suffering in a way that need not start with God or influence the decisions people make about their relationship with God. A theology that could become liberated from seeing suffering solely through the lens of a loving God is bound to be complicated. Yet there could be solid ground for reflections that join theology and science, and emergent realizations of religious and cosmic meaning, if we were so bold as to develop this line of contemplation.

Finally, existence as survival: in any evolutionary context, survival is a matter of adjustment and revision. The latest findings on human evolution, as presented earlier, bring to the fore our particular legacy of adaptability. Survival in *Homo sapiens* and our species' immediate forebears was fueled by an evolving resilience and flexibility. *Homo sapiens* is an evolved animal freed more than any other organism from biological inevitability and genetic constraint. Although cultural prescriptions can shackle with enormous force, the evolution of adaptability has conferred new degrees of freedom arrived at by complex symbolic cognition, abstract reasoning, the creation of ideas, and the accumulation of innovations contributed by many. How diverse our thoughts, how liberated our minds, so beautifully manifested in the universe of answers people offer to the question "what does it mean to be human?"

Cultural Diversity and the Options of Religious Understanding

Religion and theology are profound expressions of the freedom imparted by the human evolutionary adventure. There is a special role for these realms of faith and contemplation in shaping the implications of that freedom for people worldwide. I conclude this chapter with an observation about the options of the religious sense in this regard.

As noted earlier, the symbolic basis of cultural identity and consciousness binds people together. At the same time, the creation of unity and the social glue of *belonging* inevitably require distinctions to be made, the defining of people who are different from oneself. Diversification of cultures, beliefs, languages, and understandings of the world requires a process of divergence that separates groups of people from one another. Even as it diversified the human experience, helped to build alliances among distant groups, and heightened the survival of our early ancestors, symbolically mediated behavior also intensified the potential for conflict. Interdependence between groups, which was an essential survival tool in the origin of our species, required shared currencies of communication (e.g., languages), facilitating the meeting and, where feasible, the harmonizing of the symbolic universes of people living in neighboring and distant places. One consequence of symbolically driven cultural identity and the building of symbolic bridges between groups was that not all groups were treated equally. The powerful symbolic pull that unites people has also served to repel those construed to be outsiders. Denoted by flags, uniforms, and a vast array of colors, gestures, myths, and dialects, cultural identity is defined as much by the symbolic walls people erect between one another as by the symbolic commonalities.

In this observation lies a dilemma for religion as one of the great avenues of human symbolic understanding of the world. Theological thought and religious doctrine can be the means for exacerbating or bridging the differences. These are two of the crucial options presented by religious commitments. Like other areas of culture, religion can heighten the walls between people, the tensions that drive people apart. Or it can look to the universals of the human condition. With greater authority than nearly any other aspect of life, religious reflection has the potential to dissolve the differences and instill the coherence of human life and the unity of what it means to be human. This latter option hinges on what faith-based reflection can accomplish in a world filled with diverse religious perspectives. Will commonalities and universals ever win out across the vast variety of religious beliefs and experiences? Or does religion as part of the foundation of human life inevitably breed dissonance and indelible perceptions of "us versus them"?

The power of the theological themes and understandings advanced by van Huyssteen begins with the shared origin of all human beings. It merges the deepest reflections on God and the highest possibilities of our unique humanity with the legitimacy of our evolved ancestry. Our new origin story continues to shape our strongest notions of who we are and why it matters to continue to discover what it means to be human. The evolutionary narrative is inexorable in its implication: the story transcends human differences. We now know that our shared journey makes the distinctions among the world's peoples, as powerful as those differences are often felt, as merely the veneer on a long, shared history that matters. It is a history from which wholly new directions of meaning and purpose can be derived, the unity of a one-species worldwide narrative. In exploring what it means to be human, the study of human evolution starts with the idea that what was once the plurality of humanlike forebears is now the singularity of human.

PART 2 Philosophers and Historians

6   Persons and Humans

The Dignity and Distinctiveness of the Human Person

KEITH WARD

What is distinctive about human persons? Why, and how far, should they be treated with special respect? And does Christian faith have anything to add to our understanding of persons?

Christianity has much to add. Indeed, it introduces a perspective very different from that of a secular understanding of human nature. Christian thought should begin with an understanding of God as the one and only creator of the universe, as a creator who took human form in Jesus, and who intends that all human beings should participate in the divine nature (2 Peter 1:4).

Beginning with the idea of God means beginning with the idea of a nonphysical reality that originates the physical reality of the cosmos through thought and intention. Secular thinkers often assume that the physical cosmos is all there is, that there is nothing supernatural or other than material at all. In recent thinking about cosmology, this assertion of the sole reality of the physical has been modified considerably by the thought that all universes originate from a realm beyond the physical. This is often called the "quantum vacuum," but it is clearly beyond space and time as we understand them because all spaces and times (for some cosmological views, all possible spaces and times) originate from that vacuum.

Because this is called a vacuum, some writers claim that the universe comes into being "out of nothing"; it pulls itself into being by its own bootstraps. That, however, is a radical misuse of the physicists' concept of a vacuum. For a mathematical physicist, the quantum vacuum is not absolute nothing. It is filled with pulsating ("jittering," they sometimes say) energies in their lowest energy state. Particles flash in and out of existence continually, and some of them form universes that are more or less stable and enduring. This universe is one of them, so it does not really come from nothing. It originates by incessant oscillations of energies, from an immensely dynamic and constantly quivering supernatural reality. Physicists do not like the word "supernatural," but the quantum vacuum is certainly beyond space-time, and is the origin of all space-times, so it is at least nonphysical.

Moreover, universes come into being in accordance with pre-existent laws of quantum physics. These laws exist even before any universes exist, so they are not just descriptions of how universes actually behave. They are eternally (non-temporally) existing laws that govern how any possible universes will behave, and that determine which universes will come into existence. So the quantum vacuum is a non-temporal reality (though it has its own form of time, in which the "quantum jitters" oscillate) filled with many unknown and largely unknowable forms of energy, and governed by mathematically intricate and elegant "laws."

Why this "vacuum" should exist with just the nature it has remains a mystery, but the theory states that all physical universes originate in a nonphysical realm beyond them, which is governed by intelligible (not just random) principles or laws. This is not God, and Stephen Hawking, one of those who espouses this theory, has said that "we do not need a God to light the blue touch-paper." I suppose this means that the laws operate automatically, without any mind that envisages the laws and causes them to operate, and that decides to bring universes into being for a reason or with a purpose.

What is interesting is that many cosmologists have no difficulty in imagining the existence of laws without any universe over which they operate, and in imagining supra-temporal and supra-spatial forms of energy that are able to "act" in a non-spatiotemporal way so as to bring space-time universes into being. Yet they sometimes claim to find severe difficulty in imagining a reality that is conscious of such laws, and that envisages a goal for the sake of which it can bring universes into being. It seems obvious, however, that imagining such a reality—a supra-cosmic "mind"—is easier and more intelligible than imagining laws that exist without any mind being aware of them, and which have the causal power to bring physical universes into being. As Hawking himself asked, "What breathes fire into the equations?" That is, how can purely mathematical entities have the power to bring physical entities into existence? They are not themselves physical, so this seems to be a form of causal power by which the nonphysical brings the physical into being.

It is a stock objection to Cartesian dualism that nonphysical "minds" cannot interact with, or have causal effects on, physical realities. So, it is said, the mind, as a distinct ontological substance, cannot cause events in the physical brain. But such nonphysical to physical causality is exactly what contemporary cosmologists must postulate when they speak of universes originating from a quantum vacuum. Cosmologists apparently find little difficulty in postulating nonmaterial, non-spatiotemporal, entities and nonphysical causes not just of physical events, but of entire physical universes.

What is needed to make sense of this is the idea of some form of reality that can provide an ontological basis for the existence of conceptual truths, and that is capable of exerting causal power over physical events. It may simply be said that we cannot imagine any such thing, and the forms of reality in question, though they must be real, just cannot be described any further. Thus they are not only eternal (non-spatiotemporal), intelligible (mathematically elegant, integrated, and coherent), and causally efficacious (giving rise to physical states). They are also not fully comprehensible—that is, they cannot be fully understood by human minds.

When a secular view of reality is able to include an eternal, intelligible, causally effective, and incomprehensible origin and continuing basis for the physical universe, it seems almost irrational to object to the idea of God—an eternal, intelligible, causally effective, and not fully comprehensible origin and continuing basis for the physical universe—on the grounds that it does not make sense, or is vacuous. Of course, what the idea of God adds to the "quantum vacuum" model is consciousness and causality with a purpose. But the idea of God is not just a superfluous addition to the vacuum model, with no real function. It is hard to think of something being intelligible if it is not intelligible to some actual mind. Intelligibility requires intelligence, the capacity to envisage conceptual truths, to discriminate between them, and to apply them where appropriate. But more important, what is lacking in the purely physical cosmologists' view is the notion of value.

This is very ironic because intelligibility or rationality is itself a value. Yet the cosmologists' account of the universe does not explicitly include any idea of value. Cosmologists do indeed speak of their sense of awe and wonder at the immensity and beauty of the physical universe. The beauty of mathematics is what motivates the research of many of the most able mathematicians. Yet, as the mathematical physicist Steven Weinberg has famously said, "The more I understand the universe, the more pointless it seems."

Intrinsic Values and Worthwhile Lives

The question of whether the universe has any point is the question of whether there is anything the universe brings about that is worthwhile just for its own sake. For instance, the contemplation of a beautiful scene or piece of art, architecture, or music can be thought to be worthwhile, not for any other reason than that the contemplation is worthwhile in itself. It is of intrinsic value. There are many intrinsic values of different sorts, and a worthwhile life might consist in a combination of a range of values. I would not want a life that consisted of nothing but contemplating works of art. But a life of artistic contemplation, artistic creativity, travel and adventure, intellectual development and understanding, friendship and love, the exercise of compassion and cooperative activity—such a life might be called intrinsically worthwhile.

If anything is to be called intrinsically worthwhile, it must be known and enjoyed by some mind. Intrinsic values entail the existence of minds able to appreciate them. Moreover, some values are objective. They are such that minds should appreciate them, whether they do or not. The "should" here is not a matter of moral obligation. It is a matter of achieving some sort of excellence or fulfillment. It would be more fulfilling if someone was able to appreciate the music of Mozart than not. But it is not an obligation to appreciate Mozart. There are other things that it would be fulfilling to do, and no one can appreciate absolutely everything. We might say that it is fulfilling, it would give life a point, if we could pursue and enjoy some range of intrinsic goods. But it is not obligatory to pursue any specific intrinsic goods—not everyone needs to appreciate music, though it would be good to do so, and everyone needs to pursue some intrinsic goods. We might have to qualify this by saying that there are some goods that everyone should pursue, and we might call these "moral goods," like being compassionate, just, and charitable. Even then, people might pursue moral values in very different ways.

A life of pursuing and enjoying objective intrinsic values, some of them obligatory moral values, and many of them non-moral values, is a worthwhile life, a life worth choosing for its own sake. It seems, then, that the universe would have a point if it produced such lives. If the universe was such that it generated conscious lives that could envisage, create, pursue, and enjoy many objective intrinsic values, the universe would not be pointless. As a matter of fact, this universe does generate many such lives. So Weinberg must be saying that the universe has done so only by accident, or that no values are in fact worthwhile enough to be fulfilling (life is fundamentally boring), or that too many lives never have a chance of fulfillment through the pursuit of excellence, so the cost in suffering, pain, and death is too high a price to pay for the happiness of a small lucky few.

These are powerful objections to the postulate of objective purpose and value in the universe. But they show that we know what such a purpose and value would be, at least in a general way. A God is at least a mind that knows all possible states and chooses to actualize some for a reason. If the universe is truly intelligible, it will not only be mathematically elegant, it will have a point, an objective and intrinsically valuable goal that it will realize. What the postulate of God adds to the secular cosmologists' account is that the universe has such a goal. The goal, at least one that we can imagine, will consist in the emergence of conscious beings actually enjoying the realization of many intrinsically valuable states, including creativity, understanding, appreciation, friendship, and compassion.

That the universe has such a goal is what secularists deny. It might be more satisfying intellectually if the nonphysical basis of the cosmos, which the natural sciences suggest is intelligible in being the basis of a universe that is elegantly and rationally structured, was also intelligible in creating universes for the sake of the realization of intrinsic values. But empirical study of our universe suggests to many that there is too much randomness and suffering for that to be the case. The universe as they see it is an uneasy combination of rational intelligence and moral indifference. Perhaps there is a God, but that God is not very concerned with what happens to human beings.

At this point I will pause to take stock of what I have been asserting, and why. I began by asserting that Christian thought about human persons must begin by considering the ontological primacy of God. Whatever a full account of God may require, it is at least true that the Christian God is the creator of the universe. God must be thought of as knowing what universes can be created, and choosing one or more universes for a reason of great intrinsic value. This establishes the primacy of mind. God can know, evaluate, and bring physical states into being for a purpose, without being physical. The belief that there can be knowledge, thought, evaluation, and purposive action without any physical reality is an entailment of Christian belief. So is the belief that mental acts can cause physical states to exist.

Some philosophers are reluctant to admit even the possibility of nonphysical or non-embodied minds or mental acts. But I have shown that modern cosmologists have no trouble with nonmaterial realities (the quantum vacuum), with unembodied laws, and with the causation of physical universe by nonmaterial forces. I argued that they should therefore have no logical difficulty in thinking of a nonmaterial mind that envisages laws and causes physical universes. It would be natural, once we think of an intelligible cause of the universe, to think that such a cause would create for a reason—which would seem most obviously to be the realization of an intrinsic value or values. That is, I think, a clear logical possibility, but some would refuse to accept it because of the observed randomness and suffering in the actual universe. I do not intend to discuss that important issue here. I have not sought to prove that there is a God. What I have argued for is the ontological priority of mind over matter, and therefore the logical possibility and initial plausibility at least of the creation of the universe for a purpose of great value. More to the immediate point, I have argued that Christians are committed to accepting both the priority of mind (spirit) over matter, and the reality of purposive causation (what Aristotle called "final causality") in nature.

This conclusion is important in considering the nature of human persons because persons are precisely beings capable of knowledge, thought, evaluation, and purposive action. They are aware of objects, they can envisage absent and future states, and they can act in order to achieve future goals. It seems, then, that Christians are committed to at least the logical possibility that persons could exercise these mental capacities without physical embodiment, and that these capacities are what make persons in some ways like God, and therefore perhaps what gives them a distinctive claim to special regard and respect.

The "Physical" and the "Mental"

This may sound like a form of extreme dualism, and it does both clearly distinguish between spirit and matter, and argue for the possibility (and the fact) of their separate existence. But Christians not only believe in God (pure spirit) as creator of the physical universe. Christians also believe that "the Word became flesh" (John 1:14), and thereby affirm the unity of spirit and matter. While mental states can exist without being associated with any material states, the physical universe is one that is capable of being identified with the mental or spiritual. In human beings it is so identified. Humans are not pure spirits; they are spirits embedded in matter, so as to form one being, which is both spiritual and material.

Each human person partly consists of a unique chain of experiences—sights, sounds, touches, odors, and tastes, thoughts and feelings—which are only directly known by that person. The British empiricist philosophers were right in saying that such experiences are the basis of all knowledge. But there are two important features of such chains of experience that the empiricists tended to neglect. One is that most human experiences are intentional—that is, they are experiences *of* something, they have objects. I do not just see colors; I see objects that are colored, and these objects come to me as causes of my experiences, as other than me and affecting me, as independent existents with causal powers. I live in an objective world that is not, as A. J. Ayer at one time held, a logical construct out of my experiences. It is a reality independent of me, which provides the content of my experiences.

If this is a correct account of human perception, it makes human persons very different from God. God's primordial perceptions—the knowledge God has before or apart from creation—are not caused by something external to God, and God in no way depends on some external reality for them. Nor are they produced by anything like sense organs and a physical brain since God generates them solely from the divine being and whatever mental content that being has. Human perceptions are caused by realities external to humans, on which humans depend in order to have any perceptions at all. Human perceptions also depend on sensory organs and a physical brain, which transcribes those external realities into the world as humans perceive it.

In this way, human persons depend for their knowledge on an environment that causes knowledge through the medium of the brain, which is itself part of that environment. So human persons are not pure spirits, but part of a world of causal powers and objects that produces mental states in human beings. While one of the things that is important and distinctive about human persons is the unique chain of their experiences—their mental content—these experiences are not separate from the physical world, as if they were some sort of shadowy duplicate of the physical world. They are parts of the real world, but parts that are not physical and that largely, if not entirely, depend on the character of the physical.

In other words, the real world is both physical and mental, and the mental is in basic ways causally dependent on the physical. However, it is not entirely so, and this introduces the second feature that many empiricists neglect or sometimes even deny. Human persons have a sense of continuing agency, a sense that they make free decisions that build up into patterns and habits of action such that we can speak of a development (or, unfortunately, a degradation) of character over time. Again, this agency is not apart from the physical world since it is exercised in the physical world, causing changes that would not otherwise have come about. So it looks as though human persons are parts of the physical world with mental (nonphysical) properties, and causes that operate not only in accordance with purely physical laws, but through intention, in order to bring about future states that they consciously envisage.

Philosophers have found it very difficult to find ways of expressing this situation clearly and precisely. But a "monistic" view of reality has become increasingly favored. That is to say, the universe consists of one "stuff" that has parts that can be called physical and mental. These parts exist in a continuum. At one end, the "physical" is unconscious and changes in accordance with laws of nature that make no reference to value or purpose. At the other end, the "mental" consists of consciousness of abstract objects that may or may not exist, and causality that consists solely in the manipulation of thoughts, without having any intended physical effects. At one end is brute matter, and at the other end is pure thought. But between those extreme points there is a whole range of possible blends of the two aspects.

Evolutionary theory has enabled us to see this continuum as one in which the purely physical gradually evolves into something like a physical universe whose complexity and integration is such that it comes to express the mental more and more fully. From the extreme simplicity of the "Big Bang," the cosmos, apparently through its own innate propensities, develops complex physical and chemical forms, and intricately structured arrays of elements like RNA and DNA, the building blocks of living organisms. For billions of years, there is little that one could classify as mental in the being of the cosmos. Yet as complexity and organization intensify, nervous systems and brains begin to form, and it begins to make sense to speak of organisms responding to sensed or felt stimuli, and acting in primitive ways in order to sustain and replicate their own complex structures. In such responses and seemingly self-organizing behavior it is possible to see the beginnings of conscious apprehension and freely chosen purpose.

If this is how things are, there must be a significant "phase-change" in the process at which some form of consciousness and some form of purposive agency begin to exist. It may be very hard to make this a clear and decisive break. There will probably be many borderline cases, perhaps in the case of forms of bacterial life. But there clearly will be a difference between completely unconscious life and organisms that have some awareness of their environment and some freedom of responsiveness to that awareness. The onset of awareness and purposive agency is a crucial stage in the history of the universe, when something distinctively novel comes into being, even though we may want to say that it was always a possibility in the primordial constitution of the cosmos.

An even more significant phase-change occurs when the development of larger brains makes possible the onset of abstract thought—the envisaging of states that do not actually exist or that may exist in the future, or are purely conceptual possibilities, as in pure mathematics. Together with such abstract thought comes the possibility of choosing which possible states to try to bring about. The ideas of purpose and value come to play an important explanatory role in analyzing the behavior of large-brained organisms. We need to explain their behavior in terms of what they may be thinking about and what they may want to do. What psychologists call "a theory of mind" is born.

In the Christian tradition, this account reflects the thinking of Thomas Aquinas, who in turn adapted the thought of Aristotle to articulate a Christian concept of the soul (used in this tradition as equivalent to what I am calling "mind"). Aquinas distinguished "animal souls" from "vegetative souls" and "intellectual souls." Vegetative souls were the powers that enabled vegetation to organize material from the environment to grow and reproduce. There has been much heated debate about vitalism and the introduction of mystical forces to account for the existence of organic life-forms. But it is possible to bypass that old debate, and simply point out that living things do possess powers of self-organization and reproduction that are not apparent at earlier stages of evolution. We can bypass the debate about whether such powers are wholly reducible in principle to the causal powers of the atomic and subatomic realms. They do not seem to be, but I am not here particularly concerned with vegetables.

With animal souls, it is different. Animal souls are said to possess powers of immediate perception and the ability to respond in relatively immediate ways to stimuli. Such beings can be expected to exist in the evolutionary continuum, and such powers seem not to reduce to causal powers that do not even mention such things as perception and conscious response. These powers are emergent, in being genuinely novel in the history of the universe, non-reducible to purely physical powers, but their existence is dependent on the development of suitably complex integrated physical systems—brains.

Intellectual souls have the additional powers of abstract conceptual thought and freely chosen purpose for the sake of realizing something believed to be of value. It is characteristic of the human species to possess intellectual souls, and though the borderline between intellectual and animal is apt to be fuzzy and imprecise, it is real.

Aquinas had not thought of evolution, but the distinctions he made fit easily into an evolutionary scheme, whereby there is an emergent continuum of development in which certain phase-changes are particularly significant. For Aquinas, however, and for much Christian thought, the emergence of the intellectual soul—that is, of powers of abstract thought and free purposive agency—is of decisive importance. Animal souls have no special moral importance; so animals can be hunted for sport, and exist only for the use of human beings. Intellectual souls, however, have an eternal destiny of life with God, and they have the right not to be killed or treated merely as means to some other end.

If all life exists on an emergent continuum, then it is not so clear that there is a morally decisive difference in kind just because a specific organism has the power of abstract thought and purposive agency. Nor is it clear that the human species, just as such, deserves special treatment. There may be other species that have such powers. It is a matter for factual investigation to find out whether there are. Now that we know that we exist on a small planet in a galaxy of a billion stars, existing among billions of galaxies, it begins to seem likely that there are many other forms of evolved intelligent life. So we should distinguish "humans" from "persons." We may wish to say that all humans are persons; but they may not be the only persons there are. And other animals may be much more like persons, and have more personal qualities, than Christians have sometimes, and wrongly, thought.

This means that we would be defining a person as a living organism with the power of abstract thought and purposive agency, whatever its physical appearance and its evolutionary ancestry. These powers do give a reason for special moral regard. Only a being with a sense of a continuing consciousness can be aware that it is partly constituted by a unique chain of experiences, with potentialities that it takes time and discipline to realize. Only a being with a sense of continuing agency can formulate goals of activity, perform acts in order to realize envisaged values, and act responsibly for the good and harm of itself and others. If it is God's will that persons should realize their potentialities by their own responsible actions, then it is a human duty to aid them in this process. If it is God's will that they should exercise responsible freedom, then that freedom must not be curtailed or destroyed without good reason.

If God has created all life, then all life should be given a certain degree of respect. We should view it with gratitude and with admiration, as long as it does not actively harm other valuable forms of life. Belief in creation entails a love of nature and of sentient life, and gives rise to a prima facie moral obligation not to cause pain where we can avoid doing so, and to sustain the welfare of the lives God has created. Of course, we must destroy weeds and predators where they harm other forms of life, but our obligation is to cause the minimum harm possible.

Personal life—life with what Aquinas called an "intellectual soul"—is not only to be respected and preserved from suffering as far as possible. For the capacity of persons to grow and develop, to make moral choices, to exercise unique forms of creativity, to appreciate and understand the world, their ability to form long-standing and mutually fulfilling relations with others, and their ability to care for, sustain, and conserve the world and its inhabitants demand that persons are treated as creative and responsible moral agents.

The incarnation of the Word of God in human form does not imply that only humans are worthy of moral concern. On the contrary, it implies that humans are called to share and express God's concern for all that God has created. Humans are called to love the world and its creatures because God loves them. It is because humans have this special responsibility, to mediate the love of God and creatively to realize new values in the world, that they are special.

God loves all creatures. But only some of God's creatures—persons—are

Persons and Humans

able to love God in return by mediating God's love to others, by caring for creation, and by acting consciously and intentionally in order to realize the values that are potential in the world of which they are part.

Theistic Evolution

It is feared by some Christians that acceptance of evolution would rob humans of their dignity and their special place in creation. That is one main reason for the rise of creationist biblical literalism in modern Christianity. But when we see evolution as the progressive emergence of consciousness and responsible action from a material world, when we see this as an emergent development within the cosmos to become an expression of the values and goals of God, and when we see humans as having a pivotal role in bringing the cosmic process to a firmer grasp of its God-given purpose of realizing its inherent potentialities, the picture looks very different.

An evolutionary perspective should increase the respect that humans have for many forms of life and for the environment as a whole. But it does not at all undermine the special capacities that humans possess, and that mark them out as persons—beings that can consciously and freely align themselves with God's purposes, and mediate the creativity and compassion of God to their fellow creatures. The story of creation in the biblical book of Genesis is not literal, for the stars are not sanctuary lamps hung on the dome of the sky, and the Earth is not a flat disk floating on water. But the second creation account puts in story form the profound theological truth that the human vocation is to "till and keep" the earth (Gen. 2:15). Also the fact that Adam "gave names" to all the animals (Gen. 2:20), as it were "baptizing" them, shows that they have a kinship with humans, even though they do not have the sort of capacities that could make them "helpers" in caring for creation.

"Having a soul," on this account, is having specifically personal capacities, and the subject of those capacities is precisely the complex physical organism that is a human animal. But this is a physical organism that has developed a rich set of nonphysical properties and dispositions. And if you ask whether those properties and dispositions could exist without the physical organism that is their subject or underlying "substance," a reasonable answer would be that they did not originate as nonphysical and it does not seem that they would be quite the same sort of beings if they were completely nonphysical. Yet at least at a certain stage of development it may be possible to "peel off" the nonphysical from the physical, and perhaps give the nonphysical a different sort of physical embodiment.

If the nonphysical consists of a chain of memories, thoughts, intentions, and projected goals that are connected both through being members of one uniquely accessible set and by a sense of being in part the products of one continuing and developing agency, then that unity and causal continuity of consciousness may belong to the chain itself, and not be confined to the physical causal continuity of its physical basis.

Thomas Aquinas believed that the "soul," as subject and agent of such a chain of experiences, was capable of existing without its physical basis in a brain or physical body. But he held that such an existence would be "unnatural and improper." Human chains of experience and action are meant to be embodied, in order to give them a natural means of gaining new knowledge, of acting in an objective world, and of communicating with other persons. But their form of embodiment need not be confined to the one they have at some particular points in space-time.

Some scientists speculate that consciousness could be embodied in a variety of forms, perhaps in super-computers. At some point in the future, some imagine, a human consciousness could even be decanted into such an artificially manufactured form since different forms of hardware can already embody the same information. This is pure speculation at present, but at least it is thinkable. And it remarkably echoes what Paul says in the key passage on resurrection in the New Testament, 1 Corinthians 15. He states that we die with a *sōma psychikon*—which we could translate as an embodied mind, receiving sense-impressions from a physical cosmos subject to the laws of entropy and inevitable decay. But we are raised by God to life as a *sōma pneumatikon*—a "body of spirit," which does not inhabit a world of decay and death. This would be a quite different form of body. It could still be called a body, for it is a publicly visible form of expression for thoughts and feelings, and it does inhabit a public world in which persons are recognizable and can act and gain new information. But it is not physical in the sense in which we understand it, as it would be governed by quite different laws, which do not cause decay, suffering, and death.

In such a world, which we could either think of as a transformed creation or as a completely different form of being, one intrinsically valuable goal of creation would be realized. There would be a social community of persons who could act creatively, appreciate the beauty and intelligibility of being fully, and cooperate with others in mutually fulfilling companionship. Above all, Christians would think, they would know the supreme beauty and wisdom of God, be filled with devotion and love for the supreme goodness of God, and express the creative purposes of God without any sense of compulsion or resentment.

Such a state of being would be what Eastern Orthodox Christian theologians have called *theōsis*, a participation in the divine life. For persons in such a form of life would have an immediate and vivid sense of the presence of God, knowing the mind of God with a clarity impossible in this present life. They would mediate the creative love of God and so be finite expressions of the divine will. They would be conscious elements of the being of God, as it expresses itself in a communion of personal being. For Christians, such a life would be the full realization of "being in Christ," which is the goal of the Christian pilgrimage. That pilgrimage thus takes on not just a personal dimension, but a truly cosmic dimension, as "the whole creation has been groaning in labor pains until now," and "waits with eager longing for the revealing of the children of God" (Rom. 8:18–25).

This is a future hope that resonates well with an evolutionary perspective. But it is a perspective that requires the purposive will of God to direct it and ensure its final realization. Many evolutionary biologists reject any notions of supernatural influence or purposive causality in evolution. They insist that evolution proceeds solely by random, not goal-directed, mutation, and natural, not supernatural or intelligent, selection. If this is true, then there is a conflict between scientific accounts of human origins and the Christian belief that God has created life for a purpose, and that the purpose is achieved through the progressive emergence of consciousness, freedom, and intelligence within the fabric of the physical universe.

It does not seem to be the case, however, that the study of evolutionary biology in itself leads to the conclusion that there is no purpose or non-natural causal influence in the course of evolution. Despite the fantastic success of molecular biology in establishing the structure of DNA and tracing the genetic history of life on Earth, evolutionary biology is still a very young science, and it cannot reasonably claim to have delivered a complete and final account of how the universe and life has developed. If we look at the history of the cosmos from the Big Bang until now, it is hard not to see it as directional or purposive in some sense. Intelligence and mind, the ability of the universe to be aware of and understand itself, and to direct its future course, almost inevitably seems to be an improvement and a development of capacities that were only implicit in the original constitution of the universe.

Biologists often point to randomness in mutation, pointing out that many mutations are harmful to organisms, and they claim that no intelligence would have allowed this to happen. But that is not an argument in biological science. It is a philosophical argument that an intelligent being would not create a process that contained harmful or chance events. As such, the argument is not compelling. The main counterargument is well known to philosophers. It is that the existence of chance events (i.e., of events not wholly determined by pre-existing and unbreakable laws) is a necessary condition of libertarian free will (the ability to determine some events by undetermined choice). And the existence of some suffering is a necessary consequence of any world in which free beings have to learn by trial and error, have to exercise self-discipline to achieve worthwhile goals, and have to learn to relate to one another by love and cooperation, in the face of strong inclinations to seek their own personal welfare first.

Given these facts, an intelligent being could well create a process that contained chance events and suffering, under certain conditions. We could not be expected to know all of these. But they might include a guarantee that the process as a whole was guaranteed to culminate in a goal of overwhelming value; that all sentient beings would be guaranteed the real possibility of sharing in that goal; and that all instances of suffering, though in themselves undesirable, would have the possibility of being used in some positive way to achieve something of distinctive goodness. For Christians, the passion of Christ is a definitive clue to the nature of ultimate reality. Jesus's life culminated in the overwhelming value of the establishment of God's kingdom (still future in its fully realized form). His suffering and death were in themselves absolutely undesirable. But they were used by God for the sake of the liberation of millions of human persons from evil, and as such they were freely accepted by Jesus in the belief that they would be used for the salvation of the world.

In addition, it may well be that, as Plato once put it, intelligence is limited by necessity. God must contain in the divine being all possibilities, good and bad, that could exist. Since the being of God, according to most theologians, is necessarily what it is, it may be that all possibilities that are necessary conditions of the existence of overwhelming and distinctive values must come into being by the divine will, which is identical with the essential, changeless, and necessary divine nature. If there are to be human persons that are carbon-based gradually evolved and partly self-organizing life-forms, then it is possible that they could only exist in a world like this. And this world necessarily contains both destructive and creative possibilities, as more complex forms of being (for instance, carbon atoms) are forged in processes of vast creative, but also destructive, power (like the fusion of elements in stellar supernovas).

These are, to be sure, highly contested issues, seeking to present and contrast opposing views of the cosmos either as totally random and pointless or as consciously directed to the realization of distinctive and overwhelming values. The point is that they are not arguments within the natural sciences or within evolutionary biology. They are philosophical arguments about, among other things, possible interpretations of the facts established by the natural sciences.

Christians are of course bound, even apart from such arguments, to believe that the evolutionary history of the cosmos is purposive. But these are not arguments between science and some philosophical or religious beliefs. They are arguments that are strongly contested within the sciences themselves.

Almost all scientists would agree that the classical Newtonian worldview of a universe made of material particles governed by absolute and unbreakable laws of nature is obsolete. Of course, since the first formulations of quantum mechanics in 1935 this has been known, but its implications have rarely been taken to heart by the general educated public. This revolution in our understanding of the universe is not just a matter of quantum physics. Even more basically, it is a matter of our understanding of the basic laws of nature, and of how nature comes to have the sorts of order, integration, and organization that it does have. That understanding has changed. To put it in a brutally simple way, there are no absolute and unbreakable laws of nature at all, which determine exactly how all things will happen, so that, as the French physicist Pierre-Simon LaPlace put it, if we knew the initial physical state of the universe, and all the laws of nature, we would be able to predict everything that would ever happen.

The physical world is highly ordered, and manifests organized complexity at many levels. It is not all chaos and accident. But the principles of order in nature are much more local, diverse, piecemeal, emergent, and holistic than the old model of one absolute set of laws (which would be, basically, the laws of the "master science," physics) dictating the behavior of fundamental particles in such a way that, in principle, the behavior of all complex biological, personal, and social entities can be deduced from them.

We might even say that "law" is not the best model for explaining the order that exists in nature. Perhaps a different model like that of "power," "capacity," or "disposition" might be a better one. Objects might, for instance, have various capacities that may be realized or frustrated in different local contexts, and that are sensitive to novel background conditions that have never existed before.

What difference will this change of perspective make? There will be many specific differences in particular sciences, but the most obvious overall change will be the collapse of the model of science as one unified and totalizing program for answering every possible question about the universe. It will undermine a view of physics as the one master science to which all others reduce in the end. It will destroy the view of the physical universe as a closed causal system into which talk of human freedom and dignity fit only with great difficulty, and that God can only interact with by breaking God's own inviolable laws of nature. It will enable us to see the universe as open, entangled, emergent, and holistic, rather than as a piece of clockwork that follows a set of blind impersonal laws. The universe will be open and emergent, in that it does not run down eternally pre-set rail tracks, but inherently contains the potential for new creative endeavors. It will be entangled and holistic, in that the causal inter-relations and influences between entities are many and varied, and not reducible just to one sort of quasi-mechanistic form of causality. The emergence of new systems and contexts will have causal influence on the "lower" and simpler component parts of those systems.

People will still take various views of whether there is objective purpose in the cosmos, on whether or not there is true human freedom and responsibility, and on whether or not there is a God or something like a God. But the new perspective will enable those who see signs of objective purpose and value in the universe to feel that their views resonate positively with much state-of-the-art thinking in the sciences, and it will make it easier to see the universe as "friendly" to mind and consciousness, rather than that they are unanticipated and accidental byproducts of mechanistic processes. Where nature is open and emergent, we can never be sure that we have identified all causal factors at work in any situation. Divine and purposive influence may be a real causal factor that the techniques of biology simply have not detected, or maybe are not even suited to detect. And mutation may not be as random as many Neo-Darwinians think.

Within evolutionary biology, there are new developments, with many biologists arguing for an extended evolutionary synthesis (EES) to replace the new-Darwinian synthesis that is very widely accepted. This new synthesis would throw doubt on the pre-eminence of natural selection in the evolutionary process, pointing to epigenetics (the way in which environmental factors influence which genes get turned on or off), niche construction and convergence (the way in which evolutionary landscapes constrain successful mutations in specific directions), and advances in the understanding of how genetic change can be horizontal and not vertical (how genetic change can spread across species as well as through inheritance).

Such thinking is controversial, but its existence makes the point that there is not in fact one acceptable biological view of inheritance as purely accidental and due to a completely specifiable set of physical laws alone. The present state of evolutionary biology is compatible with postulating the existence of direction or purpose in nature, though that purpose will be probabilistic or statistical, an overall rather than a universal tendency toward complexity, consciousness, and intelligence. And scientific thought must be open to the idea of many unknown causal influences, including the influence of mental or spiritual realities, if it is to avoid the arrogance of thinking that there is nothing new to learn about nature. Thus belief in theistic evolution is consistent

Persons and Humans

with modern science, and in many ways it seems to fulfill the New Testament vision of the eventual uniting of the whole cosmos to the being of God, which is foreshadowed in the union of human and divine in the person of Jesus.

Moral Choice

The postulate of theistic evolution also offers a convincing picture of human nature as we see it, a mixture of lust and aggression with altruism and empathy. The Genesis story of a perfect Adam and Eve falling into sin by eating forbidden fruit was a way of expressing the truth that human beings seem to suffer an almost irresistible tendency to lust, hatred, and self-will. They seem to be born in alienation from knowledge of God and love of one another. The biblical story puts this down to a primal disobedience associated with the gaining of knowledge without corresponding moral maturity (eating the fruit of the Tree of Knowledge before Adam and Eve have learned wisdom). Later theologians, at least in Western Christianity, developed this into a doctrine of "original sin," according to which all persons, as descendants of Adam and Eve, are born sinful and guilty of sin, even before they have done anything.

That doctrine does seem to be morally deficient since persons should be held guilty only for what they have done in a fully responsible way, when they know it to be evil and could have done otherwise. These are fundamental principles of human morality, often enshrined in law. Theories of cognitive evolution enable us to see that as animals strive to survive in difficult and competitive situations, genetic traits for strength, fertility, and courage will be selected and so quickly spread throughout the population of successful predators, like human beings or their immediate ancestors. Early humans are therefore likely to have dispositions to fight and to propagate their species. Aggression and lust will be built into their natures.

However, the application of game theory to strategies for evolutionary success shows that limited altruism and empathy will also prove successful in enabling species to survive. Thus, dispositions to band together and form supportive groups will also be selected. It is not surprising that humans will have natural dispositions to lust, aggression, altruism, and empathy, for that is what the conditions of evolution are likely to implant in them.

This is a rather different picture from that of an originally perfect Adam falling into evil, and then passing on this trait by inheritance to all his descendants. But the Genesis story can be taken, and I think it should be, not as relating something that happens in temporal sequence (from a state of original perfection to a state of sin), but as a depiction of a battle of contrasting characteristics in human nature (the battle in every human person between the demands of patient wisdom and the temptations of power that knowledge gives). Then we can say that as societies of humanoids began to develop powers of intellectual thought and moral responsibility, they were faced with the moral choice of good (obeying the moral demands of goodness) or evil (choosing desire for power and knowledge). Unfortunately, choices of evil over good spread rapidly through those human populations. As epigenetics now suggests, the genetic dispositions to self-will were turned on and the genetic dispositions to altruism were blocked by continuing and growing social structures and personal choices. What we call "original sin," the predisposition to evil choices and the ignorance of God that follows from disobedience to God's moral demands, became rooted in human nature. All human persons are now born into a society where ignorance of God and inclinations to pride and self-will are endemic and inescapable. Such a condition results from generations of evil choices, as the human species, at or near the point of its origin as a distinctively personal species, turned away from goodness toward evil.

Human persons stand in need of redemption since their God-given capacities have been so corrupted by generations of egoistic choices that they can no longer fulfill the moral goals that God intends. The Christian gospel is that God has entered into the human world in order to heal and restore these corrupted capacities, and reunite humans to God. There are various ways of construing this within the Christian world, but all of them stress that only divine action can bring human persons to their proper function, that this is accomplished by God's own self-giving love, and that this divine action is definitively expressed in the life, death, and resurrection of Jesus of Nazareth. Despite virtually universal human moral failure, there is a realizable moral goal for human persons, and it is to be realized by the free acceptance of God's love and wisdom as the divine Spirit transforms human lives by uniting them to the divine nature—that is, by grace.

What is distinctive about human persons is that they are physical organisms with the naturally evolved capacity to understand the world in which they exist, to make free and responsible choices about the future of that world, to mediate the purposes of God and to participate in the love of God, to love God and enjoy God forever. Human persons thus have an objective moral goal, but that goal lies in a realm beyond this physical universe, a spiritual realm that will take the whole evolutionary history of this cosmos, and every human joy and sorrow, and develop from that history a continuing communion of persons in God that will fulfill and complete all the potentialities for good that this cosmos has contained. Human persons have failed to realize their moral purpose in this physical cosmos. So they will achieve their intended goal only by the divine action of self-giving love that will unite them to the divine nature and enable them to fulfill what they could not fulfill by their own efforts.

This is the traditional Christian view of human persons. But it is given a new context within the scientific perspective of modern cosmology and evolutionary thought, both cosmic and biological. Modern science can sometimes ignore religion as superstitious or discredited science. I have tried to suggest that the Christian view of persons as embodied souls, possessed of creative and responsible freedom, liberated by Christ from egoism and self-will, and destined for spiritual union with God, is a deeply intelligible interpretation of cosmic evolutionary theory, and that it guarantees the dignity and distinctiveness of the human person in a way that few other views can match. There is a distinctively Christian view of persons, and in particular of human persons. It supports and justifies treating persons with special respect for their freedom and their destiny in union with God. For "God so loved the world that he gave his only Son, so that everyone who believes in him may not perish but may have eternal life" (John 3:16).

7 Axiological Sensitivity

Its Origins, Dynamic Structures, and Significance for Theological Anthropology

WESLEY J. WILDMAN

Like my friend J. Wentzel van Huyssteen, I doubt that the human species possesses any marker of uniqueness—neurological, physiological, social, or behavioral—that defines an absolutely sharp and clear contrast between human beings and the beings of other species with whom we share this planetary habitat and a very great deal of our genetic material. A little more forcefully than he does, I also doubt that there is a theological way to describe the ontological status of human beings—chosen by Yahweh, in covenant with God, viceroys of Allah, karmically ensnared, or under the mandate of Heaven—that demarcates us as utterly unique. I take the human reliance on theological narratives of special commandments and covenants and orders and obligations, from heaven or ancestors or karmic structures or deities, to be evasive fictions. They are potent social constructions reflexively serving an instinct to orient human life in a profoundly uncertain environment, and that instinct is continuous with other creatures in our ecosphere, intensified in the human case by our cognitive capacities. Thus, they remain popular despite their more or less obvious arbitrariness.

The most serious problem with theologically potent social constructions of the kind that guide axial-age mega-cultures is not their evasiveness. It is that they tame absolute reality, masking its character as simultaneously totally other and closer than our jugular veins, anthropomorphically distorting the character of our world and anthropocentrically twisting the truth about our species until our Gods look a lot like us, seem to focus mainly on us, have feelings a bit like us, and act sort of like we can to bring about ends that these Gods conceive in much the way that we do. Speaking in Christian theological categories, this is one side of the original sin of our species, while the other side is neglect of the revelatory depth structures and dynamic flows of natural reality that disclose the wondrous and inassimilable richness of ultimate reality. Nontheistic, theistic, nonreligious, and religious people are all entangled in this web of original sin, and we can fly into it from either side.

I will dismiss these neat theological narratives for now, and only return to them much later in this chapter. I do this somewhat sheepishly because I know they are spiritual and moral food for billions of my fellow human beings. But they don't sustain me; their multiplicity and our ignorant-but-passionate attachment to favorites make me restless, aching for a more convincing story. Fortunately, there is another story to be told, encompassing both human nature and the absolute reality in which we live and move and have our very being. This chapter, written in honor of van Huyssteen, tells one version of this other, less familiar, more unsettling, and for me far more satisfying story. It is a meditation on the human condition, on what makes us distinctive rather than unique, and on the theological importance of that distinctiveness.

The connection with van Huyssteen is, to me, fitting. Like him, I am deeply impressed by the intensity of sensitivity to value and meaning that arises within the human species. Like him, I think that this perspective takes us deeply into the nature of our species and its theological significance. While he would not endorse my somewhat idiosyncratic portrayal of human nature in a relatively unruly environment, he would see the point in it. And like him, I can comfortably employ the symbol "image of God" to describe the theological significance of human sensitivity to value and meaning, though I would not confine the scope of this symbol's application just to human beings, or indeed just to living beings.

In our many conversations, particularly through his final year in Princeton, I think I learned that one pathway from the mainstream of the distressingly anthropomorphic Christian tradition to my edgy mystical marginalization is through the kinds of insights that van Huyssteen has grappled with in the past decade or so of his impressive career. Allow those insights sufficient authority and, in a way that never happened with van Huyssteen to the same degree, they drive a powerful critique of anthropomorphic and anthropocentric religion akin, in different ways, to both Karl Barth's Feuerbach-fueled protests against religion and to the so-called New Atheist's consciousness-raising objections to religion. They also evoke an infinitely unmanageable portrayal of our species as a sign of ultimate reality, in a way that never happened with van Huyssteen or Barth or Richard Dawkins or Dan Dennett—and not even with Paul Tillich, whom I take to be my theological ally, but whose picture of ultimate reality is, for me, just a little bit too neatly organized.

Consequently, I see this meditative chapter as an extension of my conversations with van Huyssteen. In exactly the way we would chat about these things over a good meal, here I am inviting him to ponder what his own insights might really imply about the conceptual instability of the Christian theological traditions, challenging him to recognize the way his method of transversal connections simultaneously surfaces these insights for theological reflection and keeps them safely at bay by permitting us to engage them or pass them by, and honoring him for his lifelong endeavor to place these insights in conversation with Christian theological traditions.

The theme of this meditation is axiological sensitivity. Axiology is the philosophical name for thinking about values—not just moral values, but every aspect of value from aesthetics to morals, from aspirational life longings to achieved life meanings, and from the mathematizability of regularities in the natural world to the stunning biological possibilities slowly uncovered through the evolutionary process. I am going to take for granted the (probably incontestable) van Huyssteen-inspired proposition that human beings are spectacularly sensitive to axiological possibilities and that pondering our axiological sensitivity and everything that comes with it, from language to art, takes us deeply into the biological and theological distinctiveness of our species. I will allow van Huyssteen's own arguments on behalf of this proposition to serve as the foundation for this meditation.[1] And I will build upward from there, narrating the story of axiological sensitivity in the way I have come to find it most compelling. This story makes me feel spiritually at home in the world.

The Origins of Axiological Sensitivity

Near as we can tell, our universe did not have any axiological sensitivity at one time, then it had some, and now it has at least as much as we human beings possess. While there may be more sophisticated forms of axiological sensitivity elsewhere in our mind-bogglingly large universe, in our little corner of reality, on the thin surface of our planetary bubble, we are the shining-yet-tragic examples of awareness of meaning and value. In fact, we are meaning-obsessed creatures, making of ourselves a constant interpretative puzzle, as Martin Heidegger might have put it; falling into despair as desperate as starvation when we lack meaning sufficient to sustain us, as Albert Camus wrote in *The Myth of Sisyphus*, or Edvard Munch painted in *The Scream*; and becoming

---

1. These arguments are set forth in J. Wentzel van Huyssteen, *Alone in the World? Human Uniqueness in Science and Theology* (Grand Rapids: Eerdmans, 2006).

paralyzed or reactively crazed through awareness of our freedom to construct meaning, as Friedrich Nietzsche and Jean-Paul Sartre described it.

Whence this axiological sensitivity? Can we look around our planetary home and discover how it emerged? Maybe the splendid array of forms of axiological sensitivity present in our living companion species can shed light on its origins. Maybe primatology would be an especially important resource, or the archaeology of human cultures, or the paleoanthropological study of prehistoric human beings and the hominid species from which they evolved.

There is a fascinating story to be told about the origins of axiological sensitivity and its stunning intensification in the species *Homo sapiens*. Unfortunately, we have to grant that we may never know most of that story in any detail, no matter how clever and diligent the scientists working on the origins of our species are. But we have good reasons to think that this fragmentary story will have at least four interwoven subplots.

First, there seems to have been something like punctuated equilibria in the evolution of axiological sensitivity: long periods of relative continuity and slow change interrupted by shorter bursts of rapid change and relative discontinuity.[2] In terms of complexity theory, the evolution of axiological sensitivity probably consists of a series of stable equilibrium regimes and rapid transitions between them.

In each equilibrium regime, evolution randomly walks through the possibility space associated with it, exploring a variety of dimensions: biochemical and behavioral, social and sexual, cognitive and axiological. In this process, the ordinary mechanisms of evolutionary change are in play, including inclusive-fitness considerations, which help to define what organism features are preserved and what features are lost within a population.

A transition from one equilibrium regime to a new stable equilibrium will be relatively rapid: a key change in organism capacities causes a cascade of changes to ripple through a population, powered by potential for novelty latent in the achieved complexity of the species in question. Such transitions can isolate certain organism features that were formally exposed to selection pressures, after which their frequency in a population may still change due to genetic drift or gene flow but is not changed by inclusive-fitness considerations. These transitions can also expose formerly protected organism features to the harsh realities of natural selection and sexual selection. Such a transition is a

---

2. Niles Eldredge and Stephen J. Gould, "Punctuated Equilibria: An Alternative to Phyletic Gradualism," in *Models in Paleobiology*, ed. T. J. M. Schopf (San Francisco: Freeman, Cooper and Company, 1972), 82–115.

game-changer, opening up a new equilibrium regime with different constraints and exposing a world of novel possibilities for evolutionary exploration.

The evidence for punctuated equilibrium in the evolutionary history of axiological sensitivity lies along two lines. On the one hand, we have circumstantial evidence: the vast gap between human beings and all other species in regard to axiological sensitivity. This is a complex consideration as there are forms of value detection in nature that are not developed in human beings because we lack an associated sensory capacity, such as the precise echo-location of bats or the refined pheromone analysis of ants. But in those cases, there are many species with related abilities. In the dimensions of mindfulness, meaning, music, mathematics, morality, and murder, however, human beings appear to have no near species neighbors. Perhaps there was a gradual intensification of these characteristics across the dozens of hominid species in a single equilibrium regime but that seems prima facie unlikely.

On the other hand, we have more specific evidence deriving from what Jared Diamond and others have called the "great leap forward."[3] This refers to a species change that left an explosion of human-made artifacts in the archaeological record around 40,000 to 50,000 years before the present (40–50 kbp), suggesting that this was a time of transition between two sharply contrasting equilibrium regimes of human cognition. In the old equilibrium regime, humans were anatomically modern but behaviorally difficult to distinguish from other hominid species, including the Neanderthals who coexisted with modern humans in Europe for a long time. Neanderthals may have been more solitary and modern humans more socially inclined, but both species lived in much the same way and DNA studies famously suggest that they even interbred at times. In the new equilibrium regime, a host of novel behavioral capacities flowered, including new hunting techniques, a host of human-made tools and toys, complex art, and elaborate burials. My assumption is that the transition between equilibrium regimes was all about axiological sensitivity, as modern humans gained the capacity to detect value possibilities latent in their living environments, value possibilities that were formerly invisible to them. Cognitively and axiologically, this is the period in which humans became the beings we take ourselves to be, though physiologically most of the key changes occurred much earlier. It makes sense to suppose that greater axiological sensitivity made for greater empathy and behavioral complexity in a way that was deeply attractive, so sexual selection probably accounts for why the corresponding genetic changes would have spread through human populations within about 10 millennia.

---

3. Jared Diamond, *The Third Chimpanzee: The Evolution and Future of the Human Animal*, 3rd ed. (London: Hutchinson, 2006).

The "great leap forward" hypothesis faces challenges from the fact that the archaeological record shows rare instances of tool construction, burial, and simple art prior to 40–50 kbp. This challenge is awkward when we assume that there had to be a hard-and-sharp transition to behaviorally modern humans. But it is likely that there would have been occasional forays into new behavioral territory that didn't "take" and possibly even several genetic false starts in the direction of behaviorally modern humans, in the same way that there were several failed migrations of modern humans out of African habitats into Eurasia prior to the one that eventually "took."

However those details get worked out in the long run, the archaeological record does suggest that something big happened around 40–50 kbp. This something had everything to do with behavioral repertoire driven by newfound cognitive sophistication and sensitivity to axiological possibilities in the living environments of modern humans. Language abilities would have been stretched by these new forms of axiological awareness just as the archaeological record shows that behavioral repertoire was transformed. People would have narrated the meaning of their lives and their environments in novel ways, altering the way humans understood themselves, establishing narrative patterns for social life, and birthing more complex cultures. This may have marked the birth of shamanic practices and the seemingly religious worldviews that go along with such practices, though supposing that we have in this period the birth of something recognizable to us as religion is even more speculative.

A second subplot in the story of the origins of axiological sensitivity relates to embodied cognition. The brain-group nexus is the biocultural miracle of our species. Our kind of brain requires our kind of group, and our kind of group requires our kind of brain. This all-important entanglement of brains and groups is a stable equilibrium built on a more basic entanglement of bodies and environments that we see across all animal species, and in a certain way also in plant species and even in microorganisms. The story of the origins of axiological sensitivity within the brain-group nexus has to be told against the background of bodily, sensory engagement with environments that afford possibilities for behavior and interpretation.

Embodiment is a common theme in the academic study of religion, and even in theological anthropology, in our era. This marks a helpful change from the abstract ideational focus of past eras, which really did distort our understanding of religious phenomena, leading us to focus on religious beliefs to the exclusion of, rather than in concert with, religious practices. Unfortunately, however, the embodiment theme in religious studies and theology rarely benefits from solid knowledge about embodiment from cognitive psychology and neuroscience. As a result, the understanding of embodiment is truncated. There is a sprinkling of embodiment spice sufficient to achieve the desired result of disrupting the blandness of an exclusive focus on disembodied religious ideas, but not enough of the embodiment flavoring to create a truly new dish—that is, to register the radically embodied character of human emotion, cognition, and sociality as these impact the beliefs, behaviors, and experiences we are willing to call religious. So how do cognitive psychology and the neurosciences make a difference in our understanding of human nature, including in its religious aspects?

While I remain unconvinced by Alfred North Whitehead's theory of causation, his philosophy of organism does begin to get embodiment right.[4] In this he is anticipated by a number of American philosophers, including Charles Peirce, William James, and John Dewey. At the root of natural reality is a kind of embodied feeling, according to Whitehead. He called it "prehension" to express the way that embodied feeling grasps the environment (*prehendere* in Latin means to grasp or seize, literally, and to take in or apprehend, figuratively). He attributed prehension to fundamental atomic moments of process, which he called actual occasions, but for present purposes I'll focus on living organisms (as it happens, Whitehead thought of living organisms as large assemblages, or communities, of such moments of process, or actual occasions).

Picture an organism in an environment. As Aristotle correctly pointed out, the form of the organism determines its range of possible functional characteristics. If it has opposable thumbs, it can manipulate objects in ways that would be difficult or impossible otherwise. If it has gills, it can live underwater without surfacing for air. Aristotle didn't emphasize the environmental side as much but it is just as important. The ecological psychologists of the twentieth century, especially James Gibson, described how the environment affords possibilities for interaction that are picked up on, or not, by organisms.[5] Because the environment affords interactive possibilities, and organisms possess bodily forms that make certain kinds of interactions feasible, the organism-environment interaction is both mutually constrained and mutually enabled. The result is that organism perception, abstractly speaking, is a collaborative achievement of organism form and environmental affordance. Organisms with flexible cognition or mutable bodily form (with limbs or wings or tails or flagella) develop habits of interaction with recognizable environments, speeding

---

4. Alfred North Whitehead, *Process and Reality: An Essay in Cosmology*, corrected ed., ed. David Ray Griffin and Donald W. Sherburne (New York: Free Press, 1978).

5. James J. Gibson, *The Senses Considered as Perceptual Systems* (Boston: Houghton Mifflin, 1966).

Axiological Sensitivity

up navigation and rendering interpretation more reliably accurate. Organisms accustomed to one environment may struggle to navigate or make sense of a new environment, but they may be able to learn through exploring, gradually building up novel competencies and eventually habitualizing them to economize on energy expenditure.

A real door affords the possibilities of handle-grasping and door-opening, which some organisms can recognize and others cannot. Among organisms that can recognize those affordances, some organisms can act on them while others cannot. Often enough, it seems to be the ability to act on an affordance that determines the ability to recognize it at all, but there are exceptions. A realistic painting of a door might momentarily confuse an organism capable of recognizing the affordances of handle-grasping and door-opening, but bodily interaction with the environment soon corrects the perceptual-inferential mistake. Going further, Gibson himself extended the idea of environmental affordances to social affordances in an attempt to make sense of social life in a more comprehensive way than seemed possible within the mid-twentieth-century behaviorist framework of stimulus-response psychology. But Whitehead, with the American pragmatist philosophers mentioned above, went further still, pointing out that a door may afford many layers of possible interaction, including engaging the valuational possibilities associated with its aesthetic design or with the promise of what's on the other side. Organism-environment interaction is always valuational (i.e., axiological) engagement. Sometimes the axiological engagement is simple and practical, as when we want to know whether we can safely navigate from one room to another. Sometimes axiological engagement is freighted with existential meaning, as when someone pauses with hand on door handle, about to abandon a family forever.

Ecological psychology's understanding of perception is all about embodied cognition, and it finds its neurological underpinnings in the work of neurologists such as Gerald Edelman, who argued for neuroplasticity in relation to the environment, even *in utero*; he called this "neural Darwinism" and described the processes of neural pruning that are employed today to make sense of human brain development in the early years of life.[6] Similarly, the enactivism of neuroscientist Francisco Varela and others explains how human cognitive capacities arise in the interaction of organism and environment.[7]

The central philosophical point made by Gibson and Whitehead and

---

6. Gerald Edelman, *Neural Darwinism: The Theory of Neuronal Group Selection* (New York: Basic Books, 1987).

7. Francisco J. Varela, Evan Thompson, and Eleanor Rosch, *The Embodied Mind: Cognitive Science and Human Experience* (Cambridge, MA: MIT, 1992).

others is just as important as discovering the neurological underpinnings of embodied cognition in the brain-group nexus: every organism-environment interaction is also a valuation, an instance of axiological engagement. Axiological sensitivity lies at the root of perception and cognition, so the story of the origins and development of axiological sensitivity is as old and tangled as the history of bodies interacting with environments. When evolutionary pathways close off perceptual capabilities such as echo-location for human beings, an entire range of axiological possibilities latent in the environment is correspondingly lost to us. Likewise, when evolutionary pathways open up for us intensifications of ordinary sense experience, we find that entire ranges of axiological possibilities latent in the environment spring to life, with attendant joy and suffering. This is why we are the species that builds art museums, enjoys fine cuisine, proves mathematical theorems, has experiences we call spiritual and religious, is plagued by suicide, and endlessly talks about everything.

A third subplot in the story of the origins of axiological sensitivity pertains to social-psychological dimensions of the process. While these considerations do not apply in any straightforward way to the simplest types of organism-environment interaction, as when bacteria navigate an environment, they certainly do apply to animals, even to largely solitary animals for which the limited sociality of sexual reproduction remains a necessity. And they apply very forcefully to cognitively complex animals with cultures, such as human beings. The human brain-group nexus is born in organism-environment interaction but it develops a life of its own, one that demands analysis in terms of the psychology and sociology of motivation, behavior, cognitive error, interpersonal relationships, social groups, and cultural heritages.

The way we value powerfully depends on the way we are taught to regard our environment as we grow up within a social setting. The social framing of valuational interpretation does not foreclose individual creativity. On the contrary, it launches it into the stratosphere, enabling sophisticated varieties of valuational sensitivity that would be impossible as solo beings. Think of the social dimensions of art history in any given culture, or of the history of music. Individual differences matter here, as temperament and cognitive gifts render individuals unusually sensitive to some types of value and relatively insensitive to others. The zero-empathy psychopath may be exquisitely sensitive to music, and the genius mathematician may be incapable of appreciating fine wines. Socially borne expertise also matters: some cultures will foster brilliance at reading the signs of animal life and navigating an environment of potentially dangerous plants, while others will grasp the laws of electromagnetism and create civilization-changing technologies. Even manners and customs are built on valuation guided by socially framed perception of a social world.

Axiological Sensitivity

Most of the time, when we talk about concretely real values, we presuppose a kind of social encoding that facilitates rapid, low-energy axiological judgments. For example, many human cultures insist on the maxim of respecting one's elders, and any child deemed "properly raised" will reflexively behave in accordance with that maxim. The fact that now and then a child fails or declines to comply with this social consensus about goodness is jarring in part because it surfaces the underlying social construction, which then just seems to demand articulate or forceful defense. The social construction of reality is the social construction of patterns of valuational interpretation, and carries with it the force of social consensus, including the violence or marginalization that social consensus facilitates.[8]

The social construction of valuational interpretation throws almost all of the responsibility for construction onto the interpreter, and very little onto the environment. I think this is misleading. In the case of navigating an environment, the need for more of a balance is obvious: the environment affords valuational possibilities that the organism recognizes and creatively realizes, or not. Forms of engagement incompatible with environmental affordances, as when I attempt to ride my bicycle from the roof of a skyscraper to the pavement below, may end in tragedy as the "feedback mechanism" inherent in the structures of environmentally borne valuational possibilities kicks in. In the case of aesthetic or moral values, the balance shifts more toward organism construction but environmentally structured axiological possibilities are still in play. Not respecting one's elders, when it is enshrined in a socially enforced maxim, will have a chilling effect on a society, as some science fiction books and films have tried to depict using worlds where people past a certain cutoff age are euthanized. In the case of aesthetic and moral values, therefore, the feedback mechanism is weaker but still present, constraining without determining the outcome of organism-environment interactions.

It is even possible to amplify the voice of this feedback mechanism. The trick is to organize social forms of inquiry in such a way that those committed to processes of cognitive training in the associated specialized discourse communities develop more refined sensitivities. Not all flavors work together in fine cuisine, given the way human taste tends to work, and specialists can refine their sensitivities in this area by means of tradition-supported specialized training. We might not have known about the circulatory system or the constancy of the speed of light for all inertial observers but socially organized and supported processes of inquiry found a way to amplify the voice of the

---

8. See Peter L. Berger and Thomas Luckmann, *The Social Construction of Reality* (Garden City, NY: Doubleday, 1966).

feedback mechanism inherent in the axiological possibilities of our natural environment, correcting mistaken beliefs, resolving disputes, and opening up new worlds of understanding.

Individual creative construction is never out of the picture when organisms engage environments. But environmental structuring of axiological possibilities is also never out of the picture. These two elements are potently entangled in human social life, which arbitrarily forecloses some valuational worlds while simultaneously sustaining life-changing inquiry into others. Groups are nothing if not ambiguous.

The fourth and final subplot I will mention here is ontological: what are values and in what precisely do values reside? Are they aspects of the world that exist independently of axiological engagement by organisms, such that organisms encounter and discover them? Are they mere expressions of subjective judgments about what is important and meaningful to an organism?

Neither the radically objective nor the radically subjective interpretation of the ontology of values makes much sense to me. As soon as we picture valuational awareness arising from organism-environment interaction, with meaning-hungry interpreters exploring environmental affordances, it is obvious that values can't lie radically on one side or the other of this relationship. Rather, values take their rise as collaborative achievements of both the value-affording structures and dynamics of an environment and the value-detecting and value-constructing capacities of organisms navigating those environments and engaging the axiological affordances within them. In this I follow Dewey and the other early pragmatists, Whitehead and other process philosophers, Gibson and other ecological psychologists, Varela and other enactive theorists, and Robert Neville's axiological theory.[9]

While my earlier analysis of organism-environment interaction demands a collaborative, relational interpretation of value, this merely constrains what we might say about the *ontology* of values, without offering many details. So I need to say something about what values actually are. This has become a deeply perplexing subject in modern Western philosophy because of pervasive physicalist commitments. It has become common to appeal to emergence in order to explain how values and meaning are aspects of the physical world, but this strikes me as philosophically rather casual. Indeed, much of Western philosophy has become blind to the need to articulate the ontology of value,

9. The key works not already cited are John Dewey, *Experience and Nature*, 2nd ed. (La Salle, IL: Open Court, 1929), and the three volumes of Robert Cummings Neville's Axiology of Thinking series: *Reconstruction of Thinking* (Albany: State University of New York Press, 1981), *Recovery of the Measure: Interpretation and Nature* (Albany: State University of New York Press, 1989), and *Normative Cultures* (Albany: State University of New York Press, 1995).

and correlatively blind to the importance of what Aristotle long ago called "form" and what Paul Tillich called the "dynamics-form" ontological element.[10]

The secular, technocratic obsessions of Western intellectual elites are so focused on whatever passes for the material dimensions of reality and so eager to protest folk ideas of disembodied intentionality, awareness, and agency that we are failing to notice something important: any serious axiology imposes strict demands on ontology. I don't object to a practical focus on materiality, though I am always reassured when that focus is accompanied by a realistic confession of profound ignorance as to what matter is, in light of what we know about nature from fundamental physics. I also don't object to a deconstructive attack on folk-psychological attachment to ontological dualism and supernaturalism; that's been far too slow in coming thanks to our species' vulnerabilities to cognitive error in this department. But I do object to a failure to account ontologically for the very conditions that make our understanding of the physical world satisfying, and possible. Those conditions include axiological aspects of reality: the mathematizable regularities that we describe as "laws" of nature, the meanings we rely on to assess plausibility, the logical underpinnings of judgments of consistency, and so on.

One fascinating consequence of intensifying our interpretative focus on materiality is that we take embodiment more seriously, and with it embodied cognition, the organism-environment interaction, and the collaborative achievement of value as organisms engage environments. That in turn drives home the explanatory importance of the dynamics and form of environments (because that is how value possibilities are afforded) and the dynamics and form of organisms (because that is how value possibilities are engaged, realized, and constructed). In this way, taking materiality with due seriousness demands that we take the ontological status of values seriously, and not merely as emergent properties of a complex system whose ontological standing is purely material (whatever that means).

My solution to this ontological challenge is akin to Whitehead's, though once again without his peculiarly idiosyncratic theory of causation. It is also indebted to the early American pragmatists, among whom James was particularly effective at naming the need for an ontology that could give due weight to both material and axiological elements of reality—more effective than Dewey who was comparatively understated in his ontology.[11] The di-polar monism

---

10. See Paul Tillich, *Systematic Theology*, vol. 1 (Chicago: University of Chicago Press, 1951).

11. See William James, *Essays in Radical Empiricism and a Pluralistic Universe* (New York: Longmans, Green, 1943).

that results still resists all dualisms as well as disembodied intentionality, awareness, and agency, and thus it remains thoroughly naturalist in character, but it welds the physical and the valuational together, so it would be misleading to call it materialist or physicalist. In Aristotelian terms, this is equivalent to keeping formal causes in the explanatory picture along with material causes. Value possibilities are inherent in the formal (and dynamical) properties of organisms and environments.

In our time, non-reductive physicalists, of both the supervenience and weak-emergentist types, have ventured in this direction but not far enough. They say that there can be emergent properties that are explanatorily non-reductive to the physical, which is correct, and certainly a very good start. But I find their insistence on ontological reductionism confusing. The reason for my confusion is that I don't know what they mean by "physical" owing to the way fundamental physics is shaping our understanding of reality in such wild ways. To the extent that they mean emergent values are ontologically reducible to materiality or physicality, the claim seems evasive until materiality and physicality are defined. But I can endorse ontological reductionism when the primal stuff of reality is understood in di-polar monist terms, as combining physicality and value. Concretely real values are emergent from complex systems of components that are always physical-valuational hybrids. In my view, reality is physical-valuational hybridity all the way down, and the formal-dynamical aspects of organism-environment interaction manifest that hybridity in a particularly potent way. So call me a di-polar monist or a non-reductive physical-valuational hybridist.

The Dynamic Structures of Axiological Sensitivity

So far, I have argued that the origin of axiological sensitivity is an evolutionary story in which human social-psychology rides atop embodied cognition, and the physical-valuational hybridity of reality manifests itself in organism-environment interaction. To speak of *concretely real values* is to refer to a process of making real certain valuational possibilities latent in an environment through an organism's creative, constructive, and often socially ordered engagement with that environment. To speak of *latent valuational possibilities* is to conjure an image of a multidimensional landscape of axiological possibilities.[12]

---

12. Process philosophers will quickly and correctly think of the divine primordial nature in Whitehead's *Process and Reality*, which is the place in that system where this insight is registered most forcefully.

Axiological Sensitivity

To speak of *engagement* is to posit life as an exploration of that axiological landscape. This line of thinking takes us directly into the next phase of this meditative reflection: the dynamic structures of axiological sensitivity.

Like a complicated gift, however we came by axiological sensitivity, we now have it, and we want to know what it is and how it works. The story of origins I have sketched has already hinted at what axiological sensitivity is and how it works. I'll now take this further by describing the dynamic structures of axiological sensitivity. As usual, we don't know as much about this as we might like, so there is something inevitably speculative about the musings that follow. Yet even speculative musings can illuminate a complex subject matter. I think it is important to attempt to speak about axiological sensitivity forthrightly, if only to contest the casual dismissal of its importance that I criticized above.

On the environmental side of axiology we have the multidimensional landscape of axiological possibilities, constraining without determining the way organisms creatively engage it. This landscape of axiological possibilities is not formless and void, with every imaginable and unimaginable possibility included. If $F = ma$, then a bunch of possibilities are ruled out. If cultures don't respect elders, highly probable consequences will ensue. Pythagoras's theorem of right-angled triangles either works in a flat plane or it doesn't. Perhaps in another universe the structured dynamics of the landscape are different from what they are in this universe, but that just means that the landscape is larger, with places we can't reach, not that it lacks dynamic structure.

People who focus their attention and efforts in one or another order of aesthetic values become expert. This is because they explore specialized valleys within the landscape of axiological possibilities, usually in the company of other experts, training one another to perceive the valuational affordances in the food, the music, the sculpture, or the moral excellence they seek to cultivate. These are traditioned processes, as a result. Sometimes tradition speaks louder than the rawer axiological affordances of the environment—this is the meaning of fads and trends. But properly rational processes of inquiry optimize the ability to detect and engage environmental affordances in such a way as to correct prevailing opinions above and beyond, beneath and around, in and through the mere shifting of trends. In fact, the cyclical rotation of conventional trends can tell us something about the underlying landscape of possibilities that we explore in our aesthetic adventures, much the way that the movement—often enough the apparent rotation—of massive objects allows us to reconstruct the underlying space-time manifold in the general theory of relativity.

The multi-vocal character of the landscape of axiological possibilities implied in the possibility of numerous conventional "takes" on the same aspect of reality is important. Cultural anthropology drives that home. All human groups have certain cultural universals, from kin structures to means of economic exchange, but the ways these cultural universals are realized in a given culture at a particular time are extremely diverse, showing that there is more than one approach to doing almost anything of value.

Empathy is our greatest ally in our efforts to discern the multi-vocal character of this strange landscape. Through the exercise of empathy, we can learn to appreciate the excellence of the saint, and with a great deal more effort the excellence of a serial killer. I would sign up to designate the former good and the latter evil, but there is a kind of intrinsic value even in evil that I want to call excellence. In fact, part of the intoxicating lure of serial killing is the realization of possibilities that are beyond the social pale and therefore not usually discerned, making the serial killer or the torturer or the heartless manipulator a kind of bold adventurer, a fact that also often makes them simultaneously dangerously arrogant and dangerously dismissive of the herd moralities on which we rely for civilizational stability.

The landscape is also mutable. We can create new life niches, after which valuational possibilities open up for us that were formerly virtually impossible to envision. When human beings started to create gardens, we unleashed a cascade of novel valuational possibilities that were latent in the axiological landscape but impossible to encounter until artificial environments allowed us to engage them.

The dynamic structures of the landscape of axiological possibilities are therefore somewhat determinate while also being multi-vocal and mutable. We can explore those dynamic structures and learn to navigate valuational affordances in our environment in such a way as to cultivate priceless expertise. What is real in the landscape are the possibilities and the dynamically structured relationships among them. This, then, makes the landscape virtual in an important sense: while concretely real values do not exist until value possibilities are engaged, the value possibilities are already latent in the environments we find and the environments we create. In the multidimensional landscape of axiological possibilities, the virtual is as much reality as there is. Gilles Deleuze means something different, though not unrelated, by his usage of the term *virtual* to describe something that is ideal rather than actual, and yet still real. This is his own way of acknowledging the axiological dimension of reality: for him, axiological engagement occurs in the real relations that constitute the actualization of the virtual.[13] In fact, the long history of all phil-

---

13. See Gilles Deleuze, "The Actual and the Virtual," in Gilles Deleuze and Claire Parnet, *Dialogues II*, 2nd ed., trans. Eliot Ross Albert (New York: Columbia University Press, 2002),

osophical traditions includes extensive meditations on the ontological status of virtual aspects of reality such as value possibilities in nature that can be concretely actualized through engagement.

On the organism side of axiology we have valuational engagement: creative, constructive, and often enough socially structured interpretative realization of some environmentally borne axiological possibilities and the foreclosure of others.

Foreclosure is an important practical point here. If I spend all my life laboring to become expert in meditation, I probably forgo the opportunity to cultivate expertise in playing the cello, and many other forms of axiological sensitivity. Each of us turns away from one valley or many valleys in the landscape and devotes effort and attention to exploring the intricate affordances of one particular valley, the valley of our choosing. When we choose, we move into the axiological landscape in such a way as to render some possibilities inaccessible and others more immediately sensible, present to us with increasing intensity in future choices. We don't get to decide to be a wide receiver or a cornerback unless we first decide to play football. And after we decide to play football, we are not likely to be able to play cricket at the level of excellence that might have been possible otherwise.

The creative moment of engaging environmentally afforded axiological possibilities has been the focus of a host of canny philosophers. Rather than focusing on the existential moment of freedom in choosing, though, I want to draw attention to the *determining character* of choice. The axiological landscape is vastly complex, a virtual world of almost endless dynamically structured possibilities. When we choose, we create values that are concretely real; we make determinate some of the possibilities we can sense in the environment. Whitehead describes this beautifully, and names it the process of concrescence: entities becoming concretely actual. My interests lie less in the concrescence of actual entities and more in the concrete realization of value possibilities. Those value possibilities are dynamically structured and real in their way yet they are also virtual until they are rendered actual in the organism-environment interaction.

Choice is awe-inspiring when we slow down enough to sense its dimensions. We can choose with or against conventional wisdom. We can choose for or against our own well-being and personal interests. We can even choose to esteem new values that seem dramatically counterintuitive against the evolutionary background of our emergence. For example, we can devote ourselves

---

148–52. This is elaborated at greater length in *Difference and Repetition*, trans. Paul Patton (New York: Columbia University Press, 1994).

to radical, unlimited compassion despite the fact that our species character only naturally supports the limited compassion of kin altruism (family comes first) and reciprocal altruism (the altruistic version of tit-for-tat). Not many of us make the choice to commit ourselves to radical compassion, and quite a few of us talk about the virtue of radical compassion more than we realize it in practice, but it is a possibility latent in our social and natural environments that we can cultivate—if we so choose.

Going beyond enshrining values that fly in the face of our ordinary evolutionarily conferred capacities, we can construct worlds of meaning and cleave to them—with devotion or desperation, or even delusion. When we tell ourselves an intimate relationship with a certain person will make us happy but the possibilities of genuine happiness and well-being are actually tragically remote, we can talk ourselves into believing that our hopes will be fulfilled anyway. We overwrite the probabilities afforded in the axiological landscape of possibilities partly because we can't sense enough of it to be sure about the future, and partly because we don't like the parts of it that our protective friends and family are only too happy to put to us in the form of dire warnings. Of course, there are also times when we think we can see a way through against all odds, a way for the relationship that everyone believes is doomed to flourish. Maybe we sensed a narrow ravine of possibilities in the landscape that our advisors missed, or maybe we were delusional but lucky.

Sometimes our constructions are so pervasive that the feedback from axiological affordances in the environment is completely drowned out in the noise of what we create. The background environment is still there but its affordances are so vague and underdetermined in our foreground life practices that our skill in axiological engagement is limited to navigating the possibilities latent in the artificial world of our making. For example, we can tell ourselves anything we want about how nature works, as when Aristotle held that women were rationally defective; we can happily explain away contraindicating data, as when Aristotle was forced to acknowledge extremely intelligent women but diagnosed them as contrary-to-nature exceptions; and we can refuse to see the effects of patriarchal social orders for millennia on end. Yet, in a suitable era, either by happenstance or through the labors of courageous genius, we can discover that we were wrong in our valuations of women and that we had constructed our worldview in such a way as to make it very difficult to detect the mistake.

Axiological engagement can be artful or artless, effortful or lazy, manipulative or receptive, distorting or deferential. It is our nature to engage our environments axiologically. We know it deep in our bones: we can't do anything we want with the world because it is axiologically ordered, but we have awesome choices at almost every moment, choices in which we realize some latent possibilities and foreclose others. So we must take responsibility for what we do, and for what we don't do. As Nietzsche and just about every existentialist philosopher have been at pains to point out, taking responsibility for our choices is daunting because it pushes into awareness the fact that we hold the meaning of our lives in our very hands. Nevertheless, for many people, taking responsibility is preferable to evading responsibility by means of the host of deceptive narratives we employ to rationalize or to mute awareness of failure and laziness. Such attempts to dull the nausea we feel when we sense our axiological inertness are a glossy patina of self-deception covering the crumbling decay of delusional deflections lurking beneath.

The dynamic structures of axiology seem most colorfully marked by their variability. This means variability in degree of determinateness or, equivalently, in power to constrain valuational interpretation, on the landscape side; and variability in degree of sensitivity, and also cultivated expertise in socially ordered traditions of inquiry, on the engagement side.

Among the more constraining aspects of the dynamic structures of axiology are what we call *laws of nature*. These are mathematizable regularities that will push back against our interpretations if we can learn to engage them with sufficient sensitivity. Even statistical regularities such as the gas laws of statistical mechanics, the laws of measurement in quantum mechanics, and statistical laws in the social sciences can push back against our interpretations, though here the landscape constraints are subtle and we have to pay particularly close attention. The easiest way to notice landscape constraints on axiological interpretation is to invest in carefully organized traditions of inquiry that accumulate understanding over centuries and train us how to engage with the necessary sophistication.

The meaning of our lives arises through our individual and corporately structured adventures in axiological engagement. This, too, is a collaborative achievement in concrete value-making, with the axiological landscape contributing latent possibilities that organisms choose to realize through engagement. The fact that most of us bring such passion to the quest for meaning is what has grabbed the attention of philosophical interpreters of the human condition: we are meaning-hungry and we'll hunt down meaning for our lives to chew on regardless of what the landscape of axiological possibilities has on offer. Here, then, with life-meaning construction, we have a premier example of the landscape appearing to be only weakly able to constrain valuational interpretation—of all places, the very locus in our lives about which we care so deeply, feel so ravenous, and need most guidance. Perhaps that is the irony of the human condition in a nutshell, as nearly as this kind of speculative meditation can express it, at any rate.

WESLEY J. WILDMAN

Axiological Sensitivity and Theological Anthropology

Who are we, then, in theological perspective? What difference does understanding the origins and dynamic structures of axiological sensitivity make to theological anthropology?

Note, first, that this is an exercise in theological anthropology from below, rooted in experience, as revealed by close phenomenological attention, rather than theological anthropology from above, in the specific sense of adhering to some received religious narrative, a way-of-seeing guiding the theological interpretation. Theological anthropology from above requires us to be very, very lucky with our received narrative ways-of-seeing because there are so many of them—even if we only count the ones that are still guiding human lives rather than the host of alternatives that have passed into the hermeneutical graveyard—and because the circumstances of birth and culture determine which of the living narratives we encounter and subsequently find most plausible. Of course, it is always possible to rely on the way such received narratives can seem internally incorrigible, clinging to groups in which nobody asks in uncomfortably pointed ways the obvious questions about arbitrary attachment to questionable narratives, and thereby shielding from our awareness the hunger that drives obviously intellectually questionable adventures in meaning construction. Such approaches are not worthy of scholarly recognition because of their brutally casual neglect of relevant information and their arbitrary embrace of favored constructed narratives to constrain subsequent interpretation. This is bias masquerading as virtue. Nevertheless, such forms of inquiry can be extremely useful in the context of religious communities who rely on a specialized subset of their members to adopt a *fides quaerens intellectum* (faith seeking understanding) approach to theological inquiry, driven and ultimately limited by intra-community interests and norms. Such confessional settings actually encourage the arbitrary neglect of relevant information. Specially trained intellectuals able to inhabit the ruling narrative sincerely can be highly prized members within such communities.

That is not that, obviously. But we can think of the current exercise in theological anthropology as being in dialogue with more confessional approaches. In fact, that's the approach I adopt here. Taking for granted the account of axiology above, how might a fruitful dialogue unfold between it, on the one hand, and a confessional tradition of theological anthropology, on the other? The confessional tradition I have selected, Christianity, is internally complex, and indeed rife with interpretative tensions. Consequently, I will focus just on one key idea from it, though this idea is itself internally complex: the theme of the *imago Dei*, the image of God.

Axiological Sensitivity

In *Alone in the World?* van Huyssteen sets up a similar dialogue structure, also connecting to traditional Christian affirmations that human beings are created in the image of God. The link between axiology and the *imago Dei* is, as he would say, a point of transversal connection that invites dialogical exploration. Perhaps he would be less willing to say, with me, that we are *morally and intellectually obliged* to explore the implications of moments of transversal connection for confessional theological viewpoints; he treats them mostly as potentially exciting opportunities rather than burdensome obligations with potentially disruptive effects. Likewise, van Huyssteen would probably be unwilling to join me in pursuing theological anthropology from beginning to end with the secular academy as its institutional home, leaving aside the authority of confessional traditions altogether and employing their wisdoms and their histories only as sources of information. I have pursued that, and justified it, elsewhere.[14] Despite our differences, here I am inspired by van Huyssteen to focus on transversal dialogue, though even this will take us into territory that he himself does not traverse in his theology.

To the extent that the story of axiological origins and dynamic structures I have related is philosophically credible, *thinking of human beings as in the image of God establishes a link between the divine nature and the story of axiology*. This in turn forces on us a fairly sharp choice.

In my story, there is no special valuational grading of the possibilities virtually alive within the axiological landscape. It is we who choose, or who inhabit socially coded choices, to make some valuational possibilities concretely real, and to interpret them the ways we want. There is no capital-g Good or capital-e Evil; no capital-b Beauty or capital-u Ugliness; no capital-l Laws of nature or capital-c Chaos. These are powerful but also misleading abstractions from the sometimes socially ordered interaction of organisms and environment. The fundamental choice we face is whether to regard ultimate reality in just this way, or as an axiological grading of the virtual landscape of valuational possibilities. In the first instance, human will, creative choosing, determines all concrete values, in a collaborative symphony with the landscape's structured dynamics. In the second instance, God represents an ordering of axiological possibilities, akin to divine moral commands and aesthetic preferences. Which way we go with the decision is all-important for understanding human beings.

I depart from both Whitehead and van Huyssteen at this point. Both of

14. See *Science and Religious Anthropology: A Spiritually Evocative Naturalist Interpretation of Human Life* (Farnham, UK: Ashgate, 2009), for the effort to which I allude here, and *Religious Philosophy as Multidisciplinary Comparative Inquiry: Envisioning a Future for the Philosophy of Religion* (Albany: State University of New York Press, 2010), for my justification of this approach.

them, in very different ways, choose the latter path. God is a morally interested and aesthetically invested being for van Huyssteen, and a naturally reflexive axiological optimization process for Whitehead. For me, God is the ground of being, understood as the condition for the possibility of the axiological landscape I have described—a virtual landscape of possibilities with dynamic structures yet valuationally ungraded. To employ and extend a term of Friedrich Schleiermacher, God is the *Whence* of the axiological depth structures and flows of reality.[15] More precisely, thinking of God in this way is our last-gasp estimation of that which necessarily surpasses cognitive grasp by any finite creature, as our apophatic mystical brothers and sisters might say. Along one of the apophatic mystical paths, the one known as the *via negativa*, or the way of negation, many other models of God need to be disposed of before this one as *even less plausible*. These discards include all of the notably anthropomorphic models, including van Huyssteen's, no matter how theologically renowned or how popular in retail religion they might be. In my account, the model of ultimate reality I am describing falls, as all ultimacy models fall, but it falls later in the plunge to silence, a mark of being closer to the truth of the matter.

It follows that van Huyssteen's approach is mistaken, on my analysis—that is, further from the unreachable mark than my analysis is. In fact, I believe there is strong evidence to support my interpretation of it as remaining in thrall to anthropomorphic tendencies and related kinds of cognitive error that plague not only folk religion but also the theological rationalizations of it that are so common in the confessional theological traditions that subserve the interests of religious communal identity. The cognitive sciences have documented these tendencies to cognitive error in our species over the past century or so, and the cognitive science of religion has applied and extended that work into the understanding of religion. While van Huyssteen's view is the more popular, and it remains logically possible regardless of any amount of evidence, this enormously impressive body of research, once fully and clearly grasped, renders that view of God implausible, and with it the idea of human beings as living in a divinely valuationally graded landscape of axiological possibilities. I can't make such a case here, and doing so is not the aim of this chapter anyway.[16]

I think Whitehead's approach is wistful and largely irrelevant to us. It is certainly *causally irrelevant* because it is only in the consequent nature of God that this axiologically optimized version of reality eternally concresces, never

---

15. See Friedrich Schleiermacher, *The Christian Faith* (Edinburgh: T&T Clark, 1928).

16. I have made that case in *In Our Own Image: Anthropomorphism, Apophaticism, and Ultimate Reality* (forthcoming) and *Science and Ultimate Reality* (forthcoming).

Axiological Sensitivity

becoming actual and so never able to be prehended in the world of actual occasions. Divine axiological optimization is a kind of metaphysical appendage that, if dropped, can make no material difference to the unfolding of the world or to human life. Charles Hartshorne saw this problem in Whitehead's system and attempted to repair it, making of God a community of actual occasions; in this way, God could become serially actual, and thereby be prehended by other entities. But in the very same moment that Hartshorne "rescued" Whitehead's God from moral and aesthetic irrelevance, he sacrificed the anti-anthropomorphic power of Whitehead's outlook. I think Whitehead's wistful way is better. I prefer practically useless wistfulness to practically powerful anthropomorphic illusions. Neville saw the problem, also, and dispensed with the concept of the divine provision of an initial aim to the concrescence of every actual occasion altogether, thereby solving the problem while remaining truer to Whitehead's spiritual sensibilities than Hartshorne was able to do.[17]

My own view, for all its plausibility relative both to the axiological story I have told and to what is known about human cognition, is deeply unpopular among religious people, and even among nonreligious people who feel the need for some absolute grading of axiological possibilities. This unpopularity expresses a profound double critique of my view. One side of the critique urges that you can't organize human social life when there is no moral foundation, no moral compass to tell us right from wrong, no final confidence that there is a way to be axiologically, and above all, morally. The other side of the critique urges that only a personally ordered divine being could be the condition for the possibility of such a marvelous multidimensional landscape of axiological possibilities, and if that's the case then it only makes sense to assume that this landscape is valuationally graded by this same personally ordered being.

The second critique betrays a lack of metaphysical imagination and a dependence on anthropomorphic reasoning. If billions of nontheists can solve that problem then I certainly don't need to address it here.

The first critique is Immanuel Kant's and it is sound as far as it goes. But it is also not really relevant to the truth of the matter. Kant himself implicitly recognized this in formulating the principles of moral reason as *postulates* for which the only rational ground is that we presuppose them in making moral judgments. But the scientific study of religion shows that human beings will behave in exactly the way we do—as meaning-making engagers of axiological possibilities—regardless of whether there is a Kant-style metaphysical foundation for morals. We will find one if it's there to be found and we'll invent

---

17. See Robert Cummings Neville, *Creativity and God: A Challenge to Process Theology* (New York: Seabury, 1980).

one otherwise and it will feel just as convincing to the inattentive. Kant didn't know about this and it would have given him pause the same way it has caused every moral thinker to pause since these discoveries were made. Whether or not there is a metaphysical foundation for morals (i.e., valuational grading of the landscape of axiological possibilities) can't be settled by the mere fact that we seem desperately to need there to be one.

Theological anthropology is deeply impacted by this metaphysical question of valuational grading of the landscape of axiological possibilities, which I have argued is forced on us as soon as we place my story about the origins and dynamic structures of axiology in transversal connection with the affirmation that human beings are in the image of God. If there is a personally ordered and morally interested God, many of the narratives guiding confessional theological traditions can be taken seriously, and (within limits) quite literally. After that, human beings are what those narratives say we are, there is a Kant-style metaphysical foundation for morals, and all axiological judgments are rightly interpreted as movements toward or away from the divine, as Karl Rahner so famously expressed the meaning of human choice.[18]

For many people, this is an extremely attractive framework for human life, reassuring, full of purpose, and packed with vibrant meaning. But I don't think it is close to being true. It depends for its plausibility on shielding ourselves from the full richness of the axiological landscape, which we discover in our very bodies as our lives unfold along strange paths, often incommensurate with the controlling narratives of the moral frameworks to which we adhere. It requires us to pretend that there is valuational grading where there is none, to impose on alternative axiological worlds whatever derogatory assessments are needed to protect our own, and to reduce the encounter among axiologically diverse cultures to a mere matter of survival of the fittest, which we silently associate with the best, the truest, and the most beautiful. Gone is testimony to axiological vagueness and plurality, to dynamic structures that open up dark truths we'd rather hide from, to the axiological wonders we uncover in our lives but keep as secret as we hold them dear, and to our ravenous hunger for meaning that drives us to destroy alternative visions of life rather than confront our responsibility for constructing the vision we inhabit. It's the secret of genocide: I'd rather not see the full landscape for what it is; it's just too bright, too intricately complex, too daunting. Contrary to the new atheists, especially Sam Harris and Christopher Hitchens, this devastating series of defense mechanisms has nothing particularly to do with religion; all humans

---

18. See Karl Rahner, *Foundations of Christian Faith: An Introduction to the Idea of Christianity*, trans. William V. Dych (New York: Crossroad, 1987).

are vulnerable to it. Religion offers convenient rationalizations for the ensuing bad behavior but we can always build convenient rationalizations—economic or moral if not religious.

This is who we are. Spiritually speaking, we need to learn to affirm it and to navigate gracefully the axiological landscape free from attachment to reassuring but illusory stories of absolute valuational grading.

Conclusion

Van Huyssteen was kind and generous to try to penetrate my axiologically driven spiritual view of the world. Over lunch, he would ask me: how, then, are we supposed to live, morally? My answer was always the same: we choose, we take responsibility for choosing, we enjoy what we engage, we use coalitions to support forceful protection of consensus values, and we always remain self-critically aware of our tendency to write the needs of our morally rapacious maws onto the axiologically ambiguous cosmos, to the peril of those less powerful than we are.

He was kind and generous, as I say, but never convinced. I think he hoped I was wrong.

8   Human Evolution

Some Tough Questions for the Christian

MICHAEL RUSE

We know a lot about human evolution (Ruse 2012). We evolved from the higher primates—not of a kind still existing—and broke with them at least five million years ago, although some now suspect it might have been as long as ten million years. It seems clear that for a while humans and chimpanzees went it alone together. So we are more closely related to chimpanzees than they are to gorillas. We know that Africa was the home of our evolution and that we got up on our hind legs before our brains started to explode up in size. There is still considerable debate about causes, although basically all agree with the need to adapt to savannah life after leaving the safety of the jungle. It seems clear that cooperation was a major factor in human evolution, and with the ability to do this came other related adaptations, for instance, the control of the more violent emotions and the loss of physical fighting adaptations like big teeth. Apparently human evolution involved a succession of exits from Africa and this led to bottlenecks, meaning small groups—although there is no reason to believe that the human population numbers ever dropped below the thousands.

Homo sapiens appeared about 500,000 years ago. Neanderthals are considered a subspecies of *Homo sapiens*. Apparently before their dying out around 50,000 years ago, there was some interbreeding with our subspecies, and so we (Europeans, that is) carry a small (less than 5 percent) number of Neanderthal genes. Recently there has been the much-discussed discovery of a species of physically small human-like beings on an island of Indonesia, *Homo floresiensis*, otherwise known as the "hobbit." It should be stressed that although this finding was unexpected, no one thinks that it challenges standard Darwinian evolutionary theory (Darwin 1859; Ruse 2006). Indeed, for human evolution generally, although obviously there are many questions asked and more answers offered, no one thinks that human evolution in any way challenges the accepted evolutionary paradigm of the natural selection of random variations.

I take these uncontroversial scientific claims as background to this discussion. My question is about the way or ways that the claims impinge on Christian theological beliefs. Of course, as we all know, Christians are all over the place on their theological beliefs. Would that they were as united as the paleoanthropologists! But I will take what can reasonably be called a fairly acceptable, conservative position. I want no truck with heresies like process theology. A creator god exists and this god is all loving and all powerful. Humans are made in the image of this god (whom I will now capitalize as "God"), meaning that we have intelligence and a moral sense and free will in some sense to go with this. We are tainted by original sin, and Jesus, who is one substance with God, came to Earth and died on the cross for our salvation. We have therefore the real possibility of eternal life. We are expected to behave properly, but doing good in itself could never be enough. For that, we need Jesus. The Bible is the revealed word of God, true throughout; but it has long been recognized (at least since Augustine) that it often needs to be understood metaphorically or allegorically. It is not a work of science.

There are three topics I want to raise. I do this in the spirit that I think has always marked the work of J. Wentzel van Huyssteen, namely, inquiry and a preparedness to go where the argument leads. I am not a believer, and I reject the central claims of Christianity (Ruse 2015). But I am not an atheist, perhaps more of an inquiring agnostic, at one with the biologist J. B. S. Haldane (1927) who said that the true meaning of the world could be a lot weirder than we could ever imagine. I do very much cherish my Quaker childhood, and I offer this chapter in the way in which I was taught to think about these things. In other words, I want to be constructive rather than destructive.

Adam and Eve

Adam and Eve are rather important for the Christian, meaning now always the Christian as characterized above. (As a Quaker—a "Junior Young Friend"—I am not sure I had ever heard of Adam and Eve!) Augustine is definitive. Jesus died on the cross. Why? For our sins. Why, if we are made in the image of an all-powerful, all-good God, are we sinful? Because we are tainted with original sin. What is original sin that would thus taint us? Adam, urged on by Eve, seduced by the serpent, ate the piece of fruit in direct disobedience to the order of God. "Therefore, just as sin entered the world through one man, and death through sin, and in this way death came to all people, because all sinned" (Rom. 5:12).

According to modern science, there was no unique Adam and Eve. All human ancestors ("hominins") were part of a larger group of conspecifics. Nor is it much help to refer to so-called Mitochondrial Eve, a female ancestor from whom we are supposedly all descended on the basis of shared mitochondrial evidence (Ayala 1995). There is no reason to think that she is the only female from whom we are all descended; she is just the one that we can pin down. The same applies to her male counterpart, Y-chromosomal Adam. He was not the only male around nor even necessarily the only male from whom we are all descended. And in any case, there is no reason to believe that this Eve and this Adam ever knew each other and had offspring. They probably lived thousands of years apart.

More troublesome really though is the fact that this Adam and Eve and everyone else would have had mums and dads and that these would have been of the same species—Darwinian evolution is gradual—and they would have been just as good and bad as their offspring. Sin did not enter the world through one man. The struggle for existence is, and always was, really tough. Being nice all of the time—more on this in a moment—simply isn't a good Darwinian strategy. Thomas Hardy, in his last novel *Jude the Obscure* (1895), had it dead-on. Sue (his common-law wife) is about to leave Jude (an honest, working-class striver who wanted to be a clergyman but who failed at every turn) and says: "Your worldly failure, if you have failed, is to your credit rather than to your blame. Remember that the best and greatest among mankind are those who do themselves no worldly good. Every successful man is more or less a selfish man. The devoted fail . . . 'Charity seeketh not her own.'"

The Augustinian solution fails in the face of modern science. It just doesn't work. As I said above, I am trying to be constructive rather than destructive. So please don't take me as saying that this will be the last word on the topic. Obviously not. But some rethinking is required and I don't think it can be just a Band-Aid solution. It just won't work to say that one day God put immortal souls in a pair of hominins and that did the job. Either every member of the species was made in the image of God, or none was. Shared characteristics is what it means to say you have a species. Horses have four legs, humans have two. The very message of human evolution is that we as a line started to get bigger and bigger brains and that means intelligence. If everyone else in the group is as thick as two short planks, then intelligence is not going to be of great help to the two with super brains. As the late Jack Sepkoski, a leading paleontologist, put it so nicely: "I see intelligence as just one of a variety of adaptations among tetrapods for survival. Running fast in a herd while being as dumb as shit, I think, is a very good adaptation for survival" (Ruse 1996, 486). As a general strategy, going with the majority is a good rule and breaking with this at every turn is a recipe for disaster.

My feeling is that you have to rethink original sin from the bottom up. Perhaps—and I really don't mean to be condescending to Christians by telling them how to run their theology—this is no bad thing. You have a rather naive chap, without any clothes on, sitting in a garden and persuaded by a wily serpent to eat a piece of fruit. And then God blasts him and his girlfriend out of the garden and they and their children are condemned for all eternity, until God takes pity on them. With respect, that seems to me to be a little bit of an overreaction, rather like the legislators of my state that delight in sending fourteen-year-olds to prison for life, without the possibility of parole. As I remember, Augustine himself was rather given to pinching other people's fruit, without such draconian consequences—although typically being Augustine a prank was more than a prank. "My desire was to enjoy not what I sought by stealing but merely the excitement of thieving and the doing of what was wrong" (Augustine 1998).

With the removal of Adam and Eve, you are not pushed to saying that we are not sinful. We are. You are pushed to saying that sin is part of human nature, part of the way in which we developed, and should not be pinned down on one dope a long time ago. (I call him a "dope" because basically that is what Adam truly is. He is not a pedophile and he is not an axe murderer. He is absolutely not a National Socialist and to blame Adam for Adolf Hitler is ludicrous.) There is of course another tradition on original sin, credited to Irenaeus of Lyons, and in favor in Orthodox Christianity, that finds this kind of thinking congenial. God knew that Adam and Eve were immature and has always taken this into account. Jesus's coming is not a function of the acts of these two but something always planned to bring God's creative intentions to fruition. Easter is not "Plan B," where God tried to correct the mistakes from the first time around.

Obviously there are still going to be theological issues here, for instance, about the meaning of the death on the cross and the resurrection if God always planned it. My point is simply that modern science challenges us here and that rethinking is necessary, along with the reflection that Christians are already one step ahead on this rethinking.

Selection

We were produced primarily through natural selection. That means, as pointed out above, it would have been virtually impossible for humans to have evolved without a dark side to their natures. But think also of the flip side, the light side to our natures. We now know, what Darwin always claimed, that humans work as individuals in our species because we are terrific cooperators—"altruists," in the language of biologists. When you think about it, it is obvious. We are out on the plain, possibly because we simply were not as good at the jungle as were others, those who evolved into chimpanzees. We face all sorts of new dangers, no longer being as concealed as before. At the same time, we are fairly hopeless at the things that lead to good plain living. We are not strong and fierce like lions, able to catch our suppers. We are not fleet like antelopes, able to escape being someone else's supper. So, in the immortal words of Benjamin Franklin on signing the Declaration of Independence, we had all better hang together or assuredly we will all hang separately. Which of course is just what we did, quite possibly as foragers in those early days. And success bred success. As we became cleverer and cleverer apes, we were able to ensure supplies of more and more protein—meaning the bodies of dead animals—and so support bigger and bigger brains. But fighting among ourselves was not the key to success. So a huge amount of evolutionary effort, if one might so put it, went into making us social animals. And we are. If you compare us say to a pack of lions we are patsies. Of course there is violence and with modern science and technology the violence has the potential and reality to be far worse than it was. But in context we humans are the hymenoptera (ants, bees, and wasps) of the primate world.

"Is" does not imply "ought." David Hume taught us that. So showing that helping each other is, thanks to our evolution through natural selection, doing what comes naturally does not in itself have deep moral implications. But it does suggest that it is part of human nature to be good, just as it is part of human nature to be bad. I am not saying we are as good as we should be. We are not. But we are not starting from ground zero. Hence, I would suggest that claims made in the name of Christianity about us being irredeemably corrupt are simply hogwash—hogwash of a rather pernicious (and too often Calvinist) nature. I am thinking here of Jonathan Edwards (2005).

> The God that holds you over the Pit of Hell, much as one holds a Spider, or some loathsome Insect, over the Fire, abhors you, and is dreadfully provoked; his Wrath towards you burns like Fire; he looks upon you as worthy of nothing else, but to be cast into the Fire; he is of purer Eyes than to bear

to have you in his Sight; you are ten thousand Times so abominable in his Eyes as the most hateful venomous Serpent is in ours.

Sorry, but in the light of modern biology that is just nonsense, and not terribly helpful nonsense either. We can improve, thanks to our abilities and our culture and much more. In fact, evolutionary psychologist Steven Pinker (2011) has given good evidence to suggest that we are improving. We are not there yet and probably never will be. But if we are abominable in God's eyes, first it is at least partially his fault, and second, I don't believe a word of it. The metaphor of God as a loving father caring for his immature children, trying to help them grow and be worthwhile adults, makes much more sense, biologically and theologically.

Darwin had a second kind of selection, sexual selection, and this played a huge role in his account of human evolution. He thought it really did confirm Victorian ideas about the sexes. "Man is more courageous, pugnacious, and energetic than woman, and has a more inventive genius. His brain is absolutely larger, but whether relatively to the larger size of his body, in comparison with that of woman, has not, I believe been fully ascertained." Continuing: "Male and female children resemble each other closely, like the young of so many other animals in which the adult sexes differ; they likewise resemble the mature female much more closely, than the mature male. The female, however, ultimately assumes certain distinctive characters, and in the formation of her skull, is said to be intermediate between the child and the man" (Darwin 1871, 2, 317–18).

I need hardly say that down through the centuries a lot of Christians have been happy with this point of view, which to be candid probably owes a lot to Christian origins—never forget that Darwin set out to be an Anglican clergyman. "Let a woman learn quietly with all submissiveness. I do not permit a woman to teach or to exercise authority over a man; rather, she is to remain quiet. For Adam was formed first, then Eve; and Adam was not deceived, but the woman was deceived and became a transgressor. Yet she will be saved through childbearing—if they continue in faith and love and holiness, with self-control" (1 Tim. 2:11–15). Let's not forget that there are no Catholic women priests, nor for that matter are there any Southern Baptist women pastors.

Right from the beginning, after Darwin published the *Descent of Man* in 1871, there were those who took up Darwin's theory and showed how often it leads to conclusions with which he would not necessarily agree. Sexual selection was at the heart of this, as commentator after commentator—often women—pointed out that if women don't get as much out of the evolutionary process as men, then they are not going to stay women for long! Never make the mistake of underestimating the fair sex. Even those who struggled to maintain the old supremacy knew this. Thus Rudyard Kipling in a poem written in 1911:

> And Man knows it! Knows, moreover, that the Woman that God gave him
> Must command but may not govern—shall enthral but not enslave him.
> And *She* knows, because *She* warns him, and Her instincts never fail,
> That the Female of Her Species is more deadly than the Male. (Kipling 1999)

Today's evolutionary biologists have taken this thinking to its conclusion, and study after study, including many on the great apes, suggests that females are as powerful and effective as males (Hrdy 1978). In chimpanzee groups, for instance, it is the older females who rule the roost and the competing males struggle to win their attention and favor (de Waal 1982).

Again, this hardly has an immediate implication for Christianity. You can still keep going with all-male pastors and priests. But if nothing else, it starts to suggest that there is something unnatural about keeping women in subservient roles, and—for Catholics especially—it has always been a central part of Christian thinking about morality that that which is natural is good (Ruse 2010). God made things to function, to work naturally, and it is our obligation to go with what God designed and wants. If God made women equal to men, then who are we to give them subservient roles?

Existence

God did not have to create anything. But he did. God did not have to create humans. But he did. Hence, although we are contingent—we did not have to exist—in some sense we are necessary—God wanted us and so we exist. It could not have been the case that an all-powerful God wanted humans but was unable to produce them. Unlike triangles with internal angles adding up to three right angles—which presumably God could not have produced even if he wanted them—we are possible beings and so if God wanted us (which he did), he could and did produce us.

But how could God have produced us and, if he did, are we still necessary? He could, I suppose, have produced us all miraculously, at one fell swoop—whoomph! First you have nothingness; then you have the whole kit and caboodle up and running. The nineteenth-century Plymouth Brethren naturalist Philip Gosse (1857) thought something like this had happened. The trouble is that what he thought was a virtue, others thought was a dreadful fault. If you make humans and presumably the rest of the world to fit us into, you make us as if evolution had occurred and that makes God seem terribly dishonest. All of those fossils in the Burgess Shale that look as though they were part of the Cambrian explosion and they are as fraudulent as Piltdown Man? What kind of trickster is God? He comes across a bit like Crow, God's evil Doppelgänger, in one of Ted Hughes's poems. When all has gone dreadfully wrong, Crow grinned and said: "This is my Creation."

Suppose then that God creates through law. How is he to do this? You can go the way of the great philosophers distinguishing between primary causation and secondary causation. Primary causation is God's deciding to make humans. Secondary causation is how this happened.

> In matters that are obscure and far beyond our vision, even in such as we may find treated in Holy Scripture, different Interpretations are sometimes possible without prejudice to the faith we have received. In such a case, we should not rush in headlong and so firmly take our stand on one side that, if further progress in the search of truth justly undermines this position, we too fall with it. That would be to battle not for the teaching of Holy Scripture but for our own, wishing its teaching to conform to ours, whereas we ought to wish ours to conform to that of Sacred Scripture. (Augustine 1982, 41)

This is all very well, but you still have the spadework of deciding how you can get humans by secondary causation. Richard Dawkins (1983) of all people has argued that the only way possible is by evolution through natural selection. The defining mark of living organisms is that they are adapted, they are as if designed for their roles in life—hands, teeth, penises, vaginas, bark, flowers, leaves, wings, feathers, scales, fins, the list is endless. But how naturally do you produce what has been called "organized complexity"? Lamarckism, the heritability of acquired characteristics, takes note of the complexity, but is false. Evolution by jumps, what is known as "saltationism," is also false and in any case would not produce the desired as-if-designed features of organisms. Large-scale instantaneous changes are always maladaptive. They don't work. And so you go through the list until the only survivor is Darwinism—evolution by natural selection working on small random variations. (Random in the sense of not produced according to need. We know a lot about the causes.)

But here's the rub! Darwinian evolution has no fixed or predetermined direction. On the one hand it is relativistic. As Sepkoski pointed out, in one circumstance being dumb as an ox, literally, is a good thing. In another circumstance it is not. If food is abundant, then it may pay to be big. If food is scarce, then it may pay to be small. If the background is tan and the predator hunts by sight, then tan camouflage pays off. If the background is black, then tan camouflage could prove fatal. On the other hand, there is the randomness of the variations. A new predator turns up, one that for the first time hunts by sight. There is no guarantee that the right variation will turn up—one of color, or desire to hide, or even ability to leave. It might, but note that it is not predetermined. Hiding behavior is not the same as having a tan backside, and when you add in all of the other features that have got to go along with the new feature, who knows what might be the result?

Theistic Evolution

So why then should humans appear? God wants humans but the only way to get them is through natural selection and that offers no guarantees. Apparently God could wait indefinitely and still be out of luck. A number of solutions have been offered and I am not very comfortable with any of them. One overall strategy is to pull out of science and keep God on the job. This kind of "theistic" directed evolution—you put the variations to work to get the results you want—was endorsed by Darwin's great American supporter, the Harvard botanist Asa Gray.

> We have only to say that the Darwinian system, as we understand it, coincides well with the theistic view of Nature. It not only acknowledges purpose ... but builds upon it; and if purpose in this sense does not of itself imply design, it is certainly compatible with it, and suggestive of it. Difficult as it may be to conceive and impossible to demonstrate design in a whole of which the series of parts appear to be contingent, the alternative may be yet more difficult and less satisfactory. If all Nature is of a piece—as modern physical philosophy insists—then it seems clear that design must in some way, and in some sense, pervade the system, or be wholly absent from it. (Gray 1876)

The trouble with this is first, as Darwin grumbled, you really are taking the matter out of science. As a Christian, you may not care—you may indeed be quite comfortable with this—but let us note that this is what you are doing. If you are a Protestant who thinks that miracles ended in biblical times, then realize that now you are bringing in something that looks very much like divine interference on a regular basis. Second, the trouble is that there is no empirical evidence for such direction. Everything we know points the other way. It could be there, but don't pretend that scientific reasons drove you to this position. Third, theologically, once you bring God into the business on a daily basis, then you are open to questions about why God doesn't do a bit more. Why doesn't he correct mutations that are going to lead to horrendous effects like many genetic diseases? If you keep God at bay all of the time, I am not saying that you are going to end these sorts of questions—nor do I personally think you should—but you do have a strategy. This is not how God works.

A hyped-up version of Gray's theistic evolution is the modern-day Intelligent Design Theory (IDT), supposing that life shows such irreducible complexity that the only way to explain it is through a divine intervention—actually, IDT supporters always protest that they don't think the intervention necessarily has to be divine, but that is what they all believe (Behe 1996; Dembski 1998). They certainly don't think that the course of life on Earth is directed by a graduate student on Andromeda who is experimenting on different planets to see the effects. Unfortunately, however, it has been shown in convincing detail that the IDT supporters' claims about irreducible complexity are just not well taken. Their paradigmatic examples, the motor of the bacterial flagellum and the blood-clotting cascade, have been shown to be reducible to smaller parts and selection has been demonstrated as the key causal factor in their nature and very existence (Miller 1999; Ruse 2003).

A third, slightly more sophisticated version of this kind of thinking comes from the fertile brain of physicist-theologian Robert J. Russell (2008). Invoking quantum theory, he suggests that perhaps God flies below the radar as it were. We know that mutations occur at a quantifiable rate. It is just that this has to be understood on a statistical basis. In time t, x percent of genes A will mutate into genes B. Now it might be that ten seconds into t, a change would make no big difference, but ten thousand seconds into t a change might make all the difference because just such a mutation would then be needed and used. Russell suggests that this is where God makes his moves. From the viewpoint of modern science he doesn't interfere—you still get the same x percent in time t—but when the actual mutation occurs is crucial and God is in charge here. So God could and does guide evolution to the production of human beings.

Again, I can only say that it seems to me that even if this works—Russell calls his position NIODA, Non-Interventionist Objective Divine Action—you are still left saddled with horrendous theological issues. Why doesn't God get to work to prevent horrible genetic diseases? Suppose that the switch of a gene in a sperm makes all the difference. Why can't God hold off switching the gene until the producer is masturbating or having sex with a female during her infertile period? The trouble is that once you get God involved on a regular basis, the theological problems start pouring in, quite apart from the fact that you are now muddying the separation between science and religion that is the mark of modern science.

Doing Things Naturally

The alternative strategy is to stay with the science, arguing that Darwinian evolution is not as undirected as you might think and that humans will indeed emerge. Along these lines, at least three solutions have been offered. First, there is an updated version of an argument initially proposed by Darwin himself. Supposedly natural selection leads to better and more efficient features and brains will win out.

> If we look at the differentiation and specialisation of the several organs of each being when adult (and this will include the advancement of the brain for intellectual purposes) as the best standard of highness of organisation, natural selection clearly leads towards highness; for all physiologists admit that the specialisation of organs, inasmuch as they perform in this state their functions better, is an advantage to each being; and hence the accumulation of variations tending towards specialisation is within the scope of natural selection. (Darwin 1861, 134)

Continuing this line of thinking, in the twentieth century (thanks particularly to the work of Julian Huxley) Darwinian evolutionists developed the idea of an evolutionary "arms race." Lines of organisms compete and their adaptations get better. The prey gets faster and so the predator gets faster. Eventually this all leads to brains and to humans. Huxley writes, "The leaden plum-puddings were not unfairly matched against the wooden walls of Nelson's day." Now however, "though our guns can hurl a third of a ton of sharp-nosed steel with dynamite entrails for a dozen miles, yet they are confronted with twelve-inch armor of backed and hardened steel, water-tight compartments, and targets moving thirty miles an hour. Each advance in attack has brought forth, as if by magic, a corresponding advance in defence." Likewise in nature, "if one species happens to vary in the direction of greater independence, the inter-related equilibrium is upset, and cannot be restored until a number of competing species have either given way to the increased pressure and become extinct, or else have answered pressure with pressure, and kept the first species in its place by themselves too discovering means of adding to their independence" (Huxley 1912, 115–16).

Today we find Richard Dawkins endorsing this kind of thinking. "Directionalist common sense surely wins on the very long time scale: once there was only blue-green slime and now there are sharp-eyed metazoa" (Dawkins and Krebs 1979, 508). This is all thanks to arms races.

> Notwithstanding [Stephen Jay] Gould's just skepticism over the tendency to label each era by its newest arrivals, there really is a good possibility that major innovations in embryological technique open up new vistas of evolutionary possibility and that these constitute genuinely progressive improvements.... The origin of the chromosome, of the bounded cell, of organized meiosis, diploidy and sex, of the eucaryotic cell, of multicellularity, of gastrulation, of molluscan torsion, of segmentation—each of these may have constituted a watershed event in the history of life. Not just in the normal Darwinian sense of assisting individuals to survive and reproduce, but watershed in the sense of boosting evolution itself in ways that seem entitled to the label progressive. It may well be that after, say, the invention of multicellularity, or the invention of metamerism, evolution was never the same again. In this sense, there may be a one-way ratchet of progressive innovation in evolution. (Dawkins 1997, 1019–20)

Explicitly Dawkins argues that evolution is cumulative. Today's arms races are ever increasingly electronic as both sides build bigger and better computers. So in the animal world. Referring to something called the Encephalization Quotient, a kind of cross-species IQ equivalent, Dawkins writes: "The fact that humans have an EQ of 7 and hippos an EQ of 0.3 may not literally mean that humans are 23 times as clever as hippos! But the EQ as measured is probably telling us *something* about how much 'computing power' an animal probably has in its head, over and above the irreducible amount of computing power needed for the routine running of its large or small body" (Dawkins 1986, 189). No prizes for guessing what that something is.

Of course, even if there is something to all of this—in point of fact, the notion of biological arms race is much contested with some evolutionists thinking them prevalent and others much more skeptical (Parker 1983; Bakker 1983)—it hardly gives you the guarantee that the Christian needs. Humans *must* appear. But even with arms races, there is an element of contingency. As Stephen Jay Gould pointed out, thanks to an asteroid hitting Earth sixty-five-million years ago, the dinosaurs were wiped out and the mammals took over. Had this not happened, one doubts that humans would have evolved. "Since dinosaurs were not moving toward markedly larger brains, and since such a prospect may lie outside the capabilities of reptilian design ... we must assume that consciousness would not have evolved on our planet if a cosmic catastrophe had not claimed the dinosaurs as victims. In an entirely literal sense, we owe our existence, as large and reasoning mammals, to our lucky stars" (Gould 1989, 318).

A second solution, endorsed by Gould himself, focuses on the constraints on evolution through selection (Gould 1985). Organisms can and can only enter pre-existing ecological niches. Since we humans occupy a niche for culture, obviously it pre-existed and so even if we had not succeeded some organism somewhere down the line would have. It is true that they might have had green skin, but one doubts that God would have been too worried about that. The Christian paleontologist Simon Conway Morris has been a recent enthusiast for this line of thinking. About us he writes:

> If brains can get big independently and provide a neural machine capable of handling a highly complex environment, then perhaps there are other parallels, other convergences that drive some groups towards complexity. Could the story of sensory perception be one clue that, given time, evolution will inevitably lead not only to the emergence of such properties as intelligence, but also to other complexities, such as, say, agriculture and culture, that we tend to regard as the prerogative of the human? We may be unique, but paradoxically those properties that define our uniqueness can still be inherent in the evolutionary process. In other words, if we humans had not evolved then something more-or-less identical would have emerged sooner or later. (Conway Morris 2003, 196)

Again, however, I am not sure that you get quite the guarantee of success that you need. I am not convinced that some line must necessarily find its way into the niche. Is every possible niche on this Earth now occupied or has been occupied? Perhaps the evolution of some organisms stops or blocks the evolution of other organisms, they bar the way to entry to some niches. Could the culture niche be like Brigadoon, open only once every hundred (or hundred million) years and if there are no takers closed again for ages? My worry is that we could have things backward. We know that there is a cultural niche because we are in it, but perhaps it did not exist without us and other beings might have been slightly different and gone slightly different ways and either missed our niche entirely or made a somewhat different niche—one that didn't make beings quite good enough for God. Assuming of course that niches do really exist independently. We find it hard to conceive of sentience except as we understand it, but perhaps using pheromones to communicate or smells or whatever, the thinking processes would be quite different. I am not saying they would be, but simply that I don't see such possibilities ruled out.

After all, Christians themselves seem to think that there are mysteries that we cannot yet grasp—"now I see through a glass darkly" (1 Cor. 13:12)—and so why should there not be other kinds of intelligence that think very differently?

A third scientific option is to rely on ideas mooted by the nineteenth-century evolutionist Herbert Spencer (1857), although hints of them can be found in early notebooks of Charles Darwin. Perhaps nature just complexifies over time and humans will appear.

> The enormous number of animals in the world depends on their varied structure & complexity. — hence as the forms became complicated, they opened fresh means of adding to their complexity. — but yet there is no *necessary* tendency in the simple animals to become complicated although all perhaps will have done so from the new relations caused by the advancing complexity of others. — It may be said, why should there not be at any time as many species tending to dis-development (some probably always have done so, as the simplest fish), my answer is because, if we begin with the simplest forms & suppose them to have changed, their very changes tend to give rise to others. (Barrett et al., 1987, E 95–97)

Stephen Jay Gould (1996), before he died, speculated along these lines. He suggested that the evolution of life was a bit like a drunkard walking along a sidewalk with a wall on the side. The drunk can never walk through the wall but at some point he will fall into the gutter. Life can never get simpler than simple but it can always get more and more complex. Recently a philosopher (Robert Brandon) and paleontologist (Daniel McShea) at Duke University have floated a version of this line of thinking. They see life's history as driven by a kind of upward momentum. Making reference to what they call the "zero-force evolutionary law" (ZFEL for short) they write: "In any evolutionary system in which there is variation and heredity, in the absence of natural selection, other forces, and constraints acting on diversity or complexity, diversity and complexity will increase on average" (McShea and Brandon 2010, 3). Acknowledging that they write in the spirit of Spencer, it seems that for them (as was the case for Spencer) things just naturally keep complexifying—one cause leads to several effects and these in turn multiply.

Of course, part of the problem here is what on earth one means by complexity. Richard Dawkins is helpful.

> We have an intuitive sense that a lobster, say, is more complex (more "advanced," some might even say more "highly evolved") than another animal, perhaps a millipede. Can we *measure* something in order to confirm or

deny our intuition? Without literally turning it into bits, we can make an approximate estimate of the information contents of the two bodies as follows. Imagine writing the book describing the lobster. Now write another book describing the millipede down to the same level of detail. Divide the word-count in the one book by the word-count in the other, and you will have an approximate estimate of the relative information content of lobster and millipede. It is important to specify that both books describe their respective animals "down to the same level of detail." Obviously, if we describe the millipede down to cellular detail, but stick to gross anatomical features in the case of the lobster, the millipede would come out ahead. But if we do the test fairly, I'll bet the lobster book would come out longer than the millipede book. (Dawkins 2003, 100)

Or is Dawkins so very helpful? Compare warthogs with millipedes. Does one count every warthog hair, or does the hair as a whole count as one? Does one count every millipede leg, or do the legs collectively count as one? Does every hair on the back of the warthog count as an individual feature, or do you take the hairiness collectively as one feature? Is a full-headed theology professor so very much more complex and hence advanced than a bald philosophy professor? I will leave this as an exercise for the reader. Although this rather weak joke does point to the real difficulty here. Complexity as such (at least of the Dawkins kind and for the want of others that is it) does not seem to have a huge amount to do with intelligence or moral sensitivity or the sorts of things that we associate with being made in the image of God. I cannot see that randomness is going to guarantee God the beings that he wants.

Multiverses

Let me try one final possible solution to the problem. We know that humans could have evolved naturally—I am now taking out guided evolution and ignoring helpful aids like arms races—because they have done so here on Earth. In some very real sense it was possible for humans to evolve through natural selection, however very unlikely it was. So, if we could think of a way in which we could keep running the trial sooner or (probably very much) later humans would evolve. It is a bit like the monkeys typing Shakespeare—not likely but certainly possible. How then could we conjure up the possibilities? What about the idea of multiverses? Universes keep repeating over and over again, simultaneously or in sequence, indefinitely (Ellis 2011). Think of a number, double it, and you have only just started. I am not myself saying that multiverses do exist, but simply that serous scientists think these a possibility and so it is legitimate to make use of them. And if they do exist, then you have the possibility of a Shakespeare play typed by a monkey and a human species produced by natural selection. Note that unlike us God is not going to be drumming his fingers impatiently waiting for results. God on the traditional Christian view is outside time and space. He is not sitting around waiting for things to happen. For him, the thought of creation, the act of creation, the product of creation are as one.

Of course, there is now the real possibility of not just one human species but an infinite number of them. While I am more than happy to have an infinite number of copies of my beloved wife, I am rather less keen on the prospect of my late headmaster being thus proliferated. But that I think is a problem we will let God resolve! As I said at the beginning I am just trying to be constructive. And whether you like my suggestion or not, drawing now to an end I think you will agree that what we now know about human evolution poses serious questions for the Christian. But as creatures made in the image of God, with the ability and obligation to think about the created world, this should be a reason for celebration rather than one for fear.

References

Augustine. 1982. *The Literal Meaning of Genesis*. Trans. J. H. Taylor. New York: Newman.
———. 1998. *Confessions*. Trans. H. Chadwick. Oxford: Oxford University Press.
Ayala, F. J. 1995. The myth of Eve: molecular biology and human origins. *Science* 270:1930–36.
Bakker, R. T. 1983. The deer flees, the wolf pursues: incongruencies in predator-prey coevolution. In *Coevolution*, edited by D. J. Futuyma and M. Slatkin. Sunderland, MA: Sinauer.
Barrett, P. H., P. J. Gautrey, S. Herbert, D. Kohn, and S. Smith, eds. 1987. *Charles Darwin's Notebooks, 1836–1844*. Ithaca, NY: Cornell University Press.
Behe, M. 1996. *Darwin's Black Box: The Biochemical Challenge to Evolution*. New York: Free Press.
Conway Morris, S. 2003. *Life's Solution: Inevitable Humans in a Lonely Universe*. Cambridge: Cambridge University Press.
Darwin, C. 1859. *On the Origin of Species by Means of Natural Selection, or the Preservation of Favoured Races in the Struggle for Life*. London: John Murray.
———. 1861. *Origin of Species*. 3rd ed. London: John Murray.
———. 1871. *The Descent of Man, and Selection in Relation to Sex*. London: John Murray.

Dawkins, R. 1983. Universal Darwinism. In *Evolution from Molecules to Men*, edited by D. S. Bendall, 403–25. Cambridge: Cambridge University Press.
———. 1986. *The Blind Watchmaker*. New York: Norton.
———. 1997. Human chauvinism. *Evolution* 51(3):1015–20.
———. 2003. *A Devil's Chaplain: Reflections on Hope, Lies, Science and Love*. Boston: Houghton Mifflin.
Dawkins, R., and J. R. Krebs. 1979. Arms races between and within species. *Proceedings of the Royal Society of London B* 205:489–511.
De Waal, F. 1982. *Chimpanzee Politics: Power and Sex among Apes*. London: Cape.
Dembski, W. A. 1998. *The Design Inference: Eliminating Chance through Small Probabilities*. Cambridge: Cambridge University Press.
Edwards, J. 2005. *Sinners in the Hands of an Angry God and Other Puritan Sermons*. New York: Dover.
Ellis, G. 2011. Does the multiverse really exist? *Scientific American* 305(2):38–43.
Gosse, P. H. 1857. *Omphalos; An Attempt to Untie the Geological Knot*. London: John Van Voorst.
Gould, S. J. 1985. *The Flamingo's Smile: Reflections in Natural History*. New York: Norton.
———. 1989. *Wonderful Life: The Burgess Shale and the Nature of History*. New York: Norton.
———. 1996. *Full House: The Spread of Excellence from Plato to Darwin*. New York: Paragon.
Gray, A. 1876. *Darwiniana*. New York: D. Appleton.
Haldane, J. B. S. 1927. *Possible Worlds and Other Essays*. London: Chatto and Windus.
Hardy, T. 1895. *Jude the Obscure*. London: Osgood, McIlvaine, & Co.
Hrdy, S. B. 1978. *The Langurs of Abu: Female and Male Strategies of Reproduction*. Cambridge, MA: Harvard University Press.
Huxley, J. S. 1912. *The Individual in the Animal Kingdom*. Cambridge: Cambridge University Press.
Kipling, R. 1999. *Collected Poems*. London: Wordsworth.
McShea, D., and R. Brandon. 2010. *Biology's First Law: The Tendency for Diversity and Complexity to Increase in Evolutionary Systems*. Chicago: University of Chicago Press.
Miller, K. 1999. *Finding Darwin's God*. New York: Harper and Row.
Parker, G. A. 1983. Arms races in evolution—an evolutionary stable strategy to the opponent-independent costs game. *Journal of Theoretical Biology* 10(4):619–48.
Pinker, S. 2011. *The Better Angels of Our Nature: Why Violence Has Declined*. New York: Viking.

Ruse, M. 1996. *Monad to Man: The Concept of Progress in Evolutionary Biology.* Cambridge, MA: Harvard University Press.

———. 2003. *Darwin and Design: Does Evolution Have a Purpose?* Cambridge, MA: Harvard University Press.

———. 2006. *Darwinism and Its Discontents.* Cambridge: Cambridge University Press.

———. 2010. *Science and Spirituality: Making Room for Faith in the Age of Science.* Cambridge: Cambridge University Press.

———. 2012. *The Philosophy of Human Evolution.* Cambridge: Cambridge University Press.

———. 2015. *Atheism: What Everyone Needs to Know.* Oxford: Oxford University Press.

Russell, R. J. 2008. *Cosmology: From Alpha to Omega: The Creative Mutual Interaction of Theology and Science.* Minneapolis: Fortress.

Spencer, H. 1857. Progress: its law and cause. *Westminster Review* 47:244–67.

9 Science, Technology, and Aesthetics

The Manifestation of Adaptive Cognitive Fluidity in Humans

JOHN HEDLEY BROOKE

It is hard to imagine a hotter topic than what it means to be human. In response to essentialist biological definitions, to alluring visions of human enhancement, and to advances in robotics, the quest for what makes us human sometimes has the appearance of a renewed hunt for buried treasure, choreographed in multiple research projects and conferences around the world. Privileged to participate in one, held at the University of Gorizia in October 2008, I witnessed a phenomenon that J. Wentzel van Huyssteen identified and addressed in his magisterial Gifford Lectures: the large gap between the theologians searching for unique human capacities that might substantiate the doctrine of *imago Dei*, and the evolutionary anthropologists content to follow Darwin in playing down, even eliminating, fundamental differences between humans and nonhuman animals.[1] In Gorizia, many characteristics were proposed as distinctively human attributes. These included rationality, linguistic facility, will, freedom, self-consciousness, moral sensibility, a power of imagination, a capacity to apprehend reality, a potential for self-improvement, and even our being co-creators with God. Proposals from the theologians were often subtle, appealing to a metalevel, as when Catholic priest and historian of science the late Stanley Jaki asserted that "only the human mind can go beyond itself by hovering over the entire landscape of what is to be

---

1. J. Wentzel van Huyssteen, *Alone in the World? Human Uniqueness in Science and Theology* (Grand Rapids: Eerdmans, 2006).

For my invitation to attend the Gorizia conference, I am grateful to Professor Antonio Russo.

known." It would of course be wrong to pretend that only theologians would be looking for examples of human uniqueness. Even Richard Dawkins in *The Selfish Gene* was willing to say that humans are unique in that we alone can resist the tyranny of our genes. Nevertheless it was striking how an anthropologist present, Volker Sommer from the University of London, protested that the long hunt for characteristics supposedly peculiar to human beings is not only scientifically sterile but also ignores the exciting work in primatology that connects humans ever more closely to their animal progenitors.

It was van Huyssteen's achievement to show how the gap might be bridged, by appropriating paleoanthropology and other evolutionary sciences to show how distinctive human characteristics had emerged naturally, including a religious capacity and awareness. He made no secret of the fact that this would constitute a challenge to traditional theological discourse on the subject, which he was finding overly abstract and elaborate. Yet he did not conceive his revisionism as a threat to a fundamental sense of theological purpose. His notion of personhood, when reconceived in terms of embodied imagination, symbolic propensities, and cognitive fluidity, would now "enable theology to revision its own notion of the *imago Dei* as emerging from nature itself, an idea that does not imply any superiority or a greater value over other animals or earlier hominids, but might express, from a theological point of view, a specific task and purpose to set forth the presence of God in the world."[2]

Time, Place, and Human Uniqueness

Theologically motivated attempts to locate timeless criteria for affirming human uniqueness face a challenge from recent as well as the most ancient history. In his reflections on *Being, Humanity, and Understanding*, Geoffrey Lloyd refers to the "unnerving rapidity" of the succession of attempts since the middle of the nineteenth century to settle on defining characteristics of what it is to be human. No sooner had one proposal been tried and found wanting than another would be advanced, only to founder in turn.[3] Reviewing several of these supposedly defining characteristics—a capacity for language, toolmaking, symbolic representation, and (with an eye on Christian tradition) the possession of an immortal soul, Lloyd shows how none has survived unscathed. For example, in the encounter with various native cultures, Christian dogma

---

2. Van Huyssteen, *Alone in the World?* 215.
3. G. E. R. Lloyd, *Being, Humanity, and Understanding* (Oxford: Oxford University Press, 2012), 9.

repeatedly left open the question as to *which* creatures were truly human and in possession of an immortal soul.[4] Perhaps, as the Thomist philosopher and theologian William Carroll jested at the Gorizia conference, humans may ultimately be unique in harboring the delusion that they are unique.

I introduce Lloyd's reflections because his comparative study of earlier cultures reveals a further complication—namely, the importance of context when examining views of human uniqueness. In China, for example, the third-century BCE writer Xunzi differentiated humans from bird and beast not by their possession of a reasoning faculty, as in Aristotle, but by their moral capacity.[5] The problem with such an approach was the diversity of views concerning what was right and wrong. A contrasting view in China was that the distinctiveness of humans consisted not in a moral capacity but in their sharing common feelings and in their seeking satisfaction of the same basic desires. Lloyd's point is that on the question of what is distinctive about humans "quite different views were expressed within ancient Greece and again within ancient China." There was "no consensus, let alone an orthodoxy, on the subject in either society."[6] In modern ethnographic literature, even more radical divergences appear. Juxtaposing the diversities of recent times with the commonalities that purportedly evolved during the Pleistocene, Lloyd expresses caution toward evolutionary theses that uncritically streamline the stories connecting present understandings of what makes us human with the original emergence of human potentialities. In particular "the recurrent urge to identify a single differentiating factor is repeatedly thwarted by the amazing proliferation of the *actual* answers that are given."[7]

It is one of the strengths of van Huyssteen's postfoundationalist approach to the question of human uniqueness that it, too, is sensitive to the issue of context specificity. Although he argues to the naturalness of religion from the Upper Paleolithic art of southwestern France and the Basque country of northern Spain, he is careful not to overgeneralize from limited locations. What he can say is that those cave paintings, however enigmatic and mysterious, offer rich data on how, *in that specific region*, "people became recognizably human."[8] He also shows himself sympathetic to critiques of transhistorical meanings of "art." Thus, "classifying prehistoric imagery exclusively as art, or as the origins or beginnings of art, does seem to limit deeper and more contextualized un-

---

4. Lloyd, *Being, Humanity, and Understanding*, 11.
5. Lloyd, *Being, Humanity, and Understanding*, 14–15.
6. Lloyd, *Being, Humanity, and Understanding*, 17.
7. Lloyd, *Being, Humanity, and Understanding*, 28.
8. Van Huyssteen, *Alone in the World?* 214.

derstandings and often reveals a highly Eurocentric view of human evolution."⁹ And yet there is a tension because what still looks like a form of essentialism survives: "In Upper Paleolithic 'art' we are dealing with the remarkable material expression of something quintessentially human, something that sets us apart from other animals, and even from our closest prehuman ancestors."¹⁰ This essentialism then allows the creation of a bridge from the remote past to the present. The quest for meaning in human prehistory is not about only the remote past. On the contrary, "it directly concerns our images of ourselves and what we see as our own distinctive humanness."¹¹ Within the continuity from past to present there is an immanent universality:

> All symbolic Paleolithic images, whether they are supposed to function in the aesthetic domain or not, certainly evoke beauty, and as such values and beliefs.... What does seem to be universal to all of us as humans is that we mark durable objects with symbols.... We make sense of our worlds by producing symbolic ones that include real and imaginary creatures, myths and beliefs.¹²

What is to be included in this universality? Connections between art and religion feature prominently in van Huyssteen's argument, religious awareness and aesthetic appreciation linked together as defining human characteristics: "When considering the crucial non adaptive, cultural aspects of human cognition, we can argue that defining human characteristics like human knowledge, moral awareness, aesthetic appreciation, religious awareness etc., in a sense transcend our biological origins."¹³ There are places in van Huyssteen's analysis where brief attention is paid to a capacity for technological innovation, as when he discusses the consequences of bipedalism and an increase in brain size.¹⁴ Interestingly, however, technological and aesthetic propensities rarely appear together in his account, as if art and technology, while both primary human pursuits, have little to do with each other.

This observation is not intended as a criticism. After all, in the modern world, art and technology have not enjoyed the same intimacy as art and religion. In most people's minds, technology is conjoined with science more than with art. As George Pattison observed in his *Thinking about God in an*

---

9. Van Huyssteen, *Alone in the World?* 174–75.
10. Van Huyssteen, *Alone in the World?* 214.
11. Van Huyssteen, *Alone in the World?* 214.
12. Van Huyssteen, *Alone in the World?* 175.
13. Van Huyssteen, *Alone in the World?* 312.
14. Van Huyssteen, *Alone in the World?* 311.

Age of Technology, "if art could take over key functions previously associated with religion, art and religion have also often sought mutual support, not least in relation to a common opposition to the world of industry and technology."[15] At the same time, it would be unfortunate if associations between art and technology were marginalized when considering the elements that combined in generating human propensities. This is because new technologies have themselves transformed what it is to be human.

My aim in this chapter is therefore to examine a few of the permutations in which science, technology, and art have come together, fulfilling human potentialities and changing what it is to be human in the process. My observations cohere with the view that human development has been facilitated and reinforced by a cognitive fluidity in the discernment of patterns and relationships in apparently unrelated information. There is of course a vast literature on art and religion, religion and science, and science and technology. There is, however, a case for reflecting on connections between technology and aesthetics and their religious connotations. This was recognized long ago by one of the earliest proponents of serious history of science. In the summer of 1851, having experienced the technological and industrial riches of London's Great Exhibition, William Whewell affirmed that God has implanted in man an impulse to go beyond utility toward artistic perfection: "So wonderfully and effectually has Providence planted in man the impulse which urges him on to his destination . . . which is, to mould the bounty of nature into such forms as utility demands, and to show at every step that with mere utility he cannot be content."[16] To be satisfied with "mere utility" was to be less than human. A modern historian of technology, Arnold Pacey, makes the point more strongly: "Every major work of engineering has something of the cathedral in it."[17]

Relations between Science, Technology, and Religion

I begin these reflections with a personal reminiscence. A first visit to Jerusalem may ignite many emotions and furnish vivid and enduring impressions. It is the city in which I first began to apprehend the complexity of the relations

---

15. George Pattison, *Thinking about God in an Age of Technology* (Oxford: Oxford University Press, 2005), 218.

16. William Whewell, "The General Bearing of the Great Exhibition on the Progress of Art and Science," in *Lectures on the Results of the Great Exhibition of 1851, First Series* (London: Bogue, 1852), 3–34 (17). For this reference I am indebted to Nicholas Fisher, "The Natural Theology of Victorian Industry," *Endeavour* 39, no. 1 (215): 1–80.

17. Arnold Pacey, *Meaning in Technology* (Cambridge, MA: MIT, 1999), 95.

between technology and religion. In one ultra-orthodox Jewish quarter, even an old-fashioned camera was an affront. Photographic images of the inhabitants were graven images and proscribed. A famous notice to that effect is placed over the entrance. My wife and I had only wished to photograph the notice, which we had seen in several guidebooks; but that was too much for one resident who gave us the fright of our lives, chasing us and screaming abusive language, which happily we could not understand. At the other extreme, one was intrigued by the appropriation of modern technology in ways that allowed observance of Jewish law with (to Western Protestant eyes) minimal inconvenience. Pre-programmed elevators and pre-programmed ovens meant that no work need be done on the Sabbath.

Quite apart from showing the extremes that can coexist in one city, these examples suggest that relations routinely drawn between technology and secularization are not as straightforward as they may seem. I had no quarrel with Peter Burke's suggestion that in nineteenth-century rural France the spread of chemical fertilizers could change the attitudes of peasants[18]—a new technology providing a new perspective on natural processes traditionally ascribed to providence. But my experiences in Jerusalem revealed complexities I had not suspected. In the case of an offensive camera, a technology was vehemently resisted; in hotels on the Sabbath, elevators pre-programmed to stop on every floor highlighted, and certainly did not remove, the distinctiveness of a religious demand.

My purpose in exposing complexity in the relations between technology and religious sensibilities is not to underline the ethical issues raised by technology. I will focus instead on something less tangible, but in its subtlety just as absorbing. This is the manner in which aesthetic considerations have played a crucial role in both scientific and technological practice. These aesthetic dimensions remind us that humans need not be objectified by technologies if, in the practices that produce them and in their appreciation, there is something of the divine spark of creativity.

There are two reasons why I have included reference to science as well as technology in my title. The first is that a history of the sciences reveals the important role played by aesthetic considerations when making scientific judgements.[19] The second is that given by the influential sociologist of science

---

18. Peter Burke, "Religion and Secularisation," in *The New Cambridge Modern History*, vol. 13, *Companion Volume*, ed. Peter Burke (Cambridge: Cambridge University Press, 1979), 293–317 (309).

19. S. Chandrasekhar, *Truth and Beauty: Aesthetics and Motivations in Science* (Chicago: University of Chicago Press, 1987); Nicholas Jardine, *The Scenes of Inquiry: On the Reality of Questions in the Sciences* (Oxford: Oxford University Press, 1991), 208–9; John Brooke and

Robert Merton. Perceptions of the authority of science are mediated by perceptions of its technological applications:

> The increasing comforts and conveniences deriving from technology and ultimately from science invite the social support of scientific research. They also testify to the integrity of the scientist, since abstract and difficult theories which cannot be understood or evaluated by the laity are presumably proved in a fashion which can be understood by all, that is, through their technological applications. Readiness to accept the authority of science rests, to a considerable extent, upon its daily demonstration of power.... The continued social support of that science which is intellectually incomprehensible to the public would hardly be nourished on faith alone.[20]

This is a deceptively simple point; but it means that to speak only of science, or only of technology, leads to false abstractions. Another way of illustrating an intimacy between them would be to show how new technologies have often been constitutive of scientific innovation—in the sense that, without them, novel lines of inquiry would not have been possible. New scientific instruments have often been preconditions of new aesthetic experiences and new forms of self-expression in the sciences. Galileo's description of the moon's surface, made possible by his telescope, would be a striking example, the depiction of a large circular crater persuading his contemporary Johannes Kepler that there might be intelligent technologists among lunar inhabitants.[21] Similarly, the microscope extended the domain of aesthetic experience into hitherto uncharted waters, as when Robert Hooke in his *Micrographia* (1665) expatiated on the beauty of fish-scales. The microscope magnified differences between nature and art since even such a delicate artifact as a finely wrought needle looked crude and blunt under the new instrument. There was an obvious spin-off for Christian natural theology in that the microscope enhanced appeals to design.[22] Robert Boyle saw the hand of God more clearly in a mi-

---

Geoffrey Cantor, *Reconstructing Nature: The Engagement of Science and Religion* (Edinburgh: T&T Clark, 1998), 207–43.

20. Robert Merton, *The Sociology of Science* (Chicago: University of Chicago Press, 1973), 260–61. For a recent discussion of science and values, with reference to Merton, see Mariano Artigas, *The Mind of the Universe* (Philadelphia: Templeton Foundation Press, 2000), 251–98.

21. Mary Winkler and Albert Van Helden, "Representing the Heavens: Galileo and Visual Astronomy," *Isis* 83 (1992): 195–217; Steven Dick, *Plurality of Worlds: The Extraterrestrial Life Debate from Democritus to Kant* (Cambridge: Cambridge University Press, 1982), 75–76, 130, 179–80.

22. Brooke and Cantor, *Reconstructing Nature*, 145–47, 217–19.

croscopic mite than in the vastness of the solar system, just as something of the divine had been seen in the beauty of a snowflake. Because elegance and beauty have often been predicated of scientific theories, it is helpful to consider how appeals to aesthetic virtue have featured in scientific discourse and how they may have theological connotations. We will then be in a position to assess whether there is anything equivalent in the production and evaluation of new technologies.

Aesthetic Virtues within the Sciences

It has long been recognized that aesthetic judgment played a crucial role in both the formation and dissemination of new forms of science in sixteenth- and seventeenth-century Europe. Copernicus contrasted the elegance of his solar *system*, in which the period of each planet could be correlated with its distance from the sun, with what he described as the monstrosity of the Ptolemaic, geocentric account in which the motions of each planet were modeled separately.[23] Historians have also observed the elegance with which a moving Earth could account for what then became merely the *appearance* of planetary retrograde motions. The observer was on a moving platform, creating the illusion that the planets reversed and then resumed their forward trajectories.[24] Kepler, who introduced elliptical orbits for the planets, despite his Neo-Platonic nostalgia for the circle, was still able to modulate the music of the spheres into modern form: each planet had its melody, the pitch changing with its orbital speed.[25] Even at the end of the period routinely described as the Scientific Revolution, Isaac Newton was so committed to the unity of God's creation that he was exploring analogies between planetary distances, the colors of the spectrum, and the intervals of a musical scale.[26] In the underlying mathematical ratios was a simplicity characteristic of "all the works of the Creator."[27]

23. Robert Westman, "Proof, Poetics and Patronage," in *Reappraisals of the Scientific Revolution*, ed. David Lindberg and Robert Westman (Cambridge: Cambridge University Press, 1990), 167–205 (182).
24. Charles Gillispie, *The Edge of Objectivity* (Princeton: Princeton University Press, 1960), 21; Thomas Kuhn, *The Copernican Revolution* (New York: Random House, 1957), 172.
25. Penelope Gouk, *Music, Science and Natural Magic in Seventeenth-Century England* (New Haven: Yale University Press, 1999), 148.
26. Gouk, *Music, Science and Natural Magic*, 148, 237–57.
27. Newton to John Harington, May 30, 1698, in *Correspondence of Isaac Newton*, ed. Rupert Hall et al., 7 vols. (Cambridge: Cambridge University Press, 1959–77), 4:274.

In the life sciences, too, appreciating the beauty and complexity of living things frequently informed scientific rhetoric. The great taxonomist Linnaeus argued that since humans *are* unique in their ability to appreciate the beauty of God's handiwork, they have a religious duty to study it in depth. Even Charles Darwin, a century later, spoke of a delight he had taken, especially as a young man, in exploring the Brazilian rain forests in all their sublimity. He had used religious language to describe the experience and, as an old man, recalled that the depth of his appreciation had indeed been connected with a belief in God that had gradually been extinguished.[28] The interpenetration of religious and aesthetic sensibilities is even more visible in another of the scientific giants of the nineteenth century, Michael Faraday. As Geoffrey Cantor has persuasively argued, Faraday's commitment to the unity of creation, especially his belief in the correlation and interconvertibility of nature's forces, was shaped and reinforced by the biblical Christianity of the Sandemanian sect of which he was a lifelong member.[29]

Nature did not always respond well. Faraday was defeated in his attempt to convert the gravitational force into magnetic or electrical effects. In the last analysis the primary test of a good scientific theory has to be its fertility over time and its consonance with new data. It nevertheless remains true that the quest for elegance, economy, symmetry, harmony, and unity in a scientific theory has often been a powerful lure, recognized by the greatest scientific minds. Einstein famously said that one of the tests he applied in judging a scientific theory was whether, had he been God, he would have made the world that way.[30]

The discussion of elegance and beauty in the sciences must not be confined to the issue of theory appraisal. As a student of biochemistry I many times heard references to the "beautiful" design of experiments, in the use of radioactive tracers, for example, in determining metabolic pathways. Satisfaction in the sciences comes not merely from solving puzzles but from solving them elegantly. Because aesthetic considerations may also shape ways in which scientific data and conclusions are transmitted to an audience, it is hard to disagree with the proposition that aesthetic appraisal has permeated every aspect of the scientific enterprise.[31] Chemists have seen analogies between polymer structures and Bach fugues; cosmologists, claiming to have

---

28. Adrian Desmond and James Moore, *Darwin* (London: Penguin, 1991), 122; Charles Darwin, *The Autobiography of Charles Darwin*, ed. Nora Barlow (London: Collins, 1958), 91–92.

29. Geoffrey Cantor, *Michael Faraday: Sandemanian and Scientist* (London: Macmillan, 1991), 161–95.

30. Chandrasekhar, *Truth and Beauty*, 68.

31. Jardine, *Scenes of Inquiry*, 208–9.

heard the sound of creation in the echoes of a Big Bang, have referred to the "music of creation."[32]

Intimations of the Transcendent?

What kind of theological meanings might be derived from this result? Some commentators see a direct connection between the appreciation of an elegantly structured world and perceptions of the divine in nature. For John Polkinghorne, the elegance of a scientific theory points beyond itself to a real beauty in nature that testifies to the divine. To put this in the form of a "proof" would scarcely be tolerated today, but Polkinghorne speaks of *hints* of the divine in the beauty (and fine-tuning) of a world comprehended through the sciences.[33] It may be safer to speak of the confirmation of religious convictions held on other grounds; but there is no denying a long tradition in which theological connotations have been entertained. In the work of Kepler the case for regarding scientific theories as more than instrumental devices, as at least potentially descriptive of physical reality, was argued historically and grounded theologically.[34] From the vantage point of a static sun, a hidden beauty could be unveiled commensurate with what might be expected of a divine creation and attainable, as Copernicus had said, in no other way. The very possibility of achieving and appreciating progress in the sciences has indicated to many a special quality in the human mind—that ability to "think God's thoughts after him," which Kepler regarded as a divine gift. In certain contexts, scientific discoveries have constituted a form of religious experience.[35] Another of Einstein's aphorisms was that the frame of mind required for a major scientific discovery had to be rather like that of a religious person or a person in love.[36]

Even in secular contexts, the religious language sometimes still remains. Werner Heisenberg spoke of a spirit of humility in which one had to accept

32. Roger Dobson and Jonathan Leake, "Scientists Hear Sound of Creation in Big-Bang Echo," *Sunday Times*, April 29, 2001, News section, 3.

33. John Polkinghorne, *Beyond Science* (Cambridge: Cambridge University Press, 1996), 92, 112.

34. Nicholas Jardine, *The Birth of History and Philosophy of Science: Kepler's A Defence of Tycho against Ursus, with Essays on Its Provenance and Significance* (Cambridge: Cambridge University Press, 1984).

35. John Hedley Brooke, "Can Scientific Discovery Be a Religious Experience?" in *The Edge of Reason: Science and Religion in Modern Society*, ed. Alex Bentley (London: Continuum, 2008), 155–64.

36. Abraham Pais, *"Subtle Is the Lord": The Science and the Life of Albert Einstein* (Oxford: Oxford University Press, 1982), 27.

the gift of an "incredible degree of simplicity" in the mathematical abstractions of physical theory. These beautiful interrelationships could not be invented: "They have been there since the creation of the world." Heisenberg's wife recalled that he had once said to her, "I was lucky enough to look over the good Lord's shoulder while He was at work."[37]

Might the same be said by a technologist who, in looking to nature for inspiration, builds machines that then challenge absolute distinctions between the natural and the artificial? If, as one writer puts it, technology "alienates a function of the natural body so that it can be rendered more powerful by prosthetic means,"[38] are there not more radical theological implications in the implicit disaffection with an original body of which the psalmist could say that it was wonderfully made (Ps. 139:14)? Are there not many objections to the transfer of aesthetic discourse from science to technology?

The Distinctiveness of Technology?

Attempts to create a space for aesthetic judgment in technological practice simply by analogy with scientific theorizing would be unlikely to carry conviction. Many early forms of technology were independent of theoretical science and were closer to the refinement of craft skills. It could also be objected that what has to count in technology is the utility of the product, not the more cerebral features of theory construction. In a recent interview, the inventor and industrial designer James Dyson said that he built no fewer than 5,127 prototypes of his vacuum cleaner before he was satisfied with it.[39] The building of successful machines may look very different from the building of successful theories, and new technologies, more overtly than new scientific knowledge, may be instruments of power. Moreover, whether a particular technology is implemented is likely to most depend on economic considerations. As Peter Mathias observed, there are sufficient striking examples of time lag, between having the applicable knowledge and putting it into action, to call into question any simple equation between laboratory technique and industrial production, where profitability becomes a condition of existence.[40] Again, the aesthetic aspects of a technological innova-

37. Chandrasekhar, *Truth and Beauty*, 22.
38. Lissa McCullough, as reported by Thomas Oord, "Science and Religion at the American Academy of Religion," *Research News and Opportunities in Science and Religion* 1, no. 5 (2001): 27.
39. *Sunday Times Magazine*, November 30, 2014, 7-8.
40. Peter Mathias, "Who Unbound Prometheus? Science and Technical Change, 1600-

tion might be considered trivial compared with its transformative power. For those who prefer the old ways of being human, it is the presumption in the new that so often attracts adverse religious comment. Within the Christian traditions would we not find as much, if not more, evidence of opposition to innovation as encouragement? Theology as we have known it in the past, writes George Pattison, "has too often functioned as a constraining and deadening force."[41] The complaints may not always have been of biotechnologists "playing god," but religious critics have not been slow to detect the sacrilegious in seeking to control and improve the world for our own convenience.

Possibly the strongest resistance to marrying a discourse of aesthetics with a discourse of technology was expressed by Martin Heidegger, whose views have been sensitively examined by Pattison.[42] For Heidegger the way matter is treated in technology is very different from the way it is treated in art. This is because in technology the material element is strictly subordinated to the specific use or purpose for which the instrument or tool is designed. It is then a question whether God or the gods are not absent from such a world shaped and dominated by utilitarian technology. By contrast, the construction of a work of art, such as the Greek temple discussed by Heidegger, does not use materials only in order to instrumentalize them. Consequently, there is a thinking characteristic of both science and technology in which purpose and use overrule an ability to bring us, as poetry and art surely can, into the nearness or presence of things. It is hard to disagree with this. And yet, as we have already seen in Whewell, it is questionable whether we should think only in terms of "mere utility" when appraising technological achievement. Pattison himself observes that a great work of architecture, such as the Sydney Opera House, is "inconceivable except as a technological product."[43] Artistic vision can be the mother of invention—the technological invention required for its instantiation.

Objections to marrying a discourse of aesthetics with a discourse of technology are not trivial, but nor are they decisive. When Ian Barbour, now more than twenty years ago, concluded that the case for the social construction of technology was stronger than that for the social construction of science, he pointed to the fact that human values are built into particular technological

---

1800," in *Science and Society, 1600–1900*, ed. Peter Mathias (Cambridge: Cambridge University Press, 1972), 54–80, 67.
    41. Pattison, *Thinking about God*, 9.
    42. Pattison, *Thinking about God*, 221–27.
    43. Pattison, *Thinking about God*, 227.

designs.⁴⁴ As such, the designs are invested with higher meaning. The range of values has included those derived from, or reinforced by, religious commitments, with the consequence that resources within Christian theism, for example, have been tapped to justify the development of technologies, which in turn have promised, as Francis Bacon famously put it, to bring glory to God and the relief of man's estate.

Sacred Technologies

Bacon's apologia for the altruistic application of the sciences included a more specific rhetoric in which technological innovations were justified in religious terms. The applied sciences promised nothing less than the restoration of a dominion over nature that had been God's original intention for humankind, but unrealized because of the fall of Adam. Bacon is often presented as the epitome of masculine aggression in the conquest of nature; but he did also see a humility enshrined within experimental methods that, in his view, was lacking in the scholastic philosophers who presumed to know, from ancient books alone, how the world must have been made. Aristotle may have thought about the world; but it was gunpowder, printing, and the compass that had transformed it.

In the early modern period medical technologies were also legitimated in religious terms, Paracelsus upholding the image of Jesus Christ as a healer. The supposed efficacy of Paracelsian chemical remedies was often contrasted with the impotence of the trained physicians who were apt to justify their laziness by pronouncing some conditions incurable.⁴⁵ That, at least, was how Paracelsus saw them. There is a question, to which I will return, whether the appeal to a rhetoric of defeating disease is not just a little too irresistible, a little too convenient, in the legitimation of otherwise controversial research programs. The question "who can afford to benefit from the promised innovations?" is not always asked. Nor are other questions of supply and demand. The appearance of total-body scanners in North America might be an example, where a public demand was fostered that could not be met.

Those who like to assert that the sciences, substantiated by their tech-

---

44. Ian Barbour, *Ethics in an Age of Technology: The Gifford Lectures Volume Two* (London: SCM, 1992), 22. The classic case for the social construction of technology had been made in Wieber E. Bijker, Trevor Pinch, and Thomas P. Hughes, eds., *The Social Construction of Technological Systems* (Cambridge, MA: MIT, 1987).

45. Owen Hannaway, *The Chemists and the Word: The Didactic Origins of Modern Chemistry* (Baltimore: Johns Hopkins University Press, 1975), 38–47.

nological applications, are necessarily locked in combat with "religion" often suppose that technological innovation must sit uncomfortably with doctrines of providence. In the colorful yet suspect example of Andrew Dixon White, first president of Cornell University, to fix lightning conductors to churches was bound to meet with clerical resistance in the eighteenth century because it was surely presumptuous to interfere with the artillery of heaven. At once mournful and triumphant, White studiously calculated the number of bell-ringers across Europe who had needlessly met their deaths as the bells they were superstitiously ringing had failed to prevent a strike.[46] And yet recent scholarship has emphasized how few were the objections to Benjamin Franklin's device based on a supposed presumption in interfering with the divine will.[47] In fact, one respect in which technologies could have something of the sacred about them would be in their supposed *fulfillment* of a providentialist scheme. That was how the natural philosopher and dissenting minister Joseph Priestley saw it in late-eighteenth-century England. Echoing earlier Protestant writers, Priestley considered human progress to be evidence of God's providence. And what better confirmation of human progress could there be than advances in science and technology? Priestley was ultraradical in his theology, dismissing the doctrine of the Trinity and excluding the possibility of divine influence on human minds. Both science and technology then had the added virtue of ridding the populace of superstition. Science and true religion were, for Priestley, fighting on the same side against outmoded forms of belief that were sustained by political establishments, by what he considered to be arbitrary power. Well might a repressive government, he once notoriously suggested, quake before an electrical machine. God was working his purposes out through the mediation of science and technology, not despite them.[48]

Machines have impinged on the question of divine activity in a more direct manner—by providing models for an understanding of God's relation to nature. To compare God's creation to the great clock of Strasbourg, as did Descartes and Boyle in the seventeenth century, was to emphasize a deity who acted regularly in the world, who was transcendent over it, and some of whose

---

46. Andrew White, *A History of the Warfare of Science with Theology in Christendom* [1896], 2 vols. (New York: Dover, 1960), 1:364–68.

47. Bernard Cohen, *Benjamin Franklin's Science* (Cambridge, MA: Harvard University Press, 1990), 118–58.

48. John Hedley Brooke, "'A Sower Went Forth': Joseph Priestley and the Ministry of Reform," in *Motion toward Perfection: The Achievement of Joseph Priestley*, ed. A. Truman Schwartz and John McEvoy (Boston: Skinner House, 1990), 21–56; Derek Orange, "Oxygen and One God," *History Today* 24 (1974): 773–81.

designs, for Boyle if not for Descartes, were discernible.[49] The analogy of the world to clockwork appealed to Boyle because it gave a degree of autonomy to the sciences in their bid to understand causal mechanisms, without compromising the theological insistence on a world dependent on a higher power for its creation and for the rules of its operation. Clocks also needed maintenance, the provision of which for an otherwise destabilizing solar system particularly impressed Newton.[50] The clock metaphor, in other words, was both rich and ambiguous.[51] Certainly it could be used to legitimate the absentee god of the deists, but just as easily the active, omnipresent deity of Newton. Clockwork was to be the watchword of William Paley in his classic formulation of the argument for design in his *Natural Theology* (1802). Paley's analogy between the world and a watch allowed him to argue for all manner of contrivance in a world that had been unified by Newton's laws—a world in which the various parts of living things could appear exquisitely crafted to meet their needs.[52]

With reference to Newton it is often said that his translation of the doctrine of providence into statements about God's intervention to maintain the stability of the solar system was to prove an embarrassing error by the end of the eighteenth century, when Laplace showed how the system could be self-correcting. Superficially it looks like a classic case of a god-of-the-gaps who would eventually prove surplus to requirements. The issues were not, in fact, that simple because Newton had never reduced the doctrine of providence to assertions about God's role in nature. The fulfillment of biblical prophecy testified to a providence at work in history.[53] Moreover, the periodic

---

49. Recent essays on Boyle's theology of nature and his rejoinder to Descartes's rejection of final causes include Margaret Cook, "Divine Artifice and Natural Mechanism: Robert Boyle's Mechanical Philosophy of Nature," in *Science in Theistic Contexts*, ed. John Hedley Brooke, Margaret Osler, and Jitse van der Meer, published as *Osiris*, vol. 16 (Chicago: University of Chicago Press, 2001), 133–50; Margaret Osler, "Whose Ends? Teleology in Early Modern Natural Philosophy," in *Science in Theistic Contexts*, ed. John Hedley Brooke, Margaret Osler, and Jitse van der Meer, published as *Osiris*, vol. 16 (Chicago: University of Chicago Press, 2001), 151–68; Timothy Shanahan, "Teleological Reasoning in Boyle's Disquisition about Final Causes," in *Robert Boyle Reconsidered*, ed. Michael Hunter (Cambridge: Cambridge University Press, 1994), 177–92.

50. For a fuller discussion of how God was conceived to act in a mechanical universe, see John Hedley Brooke, *Science and Religion: Some Historical Perspectives* (Cambridge: Cambridge University Press, 1991), 117–51; Canto Classics edition (2014), 158–205.

51. Jacques Berthoud, "Mechanical Time in Eighteenth-Century English Literature," in *Science and Imagination in Eighteenth-Century British Culture*, ed. Sergio Rossi (Milan: Edizioni Unicopli, 1987), 35–47 (41–44).

52. David Burbridge, "William Paley Confronts Erasmus Darwin: Natural Theology and Evolutionism in the Eighteenth Century," *Science and Christian Belief* 10 (1998): 49–71.

53. James Force, "Newton's God of Dominion: The Unity of Newton's Theological, Scien-

"reformation" of the solar system that Newton postulated was not naively understood as direct divine intervention (despite Leibniz's caricature of Newton's God as a second-rate clockmaker who had to make good the deficiencies of his creation). Newton's reformations involved the mediation of natural causes, including the role of comets passing close to the sun to replenish its mass. The most interesting complication, however, concerns the response of British natural theologians to Laplace's emphasis on a self-correcting system. For one certainly could argue that a self-correcting system demonstrated more wisdom and ingenuity than one in need of correction. The Cambridge scholar William Whewell, whom we have already met, and who actually invented the word "scientist," made precisely that point in his rejoinder to Laplace. Another machine, the steam engine, came to his aid and was invested with sanctity as a consequence. If irreligious men were finding solace in a self-regulating solar system, Whewell deprived them of it: "It would be as if the savage, who had marveled at the steady working of the steam-engine, should cease to consider it a work of art, as soon as the self-regulating part of the mechanism had been explained to him."[54] Whewell's contemporary Charles Babbage invoked another piece of technology, his calculating engine, to enrich, not deplete, an understanding of divine providence. In a critique of Hume's skeptical stance toward reported miracles, Babbage observed that it was possible to program his machine to generate a regular series of numbers, say 1 to 999, while also fixing it so that when the number 1,000 was due, a figure outside the normal sequence would show up. It was his way of showing that miracles should not be excluded on the basis of nature's regularities.[55]

Technological innovations could carry theological connotations for yet another reason. They might be seen as exemplifying a form of creativity that ultimately reflects an element of the divine in human aspiration. It has been perfectly possible within the Christian tradition to refer to the collaboration of man with his Maker in using the Earth's resources for improvement. Such collaboration is sometimes expressed today in the strong language of our being "created co-creators."[56] The basic idea has, however, been formulated with more modest pretensions and was expressed by the nineteenth-century Scot-

---

tific, and Political Thought," in *Essays on the Context, Nature, and Influence of Isaac Newton's Theology*, ed. James Force and Richard Popkin (Dordrecht: Kluwer, 1990), 83–90; James Force and Richard Popkin, eds., *Newton and Religion: Context, Nature, and Influence* (Dordrecht: Kluwer, 1999).

54. William Whewell, *Astronomy and General Physics Considered with Reference to Natural Theology*, 4th ed. (London, 1839), 350.

55. Charles Babbage, *Ninth Bridgewater Treatise: A Fragment* (London, 1838).

56. Philip Hefner, *The Human Factor* (Minneapolis: Fortress, 1993).

tish evangelical Hugh Miller in his declaration that man is a "mighty improver" of nature. Miller had in mind (among other transformations) the modification of domestic animals to human specification, which he saw as a case of collaboration with the divine because, made in the image of God, human beings shared the same aesthetic sensibilities with their Creator. He could make this claim because the fossil forms, in which as a geologist he took such delight, presaged and even surpassed the noblest forms of human architecture.[57]

Because of these and other resources in Christian theism for a positive appraisal of new technologies, the erection of an impenetrable barrier between religious and aesthetic considerations on the one hand, and technological imperatives on the other, would be simplistic. Rather, we might ask how aesthetic sensibilities might mediate between a religious faith and support for technological innovation. The recent study by Geoffrey Cantor of religious responses to the Great Exhibition of 1851 is particularly instructive because the profusion of exhibits showcased human inventiveness in the arts, manufacture, and industry.[58] The Crystal Palace in London's Hyde Park, where the exhibition was housed, was itself an architectural and technological marvel, revealingly described at the time as the "glass cathedral." Cantor emphasizes the variety in the religious responses, even within the same Christian denominations. Yet among the diversity of views was the reaffirmation that progress in science, technology, and industry was an aspect of, and evidence for, God's providential plan. This was the theme of a speech delivered by Prince Albert at a banquet in March 1850 when he launched a high-profile promotion of the exhibition. The scientist, the inventor, the manufacturer, and the artisan were portrayed as divine instruments—a message that, according to Cantor, proved attractive to many Christians.[59] It was definitely attractive to Samuel Wilberforce, bishop of Oxford, who valued technological progress as an ally of Christianity because it helped to ameliorate the condition of the poor. In celebrating the ingenious designs of machinery and the beauty of artifacts on display, human ingenuity and human aesthetic sensibility were conjoined as examples of propensities that were ultimately a divine gift. Prowess in technological innovation was even used polemically to argue for the superiority of those religious cultures in which its achievements were most marked.[60]

57. John Hedley Brooke, "Like Minds: The God of Hugh Miller," in *Hugh Miller and the Controversies of Victorian Science*, ed. Michael Shortland (Oxford: Oxford University Press, 1996), 171–86.
58. Geoffrey Cantor, *Religion and the Great Exhibition of 1851* (Oxford: Oxford University Press, 2011).
59. Cantor, *Religion and the Great Exhibition*, 42–43.
60. Cantor, *Religion and the Great Exhibition*, 46, 134, 146, 151.

Technology and Aesthetic Appraisal

It is not an artifice to invoke a vocabulary of aesthetic appreciation when discussing new technologies. We know how great painters of the nineteenth century, notably Turner and Monet, were captivated by steam technologies and their visual effects. Tracks as well as trains cried out to be painted. So proclaimed the French art critic Champfleury in 1859: "Leaning on a bridge, I contemplate with pleasure those grand iron tracks, which can be charming in the absence of steam engines. Bevelled slopes cut through green fields showing great sandy yellow trenches, a blue sky, rail crossings and gentle curves, are these not paintings just waiting for a new landscape painter? Industry mixed with nature has its poetic side: the point is to see it and be inspired."[61] Not all would have agreed with him; but, in this and many comparable pronouncements, art, technology, and even the potentially religious connotations of "inspiration" could come together. Many direct linkages between art and engineering are familiar from the way in which we speak of the "artist-engineers" of the Florentine Renaissance, whose concerns with the geometry of perspective were just one expression of a fertile marriage of the arts and sciences. Speaking of Brunelleschi's dome, the Italian historian of science and technology Paolo Galluzzi has said that it "unites technology and aesthetics in an astonishingly elegant way," symbolizing perfectly the union of science and art.[62] This was not only in the innovative design but also in its execution. Leonardo da Vinci was impressed by the hoists Brunelleschi had devised, which could lift loads of more than a ton to heights between 150 and 270 feet above the ground. Brunelleschi had also invented a 65-foot revolving wooden crane for positioning the marble blocks in the lantern of the dome's summit. The development of such visual and technical skills was driven in part by an aesthetic conviction—that the key to design is proportion. Both Brunelleschi and Alberti had studied the temples of pre-Christian Rome; and to study was to measure.[63]

The primacy of aesthetically defined goals in architectural engineering was often made clear through explicit references to music and to the Pythagorean correlations between musical intervals and geometrical ratios. Alberti could say:

---

61. Cited by Philip Hook, *Breakfast at Sotheby's: An A–Z of the Art World* (London: Penguin, 2013), 180–81.

62. Cited by Alasdair Palmer, "Building the Impossible," *The Sunday Telegraph*, October 10, 1999, Arts section, 7.

63. Pacey, *Meaning in Technology*, 52.

> I am every day more and more convinced of the truth of Pythagoras's saying [that] Nature is sure to act consistently, and with a constant analogy in all her operations; from whence I conclude that the same numbers by means of which the agreement of sounds affects our ears with delight, are the very same which please our eyes and our mind. We shall borrow all our rules for the finishing our proportions, from the musicians, who are the greatest masters of this sort of numbers.[64]

It has even been argued that the very origins of technology lay in music. Arnold Pacey speaks of rhythms in the world, in nature, and in machines, and warms to the aboriginal idea of the world coming into existence through song and dance. In his own words:

> The visual and musical aspects of a machine may inform its design and development at every stage. They are important for the designer's motivation, and may spark his or her creativity. We judge the final result in part by how it looks and how it sounds. In the adjustment of an engine, we talk about "tuning" it, not just by analogy with musical instruments, but also because we know that when it sounds "sweet," it is likely to be running well.[65]

Pacey is perfectly aware that a history of mechanized industry would focus our minds on inventions aimed at deskilling work and displacing muscle rhythms; but he reminds us that some of the most intriguing of all machines are those that require their users to learn new body skills and new rhythms. The bicycle is his prime example.

Pacey's reference to the motivation of the designer introduces a sense in which the spiritual can infuse the material. The building in which I was privileged to reside in Oxford, in Harris Manchester College, constitutes an example. From discussion with James Armstrong, a former president of the Institution of Structural Engineers, I learned that his involvement with the college's new wing reflected not only his own delight in Renaissance proportions but a delight also that was suffused with both musical and spiritual meaning. In a series of lectures, delivered at the college, he referred to the commissioning of music from two composers who were invited to set a text from the Wisdom of Solomon. They were instructed to use the simple harmonies incorporated into the building design. The outcome was an unaccompanied choral setting of the

---

64. Leone Battista Alberti, *De re aedificatoria* (Florence, 1485); trans. James Leoni as *Ten Books on Architecture by Leone Battista Alberti* (London, 1726), book 9, chapter 5.

65. Pacey, *Meaning in Technology*, 18.

Science, Technology, and Aesthetics

text and an instrumental sextet. Particularly moving in Armstrong's lectures was the continuum between the quest for beauty in design and the motivation to express something of the divine. In earlier technology he recognized the intention of relating the order in buildings to evidence of order in creation. He recognized a beauty "discovered by the senses, appreciated by the intellect, but coming to rest in the heart." In his 1989 Presidential Address before the Institution of Structural Engineers he dwelled on a presupposition of his work. It was the idea of elegance—"not only elegance of form, of structure, but of our expression and understanding of the first principles of our art and of the mental systems that we use to solve most effectively the problems with which we are faced."[66]

Solutions to structural problems may not always have connotations of a higher wisdom, but they can sometimes come in the form of sudden inspiration, having the character of revelation and authenticated by a sense of the fittingness, simplicity, and beauty of the resolution. There is a modern example in the Sydney Opera House. It was conceived by its architect Joern Utzon before the question how it might be made to stand was successfully addressed. How might the roof shells be made to support each other? The inspiration came when Utzon envisioned the shells as segments of a gigantic sphere. By his own account he ran to the fruit bowl, took an orange, and sliced the peel into segments: "And suddenly I had it. . . . It was so simple and so beautiful. Everything fitted together. Spherical geometry. We had a tested principle. It meant we could build the opera house."[67] Another variation, perhaps, on the music of the spheres.

Such references to the solution of problems introduces other levels at which the aesthetic may penetrate the technological. Machines designed to solve problems may have a beauty of their own. This will be obvious to anyone who has studied the beauty of astrolabes produced within medieval Arabic cultures. Amid the publicity given to Dava Sobel's book *Longitude* (1995) was a recurring explanation for the book's popularity. This was that John Harrison's clocks were intrinsically beautiful, that something of their beauty was visible from the illustrations in the book, enough in fact to make one wish to go to Greenwich to see the objects themselves. Other obvious examples might be the elegance of a large suspension bridge or the smooth curves of a modern airliner.

---

66. James Armstrong, "An Elegant Profession," Presidential Address given before the Institution of Structural Engineers, October 5, 1989, *The Structural Engineer* 67 (1989): 3–7.
67. Cited by William Langley, "Phantom of the Opera," *The Sunday Telegraph*, September 15, 2002, Review section, 5.

Technologies subservient to the production of beautiful objects can, of course, be subservient to little more than hedonism. But there are many examples from the past where technological processes have been given explicit spiritual meaning. The fireworks of the alchemist were not unattractive to Martin Luther who saw spiritual, even apocalyptic, meanings in the separation of the pure from the impure and in the fire of the furnace. It reminded him of the resurrection of the dead at the last day.[68] New technologies continue to facilitate new aesthetic experiences, expanding rather than compressing the celebration of an astounding creation. A simple example would be the way in which *Apollo* moon landings sometimes evoked gasps of wonder from the participants, who would speak of the "beautiful experience" of walking where nobody had walked before, something akin perhaps to the joy one might experience in walking through pristine snow. And a component of the technologist's joy, especially in a matter as complicated as landing humans on the moon, or a sophisticated probe on Mars, would be the sweet smell of success. Ecstasy at mission control is a phenomenon we must all have witnessed.

Technology, as with the sciences, constantly *involves* problem-solving. Finding the elegant solution brings a special kind of satisfaction. It is even claimed that "an engineer . . . is a creative artist in a sense never known by a pure scientist."[69] Whereas the theoretical scientist has to interpret nature as he or she finds it, an engineer is committed to making something. The contrast can easily be overstated in such a characterization. As Marcellin Berthelot famously said of the chemical sciences, the chemist creates his own objects of study. But the point remains that "a great deal of work in technology feels like art to those involved."[70] It does so because it regularly calls for aesthetic, quasi-intuitive judgments: "So often a car, boat, or bridge that has been well designed for its function is aesthetically satisfying to look at, not because functional shapes have an inevitable beauty, but rather because aesthetic judgment was used in achieving an effective functional form."[71]

Present Futures

Aesthetics and technology have met on one further, crucial plane: in planning futures, even the future of our own species. Humans surely are unique

68. Brooke and Cantor, *Reconstructing Nature*, 319.
69. Gordon Glegg, *The Design of Design* (Cambridge: Cambridge University Press, 1969), 1.
70. Pacey, *Meaning in Technology*, 64.
71. Pacey, *Meaning in Technology*, 64.

Science, Technology, and Aesthetics

in contemplating a future in which they might be overtaken by their own transformed and "enhanced" derivatives. Aesthetic judgment has long played a crucial role in our manipulation of nature. An obvious example would be the pigeon fanciers of Darwin's day who, in carefully selecting for the features they wished to accentuate, provided Darwin with a metaphorical and rhetorical resource for the exposition of his evolutionary mechanism of natural selection. Before the Second World War it was not uncommon for geneticists to offer the tantalizing prospect of improved human beings. There is evidence that belief in the power of genes to mold human character provided an impetus to both classical and molecular genetics.[72] In 1939 a "Geneticists Manifesto," authored by H. J. Muller and co-signed by twenty-two distinguished geneticists, envisaged a relatively near future in which "everyone might look upon 'genius,' combined of course with ability, as his birthright."[73] This alluring prospect was fatally damaged by the eugenic practices of the Nazis, which led to a postwar culture in which nurture rather than nature returned to the ascendant, with humans off limits as far as genetic determinism was concerned. As early as 1968, however, the National Academy of Sciences in America published a survey entitled *Biology and the Future of Man* in which alternative human futures were envisaged. It is impossible to miss the tacit incursion of aesthetic values in their glimpse of the future:

> We could breed for obesity or leanness, blue eyes or black, wavy or wiry hair, and any one of the obvious physical attributes in which human beings vary. Presumably, we could also breed for mental performance, for special properties like spatial perception or verbal capacity, perhaps even for cooperativeness or disruptive behavior, even, conceivably for high scores in intelligence tests.[74]

This was still a possible rather than an actual future. The report acknowledged that little use had yet been made of the power to select our own genetic constitution. A half-century later, confronted with utopian visions of human enhancement, we have a sense that biotechnology has transformed the nature-nurture debate yet again. Evelyn Fox Keller, writing in 1992, already spoke

---

72. Evelyn Fox Keller, "Nature, Nurture, and the Human Genome Project," in *The Code of Codes: Scientific and Social Issues in the Human Genome Project*, ed. D. J. Kelves and L. Hood (Cambridge, MA: Harvard University Press, 1992), 283–357.

73. Diane Paul, "Eugenics and the Left," *Journal of the History of Ideas* 45 (1984): 574; H. J. Muller, "Social Biology and Population Improvement," *Nature* 144 (1939): 521–22.

74. Philip Handler, ed., *Biology and the Future of Man* (Oxford: Oxford University Press, 1970), 926.

of a transfiguration of that debate in the light of molecular biology.[75] There is, however, an underlying issue that has remained unchanged. In 1968 the authors of *Biology and the Future of Man* declared that "to make speedy progress, reproduction should be limited primarily to those who possess genotypes for the desired traits"; but there was then the irrepressible question: "who will decide what is desirable?" Admittedly, the context was different then from today. The hypothetical question then was whether it was realistic to prohibit procreation to a majority of men and women. But the question "who is to decide what is desirable?" haunts us more than ever. Faith in technology, which has sometimes been the surrogate religion of our times, is a faith in the power we have to control and harness the forces of nature. But are we not close to losing faith in the controls by which we control our control?

In her 1992 essay Fox Keller linked the aesthetic questions to those of human freedom: "If it is our biological or genetic future that we now seek to shape, where are we to locate the domain of freedom by which this future can be charted?" She noted the disarming suggestion that this domain of freedom is to be found in the elusive realm of human choice. But there was a catch. This suggestion of the reality of human choice assumed a "democratic and egalitarian ideal somewhere beyond biology." And yet in this discourse of human enhancement there can be no domain "beyond biology" since, in popular parlance (however naively) it is our genes that make us what we are. In her perceptive commentary, Fox Keller went on to suggest that the locus of freedom on which much contemporary discussion depends is not to be found in the sphere of "individual choice" but rather in a domain protected by ambiguous assumptions about what it is for humans to be normal.

What did Fox Keller mean? Simply this: that the distinction earlier made between biology and culture, or between nature and nurture, has now come to be made by a demarcation between the normal and the abnormal. As she put it, "the force of destiny is no longer attached to culture, or even to biology in general, but rather more specifically to the biology (or genetics) of disease." Listening to the medical rhetoric by which many biotechnological promises and practices are justified, it is difficult to deny that she had a point. Far from teaching us what it means to be human, "the burden of the new human genetics turns on the elucidation not of human order but of human disorder." Hence her conclusion: "The freedom molecular biology promises to bring is the freedom to rout the domain of destiny inhering in 'disease-causing genes' in the name of an unspecified standard of normality—a standard that remains unexamined not simply by oversight but by the internal logic of the endeav-

---

75. Fox Keller, "Nature, Nurture and the Human Genome Project."

our." Attending again to the medical rhetoric it is difficult not to agree. Is the normal human being one who would live forever, if all genetic blemishes were removed? Will the book of life, as the question has been more eloquently put, help us to cheat death?[76] If Fox Keller's diagnosis was correct, there is a deep irony in our current situation—that in thinking of designer babies, designer futures, and even a post-human world we may have lost sight of the fundamental question of what it is to be human, and whether immortality might not be a qualitative rather than a quantitative concept.

Contemporary neuroscientists seeking to understand the superior cognitive skills of humans are apt to look for subtle shifts in the frontal and parietal lobes of the brain that have occurred during evolution and which have enabled abstract thinking, analytical skills, and memory retrieval—capacities that in turn are associated with what has been called "relational reasoning," the ability to discern patterns and relationships in seemingly unrelated information.[77] The emergence of such an adaptive cognitive fluidity has featured in well-known accounts of human evolution[78] and features prominently in van Huyssteen's Gifford Lectures.[79] In this chapter I have not pretended to argue an original thesis. I have, however, tried to show, from a miscellany of historical examples, how in the modern world that fluidity has been manifest in a variety of inter-relations between technology and artistry that may be less familiar than in the dualities of science and technology, science and religion, and religion and art. I have indicated how technological innovation has carried aesthetic and sometimes religious connotations. For those who believe that concepts of human nature and human uniqueness can only be adequately analyzed by examining what humans *do*, and not simply by reference to how they are biologically constituted, historical exemplification becomes not a luxury but a necessity.[80]

76. *The Times Higher*, February 16, 2001, 18–19.
77. See, for example, contributions to the journal *Neuron* for December 3, 2014, by the University of Berkeley neuroscientists Silvia Bunge and Michael Vendetti.
78. Steven Mithen, *The Prehistory of the Mind: A Search for the Origins of Art, Religion, and Science* (London: Thames and Hudson, 1996).
79. Van Huyssteen, *Alone in the World?* 193–205.
80. For a sophisticated elaboration of this point, see Roger Smith, *Being Human: Historical Knowledge and the Creation of Human Nature* (Manchester: Manchester University Press, 2007).

PART 3 Theologians

10 Moral Origins and Evolutionary Ethics

*Navigating the Maze in Conversation
with J. Wentzel van Huyssteen*

CELIA DEANE-DRUMMOND

I owe an enormous debt of gratitude to J. Wentzel van Huyssteen, whose pioneering work in the field of theology and science, and anthropology in particular, has shaped my own thinking in significant ways. I am drawing particularly for this chapter on one strand in his corpus that shows the extent to which his work encourages further questions in an arena that is likely to become increasingly important, not least for its public significance, namely, moral origins and evolutionary ethics. He refers to morality in general terms as a distinct cultural category alongside science, religion, and art.[1] Yet coming to grips with what is meant by the evolution of "morality" is extremely challenging. In the first place, deciphering this literature is difficult for all sorts of reasons. It is not always clear precisely what is meant by morality, so its appearance in evolutionary history will either be consistently vague or depend on prior assumptions. Second, biologists are prone to use the term "morality" as a shortcut that indicates agreed frameworks for types of actions in a given community, without specifying the particular ingredients that this might entail, including, for example, patterns of altruism, forms of cooperation, conscience, types of justice-making, the appearance of what look like recognizable virtues, and so on. Morality therefore appears as the broadest possible basket into which these various characteristics get placed, and it is not always clear what it might really mean to say that an agent is acting morally or not, except that a given community agrees on particular rules in these different areas.

---

1. J. Wentzel van Huyssteen, *Alone in the World? Human Uniqueness in Science and Theology* (Grand Rapids: Eerdmans, 2006), 32, 46.

Rather more fashionable has been the shift toward consideration of *cooperation* rather than *selfishness* as a core driver of evolutionary change, hence embedding morality into a discussion of not just a specific characteristic of a social community, but forming the background of evolutionary change as a whole. This is one of the reasons, perhaps, why sociobiology is so controversial in public discourse; it seems to take neuralgic issues about morality, in most cases, according to a paradigm of selfishness, and write it large over the whole of biological history, and then integrate this selfishness or cooperation paradigm in an apparently seamless way into human history. Yet even the way that cooperation is worked out in scientific terms can still have "ultimate" roots in competitive "selfish" versions of natural selection. So while the term "selfishness" is not, when used as a biological term, intended to imply from a biological perspective any kind of moral choice, the impression left is that it does just that, and sets up beings in an evolutionary trajectory that eventually comes to find expression in rampant human self-interest.

Accordingly, for theoretical biologists such as Martin Nowak, *cooperation* is defined as "a form of working together in an evolutionary population, in which one individual pays a cost (in terms of fitness, whether genetic or cultural) and another gains a benefit," while *altruism* is defined as "a form of (costly) cooperation in which an individual is motivated by good will or love for another (or others)."[2] Sarah Coakley has teased out the power in naming cooperation and altruism as far as they can be rendered mathematically precise, while at the same time such precision disguises philosophical and empirical difficulties. She recognizes the utilitarian undertones of defining both cooperation and altruism in terms of cost-benefit, while also being caught up with the narrative that is created in the mathematical laboratory culture. So Coakley seems Janus-faced in this respect: on the one hand she states admiringly that "it is already remarkable that so many different conditions of favoured cooperation have been isolated and mathematically explained"; yet on the other hand she also accepts limits of mathematically informed accounts of the evolution of cooperation, so "it abstractly prescinds from the messiness of actual empirical observation in a way that must give us pause for thought about how much, in fact, it can 'explain.'"

---

2. As defined by Coakley in her Gifford Lecture 2, "Cooperation, *alias* Altruism: Game Theory and Evolution Reconsidered," available online, http://www.abdn.ac.uk/gifford/about/2012-giff/, and to be published with Oxford University Press under the title of *Sacrifice Regained: Evolution, Cooperation and God*, forthcoming, 2016, and also in Martin Nowak and Sarah Coakley, *Evolution, Games and God: The Principle of Cooperation* (Cambridge, MA: Harvard University Press, 2013).

And the very category of scientific "explanation" is of course one that itself begs philosophical definition.³

Coakley's seeming ambivalence about mathematical accounts of the evolution of cooperation and altruism reflects just one aspect of the difficulty of navigating the maze of literature on the evolution of morality as a whole; for while on the one hand what look like mathematically precise formulas give the scientific accounts of the evolution of cooperation a precision that biologists often long for through what could be termed a form of *discipline envy*, where mathematical accounts are viewed as more precise, theoretically sound, and therefore (implicitly) better science, on the other hand there is much, much more to cooperation than such accounts might suggest. And the explanatory power that does emerge in terms of making accurate predictions in community behavior lends a practical power to the theory in a way that is hard to resist. The distinction that Coakley insists on, correctly in my view, between the evolution of cooperation and the evolution of altruism bears in an illuminating way on the current discussion of the evolution of morality in general.

Unfortunately, however, there are no terms that specify between very general notions of morality, which could be allied at least to some extent with very general notions of cooperation and in which mathematics indicates an intrinsic "rule" (or law of nature) of some sort is in place, and what seem at least to be more genuine altruistic actions where the agent is positively and actively motivated in favor of the good of the other, but this time according to certain self-conscious "rules" agreed on by a particular community. So if altruism is the activity of "super" cooperators, "super" morality is the framework in which this activity takes place. But there are extensive conceptual confusions as well. For some scholars morality will be indicated when only *some* of the various ingredients of cooperation, altruism, justice, and so on are recognized, or even partially recognized, while others demand that morality only makes sense when fully fledged rational theories of social justice are born; this of course cuts out not just the possibility of other animals having any kind of morality, but also the greater part of hominin history and our own human history given that the first anatomically recognizable *Homo sapiens* species appeared half a million or so years ago.

There is therefore an ethical dilemma in defining who or what creatures might be in or out as far as morality is concerned; where the line is drawn will impact human behavior in the present. Of course, it is possible for human beings to allow all kinds of other creatures to be *morally considerable*, quite apart from whether such beings are thought to have any *moral agency*. However, if

---

3. Coakley, "Cooperation, *alias* Altruism."

moral agency of a sort is recognized in other species, then it becomes much more difficult to justify abusive treatment toward them. The line, therefore, between "them" and "us" becomes problematized, and so challenges fixed categories of the self in relation to the other. Much of the debate about human exceptionalism could be cleared up if there was greater attention not just to the precise meaning of terms, but a greater awareness of what such terms signify in terms of human action. But it is also clear that any kind of moral life, whatever the precise definition of what such a life might mean, is impossible as an isolated individual; even virtues are expressed in relation to others, and in this sense presuppose community with others. When that community is *also* religious, then the moral demand will shift, bringing with it, most commonly, particular normative claims as to a preference for individuals to act in one way rather than another in their associations with each other.

Bringing in religious elements to debates about morality is also contested for a number of reasons. Scientists, *qua* evolutionary scientists, are generally suspicious of religious proscriptions for the moral life, refusing to accept the validity of the religious demand to act in a certain way and favoring strictly biological explanations. In other words, where such religious believers will claim *God* as agent in prompting moral actions of one sort or another, evolutionary biologists will point to this as a surface-level interpretation; a deeper, and for them, *biological* interpretation has to do with some kind of evolutionary advantage in acting this way. How do they explain, therefore, the total self-sacrificing, altruistic life of someone like Mother Teresa, now Saint Teresa, whose own body became crippled through years of dedicated service, hardship, and solidarity with those who were dying miserable deaths on the streets of mega-cities throughout the world?[4] Her reported explanation of the way her institution lived out a call to absolute poverty, so that what she tried to achieve went beyond her individual persona, was that it was *God* who provided for their everyday community needs through daily miraculous interventions in answer to specific prayers.[5] Miracles in this sense did not mean, of course, God *literally* providing manna from heaven, but that once a need was identified, and a prayer to the Almighty articulated, then, someone somewhere responded to that need and provided precisely the amount of money or quantity of food, such as a bag of rice, for example, that was required for that particular crisis. And given that the Sisters refused to accumulate any wealth or store

---

4. Renzo Allegri, *Conversations with Mother Teresa: A Personal Portrait of the Saint, Her Mission and Her Great Love for God*, trans. Marsha Daigle-Williamson (Frederick: The Word Among Us Press, 2010).

5. Allegri, *Conversations with Mother Teresa*, 59–65.

any goods, those crises happened on a regular, almost daily basis. Now, few can doubt Mother Teresa's authenticity or personal integrity, which makes it unlikely that such events as described are fabricated, even if the gloss in their description is fashioned so as to encourage Christian faith rather than doubt. So how might a nonbeliever respond?

An evolutionary biologist might respond by suggesting that what is happening here is an example of indirect reciprocity at work in the evolution of cooperation more generally, that is, natural selection favors strategies that promote cooperation where the recipient has a high "reputation."[6] Gifts, therefore, flowed to the offices of the Sisters of Charity because of the reputation of the founding member that was also theirs by association. Yet another biological process may be at work here as well, what Martin Nowak calls "network reciprocity" because cooperators form clusters that serve to protect each other and enhance their likely success.[7] The spread of the numbers of nuns who have given themselves willingly to imitate the work of their founding religious sister could not have happened without a clustering in parallel communities throughout the world. But while evolutionary biology might offer some pointers to human behavior, the question remains as to how far it is successful and fully satisfying as an explanation for totally self-sacrificing and many might say extreme behavior, or whether it is simply a description of just some of the underlying biological processes, which are also themselves subject to dispute and challenge, or even whether such explanations are totally misleading and completely miss the point. In other words, evolutionary biology can attempt *to describe* how it could possibly be the case that such an example of extreme sacrifice, one might call this "ultra-morality," might exist in a human community, but it is not even biologically adequate when it makes the claim that this is also an "ultimate" explanation in terms of a theory that relies heavily on the evolution of selfish traits by natural selection.

The selection for behavioral traits through genetic means is not the only lens through which to consider evolutionary biology. There are other biological lenses too that are also evolutionary in a much broader sense of including epigenetic, behavioral, and symbolic forms of inheritance.[8] One of the intense difficulties with this field, and what makes it a maze in more senses than one, is that

---

6. Martin A. Nowak and Karl Sigmund, "Evolution of Indirect Reciprocity," *Nature* 427 (2005): 1291–98.

7. Martin A. Nowak, "Five Rules for the Evolution of Cooperation," *Science* 314 (December 8, 2006): 1560–63. See also Martin Novak, "Evolving Cooperation," *Journal of Theoretical Biology* 299 (2012): 1–8.

8. Eva Jablonka and Marion Lamb, *Evolution in Four Dimensions: Genetic, Epigenetic, Behavioral and Symbolic Variation in the History of Life* (Cambridge, MA: MIT, 2005).

it is all too easy to assume that engaging with a dominant form of evolutionary science delivers accurately the biological and evolutionary basis of that behavior. Morality, in so far as it is densely situated in narratives about cooperation and presupposes it, is one good example where it is too easy to presume that basically genetic explanations, such as indirect reciprocity, for example, that have the appearance of precision in that they can be mathematically formulated, represent the best available science. The precise link between the genetics of behavior and the formulas in game theories of cooperation are not all that clear either, but often the assumption is that there is an association between them. Sarah Coakley has engaged extensively with the evolutionary biology literature on cooperation, and, in so much as she has recognized that these evolutionary accounts are still narrative in texture, has opened up another important philosophical vista that needs to be kept in view, as I mentioned above.

Often the assumption in the discussion of such cases is that religious belief *does* reinforce moral proscriptions and undergirds particular ways of behaving. If religious belief did nothing, that is, had no impact on human behavior in relation to others, then evolutionary biologists would be hard pressed to find an explanation for its existence, other than as a spandrel for some other favored characteristic. This is certainly an option for those evolutionary biologists who treat religion as an offshoot of moral emergence and view it as its sequel rather than as its prerequisite. Richard Dawkins is known for his claim that religious belief encourages immoral rather than moral behavior.[9] If evolutionary biologists also happen to be religious believers this may create a dilemma in terms of seeking an explanation for moral action, or they may seek to distinguish what evolutionary biology might suggest about moral capabilities in the light of the truth-claims of that faith. But it is clear to such evolutionary biologists that the claims for truth in those religious beliefs cannot simply be ignored; as Dominic Johnson and his colleagues suggest, it is the elephant in the room when dealing with questions about the evolution of religion.[10]

J. Wentzel van Huyssteen on Moral Origins

J. Wentzel van Huyssteen takes a rather different tack in seeking to find ways to accommodate philosophical and religious interpretations of moral origins

---

9. Richard Dawkins, *The God Delusion* (London: Houghton Mifflin, 2006).
10. Dominic D. P. Johnson, Hillary L. Lenfesty, and Jeffrey P. Schloss, "The Elephant in the Room: Do Evolutionary Accounts of Religion Entail the Falsity of Religious Belief?" *Philosophy, Theology and the Sciences* 1, no. 2 (2014): 200–232.

with evolutionary science. More generally, he prefers to concentrate on the broad discussion of the evolution of the person that he understands as a *self*, that encompasses a host of other characteristics, including the evolution of sexuality, cognition, imagination, music, and language, as well as the evolution of morality and religious dispositions.[11] And more recently, he acknowledges the shift among evolutionary anthropologists away from a strictly trait-based model of human behavioral change toward an understanding of evolution through niche construction.[12] He is correct to see the significance of such a shift in terms of a blurring of the boundary between biological and cultural factors involved in mapping human evolution. He is also correct, in my view, to follow Agustín Fuentes and understand human evolution in terms of a total *system evolving*, rather than narrowed in terms of specific features or characteristics of human beings that mark humanity out as unique.[13] Indeed, he is prepared to use the language of uniqueness, even though evolutionary anthropologists such as Fuentes are generally more cautious, given how much is still being uncovered not only about the behavior of our earliest hominin ancestors, but also given greater recognition of cognitive and other capabilities of other social animals as well. I share that caution and prefer to avoid using the language of uniqueness, not least because of its moral legacy in terms of human or rather *inhumane* treatment of other animals. Yet, while I agree

---

11. Of the extensive literature by J. Wentzel van Huyssteen that addresses this theme, most significant works include *Alone in the World?*; "Interdisciplinary Perspectives on Human Origins and Religious Awareness," in *Becoming Human: Innovation in Prehistoric Material and Spiritual Culture*, ed. Colin Renfrew and Iain Morley (Cambridge: Cambridge University Press, 2009); "What Makes Us Human? The Interdisciplinary Challenge to Theological Anthropology and Christology," *Toronto Journal of Theology* 26, no. 2 (2010): 143–60; "When Were We Persons? Why Hominid Evolution Holds the Key to Embodied Personhood," *Neue Zeitschrift für Systematische Theologie* 52 (2010): 329–49; "Coding the Nonvisible: Epistemic Limitations and Understanding Symbolic Behavior at Çatalhöyük," in *Religion in the Emergence of Civilization: Çatalhöyük as a Case Study*, ed. Ian Hodder (Cambridge: Cambridge University Press, 2010), 99–121; "The Historical Self: Memory and Religion at Çatalhöyük," in *Vital Matters: Religion and Change at Çatalhöyük*, ed. Ian Hodder (Cambridge: Cambridge University Press, 2013).

12. As in J. Wentzel van Huyssteen, "Human Origins and the Emergence of a Distinctively Human Imagination: Theology and the Archaeology of Personhood," in *Verbs, Bones and Brains: Interdisciplinary Perspectives on Human Nature*, ed. Agustín Fuentes and Aku Visala (Notre Dame: University of Notre Dame Press, 2016), in press. Here he states that, drawing on the work of Jablonka and Lamb, *Evolution in Four Dimensions*, 193–231: "This constructivist view moves beyond standard neo-Darwinian approaches and acknowledges that many organisms transmit information via behavior, thus acquisition of evolutionary relevant behavioral patterns can occur through socially mediated learning."

13. He cites here Agustín Fuentes, "A New Synthesis: Resituating Approaches to the Evolution of Human Behavior," *Anthropology Today* 25, no. 3 (2009).

with van Huyssteen that it is important to try to tease out what it means to be human in an evolutionary sense in more general terms, I also think that as long as sufficient caution is applied in terms of making conclusions, it is appropriate to focus in on morality as a *specific* topic to explore, especially given the dominance of discussion on this topic among evolutionary psychologists, and its potential impact on how we conceive of both human behavior and human responsibility.

So, my focus in this chapter as far as engaging with van Huyssteen's extensive literature on the human person will be van Huyssteen's more restricted work on the evolution of morality, even though I recognize that the bulk of his published works deals with broader issues about the self and personhood. Throughout his work, including his discussion of the evolution of morality, his basic philosophical starting point remains that of *postfoundationalism*, so that rather than try to pitch religiously inspired moral claims as delivering normative rules against scientific "facts," he challenges what he perceives as the wrong-headed foundationalism in both fields.[14] At the same time he seems ready to situate himself in the stream of evolutionary ethics that presuppose naturalistic interpretations of human morality. Van Huyssteen argues that, rather than a defensive stance against evolutionary naturalism in the face of supernatural explanation, theology needs to take into account what evolutionary biologists are saying about the created world as such.[15] A postfoundational philosophy of theology will therefore be much more open to insights from other sources of knowledge and seek to open up a shared space between them, even where terms mean something different. Like Coakley, van Huyssteen recognizes that the era of a fully inclusive natural theology has faded.[16] While Coakley insists that there is, as she puts it, "no *flat plane* of reality" anymore when considering the engagement of theology and science, a mistake made by the earliest natural theologians, van Huyssteen wants deliberately to create a *transversal plane* where he argues there *can* be constructive interdisciplinary conversations.[17] And this is a consistent theme in his writing: "transversal reasoning promotes different, non-hierarchical but equally legitimate ways of viewing specific topics, problems, traditions, or disciplines, and creates the kind of space where different voices need not always be in contradiction, or

14. J. Wentzel van Huyssteen, "Post-Foundationalism and Human Uniqueness: A Reply to Responses," *Toronto Journal of Theology* 27, no. 1 (2011): 73-86.

15. J. Wentzel van Huyssteen, "Should Theology Take Evolutionary Ethics Seriously? A Conversation with Hannah Arendt and Maxine Sheets-Johnson," *Nederduitse Gereformeede Teologiese Tydskrif* 54, nos. 3-4 (September-December 2013): 275-85.

16. Van Huyssteen, *Alone in the World?* 9.

17. Van Huyssteen, *Alone in the World?* 9, 18-23, 308-25.

in danger of assimilating one another, but are in fact dynamically interactive with one another."[18]

To some extent Coakley has adopted van Huyssteen's proposed transversal methodology in so far as she entered into deep and persistent conversation with evolutionary biologist Martin Nowak. Her thinking has been significantly shaped by this encounter, even though, as I indicated above, she seems to waver between enchantment and a wariness of the implications of the claims. But where diverse uses of the same phrase invite what seems to amount to a rigorous philosophical spring-cleaning in Coakley's interpretation, for van Huyssteen such uses *may* "alert us to promising liminalities between the disciplines."[19] The interpretation of what that liminality might generate in practice does seem to differ in Coakley's and van Huyssteen's accounts. So Coakley is, therefore, still prepared to retain a theologically rich account of sacrifice that she sees in some sense mirrored in the work of the scientists that she has encountered. She resists, then, giving up on deeply held even if controversial theological concepts about sacrifice, and it is worth asking how far indeed such theological concepts have, in practice, fueled her conversation with evolutionary biologists. In the light of the work of van Huyssteen it would also be worth asking how far her theological position edges toward "foundational" in so far as it reflects a strong Christology and theology of the cross. To clarify, for van Huyssteen different versions of foundationalism are typically rooted in a modernist notion of objective truth, universalist rationality, and autonomous individuality. At the same time he rejects non-foundationalism expressed in the postmodern trend towards relativism:

> Over against the objectivism of foundationalism and the extreme relativism of most forms of non-foundationalism, a postfoundational notion of rationality helps us to acknowledge contextuality, the shaping role of tradition and of interpreted experience, while at the same time enabling us to reach out beyond our own groups, communities and cultures, in plausible forms of inter-subjective, cross-cultural and cross-disciplinary conversations.[20]

Now, in this categorization Coakley is certainly not "foundationalist" in any strong sense, but an important question is raised in that it is not immediately clear what might define *acceptable* levels of universal claims that are based on metaphysically distinct premises where discourse is also aiming to be post-

---

18. Van Huyssteen, "Human Origins."
19. Van Huyssteen, *Alone in the World?* 9.
20. Van Huyssteen, *Alone in the World?* 10.

foundational.[21] Van Huyssteen deliberately tries to destabilize any strong disciplinary claims for authority by speaking of both theology and the different sciences as "reasoning strategies": "Thinking of disciplines rather as reasoning strategies enables exactly this kind of acknowledgment of permeable boundaries between different modes of thinking and opens the way for identifying shared epistemological and methodological resources within the sciences and various theologies."[22] Indeed, he makes a strong case for the boundary between theology and different sciences to be much more fluid than is usually conceived by arguing for a due account of the contextual, embodied, interpretive roots in deeply held convictions, leading to an overall transversal character of human rationality that binds experiences through rhetoric and discernment.[23]

Social scientists engaging in critical science studies will be very familiar with such arguments, but it immediately puts natural scientists who believe in the critical weight of their claims because they are perceived to be universally valid on edge. And, as I will show below, it also makes more traditionally minded theologians ill at ease as well. Anthropologists, on the other hand, because they are also humanities scholars, are less likely to find such a transversal approach problematic, and it may be one reason why transversal reasoning works particularly effectively in such a context. But the problems still remain, and in this respect, I intend to probe the particular case of morality in order to show more precisely what these problems entail. Coakley's suspicion that dialogue is rendered too easy by theology and science dialogue at least attempts to face up to the inherent problems that transversal approaches also try to solve. Van Huyssteen admits that a strong divergence between theology and the sciences is operative at the *methodological* level, so that both are different kinds of reasoning strategies in the common pursuit of reliable knowledge. If this is the case, then one would expect a particular problem, such as how human morality has arisen, to be an issue that can be tackled through different reasoning strategies. What I hope to show next is that while there are indeed some insights that can come from an interpretation of theology and science bridging through a common interdisciplinary or even multidisciplinary task of transversal reasoning, problems still remain in terms of coherence for specific, and arguably, critical aspects of understanding human selfhood. Van Huyssteen recommends looking at the specifics of a particular case, and I believe he is entirely correct to make such a recommendation.

21. This is not yet clear in Van Huyssteen, "Post-Foundationalism and Human Uniqueness."
22. Van Huyssteen, "Post-Foundationalism and Human Uniqueness," 74.
23. See also his earlier major work on this topic: van Huyssteen, *The Shaping of Rationality: Toward Interdisciplinarity in Theology and Science* (Grand Rapids: Eerdmans, 1999).

In this respect, it is worth viewing how van Huyssteen interprets the task of transversality in the concrete instance of the particular arena of the origins of human morality, where he takes up the work of philosopher Maxine Sheets-Johnson.[24] He draws in particular on her position with respect to the importance of embodiment. She argues that cognition and inclinations toward empathy and trust are embodied in a way that is not stationary but actively moving in relation to others. Further, on the origin of evil, he follows Sheets-Johnson in the way she draws on Hannah Arendt's concept of the *banality* of evil, emerging more from a mindless diligence to duty, rather than through a dramatic temptation to sin. Yet Sheets-Johnson adds to this account a deliberate parallel turning away from empathy such that cognitive and empathetic failure open the door to evil, mediated both individually and socially. Van Huyssteen concludes that humans are not born evil, but are born with a *capacity* for good or evil, thus affirming the basic position that Sheets-Johnson develops according to which evolutionary ethics accounts for the appearance of morality. Yet, at the same time, he cautions, correctly in my view, against using evolutionary ethics as a basis for the justification of moral codes. He also comes down in favor of an evolutionary explanation for the religious basis for moral codes, so arguing that accepting the objective authority of moral codes as rooted in divine principles was only feasible because of their survival value in a Darwinian sense. Such principles seem to have their origin in sociobiological constructions, even if he is still hesitant to give them any authority from such an origin. But many biologists would also do the same, that is, they resist the idea of moral codes having any authority since evolution explains how they have arisen, rather than whether they still need to be taken seriously as guides for human behavior. And biologists, such as Frans de Waal, for example, are quite ready to propose evolutionary theories to explain the existence of moral rules, without then coming to a clear judgment about what those rules should be. In so far as van Huyssteen capitulates to evolutionary ethics, his position would not be acceptable to many moral theologians, especially those who are drawn to a normative basis for ethics that has a theological root.[25]

---

24. Van Huyssteen, "Should Theology Take Evolutionary Ethics Seriously?"
25. Neil Arner, for example, insists on a normative basis for ethics. Neil Arner, Response II, "The Difficulties of Forsaking Normativity," in *Verbs, Bones and Brains: Interdisciplinary Perspectives on Human Nature*, ed. Agustín Fuentes and Aku Visala (Notre Dame: University of Notre Dame Press, 2016), in press. Now, while it is possible to combine theological norms in ethics through divine command theory with ethical theories that are, theoretically at least, more sympathetic to knowledge arising from natural science, as in modified versions of natural law, it requires intellectual agility to navigate this boundary. See, for example, Jean Porter,

But there are other scientific difficulties here in relation to van Huyssteen's transversal project that are not fully resolved in the case of moral evolution, such as a lack of resolution between biological and cultural norms in the emergence of morality. In other words, if a religious norm is a cultural construction, it is not clear in what sense it is also Darwinian in origin in the way he implies. Further, evolutionary biology is, to a large extent, undergoing something of a paradigm shift such that narrow proscriptions of behavior according to a genetic deterministic model of evolutionary theory are being replaced by a four-dimensional model that includes not just genetics, but also epigenetics, behavior, and symbol-making.[26] It is therefore problematic even in evolutionary biological terms to describe norms, especially religious norms, in a way that ties such characteristics to given traits that can be selected for through Darwinian natural selection, quite apart from the difficulty in rendering such norms woven to an evolutionary account. The attempt, in other words, to tie complex attributes of human societies to evolutionary frameworks is itself to lean edgily toward a *foundationalist* Neo-Darwinian approach to ethics that is against van Huyssteen's overall intention.

In more recent work van Huyssteen has accepted this shift in evolutionary biology, influenced by the work of Agustín Fuentes and others.[27] It remains to be seen, therefore, how far he might want to shift his own interpretation of the evolution of morality based on this newer understanding of human evolution through niche construction. But if such a shift is followed to its logical conclusions, then the whole question of human uniqueness, including the specific moral capacities that have been learned in communities, becomes much more blurred. The beginnings and glimmerings of human abilities to transcend their environment go far back into deep history, to a time when different hominin lines were much more diffuse. It is also intriguing that the sub-classification of different hominin species may actually be an artifact of the way specific morphological characteristics have been attached to certain lineages, rather than reflecting genuine differences in species in any essentialist sense.[28] So, the beginnings of human self-awareness could reach far back in time to those lineages of *Homo* that existed even before language eventually emerged in *Homo sapiens sapiens*. And even if the moral capacities of other animals are contested, it is clear that morality did not appear suddenly and all at once, but gradually, no doubt in fits and starts, in the context of a community of others.

I also find myself more resistant to endorsing a move made by van

---

"Divine Commands, Natural Law and the Authority of God," *Journal of the Society of Christian Ethics* 34, no. 1 (2013): 3–20.

26. Jablonka and Lamb, *Evolution in Four Dimensions*.
27. Van Huyssteen, "Human Origins."
28. Agustín Fuentes, personal communication, January 23, 2015.

Huyssteen that, influenced by evolutionary ethics, seems to reject outright *any* ontology of ethics, even while I am sympathetic to many aspects of postfoundationalist philosophy. And, as I argued above, the essentialism still present in post-Darwinian accounts points to a foundationalism of a more subtle kind that insists on ethical naturalism. Van Huyssteen does not make the case for the latter, but then one is left wondering: what are the sources of authority for any ethics and on what grounds? Instead, I suggest, therefore, that there is a need to be more insistent, at least for Christian believers, that there are indeed certain moral truths that are non-negotiable, such as the moral imperative to love God and neighbor, even while admitting much more flexibility and openness to evolutionary insights compared with a standard divine command theory. While I am also not as attracted to sacrifice as a theological concept compared with Coakley, at the same time the theological richness of theological concepts like sacrifice is worth acknowledging. Of course, there are, it seems to me, ethical and moral ambiguities around the notion of sacrifice in terms of precisely what kind of conduct it could affirm. Sacrifice portrayed in a positive light could, therefore, engender unhelpful forms of masochism, or even justification for violence toward other animals, for example. So, where authors such as Coakley find themselves in that transversal space that van Huyssteen correctly identifies as important, the leaning toward one or the other end of the liminal space between foundationalism and relativism will have significant bearing on the kind of theology and ethics that emerges between the disciplines.

If van Huyssteen edges a little too close to evolutionary ethics for my liking in his account of the evolution of morality, it is worth pointing out that there may be other forms of dialogue that are still in approximately the same transversal space that he suggests, but which retain a more robust theological position without falling into the trap of a fully fledged foundationalism. Further, as the work of Coakley suggests, there may still be significant and contested controversies that remain. And, although not made explicit, the fall narrative seems to have no place in van Huyssteen's account of the origins of morality and evil.[29] So the question becomes, what, in the name of transversality should be brought in or left out for theological inquirers seeking to explore the origin of morality?

---

29. I discuss this aspect in more detail in Celia Deane-Drummond, "The Birth of Morality and the Fall of Adam through an Evolutionary Inter-species Lens," *Theology Today*, 72, no. 2 (2015): 182–93.

A Case for Animal Morality

Where van Huyssteen refers to morality in other animals he generally borrows Gregory Peterson's language of "protomorality," along with "protolanguage."[30] He is also influenced by Charles Darwin, who, according to van Huyssteen, named the moral sense as marking the "highest distinction" between human beings and other animals.[31] Now, distinction does not necessarily mean there cannot be any form of morality in other animals, but Darwin's basic idea that moral and mental faculties in human beings co-evolved leads van Huyssteen to make the claim for human uniqueness, predicated not just on generalized social instincts or intellectual habits, but also on the development of language.[32] But he goes further than this in following Christian Smith's claim for moral awareness as unique in humans in so far as it is necessarily connected to self-consciousness.[33] Smith now adds to this the concept of an *emergent human transcendent consciousness*. In short, what makes humans "unique" is that they are moral, believing animals; religion is natural in so far as it is in continuity with other animal lives who lack the neurological capacities that humans have in order to display such characteristics. But he goes further: humans "must look beyond themselves for sources of moral order that are understood as not established by their own desires, decisions, or preferences, but are instead believed to exist apart from them, providing standards by which their desires, decisions, and preferences themselves can be judged."[34] Now, this view of morality is particularly prevalent among evolutionary ethicists, but it can easily slip into the next logical conclusion, namely, that any "norm" that might appear to be the case in the moral life is, in effect, constructed as "outside" the self by the human imagination. Religious belief is of a similar trope, so that "human faith in super-empirical orders that make claims to organize and guide human life is not categorically different from the fundamental and continual acts of presupposing and believing all the other assumptions and ideas that make the living of life even possible."[35] Accordingly, religion serves a function,

---

30. Gregory Peterson, "The Evolution of Consciousness and the Theology of Nature," *Zygon* 43, no. 2 (1999): 283, cited in *Alone in the World?* 42.

31. Van Huyssteen, *Alone in the World?* 74.

32. Van Huyssteen, *Alone in the World?* 74.

33. Van Huyssteen, *Alone in the World?* 290. He cites Christian Smith, *Moral, Believing Animals* (New York: Oxford University Press, 2003).

34. Van Huyssteen offers a précis of Smith's position in this citation in van Huyssteen, *Alone in the World?* 291, but what is interesting is that for him the rationale for its validity is entirely self-evident.

35. Van Huyssteen, *Alone in the World?* 291.

namely, to keep certain moral boundaries believed to exist outside the self firmly in place. It is only a relatively small step to argue that human communities devise the idea of God in order to reinforce punishment of defectors and so solve the evolutionary difficult problem of how to deal with those who refuse to cooperate.[36] Theoretically it is possible to acknowledge that morality or religion evolved without necessarily undermining whether that religion or belief is true. But this creates a problem for van Huyssteen that he does not address, namely, that sources of moral authority or belief in God when devised in this way are, from the perspective of that community, in a functional sense still *foundational*, in that they are believed to be universal, as otherwise they would not carry the weight of moral authority over that community. Elsewhere he argues that evolutionary epistemology is postfoundational in as much as it moves away from strict scientific positivism.[37] But how far is it entirely convincing that the strong narratives embedded in evolutionary accounts are benign in the way that van Huyssteen implies? Certainly, in so far as they seek to explain the emergence of morality and religion they are not benign at all. In other words, evolutionary epistemology is, it seems to me, complex in so far as different philosophical positions will attach to different versions of evolutionary theory.

In addition to these problems there is also an underlying account about the human that defines human uniqueness in terms of a possession of a range of capacities that are then found to be lacking in other animals. In as much as the intellectual capacities and powers of self-reflection in humans are distinct from those of other social animals such an account achieves a common consensus across a range of scientific disciplines. It also coheres with traditional accounts of human reason, such as that found in Aristotle and Aquinas, as well as his teacher Albertus Magnus, who all, in their slightly different ways, recognized that the supreme powers of self-reflection in humans gave them a distinct capacity to control their emotions in a way that was not possible for other animals. However, and this is important to recognize, they had not yet characterized such animals as machines, but understood that observations on animals are illuminating for the human condition.

Those evolutionary theories that project human behavior in terms of natural selection of genetic traits have dominated the literature until very recently. The evolution of morality is no different in this respect since, according to this view, the real underlying cause is related to gene selection; proximal causes

---

36. Johnson, Lenfesty, and Schloss, "The Elephant in the Room."

37. J. Wentzel von Huyssteen, *Duet or Duel? Theology and Science in a Postmodern World* (Harrisburg, PA: Trinity, 1999).

are therefore disregarded. I suggest that such views betray a subtle (or in the case of authors such as Dawkins,[38] not so subtle) version of scientific foundationalism that is hard to dislodge. Part of the problem of the engagement of theology with any science *even* in a transversal mode is the tendency for that science to move and change, just as the philosophical and theological implications of that science are wrestled with through a process of reflection. As I discussed earlier, evolution in four dimensions changes this reductionistic and somewhat mechanistic account in so far as recognizing that the influences on natural selection are not about a given set of traits in relation to an external "outside" environment, but that in human evolution a complex suite of social characteristics emerge that are reciprocally and mutually conditioned by inter-relationships with other creatures and the ecological landscape—what scientists are calling the dynamic evolutionary "niche."[39]

Why is this significant for an account of the evolution of morality? I suggest this is significant since human moral and religious life did not happen in isolation from other animal kinds, but was parsed and shaped through human interactions with them. I have elsewhere named this kind of emergent morality as "*inter*-morality," thus naming the interactions with other species that such a morality specifies.[40] Now, this thesis on inter-morality would hold to some extent regardless of whether other animals do, in fact, have their own moral worlds and moral norms. But I suggest that it is worth considering whether this is indeed the case since if it is, then inter-morality reflects a transversality of a different sort, this time between agents that are occupying different and distinct ecological niches, but at the same time, interlacing niches. With the advent of domestication there is the total incorporation of two niches, that of the domesticated creature and that of the human, but one comes under the umbrella of the human niche but resists straightforward incorporation. By this I mean that the other animals' life and agency still impinge on the human in a way that impacts on the moral lives of those humans who have chosen to bring those animals into their human worlds. Overall, there has been an anamnesis

---

38. Richard Dawkins's *Selfish Gene* was highly influential in this respect; Richard Dawkins, *The Selfish Gene* (Oxford: Oxford University Press, 2006).

39. For further discussion of niche construction, see Celia Deane-Drummond and Agustín Fuentes, "Human Being and Becoming: Situating Theological Anthropology in Interspecies Relationships in an Evolutionary Context," *Philosophy, Theology and the Sciences* 1, no. 2 (2014): 251–75.

40. "Evolutionary Perspectives on Inter-Morality and Inter-Species Relationships Interrogated in the Light of the Rise and Fall of *Homo sapiens sapiens*," *Journal of Moral Theology* 3, no. 2 (2014): 72–92; Celia Deane-Drummond, *The Wisdom of the Liminal: Evolution and Other Animals in Human Becoming* (Grand Rapids: Eerdmans, 2014).

of the long history of entangled lives of humans and other creatures, so much so that in our present societies there is a tendency to reject animals that come to live in association with human spaces, even though arguably it is as much their space as that of humans.[41]

Frans de Waal's Tower of Morality

Frans de Waal, more than any other primatologist, perhaps, has helped put animal behavior on the map as far as consideration of morality is concerned. Not only is he a prolific author, he also has succeeded where others have failed in denting a popular paradigm that has ingrained itself into public consciousness, namely, that human beings are basically at root selfish and sinful. While the disjunction between those who think of human nature as deeply sinful and those that think of that nature as basically good goes back even further than the famous argument between Augustine and Pelagius, de Waal plays into the sensibility of those who lean more toward Pelagius. Most sensible theologians think of human beings as a mixture of good and bad tendencies, rather than being at root one or the other. De Waal sees his role as a corrective one. Given the stress on the *viciousness* of animal natures, he wants to present the other cooperative side and show that the cooperative tendencies that we find in other animal societies are "building blocks" for the human moral world.

De Waal's repeated message is that what we observe in other social primates gives us clues about human behavior. In one of his first works on the social politics of chimpanzees he says this: "When Aristotle referred to man as a political animal he could not know just how near the mark he was. Our political activity seems to be a part of an evolutionary heritage that we share with our close relatives. . . . What my work at Arnhem has taught me, however, is that the roots of politics are older than humanity."[42] And against those who might challenge such a supposition as reading into chimpanzee behavior that of human beings he says this: "my knowledge and experience of chimpanzee behavior have led me to look at humans in another light."[43] And it is actually this movement, from chimpanzee to conclusions about the human, that is rather more controversial, it seems to me, since it implies that what we see in chimpanzees does give us clues about human behavior. The difference, ac-

---

41. A point that Marc Bekoff makes forcefully in Marc Bekoff, *Re-Wilding Our Hearts: Building Pathways of Compassion and Co-Existence* (Novato: New World Library, 2014).

42. Frans de Waal, *Chimpanzee Politics: Power and Sex among the Apes*, 25th anniversary ed. (Baltimore: Johns Hopkins University Press, 1998), 207.

43. De Waal, *Chimpanzee Politics*, 208.

cording to de Waal, is that while chimpanzees are far more blatant about their desires for power and influence, human beings are much more adept at either hiding or disguising their motivations from others. De Waal is also aware that any link between chimpanzees and humans might seem insulting to humans, used, as we are, to considering ourselves as superior to other animals. But the hierarchy that exists in chimpanzee societies in accordance with particular ranks gives, for de Waal, a measure of stability to the social structure:

> All parties search for social significance and continue to do so until a temporary balance is achieved. This balance determines the new hierarchical positions. Changing relationships reach a point where they become "frozen" in more or less fixed ranks. When we see how this formalization takes place during reconciliations, we understand that the hierarchy is a cohesive factor, which puts limits on competition and conflict.[44]

While such a hierarchical view might seem hard to stomach, de Waal also insists that such hierarchies are not fixed, and their existence brings stability to the social structure, allowing other activities such as childcare, sex, play, and cooperation. But it is possible to challenge the presuppositions in making conclusions about what such observations indicate about human behavior. In the first place, are hierarchical political arrangements and the stability that ensues *necessarily* a good in the human community in the way that de Waal implies? While he qualifies this by saying that such hierarchies are "tested daily," this does not render them necessarily some sort of prelude for human political systems. There are problems in making this a proto-political system for humans, in that it implies that the most "natural" systems of organization are also hierarchical ones, thus opening the door to the justification of oppressive regimes. Indeed, the only reason for a dominant to be toppled in chimpanzee politics seems to be that another, stronger individual wins out, even if that rank ordering is qualified by coalitions and networks of influence.

In subsequent works, de Waal explores other aspects of what look like elements of proto-morality found in primate behavior, including altruism and justice, that he prefers to term "other regard" and "fairness," respectively.[45] Again, as in chimpanzee politics, he makes the case for a tower of morality approach, so that the elements that can be observed in other animal societies

---

44. De Waal, *Chimpanzee Politics*, 208.
45. Frans de Waal, *The Age of Empathy: Nature's Lessons for a Kinder Society* (New York: Harmony, 2009); Frans de Waal, *The Bonobo and the Atheist: In Search of Humanism among the Primates* (New York: Norton, 2013).

are preludes to what is the case in human societies. What he argues for, then, is a bottom-up rather than top-down view of morality, where the basic elements for what makes human beings moral is that which emerges from our biological natures rather than that which is given to us from sociocultural narratives like religion, science, or abstract human reason.[46] Against such a view of top-down directives, he argues for a view of morality created through day-to-day interactions, grounded in the emotional life and visceral reactions that we share with our primate cousins. Of course, the view that our moral life is primarily grounded in emotions is not new, ever since David Hume proposed as much centuries ago. The difference in the case of de Waal is that he insists that morality emerges from similar kinds of behavior that we find in other animals. Of course, there is a certain irony here in that the politics of chimpanzee behavior is strictly hierarchical and top down according to rank, while the immediate reactions between individuals are based on emotion, rather than reason. So the rank order is one arrived at less through reasoned decision-making and more through visceral reaction to a sense of power in the other.

Yet, there are all kinds of other ironies embedded in this account, not just that the top-down approach to power that he still accepts seems to be arrived at through bottom-up visceral reactions. A second is that he rejects science as a player in shaping what morality is like in the place of religion, so "even avowed atheists are unable to wean themselves from a semireligious morality, thinking that the world would be a better place if only a white coated priesthood could take over from the frocked one."[47] But whom is he referring to? Those new atheists who reject religion as the basis for morality but then put scientific or secular reasoning in its place? But if that is the case, then what about the very scientific reasoning that leads to the kinds of conclusions arising from animal ethology that he adheres to himself? This is certainly a form of *reasoning*, even if it is reasoning in favor of more weight to visceral emotions in consideration of morality. And how scientifically justifiable is de Waal's case for building a tower of morality? His comparison between human beings and social animals presupposes a link between them that is not really justifiable, given how long ago the two lines diverged. Fuentes agrees with much of de Waal's arguments for finding altruistic and other behaviors in bonobos and other primates. But he concludes that this still says very little about what human beings are like or the evolution of morality. Based on the millennia since humans and other primates had a common ancestor, "the human lineage is characterized by a distinctive capacity to alter and shape our niche, by language, symbols, and

---

46. De Waal, *The Bonobo*, 23.
47. De Waal, *The Bonobo*, 23.

meanings derived from more than the materiality of our social and ecological surroundings. Human moral systems do not need religion to exist, but they do need humans. In the end, bonobos cannot tell us very much about being human at all."[48] That does not mean, however, that observations in bonobos are not fascinating for humans to consider, but it does mean a high degree of caution about building a tower of morality. In the end that tower starts to resemble more closely the tower of Babel, a chattering of confused voices.

There are also striking difficulties in constructing such a tower approach from the perspective of moral theology. In the first place, a tower implies that human beings are superior to other animals, in that their morality is the top of a tower, while the morality, such as it is present in other animals, is of a lower rank, a beastly kind. The legacy of such a view reaches right back to the earliest Christian writers, and de Waal may not be aware that he is implicitly drawing on work from ancient traditions; he is prepared to acknowledge Aristotle, for example, in naming humans political animals, but less frequently Christian authors. Such a legacy has considerable ambivalence, and the negative aspects of it are well known. Thus, David Clough insists on pointing out the implicit ethical dangers of ancient ideas such as the Chain of Being that put human beings in between animals and God in a hierarchical structure.[49] And the problems in this case relate to the positioning of human beings as superior to other creatures, a view that de Waal seems to want to resist. Although many reading de Waal's work will be sympathetic to his close attention to the lives of other animals and appreciate his determination to recognize their significance, ironically his view leads in the direction of reinforcing models of human exceptionalism. In the tower of morality humans are still on top. Yet, there is another danger as well related to how we conceive of human morality, and it is this. Lurking in the background of genetic deterministic accounts of human behavior are essentialist narratives that did so much damage in promoting eugenics in the past century. De Waal's approach is far more sophisticated in that it is about the evolutionary emergence of complex systems of cooperation, rather than explicit traits that are purely biologically given. But he still believes that the chimpanzee culture is rooted in their biology, and in that respect he is essentialist about their nature and ours. And on that basis his is an evolutionary ethic that falls into the category of ethical naturalism.

Does it matter that he is an evolutionary naturalist? Not if he was pre-

---

48. Agustín Fuentes, "Book Review: The Bonobo and the Atheist: In Search of Humanism among the Primates. By Frans de Waal," *American Journal of Physical Anthropology*, 2014. DOI: 10. 1002/ajpa.22499.

49. David Clough, in *Animals as Religious Subjects*, ed. Celia Deane-Drummond, Rebecca Artinian-Kaiser, and David Clough (London: Bloomsbury, 2013).

pared to be qualified about such matters, but unfortunately that is not always the case. The behavior of other primates becomes guides for human behavior, even if only in a loose way.[50] While Robert Audi argues that ethical naturalism is perhaps the only real option among philosophers today, he does not discuss evolutionary ethics specifically.[51] And evolutionary ethics is *realist* with respect to the psychological roots of human action, as is clear from de Waal, but *anti-realist* when considering the ontological or normative basis for moral systems, making moral claims neither true nor false.[52] For Audi a non-reductive naturalism means that a theologically orientated ethics is still possible, for goodness and obligation can still be connected with natural properties without being reduced to them.[53] But for de Waal this is impossible, for the tower of morality trumps other sources of authority, even though, at the end of the day, he resists coming out with normative bases for morality. And the tower, as its name implies, suggests emergent properties in the "higher" systems, so one-on-one morality is most characteristic of animals other than humans, but he believes that community concern is only very rudimentary in other animals.[54] That rudimentary element involves things like females interceding for another when a male is trying to force her to have sexual intercourse, or females forcing a rock out of a violent male monkey's hand.[55] It is hard not to make comparisons with human interventions in unwanted male behavior. De Waal concludes, "Moral transgressions, even those that don't directly affect us, are bad for everyone."[56] So while morality is bottom up, rooted in visceral emotions, it is still ultimately *normative*, and for de Waal, "social animals strive for harmonious relationships."[57] There seems, then, to be an inner sense about how things ought to be, so when fighting does break out, there are almost im-

50. De Waal, *Age of Empathy*.

51. Robert Audi, "Ethical Naturalism as a Challenge to Theological Ethics," *Journal of the Society of Christian Ethics* 34, no. 1 (2013): 21-39.

52. Audi in "Ethical Naturalism" considers the particular case of noncognitivism, where normative elements are thought of in motivational, psychological terms. This is probably the closest position to that favored by evolutionary ethicists, for a realist reductive naturalism in the manner of J. S. Mill, where moral properties are considered broadly equivalent to some natural ones, is not an option and Audi's assessment that it "almost certainly fails" (24) is warranted.

53. Audi, "Ethical Naturalism," 32.

54. "This is the level at which human morality begins to depart from anything else encountered thus far, even though some animals show rudimentary forms of community concern." De Waal, *The Bonobo*, 172.

55. De Waal, *The Bonobo*, 173.

56. De Waal, *The Bonobo*, 173.

57. De Waal, *The Bonobo*, 227.

mediate attempts to repair the damage done.[58] And yet, while de Waal insists on a bottom-up view of morality, surprisingly, perhaps, he still adheres to a principled view that comes close to one that is fully realist:

> the moral law is not imposed from above or derived from well reasoned principles; rather it arises from ingrained values that have been there since the beginning of time. The most fundamental one derives from the survival value of group life. The desire to belong, to get along, to love and be loved, prompts us to do everything in our power to stay on good terms with those on whom we depend. Other social primates share this value and rely on the same filter between emotion and action to reach a mutually agreeable modus vivendi.[59]

This commonsense view of morality derived from a study of bonobos seems to cohere with what we might expect: no one likes a fight. But to say that such laws have been there forever implies a normativity that sounds almost religious in its commitment. Further, to arrive at conclusions about the evolution of human morality from observations of primate behavior short-circuits considerations of early hominin evolution and forgets, too readily, the social and biological divergence between humans and social animals. If anything we might say there are remarkable *convergences* in the behavior of social animals and human beings that imply that there are some restraints, at least, in the way a well-functioning morality could develop. But convergence is not the same as evolution; in fact, it derives from very different phylogenetic lines. This is another reason why the tower of morality collapses since it turns what seem like analogies or convergences into implied homologous relationships. So while de Waal does recognize there are differences between humans and primates, he still assumes that they both build on the same base: the rock of morality is the same for each.

Evolution and the Fall of Adam

I believe, therefore, that de Waal is correct to consider the social lives of animals as being significant for human morality, but for different reasons. Social primates do not show any preludes for human moral behavior, however tempting it might be to come to such conclusions. But they do show us how

---

58. De Waal, *The Bonobo*, 228.
59. De Waal, *The Bonobo*, 228.

remarkably sophisticated their social lives have become. They have converged in certain respects with human moral systems, even though there are both similarities and differences in their derivation. And the convergence appears because the systems in place promote cohesive communities. That does not mean, however, that morality in human societies is derived purely from abstract principles. Rather, our emotional lives do register with those of other animals, and, as far as we can tell, we share in at least some of the same tendencies. How far these tendencies are also evolved tendencies is difficult to assess, but the theological tradition at least has always allowed for humanity being considered both a living creature and a living animal. We are animals and, as such, sentience, care for our young, and reproduction are all features of our existence. Should any of this matter for morality? The natural law tradition has always said "yes" to that question; divine command theories have said equally firmly "no." And while there is not scope in this chapter to dwell on the different varieties of natural law tradition, the fact that natural law has become secularized and even politicized shows that there are respectable arguments for weaving biological aspects of human existence into how we think of ourselves as moral agents.[60] Alasdair MacIntyre has termed this reminder of our animality the capacity for dependence, so that we are dependent, rational animals, learning our *dependence* from our shared social life with each other and other creatures, and our particular form of *rationality* from being schooled in the ways of virtue.[61] And it is the failure of de Waal to admit to rationality being important in human morality that makes his case in the end one that is derived from the authority of his experience, rather than the authority of evolutionary science as such. So it is possible to criticize him, as Fuentes does, for not being sufficiently *evolutionary* in his thinking. And it is possible to criticize him, as I do in this chapter, for deriving fundamental norms about human morality from his own experience with primates, with the allure that such authentic experience brings.

Yet the Christian tradition, at least, is reliant on a narrative about the fall into sin of humanity and its salvation in Christ for its theologically orientated ethics. So, even though Thomas Aquinas, for example, was content to speak of natural law, that natural law was still oriented toward the divine law, the law of God, and its ultimate principles came from that law. Theologians, unless they are prepared to rescind on their belief in God, at some stage will refer back

---

60. See Celia Deane-Drummond, "Natural Law Revisited: Wild Justice and Human Obligations for Other Animals," *Society of Christian Ethics* 35, no. 2 (2015): 159–73.

61. A. MacIntyre, *Dependent Rational Animals: Why Human Beings Need the Virtues* (Chicago: Open Court, 1999).

to the fall of humanity or the possibility of human sinfulness. So, I agree with de Waal that morality and wild justice exist in other animals. But that does not make it the *same* as that found in human societies, for humans have the possibility of deliberative forms of sin in the way that other animals do not. I also think that it is reasonable to presume that sin did not happen suddenly in very early hominin societies, but that there was a gradual intensification of tendencies to harm, culminating eventually in a self-conscious turning away from God and each other. But I suggest that it is the *collective* and *community* sense of sin that has been lost in the post-Enlightenment era in a way that was quite clearly not characteristic of the earliest Christian communities.[62]

If evolutionary biology has done anything, it has reminded us of the collective sense of morality, including the tendency to sin, that marks the beginning of a distinctive and deliberative collective will to err in the human community. And that collective will to err is also one that each and every individual makes his or her own in the course of a life lived; the moral life is a life lived conscious of the temptation to sin but choosing to do otherwise, choosing the good. What that good means will need to be worked out in accordance with particular norms of social justice where the needs of the most vulnerable members of society are protected. A theological ethic and account of morality cannot afford to waver on what those principles might look like, even while acknowledging the insights arising from evolutionary perspectives on the human.

---

62. See Celia Deane-Drummond, "In Adam All Die? Questions at the Boundary of Niche Construction, Community Evolution, and Original Sin," in *Evolution and the Fall*, ed. William T. Cavanaugh and James K. A. Smith (Grand Rapids: Eerdmans, 2017).

11 What Makes Theology Theology?

Conviction, Communicability, and Comprehensibility

MICHAEL WELKER

In the past twenty years J. Wentzel van Huyssteen and I have been—individually and together—very much engaged in projects that brought theology into international and interdisciplinary dialogue and cooperation. The dialogue with the sciences was of particular importance, but we also sought constructive interactions with other areas of research. Our common conviction has been that such projects require a strong sense of theological identity and that the theological topics should be very carefully selected in order to be fruitful for both sides.[1] It is in the light of these common interests and convictions that I want to contribute the following thoughts to this festschrift in van Huyssteen's honor.

The simplest definition of theology says, "Theology is talk about God." This basic definition, simple as it is, however, demonstrates the necessity for a more sophisticated answer because it is obvious that not each and every remark about God is a theological one. There is talk about God or about religious matters which, for instance, is purely statistical or fact-related, and whose speaker can be totally indifferent to the statement. Examples of such an

---

1. J. Wentzel van Huyssteen, *The Shaping of Rationality: Toward Interdisciplinarity in Theology and Science* (Grand Rapids: Eerdmans, 1999); *Alone in the World? Human Uniqueness in Science and Theology* (Grand Rapids: Eerdmans, 2006); see also our contributions to *Concepts of Law in the Sciences, Legal Studies and Theology*, ed. M. Welker and G. Etzelmüller (Tübingen: Mohr Siebeck, 2013), 205-24, 319-38.

This chapter was originally published in *Theology Today* 72, no. 2 (July 2015) and is reprinted by kind permission.

attitude would be sentences like: "In this African country, about 90 percent of the population seem to believe in a god." Or: "According to Greek mythology, Zeus was the highest Olympic god." These statements talk about a god, but they can hardly be regarded as truly "theological."

So what is the minimum requirement for an utterance to be acknowledged as theological? I should like to argue that at least two elements are necessary if a reference to God or to religious matters is to be qualified as a "theological" one. First, a theological utterance about God must show at least "a minimum level of conviction to relate to an encompassing sustaining, saving and ennobling power, at least a minimal degree of having been existentially grounded."[2] If this is not the case for the speaker, it should at least hold true for the persons or contexts the talk refers to — directly or indirectly. The second requirement for an utterance to be considered theological is that it is formulated in words and is comprehensible. Thus a silent prayer or a sigh directed to God cannot be regarded as a theological utterance. These two minimum requirements seem to be very simple, even trivial, but in their combination they are actually quite demanding. In order to reach the level of theological propositions, religious utterances must express religious certainties that are communicable and comprehensible. They must be open to communication and development with regard to their content.

To be sure, theological utterances do not necessarily have to show a well-developed faith. They do not have to reach the levels of a confession or a proclamation. They can be fragmentary, rudimentary, and even distanced. But they have to unite at least a minimum of consistency of conviction and a minimum of consistency of subject matter. This means that theology does not only look for individual certainty and a common certainty in consensus. Nor does it look only for topic-related coherence and correctness. It has to connect both dimensions — subjective certainty and objective content and coherence — and thus it opens up the search for truth. Truth is often confused with mere certainty, particularly in religious matters. It is also often reduced to consistency and correctness, particularly in the academy. But theology requires both dimensions, subjective certainty and objective content and coherence. The mutual challenge of both sides takes theology into the search for truth.

Many good Protestants love the famous statement attributed to Luther at the Diet of Worms before the emperor and the empire in 1521: "Here I stand. I can do no other. God help me. Amen." It is fairly uncertain whether Luther

---

2. See Michael Welker, "Is Theology in Public Discourse Possible Outside Communities of Faith?" in *Religion, Pluralism, and Public Life: Abraham Kuyper's Legacy for the Twenty-First Century*, ed. Luis E. Lugo (Grand Rapids: Eerdmans, 2000), 110-22 (112).

said these words at all. What is documented is his statement, "If I cannot be convinced by testimonies of Scripture or overt arguments of reason, my conscience is captivated in the words of God." This statement connects exactly the search for certainty and the search for rationally consistent and scripturally bound theological insight. In an exemplary way it marks the theological search for truth and the challenge that theology should be practiced in "truth-seeking communities."

With this basic challenge in mind, we will investigate the inner texture of an academic and ecclesial theology, the "theology" that we try to cultivate in seminaries, in universities, and hopefully also in churches. How do individual religious insights and remarks reach the level of what we regard or should regard as "theology" in the strictest sense in the academy and in the churches? My own understanding has greatly profited from a multi-year exchange and dialogue with colleagues from the Max Planck Institute for Comparative and International Law at the University of Heidelberg on the topic "Legal Dogmatics and Theological Dogmatics." Moreover, a guest professorship at the Center for the Study of Law and Religion at Emory University, Atlanta, gave me the opportunity to elaborate the astounding communalities in the areas of legal and theological dogmatics. No fewer than nine interdependent levels of normative impact are necessary in order to establish the great weight of legal and theological normativity. It has been interesting to see that both legal and theological scholars tend to select only some of these levels when they deal with the question, What makes theology theology? or, respectively, What makes jurisprudence jurisprudence? To be sure, in the following discussion of the nine interdependent levels of normative impact, I will concentrate on theology only.

Level 1: Concentration on Integrating Concepts of God

On the first level, the seemingly trivial insight that "Theology is talk about God" is taken seriously. This level is concerned with the identification of integrating ideas, concepts, or narratives of God, or of the divine. Even on this level, the spectrum of opinions is broad. Some theologians propagate integrating concepts of God such as "God is the ultimate point of reference," or "God is the ground of being." Others prefer religious ciphers— "the transcendent," or "the numinous"—and demand respect for the apophatic and the unknown. Even among the group who searches for theological clarity, there is a vast difference between those who insist, for example, on a Trinitarian theological basis or on other concepts of God that are compatible with revelation and Christology, and those who are quite satisfied with a *prima causa* or an "all-determining reality."

A recent contribution of a philosopher at the Heidelberg Academy who tried to argue for a strong "theological" interest of all serious philosophy opened my eyes to a very important fact.[3] Theology should insist on a clear differentiation between theology and a totalitarian metaphysics that works with all sorts of concepts of "the absolute." It should insist on the insight that a serious concept of God cannot remain soteriologically empty. A "first cause" or a "ground of being" without any saving, elevating, and ennobling powers cannot be regarded as "God," and the best reflections on it do not make a theology.

Once we have seen this, it is clear that the mere search for an "ultimate thought" is not at all sufficient to make theology. You cannot pray to an "ultimate thought" and you cannot expect salvation from an "ultimate thought." If the question, What makes theology theology? asks for Christian theology, it has to insist on a differentiated unity of God that makes sense of the revelation of God in Jesus Christ. This differentiated unity is expressed by Trinitarian theology. Even a more general answer than the Christian one to the question, What makes theology theology? should insist on a differentiated integrating thought or idea of God. If theology is "talk of God" or even "teaching about God," a merely apophatic or numinous or radically monistic and absolutely simple entity will not suffice on this first level.

Level 2: Respect for the Weight of the Biblical Canon

The fact that a mere "ground of being" cannot be regarded as "God" becomes very clear when we focus on the second level needed for an understanding of what theology is, namely, the normative weight of the codified and canonical texts. In some churches the church fathers belong to the ecclesial-theological traditions to be considered on this level, and many churches hold confessions in high esteem. Serious academic and ecclesial theology grounds its talk about God above all on the weight of the biblical canon. It cooperates with exegetical and historical research. I have proposed to speak of a "fourfold weight" of Scripture in order to explain the Reformation principle *sola scriptura* in contemporary contexts.[4] First, there is the great historical weight of the bibli-

---

3. Jens Halfwassen, "Gott im Denken: Warum die Philosophie auf die Frage nach Gott nicht verzichten kann," in *Gott-Götter-Götzen*, ed. Christoph Schwöbel (Leipzig: EVA, 2013), 187-96.

4. Michael Welker, "Sola Scriptura? The Authority of Scripture in Pluralistic Environments," in *A God So Near*, ed. B. Strawn et al. (Winona Lake, IN: Eisenbrauns, 2002), 375-91.

cal canon that grew over one millennium and includes an enormous array of witnesses to God and God's workings in the most different traditions of peace and war, times of tyranny and chaos and times of freedom and joy, individual suffering, sorrow, and distress, but also experiences of deep gratitude and the fecundity of life.

Next, there is the enormous cultural weight of Scripture. It radiates not only into the area of religion, but also into the arts, into the general culture, the academy, and education in vast parts of the world. This radiation, to be sure, was not only and not always for the good of humankind. Reference to Scripture was also used in religious, political, and moral oppression. But in any case the overwhelming cultural powers of biblical rationalities, symbols, and imaginations can by no means be denied.

Then there is the canonical weight. The different biblical traditions do not follow one line of thought. They do not simply support one idea or one value. But in multifarious ways they are deeply interconnected and cultivate a whole network of interconnected values. They combine complexity of insight and coherence of religious, social, cultural, and moral orientation.[5] This canonical weight is one of the reasons for their great orienting power over the ages and their normative gravity.

The historical, the cultural, and the canonical weights in their turn are grounded in the decisive theological weight of Scripture, in its reference to God, God's revelation, and God's sustaining, saving, and elevating relation to creation and to humankind. It is therefore correct to say that the relation to Scripture makes theology theology. This is not yet the whole answer, but an indispensable part of it. Under the rubric of "biblical theology" we have organized many processes of international and interdisciplinary theological cooperation.[6] We wanted to work against a tendency in Old and New Testament exegesis to develop itself into merely philological, historical, and cultural studies disciplines. Moreover, we wanted to work against all sorts of reductionist systematic and practical theological thinking that often replaces theology with self-made popular religious philosophies and leads to self-secularization and self-banalization in contemporary theologies and churches. We learned that serious work with the biblical traditions can very much improve the standing of theology in the general academy, even in dialogue with the sciences. And yet this move alone does not provide a sufficient answer to our question.

---

5. See Jan Assmann, "Fünf Stufen auf dem Wege zum Kanon: Tradition und Schriftkultur im alten Israel und frühen Judentum," in idem, *Religion und kulturelles Gedächtnis* (Munich: Beck, 2000), 81–100.

6. See as one successful example among many the *Jahrbuch für Biblische Theologie* (Neukirchen-Vluyn: Neukirchener Verlag, 1986–2015).

Level 3: The Orienting Power of the Dogmatic Loci

If theology had nothing but a concept of God (level 1), it would be dried out by reductionism. If theology had nothing but Scripture (level 2), it would be flooded by and drowned in an ocean of narratives and disparate insights. On the third level, theology in general and theological dogmatics in particular have to concentrate on a selection of interdependent specific topics that demonstrate the orienting value of the first two levels in specific contexts and with respect to specific questions and problems.

The third level has to show the topic-centered weight of theology. A classic form to do this was and still is a multi-loci dogmatics. Theology has to unfold its leading and integrating general thoughts of God, and it has to reduce and structure the enormous complexity of the witnesses of Scripture. A sound and fruitful theology has to deal with a limited polyphony of topics and perspectives. The biblical canon, the multi-loci dogmatics, the voices of the church fathers, the positions of the reformers, the ecumenical constellations—they all require coming to terms with what I have called a "structured pluralism."[7] This structured or organismic pluralism should not be confused with a diffuse "plurality," with radical individualism and relativism.

On this level, the exegetical, historical, and systematic approaches of theology have to bear fruit. These fruits do not necessarily have a direct contemporary relevance. They are not necessarily plausible to everyone in today's concrete environments. This is why we need the further levels (4–9) for a satisfactory answer to the question, What makes theology theology?

These further levels suffer from the great divide between academic theology and ecclesial theology. Ideally, both types should support each other, correct each other, and demonstrate the wonderful power of two different yet related "truth-seeking communities."[8]

Level 4: A Purely Academic Theology

In reality, however, we often see a divide between those who think that theological truth-claims are best articulated and best tested in the church and those

---

7. M. Welker, *Kirche im Pluralismus* (Kaiser: Gütersloh, 1995; 2nd ed., 2000); "Calvin's Doctrine of the 'Civil Government': Its Orienting Power in Pluralism and Globalization," in *Calvin Today: Reformed Theology and the Future of the Church*, ed. Michael Welker, Michael Weinrich, and Ulrich M. Lier (London: T&T Clark, 2011), 206–14.

8. John Polkinghorne and Michael Welker, *Faith in the Living God: A Dialogue* (London: SPCK, 2001).

who prefer the academy and the orbit of highly interdisciplinary universities, which makes it the theologians' duty to justify their claims in philosophical, psychological, sociological, philological, historical, and even scientific discourses. In the second perspective, a purely academic theology would be what makes theology theology. This answer, however, is easily misleading because in this development we often witness a loss of dogmatic responsibility and content. In our days, many colleagues are quite happy to see themselves transformed into scholars of religious or cultural studies, into philosophical theologians, historians, or sociologists—maybe with a specific competence in theological issues. But with all due respect to a seemingly pure academic ethos, we should calmly acknowledge that this approach offers many ways not to "make," but rather to distort or even destroy theology within theology.

Level 5: Academic Theology's Educational and Practical Responsibilities

We need the complicated connection of an academically well-trained systematic, biblical, and historical theology with a practical theology. We need the strong understanding that the former should not only contribute to the development and flourishing of the academy, but that it should also reach people outside the academic orbit, people who are deeply interested in theological and spiritual issues or who should become convinced that these issues are of great importance. The fact that in the academy future pastors and teachers are trained makes this task of reaching out beyond the academy indispensable for academic theology. It is, however, not only the training of the academic elite of the future that sets the standards for a good theology in universities and seminaries. It is above all the elite of practical theology in churches and educational institutions that is the test case for an answer to the question, "What makes theology theology?" To be sure, the answer can by no means be that the education of mere theological practitioners and theological technicians makes theology theology. It is exactly the bridging between two types of truth-seeking communities—that is, the academy and the church—it is their mutual support and their mutual constructive critique that should be cultivated by a good theology.

Level 6: Practical Theology in Ecclesial and Concrete Cultural Contexts

On the sixth level, it is not satisfactory to argue that it is the theology of individual pastors, of teachers of religion, and of church leaders that makes theology theology. We should certainly acknowledge the enormous normative power of theology exercised in and by these professional individuals and groups. It is their respect of and their constant work on a good dogmatic orientation, on adequate concepts of God, on an adequate scriptural, exegetical, and historical grounding, on a constant dialogue with the ongoing academic theological research, which offer the first part of a comprehensive satisfying answer to the question, "What makes theology theology?" Here it is a responsibly practiced theology that comes before our eyes. It is a theology that constantly relates to practiced piety, to general theological claims and doubts, and to religious indifference and skepticism in today's ecclesial and secular environments.

On this level we have to deal with the tempting answer, "It is ecclesial theology that makes theology theology." This answer is not false, but without a differentiated qualification it can become as one sided and misleading as the reference to the integrating concepts of God and the Bible. All too easily "ecclesial theology" can turn into a domination by church hierarchies, by academic professionalism, by institutional normative powers, by religious moral moods, or pressing actual problems that can be related to the life of the church. We have to take all the other levels into account in our search for an answer to the leading question in order to overcome these dangers.

Level 7: Institutionalized Theology with a Differentiated Professional Ethos

Practiced theology is not just a poly-individual enterprise of more or less inspired religious leaders with more or less developed inclinations to serve as theologians proper. In a multitude of forms and with many cultural means, the academy, the church, the ecclesial communities, but also other parts of modern societies want to ensure the specific quality of practiced theology in churches, schools, and beyond. Practicing theologians have to pass exams, ordinations, and visitations; as a rule they work in schools and not in parks, in churches and not in coffee houses—that is, they operate in the framework of institutions and in what is known as "public places." They are under many forms of public and professional control.

Since we want to invite the communication and participation of potentially all individuals in our societies in the practicing of theology, we as a rule do not over-emphasize the fact that theology is a very seriously organized and institutionally loaded business. Thus we do not rub it in that "it is its discipline and its seriousness and its institutional powers that make theology theology." In a more sublime way, we refer to and address all the other levels when we say, "It is the respect for the word of God that makes theology theology." It is the orientation toward Scripture that makes theology theology. It is the concentration on specific central theological topics (for instance, Christology) that makes theology theology. It is the serious study in the search for truth that makes theology theology. It is the orienting power in the life of the community and the church that makes theology theology.

If we try to avoid the reference to the word of God, the revelation of the triune God in Jesus Christ, grace, and faith (the famous "four *solas*" of the Reformation) we easily run into the danger of idolizing institutional and cultural artifacts as making theology theology.[9] Although we should not underestimate the power of church buildings, church music, well-orchestrated worship, good techniques of education and social organization in the life of the church—it all remains on the levels of supporting theology, but it cannot make or even replace it.

Level 8: A Theology with Orienting Power in Existential Situations

The penultimate answer takes us to a decisive test of all dogmatic, academic, and ecclesial theology: Does it help and orient and inspire people in their search for God, for God's guidance, in their quest for comfort and salvation, in their attempts to understand the sustaining, saving, and ennobling work of God in the midst of an ambivalent creation and in the midst of massive sin and pain among human beings? In late modern societies, most professional and practical theologians seem to be far too little pressed by burning theological questions. To be sure, many people contact them in situations of important transitions in their lives such as birth, maturation, marriage, and death; very often they not only seek good and pleasant rituals, but also solid theological messages and answers that can comfort their hearts and souls, give peace to their conscience, satisfy the demands of their reason, and illuminate their spirit.

---

9. See Berndt Hamm and Michael Welker, *Die Reformation: Potentiale der Freiheit* (Tübingen: Mohr Siebeck, 2008); M. Welker, "Die Reformation als geistliche Erneuerung und bleibende Aufgabe in Theologien und Kirchen," *Evangelische Theologie* 73 (2013): 166-77.

People in complicated existential and ethical situations not only seek pragmatic practical solutions, but they also want to get truly comforting and truthful theological insights that can orient or reorient their lives. In such existential and pastoral situations there is no single and no simple answer to the question, What makes theology theology? Still it is clear that in such cases people do not primarily look for the individual answer of a good pastor or teacher, but for the word of God. And without sound orientation provided at the other levels of theological normativity, relevant theological questions and answers are hard to articulate.

Level 9: A Theology That Shapes the Religious and Theological Mentalities

On the ninth level, we have to acknowledge that the professional theology on which we have concentrated in the search for an answer to the question, What makes theology theology? has to serve the serious nonprofessional theological search we set out with. It has to respect the individual search to understand God, God's word and work, the search for comfort and illumination, the attempt to develop faith in God's revelation and to live a life in its light, or at least, to cultivate an honest religiosity that stands firm in the diversity of cultural life with claims both from strict fundamentalism and aggressive atheism at its edges.

On the other hand, the isolation of the ninth level is one of the greatest threats to theology in our days. Many well-meaning people, but also many Neo-Protestant theologians, would answer our question by saying, "It is subjectivist faith which makes theology theology."[10] However, the reference to my inner voice, my "inner Other," the reference to my religious certainty, is as problematic as the isolated ultimate God-thoughts that we discussed on the first level. The concrete individual attempt to relate to God, the search for religious certainty, is indeed an essential element for all theology, but it does not make theology. It can rather destroy all theology in its very beginning. We therefore have to serve on all the other levels in order to make sure that the various religious searches in all environments can reach the level of theology. And this means that they can talk of God and teach about God in ways that allow for shared spiritual communication in the individual and common search for truth and salvation.

---

10. See my detailed critique of "subjectivist faith as religious trap" in *Gottes Offenbarung: Christologie* (Neukirchen: Neukirchener Verlag, 2012) (ET = *God the Revealed: Christology* [Grand Rapids: Eerdmans, 2013]).

It is on all these nine levels that the question, What makes theology theology? has to be answered. This differentiation makes us understand that different people privilege only some and certain of the nine levels over against others, depending on their interests and concerns. We can explain why theology taught in seminaries and at universities needs a differentiation of disciplines for its flourishing. On this basis we can work on a mutual strengthening of the different attempts to give a satisfying answer to the burning question, What makes theology theology? There is no simple answer to this question. But we can identify consistent and fruitful connections between the different answers that address different aspects in the attempt to serve the word of God, to serve the search for truth, and to serve the well-being of fellow human beings. And we can aim at a polyphonic consonance of the different perspectives and their truth-seeking contributions to the great task that makes theology theology.

12 Are We Alone? And Does It Matter?

The Narrative of Human Particularity

DAVID FERGUSSON

The intriguing title of J. Wentzel van Huyssteen's 2004 Gifford Lectures is set in interrogative mode—*Are We Alone?*[1] This was repeated in the published version two years later. Its subtitle suggests the direction of his argument—human uniqueness in science and theology is described in an interdisciplinary conversation around the model of a transversal rationality.

A carefully constructed case for human distinctiveness is assembled in close conversation with paleobiology and anthropology. This locates human uniqueness historically in the development of linguistic capacities in Upper Paleolithic life, particularly its art, for example, in the cave paintings at Lascaux from almost 20,000 years ago. The biological explanation for this includes reference to developments in the brain of *Homo sapiens* that make symbolic activity possible, perhaps quite suddenly in evolutionary terms. Though in part conjecture, it is suggested that this may have conferred on *Homo sapiens* an evolutionary advantage that ensured its survival. Following Ian Tattersall, van Huyssteen writes, "If there is one single thing that distinguishes humans from

---

1. *Alone in the World? Human Uniqueness in Science and Theology* (Grand Rapids: Eerdmans, 2006). Delivered in the historic Playfair Library at Old College, Edinburgh, in the spring of 2004, these lectures were distinguished by the growth in audience each evening.

This chapter was originally published in *Theology Today* 72, no. 2 (July 2015) and is reprinted by kind permission. I am grateful to my colleague Mark Harris and also to fellow symposiasts in Princeton for their comments on an earlier version of this chapter. And not least Margot and I owe Wentzel and Hester themselves a debt of gratitude for their valued friendship and support across three continents and twenty years.

all other life-forms, living or extinct, it is the capacity for symbolic thought, the ability to generate complex mental symbols and to manipulate them into new combinations."[2] Accompanying this development, there is a further shift in the capacity for self-awareness and consciousness by which humans are capable of reflecting on their experiences in categories of meaning, intention, and purpose.

Allied to these claims drawn from other disciplines is the theological notion that human beings are created in the image of God. This is explored in some depth. Various historical formulations are found wanting owing to their abstractionism and failure to recognize the embodied and social setting of human life. Yet the *imago Dei* is reaffirmed in an evolutionary setting as the capacity for symbolic expression and the subsequent ability to represent both theoretically and practically the sense of God. This capacity carries ethical responsibilities for fellow humans, other creatures, and the Earth itself. Yet there is also a shadow side to our existence; our lives are entangled in violence, sin, misfortune, and suffering. These are all inflected and compounded by our human capacities, but so also are possibilities for grace, forgiveness, and hope. In the conclusion to van Huyssteen's study, a narrative of creation and redemption emerges with the claim that theologies rooted in particular traditions can go beyond the province of science by offering their own resources and insights. These have a particularity that is enabled by evolutionary processes but not reducible to them, as, for example, in the skepticism of Pascal Boyer's *Religion Explained*. Religion may be natural, but it is not exhausted by a naturalist explanation. Hence the space is mapped out for a stronger theology than has sometimes been recognized.

What makes this thesis so intriguing is its capacity to engage in a patient and cautious conversation with paleoanthropologists while also advancing some modified theological conclusions that are rooted in classical Hebrew and Christian traditions. These theological claims retain some strong notions about human distinctiveness as intended by God and as conferring on human beings alone the status of covenant partners (my words, not his). What emerges is a tentative exercise in a kind of natural theology. The emergence of human symbolic activity as the site for religious awareness and expression meshes with theological claims about creation, providence, and creatures who reflect the divine image. "For the theologian this interdisciplinary move implies that God used natural history for religion and for religious belief to emerge as a natural phenomenon."[3] We should note here the language of divine intentionality and teleology.

2. Van Huyssteen, *Alone in the World?* 190.
3. Van Huyssteen, *Alone in the World?* 322.

DAVID FERGUSSON

Is Anthropocentrism a Problem?

In its classical expressions, Christian theology has been heavily invested in claims about human distinctiveness. This appears to be a feature of the two creation stories in Genesis and also the brief allusions to the *imago Dei* that follow. Parallels can also be found in Psalm 8 and in the ways in which human beings are frequently summoned and addressed by God in the law, the prophets, and wisdom teaching. This attention to human uniqueness appears to be affirmed by the incarnation. The Word of God becomes enfleshed as a human being, Jesus of Nazareth. This is the focal point of God's dealings not only with *Homo sapiens*, but with the entire cosmos. To this might be added eschatological claims that are traditionally focused on the judgment and final destiny of human beings. Despite the presence of other creatures in the Apocalypse, artistic depictions of the last judgment, such as that of Michelangelo in the Sistine Chapel, are concentrated on the fate of human beings alone. We might then say that the traditional scheme of election, creation, providence, sin, redemption, and eschatological consummation requires some strong assumptions about human uniqueness in the divine economy. Without these, the rug is pulled from under the feet of the theologian.

Nevertheless, claims about human uniqueness face concerted attack in recent literature. "Anthropocentrism" has emerged as a critical term to challenge earlier assumptions that privileged human beings. Several related strands can be detected in such criticisms of the tradition.

First, it is argued that the cognitive capacities of human beings have become isolated and over-determined. This has set humans apart from all other creatures, with the exception of angels. At different times, this has been detrimental to women, the disabled, and nonhuman creatures. These fail a benchmark test by which a true and distinctive humanity is measured, usually in terms of rationality. Such privileging of the cognitive reflects a faulty anthropology. As van Huyssteen argues, the person is embodied, active, and relational and not merely a thinking thing.

The exclusive focus on human beings has also been environmentally hazardous in the ways in which it has presented the world and animals in proprietorial terms. The creation is given to us to regulate, use, and dispose of us as we judge fit. This is arguably a consequence of ontologies in which human beings belong to a different order from other creatures by virtue of their rationality or some other distinctive feature. Even when more benign notions of stewardship or humans as priests of creation are introduced, these are still challenged as overly anthropocentric. Each represents the claim that the world and other creatures cannot be fulfilled except through human guardianship and representation before God. This is hubris on our part.

Finally, assertions of human uniqueness are held to represent a bias by which we confer on our own kind qualities that render us superior to every other species. This speciesism is indefensible, it is argued, and leads to ethical distinctions that result in harmful practices and gross moral distortion. David Clough's recent systematic theology of animals works from within the tradition but argues that its reform is urgently needed in order to eradicate all forms of anthropocentrism.[4] This requires several shifts: a muted and functional account of the *imago Dei*; a stress on incarnation and redemption as creaturely rather than human; and an eschatology for all creation rather than its human occupants only. One can of course find precedents for all of these in the tradition—it is no coincidence that much attention has been devoted recently to Maximus the Confessor—and these are cited in an attempt to overcome Western anthropocentrism. While not erasing all evidence of anthropocentrism, this approach to theological anthropology is at least alert to the problems. Human vocation and destiny cannot be articulated except in relation to the whole creation—these are forever bound together.

Anthropocentrism and Hominid Evolution

In recent literature on the science-religion interface, further support for this criticism of anthropocentrism is evident. On some accounts at least, the scientific evidence indicates that many of the elements belonging to the Upper Paleolithic revolution were already widespread around 80,000 years ago. These include blade technology, bone tools, use of pigment, art, decoration, and long-distance trading.[5] In itself, this revision seems to make little difference to any philosophical or theological claim. If it points to an earlier and greater gradualism rather than a sudden explosion (relative to an evolutionary timeframe), this in itself may be irrelevant to claims for human distinctiveness. What may be more significant though is the claim that many of these characteristics were shared by other hominin groups who coexisted with *Homo sapiens* over many millennia, including those whose genetic material some of us have perpetuated.

Claims for a greater gradualism make the case for shared characteristics

---

4. David L. Clough, *Systemic Theology*, vol. 1, *On Animals* (London: T&T Clark, 2012).
5. See Joshua Moritz, "Human Uniqueness, the Other Hominids, and 'Anthropocentrism of the Gaps' in the Religion and Science Dialogue," *Zygon* 47, no. 1 (2012): 65–96 (84).

more plausible. In the case of four hominin groups, it is argued that we are dealing with different species though with a common lineage shared also by *Homo sapiens*. Each of these species had large brains, bipedal gait, and a developed material, social, and symbolic culture. Of greatest interest has been *Homo neanderthalenis*, who lived alongside *Homo sapiens* for approximately fifteen millennia before their disappearance. Anatomically and genetically, the key features that facilitate speech are found in Neanderthals, including the FOXP2 gene, though Tattersall in his recent study suggests that this is overly simplistic. There is no "silver bullet" that provides a sufficient condition for the emergence of language.[6] Nevertheless, the archaeological evidence suggests a material, social, and symbolic culture similar to that of early human beings, with evidence for empathy, care, and an awareness of death. Even if some of this evidence is thin in places and can be contested, it seems unwise to rule it out of court simply for the sake of maintaining a thesis about human distinctiveness. At the very least, the boundaries between these hominin groups now appear fuzzier. This is illustrated by the oft-quoted comment of Stringer and McKie. If a Neanderthal "could be reincarnated and placed in a New York subway—provided that he were bathed, shaved, and dressed in modern clothing—it is doubtful whether he would attract any more attention than some of its other denizens."[7]

Such claims for hominin forms of life are intended to arrest any simple claim for either anatomical, biological, cognitive, or behavioral uniqueness. Anything that we have done has its adumbration in other species. *Homo sapiens* may have survived while others did not, and proceeded to evolve culturally in quite dramatic ways. But this functionality may not have been on account of any startling difference or superiority to other hominin groups that made one outcome inevitable. Like the Battle of Waterloo—a "damned close run thing" according to Wellington—it could easily have gone the other way with dramatically different outcomes for subsequent world history.

To add to these concerns, we need to factor in two further sets of considerations. The first is more mundane and is the aforementioned claim of Clough and others that most of what has historically been claimed as unique to humans is mirrored in species other than hominins. This includes learning, communication, cooperation, empathy, aesthetic sensibility, and even sinfulness. Particularly among the higher primates, these qualities can be discerned. Characteristic human forms of life thus have their analogues in the capacities

---

6. Ian Tattersall, *Masters of the Planet: The Search for Our Human Origins* (New York: Palgrave Macmillan, 2012), 211–12.

7. Quoted by Moritz, "Human Uniqueness," 88.

and activities of other species. This is confirmed not only by a shared genetic inheritance but also by studies of animal behavior. Appealing to a substantial body of research, Clough writes:

> We now have reason to believe that sheep are capable of recognizing hundreds of faces; crows are able to fashion tools in order to solve problems; chimpanzees exhibit empathy, morality and politics, and can outdo human subjects in numerically based memory tests; dolphins are capable of processing grammar; parrots can differentiate between objects in relation to abstract concepts such as colour and shape; and sperm whales have developed culturally specific modes of life and communication.[8]

The search for a single quality or set of characteristics that isolates human beings and sets them apart in the created order is misplaced, according to this line of argument. The drawing of a line between the human and the nonhuman will have two deleterious consequences. The first is the obvious one that the nonhuman will be relegated to a disposable or instrumental status since it lacks what differentiates the human as of unique worth. The second is less obvious but at least as important. This is the danger of flattening out the difference between other creatures by assigning them to the common status of nonhuman. There is a vast difference between an ant and a chimpanzee, which is important for the ways in which we should treat them. This can be occluded by introducing a binary line in creation whether between human and nonhuman, rational and non-rational, spiritual and material. We may be alone as the last hominin group standing, but our deep affinities with other species together with our ancestral and genetic links to extinct evolutionary relatives place us firmly within the natural world, its haphazard processes and forms of animal life.

Extraterrestrial Possibilities

There is also an extraterrestrial dimension to this debate that has increasingly come to the fore. Human distinctiveness may be relative to the history of evolution on our planet, but what about other planets that populate distant galaxies? What would be the outcome of the discovery of extraterrestrial intelligence in terms of how we view human capacities and their place in the story of creation? Here we enter a more speculative field of inquiry though

---

8. Clough, *On Animals*, 30.

one that attracts increasing attention from scholars. Expert opinion appears divided and it is no doubt rash to hitch one's theological wagon to either side. Simon Conway Morris speaks of humans as inevitable but in a lonely universe.[9] Given the constraints of life on Earth, he regards the appearance of something like our species as highly probable. But these conditions require such a complex concatenation of events that he is inclined to believe it unlikely that they are repeated elsewhere in the cosmos. Others are more confident that, given sufficient time and space, the probability of intelligent life emerging more than once is quite high.

David Wilkinson notes how place and status were closely associated in earlier theological anthropologies. If human beings were situated at the center of the cosmos in a prime position on planet Earth, then their status as uniquely created in the image of God seemed secure. This appeared to privilege humans while also casting doubt on the possibility of unconnected extraterrestrial life-forms. The decentering of our planet in modern science, however, severs any link between status and place. This appeared to be a consequence of early modern science and it coincided with a period of intense reflection on the possibility of extraterrestrial life. If God had created distant stars and planets that conformed to the same laws of physics, then perhaps other life-forms with their own particular histories and relatedness to the divine could be conceived. The distinctiveness of human beings, moreover, was increasingly viewed not in terms of being either alone or at the center of the cosmos but as related in particular ways to the action and purposes of God.[10] This could be affirmed while remaining open to the prospect of other life-forms with their own histories that remain forever unknown to us.

At the very least, it seems unwise to rule out this empirical possibility a priori, on account of theological predispositions about human uniqueness. We might face a future scenario in which theology will have to reckon with a creation in which intelligent forms with their parallel but unrelated stories are also governed by God's providential purpose. Human distinctiveness would then become at most relative to the history of our planet rather than to the entire creation. We would no longer be alone from either a cosmic or a theological perspective, though it is worth recalling that Christian theology since the time of Origen has imagined such possibilities.

---

9. Simon Conway Morris, *Life's Solution: Inevitable Humans in a Lonely Universe* (Cambridge: Cambridge University Press, 2003).

10. David Wilkinson, *Science, Religion and the Search for Extraterrestrial Intelligence* (Oxford: Oxford University Press, 2013), 18–25.

The *Imago Dei* Reconsidered

Most of the theological discussion of these issues revolves around the locus of the *imago Dei*. If it denotes a set of characteristics or activities or biological features that set human beings apart from other creatures, then it appears to be in trouble. Two rejoinders might be possible here. Either we continue to seek out a vital human ingredient that isolates our species from others or we extend the *imago Dei* to include other creatures, perhaps along a graduated spectrum of capacities. But neither of these options is immediately appealing. The quest for a single or aggregate set of distinguishing features seems doomed to face an array of counterexamples from zoology. Any activity will find its correlate and adumbration elsewhere in animal life. Meanwhile, attempts to spread the *imago Dei* through a more capacious inclusion of higher primates and other species will also suffer from the problem of fuzzy boundaries. Such a move is likely to lead to an evacuation of any useful meaning or function for the concept beyond some notion of participation in a divine order that could in principle be extended to all creatures, as well as straining the meaning of the biblical text.

Part of the problem here is an exegetical one. The Bible gives us no clue as to what elements of our anthropological makeup constitute the *imago Dei*—though many theologians have tried very hard to fill this lacuna, often through the assistance of philosophy. Yet this may never have been the intention of the biblical writers in introducing the notion in the first place. In a surprisingly small number of passages in the opening chapters of Genesis, the *imago Dei* is cited more in relation to functional aspects of human life in God's world than with respect to some vital ontological ingredient. It is a kind of marker or bookend for a narrative of divine-human interaction. This more functional approach may lead to some deflation of earlier strategies to explicate the *imago Dei*, but it seems to me the right way now to proceed.

All this is recognized in van Huyssteen's patient exploration of the history of the *imago Dei* in the third chapter of his Gifford Lectures and in his subsequent response to critics.[11] There he offers several considerations that may point beyond the impasse. First, he notes what might be called the "particularity" of the relationship between God and human beings. This is a theme that characterizes not only the crucial *imago* text in Genesis 1:26–27 but also the covenant language that is more pervasive in Scripture. The divine-human

---

11. J. Wentzel van Huyssteen, "Primates, Hominids, and Humans—From Species Specificity to Human Uniqueness? A Response to Barbara J. King, Gregory R. Peterson, Wesley J. Wildman, and Nancy R. Howell," *Zygon* 43, no. 2 (2008): 505–24.

relationship is one that has to be narrated; this is a feature of the contextual and embodied nature of our existence. The knowledge of God and of ourselves unfolds in storied form, particularly in the narratives of Jesus's crucifixion and resurrection. This story is not one that insists on human superiority to other creatures; it includes a call to responsibility, stewardship, and concern for those with whom we share the Earth and a common animal existence. And it recognizes that there are warped and tragic features of human life that do not appear to infect other creatures to anything like the same extent. If there is a human distinctiveness, it is less in terms of a qualitative difference or foreordained isolation. Instead, it inheres in forms of life that have their own particularity but that belong alongside other creatures. "The embodied human person has biologically emerged in history as a center of self-awareness, religious awareness, and moral responsibility."[12] Yet this implies neither the discarding nor relativizing of other life-forms, nor our deep connections with them.

We might describe this as a weak or benign form of anthropocentrism, over against those stronger and more strident versions that have undoubtedly led Christian thought and practice astray at earlier periods. It is matched by Tattersall's strong claims for the sudden and unprecedented emergence of symbolic behavior in evolutionary history, though he admits that the causal explanation for this remains elusive. That there could be such a qualitative leap in any cognitive state is only believable, according to Tattersall, because it has in fact happened once in history and after our biological form was settled.[13] Others favor a longer and more gradualist account, focusing on the evolution in language in Africa from 250,000 years ago. Not surprisingly, this reading is more open to stressing the continuities with other hominin populations, by contrast with a narrative that describes a sudden emergence of new cognitive functions at a late date in Europe. Instead of a single leap during the Upper Paleolithic period in Europe, a more cumulative if uneven process of biological, cultural, and historical change is discerned, in much of which *Homo sapiens* is accompanied by other hominin groups.[14] Nevertheless, whatever the outcome of these scientific debates, the functional particularity of our species remains by virtue of the contingent outcome that it survived while closely related groups perished.

It is difficult to see how theology can avoid some commitment to a weak form of anthropocentrism. But, if we think in terms of human particularity,

---

12. Van Huyssteen, *Alone in the World?* 161.
13. Tattersall, *Masters of the Planet*, 199.
14. See, for example, the essays in Rudolf Botha and Chris Knight, eds., *The Cradle of Language* (Oxford: Oxford University Press, 2009).

then this might offset the overdetermination of uniqueness as either superiority to or exclusion of other forms of life. Creatures have their own particularity, often with no reference to human stewardship or domestication. The book of Job points us in this direction with its closing meditations on the power of the crocodile and the hippopotamus. These reflect God's wisdom—though not in ways that we can understand and, far less, accommodate to our human forms of life.

Yet human particularity does present a complex narrative unlike other creaturely histories. This does not make us better—in some ways, it makes us much worse—nor does it indefinitely guarantee our survival. But it generates the phenomena of religion and theology, relatively recent developments that are novel in the story of evolution, even if we can discern some protological features of religion in other hominin groups. The particularity of our story can be affirmed without implying that we are alone as the object of God's concern or alone as God's creatures in the cosmos, or alone as the single intention of God in making the world out of nothing, or alone as the sole purpose of God in evolutionary processes. All these claims of exclusivity can be abandoned without disturbing the appropriate reading of our particular course in evolutionary history. What evolutionary history reinforces, however, is the extent to which our particularity is embodied and embedded in a wider narrative about creaturely existence. And the account we offer of that particularity will reveal strong links to other life-forms.

Incarnation, Providence, and Eschatology

In this closing section, I consider briefly three further theological features of human particularity—these relate to incarnation, providence, and eschatology.

Within the history of religion is the story of the incarnation of the Word of God as a human being. This can be aligned to the aforementioned weak anthropocentrism. The related claim that the incarnation involves the assumption of creaturely flesh can offset the exclusive exaltation of human beings in the scheme of redemption. As already noted, this is a feature of much Orthodox theology and is part of the current interest in thinkers such as Maximus the Confessor. Ian McFarland points to Maximus's image of creation as a single arch.[15] Though composed of different stones, these together form an architectural whole, each holding the other in place. It is not as individual units but

---

15. Ian A. McFarland, *From Nothing: A Theology of Creation* (Louisville: Westminster John Knox, 2014), 80.

as the arch in its entirety that the creation is redeemed and finally exalted by Christ. His work of redemption reaches out to all material existence and not merely to humankind. Admittedly, human beings form the keystone in the arch for Maximus and are pre-eminent in the way in which they represent the creation. This priestly role is arguably too anthropocentric in its implication that other creatures need us to fulfill their telos. For much of the time, they may be better off without us and apart from us. It is hubris to suggest that the crocodile and the hippopotamus need the priestly mediation of human beings to fulfill their appointed place in creation. Yet in its more extensive scope, this account of redemption points to ways in which the incarnation of the Word of God may determine not only human beings but all material forms.

Nevertheless, the question remains whether there was something fitting (as Thomas Aquinas would have put it) in the Word of God becoming incarnate as a human person rather than as another creature. I cannot see how Christian theology can avoid recourse to a weak anthropocentrism. The claim that Christ's humanity is no more necessary to the work of redemption than his gender is misplaced. It must lead to an impersonal and subconscious account of salvation that no one could know or attest. What would it mean to speak of the second person of the Trinity becoming incarnate as a crocodile or a hippopotamus? We can imagine the Word of God as a woman but hardly as another creature. It would be a Word incarnate that neither taught nor prayed nor healed nor forgave sins.

The incarnation is mediated through human speech, intentional action, and personal encounter, and in the cultural context of first-century Palestinian Judaism. Its reception in the church through its proclamation, sacred texts, and sacramental actions belongs to the particularity of the human story. This does not entail that its significance is human only or that it constitutes an aggrandizement of the human at the expense of other life-forms. On the contrary, as an act of abasement on God's part, the incarnation is an accommodation to our creaturely condition, especially to that one part of the animal world that is most culpable for the disorder and spoiling of creation. As an adaptation on God's part, it is an act of grace rather than a recognition of our elevated status. And yet at the same time, its form and content are inextricably bound to embodied culture, language, and religion. These do not confine its scope to a single species. Yet without these, a hypostatic union could have little if any of its perceived significance, at least as far as we can imagine.

A second type of anxiety surrounds the idea of providence. The intuitive appeal of strong forms of anthropocentrism in Christianity has much to do with the sense that God intended and determined a creation in which human beings would emerge as endowed with the *imago Dei*. A special act of the creation on the sixth day still shapes many of the assumptions that are held by Christian people today, as well as those of the other Abrahamic faiths. The economy of creation and salvation seems to require the appearance of *Homo sapiens* as the bearer of the divine image. Without this commitment, the subsequent story of incarnation and redemption is somehow relativized if not randomized. The parallelism of Adam and Christ requires as its prequel the setting apart of human beings as the addressees of God with their particular endowments, opportunities, and failures. In this way, a strong reading of the *imago* doctrine is essential to the fabric of the Christian faith and this sits uneasily alongside a more messy evolutionary account that sees higher primates and other hominin groups as sharing many of the features that characterize the makeup and behavior of *Homo sapiens*. The scientific story of our emergence seems to fit rather ill with the more deterministic anthropology of the Christian worldview.

It is difficult to articulate this anxiety clearly but it is deeply felt by many students of Christian theology. To respond to it, one might recall Charles Hodge's complaint about Darwinism in Princeton in 1874. For Hodge, Darwinian evolution was quite compatible with the idea of creation but he felt compelled to reject it on account of its diminution of providence. In the randomness that it perceived in the trajectory of life-forms, evolution cannot be held in tandem with the providential faith of Christianity. Hodge argued that in essence it is atheist with respect to the scope it assigns to chance. The best response to this came from those such as Asa Gray at Harvard who argued for a providence that worked in and through the natural processes of the world. An evolving world may not be wholly deterministic but it can be adapted by divine providence in ways that make it a fitting arena for the works of creation and redemption. We can avoid embracing both a deterministic outlook and a deism that merely allows the world to run its course. Providential action does not require a wholly determined universe, willed in every detail from an eternal perspective. An evolving world in which not all outcomes are fixed is open to the presence, force, and movements of God's two hands—the Word and the Spirit. The survival of *Homo sapiens* rather than *Homo neanderthalensis* may be an outcome not of divine intention but of evolutionary accident. But this claim does not exclude a divine adapting of the human story to a particular set of ends, nor does it prevent us from affirming the symbolic and cultural accommodation of the divine Word to our creaturely condition. To this extent, the distinctive claims of much Christian theology may be less closely bound to the strong forms of anthropocentrism and determinism that have characterized our theological traditions and which remain surprisingly persistent. It may be an accident that we are alone, or we may not be alone in terms of the longer run of cosmic history. But neither, I submit, would be fatal to the particularity of our species as this is understood in terms of the divine-human encounter that is presented in the Christian religion. As Asa Gray argued, theologians should not "waste their strength in the obstinate defense of positions which have become unimportant, as well as untenable."[16]

The particularity of our history denotes features that are absent from other creaturely forms of life. In this sense, we may be alone as outliers in the story of life at least on this planet. But in other respects, Christian theology can profitably forsake strong forms of anthropocentrism without abandoning its own core commitments. Finally, what of eschatology? Given that the study of the early history of *Homo sapiens* is characterized by uncertainty and contested interpretations, it seems that pronouncements about our final destiny should be tempered a fortiori by an awareness of the limits of our knowledge. The future is even more impenetrable than the past; the study of our human evolution seems to evoke this realization. Furthermore, many of the eschatological images that have dominated the traditions of Christian thought, for example, the last judgment, have been situated within a worldview that has now been surpassed in relation to the age of the Earth, the span of human history, the size of the cosmos, and its likely duration. In the realm of eschatology, Bultmann's demythologizing imperative remains with us and deserves some revisiting.

Images of resurrection, judgment, and fulfillment may have regulative force in providing a directionality for human speech and action. "In all you do, remember the end of your life, and then you will never sin" (Sir. 7:36). But what is the cognitive status of such recollection? Here the theologian may have recourse to two types of consideration. The first involves the symbolic mapping of eschatological notions in relation to themes of transcendence, forgiveness, redemption, and love that have emerged in the evolution of religion. These are directed spatially, as it were, toward a dimension that is not reducible to the material and the sensory, and temporally toward a future in which they can be better realized than here and now. Alongside this are more particular claims of the Christian faith proceeding from its conviction of the presence of the resurrected Christ, as the fullest expression of the image of God. These claims are future directed and extensive in their scope. Perhaps this is best expressed negatively. The Easter faith cannot project a future that is finally devoid of meaning and fulfillment, nor can its significance be restricted to a portion of embodied creatures only.

What this entails in terms of eschatological specifics must remain hidden

---

16. Asa Gray, "Evolution and Theology," *Darwiniana* (Cambridge, MA: Harvard University Press, 1963), 215.

from us. We can point toward it only with images and symbols rather than delineate it with any measure of clairvoyance. Thomas Reid's epistemology committed human subjects to "living wisely in the darkness."[17] By the providence of God, we are given sufficient intellectual capacity for the business of life here and now, but remain in the dark about a good deal besides. This might be transposed into terms appropriate to the second theological virtue. We can learn "to live hopefully in the darkness." Eschatology has its place, but its limits and function need to be delineated. In important respects, van Huyssteen's Gifford Lectures represent those virtues. They may seem *Christo remoto*, but this is in appearance not reality. In its pursuit of interdisciplinary findings, his work is rightly tentative while striking notes that remain faithful, cheerful, and hopeful.

---

17. See Nicholas Wolterstorff, "God and Darkness in Reid," in *Thomas Reid: Context, Influence, Significance*, ed. Joseph Houston (Edinburgh: Dunedin Academic Press, 2004), 77-102.

13   Postfoundationalism and the Ethic of Responsibility

Duet or Duel?

D. ETIENNE DE VILLIERS

When I spent six months in 2002 doing research at Princeton as a member of the Center of Theological Inquiry I had to present a paper on the research I was doing. My research at that time focused on the views of Christian ethicists who in the aftermath of the publication of Hans Jonas's book *The Imperative of Responsibility* developed their own Christian versions of the ethic of responsibility.[1] J. Wentzel van Huyssteen attended the presentation of my paper. Afterward he, in a manner characteristic of him, expressed words of encouragement to me as his friend and voiced the opinion that there are clear resemblances between my view on the ethic of responsibility and his own view on postfoundationalism. I took a firm resolution at that time to explore the relation between these two views.

During the next decade or more nothing came of my resolution. In the meantime, I have become fascinated with Max Weber's view on the ethic of responsibility, developed by him already in 1919 in a famous speech "Politics as a Vocation." As a result, I have during the past three years been working on a monograph on Weber's ethic. Van Huyssteen has in the meantime shifted his research attention and applied his postfoundationalist approach to the dialogue between theology and primatology, paleontology and evolutionary epistemology, and in 2004 delivered the famous Gifford Lectures, published in 2006 in book format as *Alone in the World? Human Uniqueness in Science and Theology*.

---

1. See the references for full details of three articles in which the findings of this research were published in 2006 and 2007.

It was only after I was invited to contribute to this festschrift in honor of van Huyssteen that I started to seriously explore the relation between his postfoundationalist approach and my own approach to the ethic of responsibility. Without denying that he and I have different research foci, I must say that I have been surprised at the resemblances. I have also realized that I have much to learn from van Huyssteen's postfoundationalist approach in my effort to develop an appropriate contemporary ethic of responsibility. In the end I have also started to wonder whether the ethic of responsibility approach, in both philosophical and Christian ethics, could not be regarded from the side of proponents of postfoundationalism as fulfilling the requirements for an appropriate contemporary approach to normative ethics.

In this chapter, first of all, I provide a brief exposition of relevant aspects of van Huyssteen's postfoundationalist approach and his application of this approach to ethics in some of his recent works. Then a brief exposition of my view on an appropriate contemporary ethic of responsibility follows. Lastly, I point out some resemblances, discuss aspects of van Huyssteen's postfoundationalist approach that could be helpful in the development of a contemporary ethic of responsibility, and argue why proponents of the postfoundationalist approach ought to be sympathetic to the ethic of responsibility approach.

Postfoundationalism and Ethics

In the introduction of his book *The Shaping of Rationality: Interdisciplinarity in Theology and Science* van Huyssteen indicates that he intends to develop an argument for moving "beyond the absolutism of foundationalism and the relativism of nonfoundationalism, to *a postfoundationalist notion of rationality* for which notions of intelligibility and optimal understanding, responsible judgment, progressive problem-solving, and experiential adequacy will be crucial" (van Huyssteen 1999, 12). When reading *The Shaping of Rationality*, but also some of his earlier books such as *Essays in Postfoundationalist Theology* (van Huyssteen 1997) and *Duet or Duel? Theology and Science in a Postmodern World* (van Huyssteen 1998) it soon becomes clear that he shares much of the criticism of postmodernist philosophers and theologians against modernist assumptions about the possibility of arriving at indubitable foundations for knowledge and the singular, universalist nature of rationality. He, however, also disagrees with postmodernist assumptions about the incommensurability of beliefs in different communities and academic disciplines, the incompatibility of a plurality of "rationalities" operating in different life spheres and disciplines, and the impossibility of accounting for beliefs to those who do not share them. He rather accepts that rationality, wherever it operates, has certain common traits and a universal intent, that certain coherence and even overlapping exist between beliefs in different communities and disciplines, and that some form of accounting for beliefs outside the community of those sharing such beliefs should not be avoided. In this way he with his postfoundationalist approach attempts to achieve a satisfactory and convincing "splitting of the difference" between modernity and postmodernity—to use the words of Calvin Schrag (Schrag 1992, 129).

It is not possible, and also not necessary, for me to provide a comprehensive exposition of van Huyssteen's view on postfoundationalism in this chapter. I will rather highlight certain features relevant for my comparison with the ethic of responsibility.

On the postfoundationalist view embodied persons, and not abstract beliefs, should be seen as the locus of rationality. As embodied rational agents we perform rationally by making informed and responsible judgments in very specific personal, communal, but also disciplinary and interdisciplinary contexts. On this view rationality is alive and well in *all* domains of our human lives. Rationality thus, on the one hand, turns out to have many faces. On the other hand, it is precisely in our ability to make informed judgments, based on what we perceive to be good reasons, in all areas of life that we find shared resources of human rationality.[2] In fact, one may say that rationality in all domains of life is about *epistemic responsibility*: the responsibility to pursue clarity, intelligibility, and optimal understanding, as ways to cope with ourselves and our world.[3] In his recent work van Huyssteen has argued that all the many faces of rationality relate to a pretheoretical reasonableness, a "commonsense" rationality that informs and is present in all our everyday goal-directed actions. The origins of a rationality of interdisciplinarity therefore lie not in abstract theories of reason but in the everyday and ordinary means by which we make rational judgments and decisions, that is, the performance of rationality in everyday activities. From these everyday activities we can identify epistemic

---

2. "Rationality thus emerges as not only a protean, complex notion, but also as inextricably linked to having good reasons for making the most responsible choices in concrete situations" (van Huyssteen 1999, 131).

3. Already in *The Shaping of Rationality* van Huyssteen concurs with Nicholas Rescher's view that "intelligibility naturally arises through evolutionary processes because it provides one very effective means of survival. Rationality, in this broadest sense of the word, can therefore be seen as conducive to human survival, and the explanation for our cognitive resources as fundamentally Darwinian" (van Huyssteen 1999, 131; cf. Rescher 1992, 3–4). In *Alone in the World?* he provides further justification for this view in dialogue with evolutionary epistemology (van Huyssteen 2006, 37–39, 79–93).

values like intelligibility, discernment, responsible judgment, and deliberation, which guide us on an intellectual level when we come to responsible theory choice and commitment. It is in the pursuit of these goals and ideals that we become rational persons as we learn the skills of responsible judgment and discernment, and where we articulate the best available reasons we have for making what we believe to be the right choices, those reasons we have for holding on to certain beliefs, and the strong convictions we have for acting in certain ways (van Huyssteen 1999, 145ff., 171; 2006, 1–2).

According to van Huyssteen, "rational accountability and the way this is exemplified by the *rational role of responsible judgment*" is crucially important for defining what he means by a postfoundationalist model of rationality (van Huyssteen 1999, 141). Rationality is about intelligibility and rational accountability, and we need to make responsible judgments precisely in those situations where we lack sufficient foundations or rules to determine our decisions and actions. Although judgment in this postfoundationalist context is never rule-governed, it also is not arbitrary, but is always based on quite specific information from very particular shared contexts (van Huyssteen 1999, 143–44). The idea of responsible judgment is, in his opinion, enhanced by Schrag's notion of the performance of the *fitting response* (van Huyssteen 1999, 147; Schrag 1994, 76; 1997, 98, 107–8). The performance of a fitting response, as a proper rational judgment, is not to be confused with simple accommodation, but rather involves discernment, evaluation, and critical judgment. The reason why this does not imply epistemic relativism is that our criteria, as resources for critical evaluation and grounds for critique, are *conditioned* by historically specific contexts, but they are not completely *determined* by such contexts. Although conditioned by its context, human thought is nonetheless able to transcend the particularities of its social and historical contexts. As a result, we are able to critique our traditions while standing in them.

This points to van Huyssteen's conclusion that the model of postfoundationalist rationality means at least the following: "while we always operate in terms of concepts and criteria that appeared in a particular culture, we are nonetheless able to transcend our specific contexts and reach out to more intersubjective levels of discussion, without necessarily falling back into any of modernity's typically totalizing metanarratives" (van Huyssteen 1999, 140). He also makes use of two other notions to support this conclusion, namely, the notions of *transversal rationality* and *wide reflective equilibrium*. The term "transversal rationality," as used by Schrag, refers to a lying across, an extending over, a linking together, and an intersecting of various forms of discourse, modes of thought, and action. Transversal rationality thus emerges as a place in time and space where our multiple beliefs and practices, our habits of thought and attitudes, our prejudices and assessments, converge. "What is at stake in this notion of transversal rationality is to discover, or reveal, the shared resources of human rationality precisely in our very pluralist, diverse assemblages of beliefs and practices, and then to locate the claims of reason in the overlaps of rationality between groups, discourses, or reasoning strategies" (van Huyssteen 1999, 136; cf. 2006, 23).

Van Huyssteen also calls the tentative and shared understanding that we achieve through communicating across boundaries, from context to context, from one form of life to another, from one discipline to another, a "wide reflective equilibrium"—a term originally used by John Rawls in his *A Theory of Justice* (Rawls 1971, 20–21) that has found wide acceptance among scholars (van Huyssteen 1999, 277–78; 2006, 31–32). In this "wide reflective equilibrium" we finally find the safe but fragile public space we have been searching for: a space of shuttling back and forth between deep personal convictions and the principles resulting from responsible interpersonal judgments. The postfoundationalist view on rationality, however, also accepts a certain genuine religious, theological, and scientific pluralism, as allowance ought to be made for conversations between people from different traditions or cultural domains who may enter the conversation for very different reasons and who may in fact disagree about many issues. On account of this legitimate diversity we must accept that also, and maybe especially, in theology, complete cognitive agreement or consensus is unattainable. Van Huyssteen therefore agrees with Nicholas Rescher (1993, 3–4) that *dissensus tolerance* will prove to be a positive and constructive part of the theology and science dialogue. In the theology and science dialogue, the most sensible posture is to accept the reality of cognitive pluralism within a shared public realm of discourse, to accept the unavailability of complete consensus, and to work at creating an optimally coherent, communal framework or wide reflective equilibrium of thought (van Huyssteen 1999, 279–80; 2006, 33).

Having worked out a comprehensive theory of human rationality from a postfoundationalist perspective in especially *The Shaping of Rationality*, van Huyssteen in *Alone in the World?* used the opportunity to apply his postfoundationalist approach to the interdisciplinary dialogue between theology and sciences like primatology, paleoanthropology, and the neurosciences on the distinctiveness of human beings, but also to demonstrate the fit of his postfoundationalist view on rationality with the findings of these evolutionary sciences on the emergence of human rationality. One of his conclusions is that with the emergence of self-consciousness and the ability to use language, not only human rationality, but also a moral awareness and a natural propensity for religious belief took shape. In two later articles he, in the same vein, explored the relation between evolutionary ethics and Christian ethics: "Ethics and Christology—Rediscovering Jesus in Evolutionary History" (van Huyssteen 2008, 492–506) and "Should Theology Take Evolutionary Ethics Seriously? A Conversation with Hannah Arendt and Maxine Sheets-Johnstone" (van Huyssteen 2011). One of the main aims with these articles is to demonstrate how "genuine evolutionary ethics" (van Huyssteen 2011, 463) supports his postfoundationalist view of rationality also when it comes to ethics. His arguments are especially directed against two foundationalist versions of normative ethics: sociobiological ethics, which attempts to provide an evolutionary justification of moral codes, and versions of Christian ethics that depart from the view that absolute moral principles are given in God's revelation.

Van Huyssteen starts his exposition with the assertion: "Thanks to contemporary primatology, paleoanthropology, and also the neurosciences, we know today that the embodied human mind has a capacity for moral awareness, an innate sense for 'right' and 'wrong' that is embedded in evolutionary history." In his article on the views of Hannah Arendt and Maxine Sheets-Johnstone he demonstrates that a genuine evolutionary ethics makes explicit the epistemological structures of caring while at the same time it anchors those structures in the corporeal facts of evolutionary life and thus enables the living of a moral life. "In this sense one could say that the starting point of evolutionary ethics is the insight that morality has a biological, evolutionary basis" (van Huyssteen 2011, 463).

Although it cannot be denied that certain traits of our moral behavior may be derived from archaic behavioral patterns and from the intense drive to survive (van Huyssteen 2011, 464), evolutionary epistemology also reveals that we humans can indeed take on cognitive goals and moral ideals that cannot be explained or justified in terms of survival-promotion or reproductive advantage only (van Huyssteen 2008, 494). What now becomes clear is that ethical behavior is indeed a product of our biological evolution, but that this fact by itself does not entail any normative assertions: from the fact that morality has developed we cannot conclude that any particular trait of human behavior is good or bad (right or wrong). "We should therefore be careful to always distinguish between the *evolution of moral awareness*, and the *evolutionary justification of moral codes*. Evolutionary ethics in this second sense has a bad history and has resulted in ideologies like Social Darwinism" (van Huyssteen 2008, 495). Evolutionary explanations of human moral awareness cannot explain our moral judgments, or justify the truth-claims of any of our moral judgments. Why and how we make moral judgments can only be explained on the level of cultural evolution, and by taking into account the historical embeddedness of our moral codes in religious and political conventions (van Huyssteen 2011, 465).

Van Huyssteen, however, also takes foundationalist Christian ethicists to task. First of all, those who think that tracing a belief's evolutionary origins automatically undermines its epistemic warrant, in his opinion, commit the so-called genetic fallacy (van Huyssteen 2011, 464). Second, they are wrong in not accepting the evidence that our moral awareness has evolved, and that such evidence implies that our moral codes may not be fixed forever as unchangeable entities (van Huyssteen 2008, 495). In an evolutionary approach to ethics the status of the belief that ethical norms are unchangeable and derivable from a set of eternal divine principles will rightly be challenged, and the creation of moral norms, in an a posteriori sense (to use Kantian terms), will be found to lie on a constructive, cultural level. This means that humans in principle are free to change their moral codes, but also that they carry great responsibility for themselves—a responsibility that cannot and should not be easily delegated to "objective divine moral codes." In this sense even the Ten Commandments and Jesus's love command are historically revealed as a posteriori moral, even when they have acquired over time the authority of biblical truth. This also frees us from the foundationalist need for an idea of absolute moral truth: our idea of truth is relative to our historical and social contexts, and their histories, and only a coherentist, postfoundationalist approach can sufficiently explain this.[4] What we find here, then, is an open view of evolution: basic patterns of our behavior depend on, and have been developed through, our evolutionary past. But this is *not* a deterministic view because we humans have the responsibility to make our own decisions on what count as the norms and limits to our behavior. We are, therefore, constrained, but not determined by our evolutionary past (van Huyssteen 2011, 464).

---

4. Van Huyssteen concurs with David Lahti's claim that he has found an intriguing and creative example for the adaptive role of moral evolution through cultural transmission in Jesus's Sermon on the Mount (Matthew 5–7). Lahti (2004, 140–43) argues that Jesus used his Sermon on the Mount as a way of challenging the traditional Hebrew understanding of "culture," ancestry, and "in-group" by turning away from notions of kin-relatedness to a new notion of relatedness based on shared values instead. The moral reform of Jesus as portrayed in the Sermon on the Mount thus reflects an adaptive adjustment to a new social environment (the Roman Empire, with its dominant Hellenistic culture), and lifts up a deliberate contrast between new norms being presented and the norms that would have been familiar to the Jewish people (van Huyssteen 2008, 504–5).

The Ethic of Responsibility

I have developed my view on an ethic of responsibility in critical dialogue with the German sociologist Max Weber's view of such an ethic.[5] He was the first to coin the term "ethic of responsibility" in his famous speech "Politics as a Vocation" in 1919. In this speech he proposed the ethic of responsibility as an ethics more suitable for late-modernity than the "ethic of conviction." He called the ethic he proposed the ethic of *responsibility* because it is fundamentally qualified by responsibility in two ways. It expresses Weber's conviction that in late-modernity (1) the charismatic political leader has a special responsibility to uphold ethics in the social sphere of politics, and by doing that also influence the ethical course of the nation, and (2) the ethical approach adopted in politics should be new and different in that it should be executed in a comprehensively responsible manner. According to this ethic, the political leader should exhibit prospective responsibility first of all by *selecting the ultimate values* that would form the basis of his political decisions *responsibly* and, second, *making ethical decisions* in politics *responsibly*.

Weber introduced the ethic of responsibility mainly to counter the prevalent threats to the ethical dimension of human existence in particularly politics, while not ignoring irreversible developments in modernity as the proponents of the ethic of conviction did, but fully acknowledging them. In our time the ethical dimension of human existence is also, if not more, under threat as a result of further developments in late-modernity. For one, the two threats to the ethical dimension that formed the backdrop of his ethic of responsibility proposal are still present today. Although the process of state and company bureaucratization has turned out differently than Weber anticipated, the process of rationalization, of which it is part, has in many respects diminished the freedom of individuals to live an ethical life, and especially to exert an ethical influence on broader societal developments (cf. Müller 2007, 141). To mention just one example: as a result of the imperialist influence of economic values such as materialism, consumerism, and competition on family and personal life, individuals find it difficult to even in their private lives live consistently in accordance with the ethical values of their religion or view of life. As Michael Sandel has convincingly demonstrated in his book *What Money Can't Buy*, purely economic considerations today increasingly also tend to replace moral

---

5. I gave lectures on my view of an appropriate contemporary ethic of responsibility at the Radboud University Nijmegen and the Free University Amsterdam, respectively, in May and June 2014. For a brief exposition of my view see "In Search of an Appropriate Contemporary Approach in Christian Ethics: Max Weber's Ethic of Responsibility as Resource," *HTS Theological Studies* 71, no. 1 (2015), Art. #2948, 8 pages.

considerations in public practices (Sandel 2012, 21–24). And as a result of not only the diminishing influence of religion in the lives of people, but also of cultural globalization, the diversity of ethical belief systems in modern societies is even more pronounced than at the time of Weber. It is not only that we find increasing numbers of groups professing different views of life in society, but also that within one religious denomination, even within one family, people have different views with regard to ethical issues. This makes cooperation within personal relationships, institutions, or broader society difficult when it comes to joint initiatives based on ethical values.

Attempts of present-day religious fundamentalists to counter these threats show a strong resemblance to the inadequate attempt of the proponents of an ethic of conviction to do so in Weber's time. They try to salvage the adherence of their group members to their "thick" ethical beliefs in a globalized world by completely ignoring irreversible global societal changes, isolating their members from the influence of contemporary cultural developments, and reverting to authoritarian practices of times gone by. At the core of this response to modernization lies the same sort of ethical absolutism that Weber found wanting in his time and in our time can only cause havoc in the world society.

Without denigrating the efforts of philosophers to develop first-level normative theories that could help us to find and justify universally valid moral principles, we have to conclude that such efforts have not been very effective in stemming the tide of the threat to the ethical dimension of life. It is not only a case of philosophers still not being able to agree on foundational moral principles and their justification, but also that many philosophers with a postmodernist approach are convinced that it is in any case impossible to provide rational justification of universally valid moral principles. More important, people still today do not turn to the first-level normative ethical theories of philosophers for ethical guidance in their everyday life. From my experience of teaching professional ethics to engineering students for a number of years it has become clear that the mere exposure of such students to the different options regarding normative ethical theories does not really help them to effectively deal with the ethical issues in their profession. The main problem is that such students do not come to the classroom with minds that are tabula rasa with regard to ethics. They already have their personal ethical convictions and are not desperately in need of moral principles. As they are already convinced about the rightness of their ethical convictions, they are also not in need of the justification of moral principles by means of a particular normative ethical theory. What they are primarily in need of is ethical guidance on *how* they could in a meaningful way relate their own moral convictions to the ethical problems of their profession. In other words, what they need is second-level normative ethical guidance on how they should deal with their own ethical convictions in a professional context and how they should make use of them in deciding on ethical issues in this context.

To put it in a more general way: what we need today, even more than efforts in first-level normative ethics to identify rationally justified ethical principles, is a second-level normative ethics that could provide guidelines on the best approach in dealing with the existing diversity of ethical values and intra-systemic values and on the measures that should be taken to ensure effective ethical decision-making. We urgently need such an ethics not only for the reasons I have already mentioned, but also to counter a serious new threat that still had not been identified in Weber's time, namely, the threat to all life on Earth as a result of the negative impact of the rapid development of modern technology. Such a threat can only be effectively countered on the basis of sufficient consensus on goals, norms, and decision-making processes.

Although Weber provides us in his ethic of responsibility with a helpful model of such a second-level normative ethical approach we have to take into account that his approach is ridden with a number of serious problems we should try to avoid in our own efforts to develop a contemporary ethic of responsibility. I mention three of these problems:

1. *Weber's formal concept of ethics makes allowance for a strong nation-state as ultimate value of the ethic of responsibility*

I do not believe, as someone such as Peter Breiner (1996, 199) does, that Weber's ethic of responsibility is intrinsically linked to his nationalism. However, what one can say is that Weber in the way he constructs the ethic of responsibility, creates room for the political leader acting in accordance with this ethic to elevate an internationally strong German nation to ultimate value. In the light of the extremely negative experience of the consequences of German and other examples of nationalism since 1919 this is problematic. Providing safeguards for avoiding the elevation of a group entity such as a particular nation, race, or gender group to ultimate value and providing it with ethical status should be a prerequisite for any present-day attempt to formulate an ethic of responsibility.

In my opinion the only way to provide such safeguards is to take leave of Weber's formal understanding of ethics purely in terms of the moral agent's subjective attitude of subordination and devotion to an ultimate value. It is for him this attitude that renders the actions of the moral agent "ethical," no matter what the content of the concerned ultimate value is. In my opinion it should today be regarded as irresponsible to call the actions that follow from the devotion to whatever chosen ultimate value "ethical." Part of the task of a contemporary ethic of responsibility is therefore to seek an understanding of ethics that would entail limits to the choice of ultimate values and to calling actions "ethical."

It might be fruitful to take as point of departure two concepts of morality or ethics that are still influential today: a wider concept relating to "the good" and a narrower one relating to "the right" or "the just" (see Bayertz 2004, 37–39; Putman 2002, 93–94). In my opinion the need for both "thick" group-specific moral guidelines (related to what is regarded as "the good" in a religious or cultural group) and "thin" general moral norms (related to what is acknowledged as "the just" in inter-cultural and inter-religious relationships and institutions, secular societies, and the global society) should be recognized in a contemporary ethic of responsibility. Even if we conduct our personal lives mostly in accordance with the thick ethical values of our respective views of life—and rightly so—we also need consensus or agreement on at least a minimal morality that would enable us to live peacefully together in relationships, groups, organizations, and societies characterized by cultural, religious, and moral diversity. In my opinion part of what is involved in responsibly dealing with values today is not only to strive in different social circles to negotiate agreements or covenants on shared moral values and commit oneself to such agreements, but also to self-critically examine the thick ethical values of one's own group in terms of such agreements. It also involves the active promotion of a growing moral consensus in all the social circles one is involved with to strengthen the basis for joint ethical initiatives, for example, with regard to the protection of the natural environment (see De Villiers 2014, 161–74).

2. *The designation of the charismatic political leader as the sole agent of the ethic of responsibility is elitist and authoritarian and one-sidedly political*

Weber's designation of the charismatic political leader as sole agent of the ethic of responsibility is based on several presuppositions: social cohesion in society is dependent on a single dominant and uniform ethical value system; not only religious leaders, but also leaders from social spheres other than politics, are not in a position in modern societies to exert enough influence to help bring about the acceptance of such a dominant ethical value system; ordinary citizens are too caught up in and preconditioned by processes of instrumental rationalization to initiate any effective "from the bottom up" moral renewal of society; and, lastly, in a pluralist society such a dominant ethical value system could only be achieved by a political leader who uses his demagogic skills and political power to ensure general acceptance by the citizens.

From a present-day perspective all of these presuppositions should be criticized or at least strongly qualified. We realize today that the establishment of one dominant and uniform "thick" ethical value system, whether it relates to the ethical values of a particular religious or cultural group or the personal ethical values of a particular political leader, is not viable in modern societies, at least not in ways that are democratic and non-authoritarian. Instead, we have settled for the democratic recognition of a set of "thin" moral values and human rights to regulate the public sphere.[6] We are not so pessimistic anymore of the role leaders from other social spheres than politics, for example, in education and the media, and even citizens, individually or in organizations, can play in the ethical renewal of society. And we are especially wary of authoritarian political leaders who use their demagogic skills to sway the so-called masses. We therefore would not—and also should not—support an ethic of responsibility that has the charismatic political leader as sole agent. An appropriate contemporary ethic of responsibility would call on all individuals to fulfill their responsibility regarding morality in society in all spheres of life.

3. *Weber overemphasizes the autonomy of social spheres and the contradictory nature of value systems*

Weber provides a sketch of the differentiation process of social spheres in which these spheres increasingly become separated and insulated from one another, each with its own distinctive value system. He does not make allowance for much interpenetration of the different social spheres by the values of other spheres (see Münch 1980, 18–53; 1991, 309–35). As traditional Western moral values are closely associated with the Christian religion they are, according to him, also increasingly excluded from other social spheres as secularization proceeds. Sociologists today make much more allowance for the interpenetration of social spheres by values from other spheres. It is also more strongly accepted that moral values can and ought to be recognized in the different social spheres, especially when these moral values express the moral consensus in the particular social sphere or society. Using the terminology of the sociologist Peter Beyer one may even attribute to at least a certain set of globally recognized moral values special status by asserting that they are "all-encompassing" in nature (Beyer 2001, 266). This, however, means that

---

6. Michael Walzer first introduced the distinction between "thick" and "thin" morality in his book *Thick and Thin: Moral Argument at Home and Abroad*. He utilizes the term "thick" to point to a kind of moral argument that is "richly referential, culturally resonant, locked into a locally established symbolic system or network of meanings." "Thin" is simply the contrasting term (Walzer 1994, xi).

Weber's assertion regarding the strong contradictory nature of value systems also has to be questioned. Even the ethical value systems of competing views of life to some extent overlap. Otherwise it would not have been possible for religions—and secular views of life—to take over ethical values from one another as all of them have done in the course of history. It is also not true that the value systems of different social spheres are always or in all respects in conflict with one another. For the most part the values they consist of are rather complementary to one another. Otherwise it would not have been possible for a good politician to also be a good artist, or a good Christian or Muslim to also be a good businessperson.

In the light of my criticism of Weber's version of the ethic of responsibility I want to plead for the recognition of a second-level ethic of responsibility that would retain the main foci of his version, namely, taking responsibility for maintaining the ethical dimension in all spheres of life and doing ethics responsibly (i.e., responsibly dealing with values and making ethical decisions in accordance with prevalent circumstances), but avoid the problematic aspects of his version. Such an ethic of responsibility should be conceived in such a way that it applies not only to politics but also to other social spheres and personal life. It should make provision not only for the responsibility for ethics of political leaders, but also for those of other role-players in politics and in other social spheres, as well as the responsibility of individuals involved in personal relationships. It should not proceed from the assumption that all value systems are in conflict with one another, but rather from the assumption that they are for the most part compatible and complementary. It should not grant ethical status to values that would lead to conduct that is harmful to human beings and the natural environment. And finally it should distinguish between comprehensive sets of ethical values that are part of views of life and a minimal morality on which consensus has been reached and grant to the minimal morality relative priority over the ethical values provided by views of life in public life.

Postfoundationalism and the Ethic of Responsibility

The brief expositions of van Huyssteen's postfoundational view on rationality and my own view on the ethic or responsibility, in my opinion, clearly show that the relation between the two has to be described in terms of a duet rather than a duel. Although the foci of the two research projects are different there is also tangency (or should I rather say "transversality") with regard to assumptions and intent. In this last part of my chapter I first of all point out some of the resemblances. Second, I discuss ways in which the postfoundationalist approach of van Huyssteen can enrich the attempt to formulate an appropriate contemporary ethic of responsibility. And third, I would like to argue the case that proponents of the postfoundationalist approach ought to support the search for an appropriate contemporary ethic of responsibility.

Resemblances

I mention four ways in which postfoundationalism resembles the ethic of responsibility:

1. *Postfoundationalism and the ethic of responsibility share insights from constructive postmodern thinking*

Van Huyssteen makes no secret of the fact that his postfoundationalist approach shares many of the insights of what he calls "constructive postmodernism." The most important one—clearly expressed in the word "postfoundationalist"—is that it is not possible to find indubitable foundations for our knowledge-claims as proponents of modernism believe. In his two articles on ethics, discussed in this chapter, he also explicitly denies that indubitable foundations for normative ethics can be found in the nature of human beings as it evolved in the evolutionary process, as sociobiology and Social Darwinism claim, or in objective divine moral codes as fundamentalist versions of Christian ethics claim. According to van Huyssteen, the reason for this—and here he falls back on a second insight of postmodernism—is that our idea of truth is relative to our historical and social contexts. This is also true with regard to moral beliefs on right and wrong attitudes and actions we personally hold. They are derived from the traditions of the communities we belong to. This embeddedness of our moral codes in religious and political conventions is, in van Huyssteen's opinion, also not contradicted by the evolutionary origins of morality as only the origin of our "moral awareness" can be traced to evolution, but not the origin of our moral codes. He also relies on a third insight of postmodernism when he introduces the notion of the *fitting response* as an integral part of his postfoundationalist approach, namely, the insight that close attuning to the concrete context or situation is of the essence in judgment, including ethical judgment.

To assert that Max Weber in formulating the first version of the ethic of responsibility relied on insights from postmodernism would be blatantly anachronistic. It would also ignore the elitist and authoritarian assumptions on which his exposition of the ethic of responsibility is based, which clearly sets him apart from postmodernism. Nonetheless, it would not go too far to assert that in some other respects he, like other contemporary representatives of the so-called *via media* like Wilhelm Dilthey, Henry Sidgwick, William James, and John Dewey, could be regarded as a forerunner of postmodernism.[7] Like these other philosophers he did not believe that science could fill the gap left by religion in providing meaning and ethical guidance to life (Kloppenburg 1986, 5). Like them he was not convinced by the two major normative ethical theories of the Enlightenment, the deontological theory of Kant and the utilitarian theory of Bentham and Mill. Kant's ethics was found to be too formalistic and abstract to provide ethical guidance in real life and the hedonism and psychological egoism of utilitarianism an inadequate foundation for ethics (see Kloppenburg 1986, 119, 121–22). His oft-repeated assertion that the choice of ultimate values is purely a matter of faith also points to the fact that he rejected the view that rationally justified universal moral principles should be the point of departure in ethical deliberation. He rather believed that in choosing the ultimate values of our personal ethics we have to fall back on the worldviews (*Weltanschauungen*) we were socialized in. Added to that, one of the main differences between the ethic of conviction and the ethic of responsibility—as sketched by Weber—is the extent to which the concrete situation is taken seriously. Whereas the ethic of conviction in an abstract manner applies given moral values to the situation without taking into account the consequences of the actions decided on, the ethic of responsibility carefully analyzes the concrete situation to decide on the applicable moral and functional values and to carefully estimate the foreseeable consequences of options for action, before deciding.

In my own efforts to formulate an appropriate contemporary ethic of responsibility I concur with van Huyssteen's view, in a less clear and nuanced way already present with Weber, that no universally valid normative foundation for ethics can be found, that our ethical beliefs are embedded in our views of life, which in turn are influenced by the traditions of the communities we have been socialized in, and that careful analysis of the concrete situation of ethical decision making is of the essence, both with regard to the responsible choice of applicable values and the optimal estimation of future consequences.

2. *Postfoundationalism and the ethic of responsibility both reject certain assumptions of deconstructive postmodernism*

[7]. For a comprehensive study on the resemblances between the philosophers of the so-called *via media* (including Weber), see Kloppenburg (1986).

By denying the incommensurability of rationalities operating in different life spheres and academic disciplines and of beliefs held in these life spheres and disciplines van Huyssteen in his postfoundational approach clearly transcends deconstructive postmodernism. He is rather convinced that a certain transversality with regard to rationality operating in different life spheres and disciplines can be pointed out. In fact, he believes that in all rationality a certain universal intent is at work. As a result, we are able to transcend our specific contexts and to reach out to more intersubjective levels of discussion and to achieve a certain wide reflective equilibrium.

In this respect Max Weber would have been quite comfortable in the company of the deconstructive postmodernists. He was adamant about the unbridgeable conflict between value systems and values, especially when it comes to the choice of ultimate values. Although he found agreement on ethical values in politics indispensable for achieving strong social cohesion in the nation, he was convinced that the only way that it could be achieved was through the charismatic political leader successfully promoting his own ultimate values and political goals and convincing the voters of them.

As I have already indicated, Weber's view of the conflictive nature of values cannot, in my opinion, be the point of departure in the search for an appropriate contemporary ethic of responsibility. Of course, we cannot but start out from the "thick" moral beliefs we have made our own in interaction with the traditions of the communities we have been socialized in. There is also nothing wrong with systematizing and applying our "thick" moral beliefs, for example, in Christian ethics if we are Christian believers. But there is also no reason to believe that we are caught up in our "thick" moral beliefs and that it is impossible to find any moral agreement outside our primary communities. In fact, if we want to be rational and contribute to peaceful coexistence and effective cooperation in pluralist societies, we also have to take on the responsibility to be involved in efforts in different social contexts to achieve optimal agreement on the values that should guide our attitudes and actions (see De Villiers 2014).

3. *Postfoundationalism and the ethic of responsibility agree that moral codes are not absolute and fixed, but need to be adapted*

In criticizing the view of foundational Christian ethicists who believe that an objective and absolute divine moral code is given through revelation van Huyssteen does not shy away from calling them wrong in not accepting the evidence that our moral awareness has evolved, and the implication that our moral codes may not be fixed forever as unchangeable entities. In his opinion we should rather accept that human beings have since their evolvement as rational beings adapted their moral codes in the effort to survive in ever changing circumstances.

I fully concur with van Huyssteen's view in this regard when it comes to the formulation of an appropriate contemporary ethic of responsibility. Although Weber was not convinced by the efforts of the prevalent normative ethical theories of his time to provide universal moral values, he still clung to the traditional view that the ultimate values we make our own are absolute and ought to be served and obeyed unconditionally. I rather agree with van Huyssteen that although each tradition has certain core beliefs and values with a higher authority and permanency than other beliefs and values on the fringes of the tradition, it does not mean that they may never be adapted. Especially when drastic changes in circumstances take place a certain reinterpretation and reprioritization of core beliefs and values are needed in order to ensure the survival not only of the members of the community involved, but of the tradition itself and the integrity of the community adhering to the tradition.

4. *Postfoundationalism and the ethic of responsibility agree that human beings have a responsibility to ensure the viability of ethical living*

Van Huyssteen explicitly states: "humans in principle are free to change their moral codes, but this also means that humans carry great responsibility for themselves and that this responsibility cannot and should not be easily delegated to 'objective divine moral codes'" (van Huyssteen 2011, 464). I take it that what he has in mind is not only the responsibility to live ethically by adhering to existing moral codes, but also the responsibility to adapt moral codes and even to formulate new moral virtues and norms when the circumstances demand it.

Again, I fully concur with van Huyssteen's view in this regard. From the perspective of the ethic of responsibility I would like to add that the circumstances in late-modernity not only demand the constant reevaluation and reformulation of existing moral codes, but also effective efforts to maintain the ethical dimension in all spheres in life. In the late phase of modernity the ethical dimension of life itself is under threat, among others, as a result of the tendency to exclude ethical considerations in independent social spheres like politics, the economy, science, and technology; the creeping imperialism of the functional economic values of consumerist capitalism in other spheres of life; and a rampant pluralism and individualism. All individuals, groups, organizations, companies, and governments thus also have the fundamental responsibility to ensure the effective maintenance of the ethical dimension of life.

What the Ethic of Responsibility Can Learn from Postfoundationalism

Van Huyssteen has convinced me that rational accountability, the willingness to provide reasons for values chosen and decisions taken, should be an integral part of the ethic of responsibility. If I understand him correctly, rational accountability does not only mean providing reasons to others who belong to the same community and share the same beliefs, but also to those in other communities who do not share one's religious, cultural beliefs. It also includes the willingness to not just blindly follow traditional beliefs, but to critically examine them in the light of changed circumstances and insights gained in communicating with members of other religious and cultural communities. So we can state:

For ethical deliberation to be counted as rational it has to account for values taken as point of departure and actions decided on

In my opinion some of the important implications of incorporating rational accountability in the ethic of responsibility are the following:

1. When accounting for one's choice of values and action decisions to members of other communities one should use reasons that they can accept, or at least understand. This does not mean that we can and should find reasons that are universally evident. It does mean, however, that we should strive to provide reasons that would be acceptable or understandable for the particular persons we are communicating with. This can, inter alia, be done by pointing out the overlapping consensus with regard to the different sets of values we adhere to or with regard to the action decisions we come to. It can also be done by pointing out the mutual beneficial consequences of our action decisions for all involved in a particular situation. And it can be done by demonstrating that our action decisions comply with moral values or human rights we have already agreed on through negotiation.

2. Accounting for one's choice of values and action decisions also means to critically examine them. One should ask questions such as: do they lead to consequences that are negative to some people, and do they comply with agreed-on moral values or human rights? If some persons or groups are negatively affected or one's action decisions violate moral agreements we should seriously consider adapting or changing our personal values.

3. Accounting should, however, also be done over against members of one's own community. It is not only the case that one should be willing to provide proof to them that our action decisions comply with the values shared

within the community. It is also the case that we should convince them that it is necessary to seek moral agreement with other communities in local, national, and global contexts and that it is necessary to adhere in the public sphere to the "thin" moral values agreed on. In the South African context, for example, far too little is done in certain church denominations to motivate their members to support and adhere to the bill of rights contained in the constitution of South Africa. It would go a far way if churches were willing to provide good reasons, based on "thick" Christian beliefs, why members should support and adhere to "thin" human rights.

Why Postfoundationalists Should Support the Ethic of Responsibility

I mention two major reasons why proponents of foundationalism should support the ethic of responsibility:

1. *The central postfoundational notion of epistemic responsibility implies on the level of normative ethics an ethic of responsibility approach*

According to van Huyssteen, "epistemic responsibility" entails the responsibility to pursue clarity, intelligibility, and optimal understanding as ways to cope with ourselves and our world. For me this implies on the level of normative ethics that we should adopt a normative ethical approach that is intelligently attuned to the particular circumstances in which we have to live ethically, or to put it differently, in which we attempt to cope in a truly ethical manner. In late-modernity we live in a situation not only of rapid technological change that poses a threat to all future life on Earth, but of rampant pluralism. In such a situation the ethical dimension of life is constantly under threat. The appropriate approach to normative ethics would be, first of all, one of taking responsibility for *effectively maintaining the ethical dimension* in all spheres of life. It would, second, be one expecting of us to take responsibility for *choosing the values* on which our ethical decisions are based *in a contextually appropriate manner*. Among others, this would mean choosing the mix of moral and functional values that fits the concrete situation and deciding on whether it would be appropriate in the situation to base our action decisions on our own "thick" moral beliefs, or rather on shared "thin" moral beliefs. It would, third, be one expecting of us *to make ethical decisions in an appropriate manner*, doing justice to the present situation and taking into account foreseeable future consequences of options for action—especially taking into account the impact different options for action would have on the sustainability and quality of life in future. And lastly, it would be one expecting of us to take responsibility for, on the one hand, the maintenance, as well as the suitable adaptation of the "thick" moral beliefs we adhere to on account of socialization, but on the other hand also for negotiating optimal moral agreement on values and actions in the different social spheres we are involved with to ensure cooperation on an ethical basis. As all of these normative ethical implications of the central postfoundational notion of "responsible judgment" are what the ethic of responsibility stands for, support of this approach to normative ethics by proponents of postfoundationalism seems to be advisable.

2. *The postfoundational acceptance of both the inevitability of departing from beliefs based on the traditions of communities and the need to transcend such beliefs in search of transversality, points to the second-level normative ethical approach of the ethic of responsibility*

On a normative ethical level the flip side of van Huyssteen's postfoundational rejection of indubitable foundations that could provide universal rational justification for moral principles is that the normative status of the "thick" moral beliefs of, for example, religious communities are fully restored. Not only may Christians, for example, rightfully depart from their "thick" moral beliefs when they have to decide on ethical issues, but they may rightfully claim that they first of all find justification for their own personal moral beliefs and their ethical decisions based on these beliefs within the Christian community. In fact, I think that one may conclude that from a postfoundational perspective particular communities, whose members share moral beliefs based on certain religious, cultural, or philosophical traditions, are the prime social spaces for the justification of first-level moral principles—that is, moral principles that prescribe specific actions as right, desirable, or appropriate. As postfoundationalism also emphasizes the need to give account for one's moral beliefs and ethical decisions in fora outside one's own primary communities, this does not exclude the obligation to provide optimal justification of one's moral beliefs and ethical decisions to whoever asks for it. We have already discussed some of the ways in which accounting of one's moral beliefs and ethical decisions can take place. Such accounting or justification would, however, always be incomplete or partial, as there are also aspects of "thick" moral beliefs that cannot be fully shared by those outside our primary communities. The extent to which "thick" moral beliefs can be justified over against members outside primary communities, of course, also depends on how effective processes of finding and formulating "overlapping consensus" and negotiating moral agreements or covenants had been in the past.

In my opinion this two-level justification of moral beliefs advocated by postfoundationalism provides support for my view that the ethic of responsibility should be regarded as a second-level normative ethical theory. The ethic of responsibility does not claim to provide justification of first-level moral principles, as it is accepted that the justification of such principles takes place, first of all, and in the most complete manner, in communities, which are composed of people sharing the same religious, cultural, or philosophical beliefs. The ethic of responsibility as second-level normative ethical theory does, however, provide guidance on *how* we should regard our own "thick" moral beliefs (as not absolute, but fallible and with only relative priority in that the validity of functional values is also recognized), on *how* we should regard the "thick" moral beliefs of outside communities (with tolerance, and as possible sources of moral wisdom), and on *how* we should go about when taking ethical decisions (thoroughly analyzing the concrete situation, taking into account foreseeable consequences of options for action, and testing our own opinion on what ought to be done by consulting other role-players).[8] It also points to our responsibility to seek "overlapping consensus" and negotiate moral covenants to enable wider justification of moral beliefs and ethical decisions and stronger cooperation in ethically desirable projects.

Conclusion

I hope that it has become clear that van Huyssteen was right when he made the remark more than a decade ago that there are resemblances between his view on postfoundationalism and my view on the ethic of responsibility. To me, at least, it has become crystal clear. What has also become clear to me is that I have much to learn from postfoundationalism for my research project on an appropriate contemporary ethic of responsibility. In fact, I believe that such an ethic can count as an expression of postfoundational intentions on a normative ethical level.

References

Bayertz, K. 2004. *Warum überhaupt moralisch sein?* Munich: Beck.
Beyer, P. 2001. The global environment as a religious issue: a sociological analy-

---

8. For the case I have made out that the German Christian ethicist Eduard Tödt has already done invaluable work in developing an ethic of responsibility approach to ethical decision-making, see my contribution to the festschrift for Dirk Smit (de Villiers 2011; cf. Tödt 1977, 1979, 1988a, 1988b).

sis. In *Religion and Social Transformations*, edited by D. Herbert. Aldershot: Ashgate.

Breiner, P. 1996. *Max Weber and Democratic Politics*. Ithaca, NY: Cornell University Press.

De Villiers, D. E. 2006. Prospects of a Christian ethics of responsibility (part 1): an assessment of an American version. *Verbum et Ecclesia* 27(2):468–87.

De Villiers, D. E. 2007a. Perspektiven einer christlichen Verantwortungsethik. *Zeitschrift für Evangelische Ethik* 51(1):8–23.

De Villiers, D. E. 2007b. Prospects of a Christian ethics of responsibility (part 2): an assessment of three German versions. *Verbum et Ecclesia* 28(1):88–109.

De Villiers, D. E. 2011. An ethics of responsibility reading of Eduard Tödt's theory on the formation of moral judgements. In *Living Theology: Essays Presented to Dirk J. Smit on His Sixtieth Birthday*, edited by L. Hansen, N. Koopman, and R. Vosloo. Wellington: Bible Media.

De Villiers, D. E. 2014. Christian and cosmopolitan ethics: friends or foes? In *Cosmopolitanism, Religion and the Public Sphere*, edited by S. Kim and M. Rovisco. Abingdon: Routledge.

De Villiers, D. E. 2015. In search of an appropriate contemporary approach in Christian ethics: Max Weber's ethic of responsibility as resource. *HTS Theological Studies* 71(1), Art. #2948, 8 pages. http://dx.doi.org/10.4102/hts.v71i1.2948.

Kloppenburg, J. T. 1986. *Uncertain Victory: Social Democracy and Progressivism in European and American Thought, 1870–1920*. New York: Oxford University Press.

Lahti, D. 2004. "You have heard . . . but I tell you . . .": a test of the adaptive significance of moral evolution. In *Evolution and Ethics: Human Morality in Biological and Religious Perspective*, edited by P. Clayton and J. Schloss. Grand Rapids: Eerdmans.

Müller, H.-P. 2007. *Max Weber: Eine Einführung in sein Werk*. Cologne: Böhlau.

Münch, R. 1980. Über Parsons to Weber: von der Theorie der Rationalisierung zur Theorie der Interpenetration. *Zeitschrift für Soziologie* 1:18–53.

Münch, R. 1991. *Dialektik der Kommunikationsgesellschaft*. Frankfurt am Main: Suhrkamp.

Putman, H. 2002. Must we choose between patriotism and universal reason? In *For Love of Justice*, edited by M. Nussbaum. Boston: Beacon.

Rawls, J. 1971. *A Theory of Justice*. Cambridge, MA: Harvard University Press.

Rescher, N. 1992. *A System of Pragmatic Idealism*. Vol. 1. Princeton: Princeton University Press.

Rescher, N. 1993. *Pluralism: Against the Demand for Consensus*. Oxford: Clarendon.

Sandel, M. J. 2012. *What Money Can't Buy: The Moral Limits of the Market*. London: Penguin.
Schrag, C. O. 1992. *The Resources of Rationality: A Response to the Postmodern Challenge*. Bloomington: Indiana University Press.
Schrag, C. O. 1994. Transversal rationality. In *The Question of Hermeneutics*, edited by T. J. Stapleton. Dordrecht: Kluwer.
Schrag, C. O. 1997. *The Self after Postmodernity*. New Haven: Yale University Press.
Tödt, H. E. 1977. Versuch zu einer Theorie ethischer Urteilsfindung. *Zeitschrift für Evangelische Ethik* 21:81–93.
Tödt, H. E. 1979. Kriterien evangelisch-ethischer Urteilsfindung: Grundsätzliche Überlegungen angesichts der Stellungnahmen der Kirchen zu einem Kernkraftwerk in Wyhl am Oberhein. In idem, *Der Spielraum des Menschen: Theologische Orientierung in den Umstellungskrisen der modernen Welt*. Gütersloh: Verlagshaus Gerd Mohn.
Tödt, H. E. 1988a. Versuch einer ethischen Theorie sittlicher Urteilsfindung. In idem, *Perspektiven theologischer Ethik*. Munich: Chr. Kaiser Verlag.
Tödt, H. E. 1988b. Die Zeitmodi in ihrer Bedeutung für die sittliche Urteilsfindung. In idem, *Perspektiven theologischer Ethik*. Munich: Chr. Kaiser Verlag.
Van Huyssteen, J. W. 1997. *Essays in Postfoundational Theology*. Grand Rapids: Eerdmans.
Van Huyssteen, J. W. 1998. *Duet or Duel? Theology and Science in a Postmodern World*. London: SCM.
Van Huyssteen, J. W. 1999. *The Shaping of Rationality: Toward Interdisciplinarity in Theology and Science*. Grand Rapids: Eerdmans.
Van Huyssteen, J. W. 2006. *Alone in the World? Human Uniqueness in Science and Theology*. Grand Rapids: Eerdmans.
Van Huyssteen, J. W. 2008. Ethics and Christology—rediscovering Jesus in evolutionary history. *Verbum et Ecclesia* 29(2):492–506.
Van Huyssteen, J. W. 2011. Should theology take evolutionary ethics seriously? A conversation with Hannah Arendt and Maxine Sheets-Johnstone. In *Living Theology: Essays Presented to Dirk J. Smit on His Sixtieth Birthday*, edited by L. Hansen, N. Koopman, and R. Vosloo. Wellington: Bible Media.
Walzer, M. 1994. *Thick and Thin: Moral Argument at Home and Abroad*. Notre Dame: University of Notre Dame Press.
Weber, M. 1994. The profession and vocation of politics. In *Weber: Political Writings*, edited by P. Lassmann and R. Speirs, 306–69. Cambridge: Cambridge University Press.

14 Living with Strangers?

On Constructing Ethical Discourses

DIRK J. SMIT

In late August 1983 J. Wentzel van Huyssteen invited me to Port Elizabeth for public lectures on "the need behind the writing of confessional documents."[1] The theme only sounds abstract and innocent. In reality, the times were filled with tension and controversy and the topic was at the heart of intense conflict in church and society in South Africa. The lecture halls were packed. The tension was tangible. Public media were present and reported extensively in the daily press on what seemed to be a sophisticated question of Reformed doctrine.

The background was the adoption of the *Belhar Confession* by the Dutch Reformed Mission Church just months before, rejecting the theological justification of the ideology and politics of apartheid in the name of the gospel, claiming that the church of Jesus Christ is called to hear, trust, and obey a message of unity, reconciliation, and justice.[2]

---

1. J. Wentzel van Huyssteen served as professor and chair of the Department of Religious Studies (earlier Biblical Studies) at the University of Port Elizabeth (UPE; now the Nelson Mandela Metropolitan University, NMMU) from 1972 to 1992, when he was appointed as the first James I. McCord Professor of Theology and Science at Princeton Seminary. At the UPE he initiated a Study Group for Theology that often organized events, lecture series, and short courses for students, ministers, and the general public.

2. On the history, content, and reception of the *Belhar Confession*, see the award-winning theological work by Piet J. Naudé, van Huyssteen's successor in Port Elizabeth, *Neither Calendar Nor Clock: Perspectives on the Belhar Confession* (Grand Rapids: Eerdmans, 2010), as well as the more historical study by Piet J. Naudé and Johan G. Botha, *Good News to Confess: The Belhar Confession and the Road to Acceptance* (Wellington: Bible Media, 2010).

The issue at stake was how to live together in a deeply divided society. Apartheid literally meant separateness. It enforced the strictest of political, social, economic, cultural, and personal separation of people based on race—and thereby produced alienation, distrust, and bitterness, but also exclusion, marginalization, oppression, and injustice. People were deliberately and forcefully further estranged from one another, after centuries of colonization, inequality, cultural differences, and conflict—in church *and* society. The envisaged dream of the apartheid imagination was the exact opposite of notions of unity, reconciliation, and justice. Borders, boundaries, and separation bring peace, was the apartheid credo.[3]

For many, this was both a moral and a political crisis. The ecumenical church resisted in diverse and many ways. True to their own tradition, black Reformed Christians finally declared a *status confessionis*—claiming that the gospel itself was at stake when the biblical message was used to justify such a social and political system—and confessed their own faith anew in Jesus Christ as Lord, over against what they regarded as a false gospel.[4]

One day after these lectures the United Democratic Front (UDF) was formed in Cape Town, the mass democratic movement that would eventually contribute so much within South Africa to the downfall of apartheid, while the liberation movements were banned and exiled.[5] The question concerning

---

3. For more general background on apartheid, on the struggle in church and society, and on the challenges for theology at the time, see from the abundant literature available the conference proceedings by Robert Vosloo and Mary-Anne Plaatjies-Van Huffel, eds., *Reformed Churches in South Africa and the Struggle for Justice: Remembering 1960-1990* (Stellenbosch: Sun, 2013); the very helpful volume of essays by Johann Kinghorn, ed., *Die NG Kerk en Apartheid* (Johannesburg: Macmillan, 1986); the widely read historical account by John W. de Gruchy with Steve de Gruchy, *The Church Struggle in South Africa* (Minneapolis: Fortress, 2005, 25th anniversary ed., revised and expanded); the theological analysis of John W. de Gruchy, *Liberating Reformed Theology: A South African Contribution to an Ecumenical Debate* (Grand Rapids: Eerdmans, 1991), his 1990 Warfield Lectures at Princeton Seminary; and for brief surveys, Dirk J. Smit, "South Africa," in *Encyclopedia of Politics and Religion*, vol. 2, ed. Robert Wuthnow (Washington: Congressional Quarterly, 2007), 840-44; "Apartheid," in *Religion Past and Present*, vol. 1 (Leiden: Brill), 293-95.

4. For the historical context and the meaning of *status confessionis*, see Gerhard D. Cloete and Dirk J. Smit, eds., *A Moment of Truth: The Confession of the Dutch Reformed Mission Church* (Grand Rapids: Eerdmans, 1984); also the doctoral dissertation from Lund by Lennart Henriksson, *A Journey with a Status Confessionis* (Swedish Institute of Missionary Research, 2010).

5. I vividly remember how we informally discussed the crisis in the country and the launch of the UDF the following day during our private conversations during that visit. For historical information and theological reflection, see the criticism of the present government in the light of the spirituality of the struggle, including the intentions and role of the UDF,

the need for new confessional documents only seemed innocent and abstract. For many, human life and, indeed, humanity itself, being human, was at stake.

In January 1984, just a few months later, van Huyssteen gave a plenary paper during the annual conference of the Theological Society of South Africa at the University of the Western Cape. The overall theme of the conference was the *Belhar Confession*. The struggle in church and society was intensifying. The theme of his paper was "Confession as Model of Thought—Theology between Insight and Experience."[6] He argued for a model of theology that would fulfill three criteria. It should take real problems seriously, it should be problem-solving, and it should be constructive and strive for progress.[7] The problems calling for such theological reflection, he explained, could be cognitive (or conceptual) but also empirical (or contextual, namely, ethical or existential).[8]

Van Huyssteen mentioned ethics only in passing, but it became the focus of John de Gruchy's official response and it dominated the ensuing discussion. The real problems and struggles facing South Africa at the time, de Gruchy claimed, were matters of "life and death" and therefore his question

---

in Allan A. Boesak, *The Tenderness of Conscience: African Renaissance and the Spirituality of Politics* (Stellenbosch: Sun, 2005); for Boesak's own role and the texts of his speeches at the time, see his memoirs, *Running with Horses: Reflections of an Accidental Politician* (Cape Town: Joho, 2009).

6. He spoke in Afrikaans, "Belydenis as Denkmodel—'n Teologie tussen Insig en Ervaring," in *Teologie—Belydenis—Politiek. Theology—Confession—Politics*, ed. Dirk J. Smit (Bellville: UWC, 1985), 7–28.

7. At the time, he was already involved in the research that would result in his widely acclaimed and influential publication, the second volume in a new series on research methodology by the national Human Sciences Research Council (HSRC), entitled *Teologie as Kritiese Geloofsverantwoording: Teorievorming in die Sistematiese Teologie* (Pretoria: RGN, 1986). An English translation was later published by Eerdmans as *Theology and the Justification of Faith: Constructing Theories in Systematic Theology* (Grand Rapids: Eerdmans, 1989) and probably contributed a great deal to North American readers becoming acquainted with him and his work—after all, translation is an important tool to make strangers more familiar to us, especially where "the gift of the stranger" is not available through foreign-language learning itself. See David I. Smith and Barbara Carvill, *The Gift of the Stranger: Faith, Hospitality, and Foreign Language Learning* (Grand Rapids: Eerdmans, 2000). In 1987 van Huyssteen was the first recipient of the newly established Andrew Murray Prize for Theological Literature for this study. It was also the catalyst behind the national and interdisciplinary conference hosted by the HSRC on paradigms and progress in theology. For the proceedings, see Johann Mouton, Andries G. van Aarde, and Willem S. Vorster, eds., *Paradigms and Progress in Theology* (Pretoria: HSRC, 1989).

8. Van Huyssteen, "Denkmodel," especially 14–23; he would develop the same thoughts in much more detail in the final chapter, "Criteria for a Critical-Realist Model of Rationality in Systematic Theology" in *Theology and the Justification of Faith*, 143–97.

was whether van Huyssteen's model of theological rationality would allow for believers and churches to speak concretely, directly, passionately, and with conviction—in other words, confessing their faith in Jesus Christ—in such historical moments.[9] Van Huyssteen found the question "extremely difficult" because he regarded such moments of confession as possible in theory but problematic in practice.[10]

Refiguring Moral Codes?

Initially, over the following years, ethical problems—including social, political, and moral questions—were seldom central to any of van Huyssteen's writings,[11] although morality was of course always implicit in his focus on questions concerning rationality, humanity, and being human.[12] Gradually, however, that would change and questions of humans also being *moral* beings increasingly came into focus as well.[13] Recently, in his contribution to a festschrift for my

---

9. For de Gruchy's response and a summary of the discussion, see *Theology—Confession—Politics*, 28–33.

10. Van Huyssteen, "Denkmodel," 33.

11. There was hardly any mention of social, political, and ethical issues in his own papers and publications and his doctoral students did not work on ethical issues. In some of his earlier essays and in several of his letters in the official church magazine he dealt with the use of Scripture and with appeals to the authority of Scripture, and at the time these public debates obviously had political and ethical backgrounds and implications, but it was not his concern to focus directly on these ethical implications. See Kenneth A. Reynhout's account of this initial phase, based on an interview with van Huyssteen himself, "The Evolution of van Huyssteen's Model of Rationality," in *The Evolution of Rationality: Interdisciplinary Essays in Honor of J. Wentzel van Huyssteen*, ed. LeRon Shults (Grand Rapids: Eerdmans, 2006), 2–7. For South African readers these ethical implications were indeed glaringly present and important. It was not surprising that the contributions to this festschrift on the occasion of his sixty-fifth birthday therefore also did not address ethical issues explicitly, with the only exception being the essay by George Newlands (on public theology and experiences of truth and reconciliation in South Africa) and indirectly those of Keith Ward (on reason, including aesthetics and ethics as well) and Christopher Southgate (on ecological concerns).

12. The earlier phases of his development have been well documented by Reynhout ("Evolution"), who in 2006 (correctly) divides the process between a first phase (of critical realism as a rationality model for theology, 1970 to 1989), a second phase (of interdisciplinary shaping of rationality in a postmodern context, 1990 to 1999), and a third phase (of interest in the evolutionary origins of rationality and human uniqueness, since 2000). Since 2006, continuing this third phase, questions concerning morality and ethics have now come to the fore in very deliberate and explicit ways.

13. His first published essay dealing with ethics was "Ethics and Christology—Rediscovering Jesus in Evolutionary History," *Essays in Honour of Conrad Wethmar, Verbum et Ecclesia* 29,

sixtieth birthday, he dealt explicitly with the question whether and how evolutionary ethics could contribute to theology.[14]

Evolution by natural selection, he says, can indeed explain our tendency to think in normative terms, that is, our innate sense of moral awareness, but it cannot replace our own moral judgments and our challenge to argue and justify the truth-claims of our moral convictions and actions.[15] Why and how we make our own moral judgments today—in the face of our own moral challenges—can only be argued in terms of our cultural evolution. We face the task of making intelligent moral judgments in the light of our own historical embeddedness within the moral codes of our religious, philosophical, social, and political conventions.[16]

---

no. 2 (2008): 492–506; a more extended version was published as "Should We Do What Jesus Did?" in *Christology and Ethics*, ed. LeRon Shults and Brent Waters (Grand Rapids: Eerdmans, 2010), 149–78; then "Should Theology Take Evolutionary Ethics Seriously? A Conversation with Hannah Arendt and Maxine Sheets-Johnstone," in *Living Theology: Essays Presented to Dirk J. Smit on His Sixtieth Birthday*, ed. Len Hansen, Nico Koopman, and Robert Vosloo (Wellington: Bible Media, 2011), 454–67; and more recently "Construction and Constraint: What Do the Laws of Nature Teach Us about Moral Laws?" in *Concepts of Law in the Sciences, Legal Studies, and Theology*, ed. Michael Welker and Gregor Etzelmüller (Tübingen: Mohr Siebeck, 2013), 319–38; as well as an essay with ethical implications, "From Empathy to Embodied Faith? Interdisciplinary Perspectives on the Evolution of Religion," in *Evolution, Religion, and Cognitive Science*, ed. Fraser Watts and Leon P. Turner (Oxford: Oxford University Press, 2014), 132–51. He is now increasingly drawing out the important moral implications of his interdisciplinary work during all these past years, and specifically of his more recent interest in evolutionary theory, paleoanthropology, and humanization in general. Still, of course, he never deals with any contemporary moral challenges or ethical problems, and he never engages in ethical argumentation or ethical discernment either. His own academic focus is on arguing *why* and *how* it could be justified to engage in ethical discourse and even more, *why* and *how* it could even be justified to appeal in this process to "what Jesus did": "Might there be evolutionary and theological reasons why what Jesus said and did are normative for us today as we construct our moral codes and ethical norms?" ("Ethics and Christology," 493). As part of his own scholarship, accordingly, he never pays any attention himself to *what* Jesus actually did and *how* that could actually be appropriated in contemporary ethical discourses (or even less why and how that could function for the whole of the Christian perspective on the normative content of the biblical message)—he obviously leaves that task for others, those actually engaged in moral construction and ethical argumentation. For an overview of contemporary literature for different ways to construe the implications of Christology for ethics, see my "'Jesus' und 'Politik,'" *Evangelische Theologie* 74, no. 1 (2014): 57–70.

14. Van Huyssteen, "Should Theology Take Evolutionary Ethics Seriously?" 454–67.

15. He often describes precisely what he understands under the term, for example, in its briefest form: "When I use the term evolutionary ethics I use it to characterise specifically the view that morality has evolved and there are clear pointers to the biological roots of moral behaviour in pre-human history" ("Should Theology Take Evolutionary Ethics Seriously?" 463).

16. "Should Theology Take Evolutionary Ethics Seriously?" 464–66.

For him, one could perhaps say, constructing moral codes today as part of our cultural evolution is an ongoing task, a project, "an interpretive enterprise, shaped experientially through our embeddedness in communities and cultures."[17] For him, moral codes and ethical judgments today therefore build on "our innate sense of moral awareness," on the human "tendency to think in normative terms," which developed through evolution by natural selection, but they remain an ongoing challenge and task in the light of our real, contemporary problems and challenges.[18]

The task is therefore never-ending; we are always constructing, reconstructing, rebuilding, refashioning our moral codes, with their visions, values, and virtues, with their crises and their judgements, their challenges to discern, to act, and to embody, in the light of new, contextual, and existential problems. We most certainly stand within our own communities and traditions, and self-critically and constructively make use of their riches and resources since they form "the boundaries of our habitation," but they do not function as final answers or a-historical authorities, but as part of who we have become.[19]

One could probably argue that Van Huyssteen is now applying his early insights on the task of theology explicitly to the ethical task. His claim remains the same. Ethics is an ongoing historical project—rooted in natural evolution but fulfilled by way of cultural evolution—in which human beings refigure and construct moral codes in the face of ever-changing and real problems, both conceptual and empirical, which also means contextual and existential.

---

17. "Should Theology Take Evolutionary Ethics Seriously?" 466.

18. "Should Theology Take Evolutionary Ethics Seriously?" 465.

19. Over the years he often approvingly made use of Delwin Brown's *Boundaries of Our Habitation: Tradition and Theological Construction* (Albany: State University of New York Press, 1994). He makes a similar point by positively using Kevin Hector's interpretations of Schleiermacher, stressing the interpretive nature of our ethical constructions: "What we have here, then, are socially mediated, experientially interpreted norms filtered through the history of the church and mediating to us *aposteriori* moral codes and normative judgments.... This critical, postfoundationalist evaluation of the tradition as we stand in the tradition, is our only fallible way of judging whether or not certain beliefs and actions count as really following (Jesus), as qualifying to do 'what Jesus did.' In this way belief and interpretation fuse in the ongoing task of Christology and Ethics.... It necessarily implies that our current beliefs, actions, and judgments, are also constrained, but ultimately not determined, by previous networks of interpretations. Learning to follow Jesus, learning 'to do what Jesus did,' is to learn to find the trajectory on which others preceded us in interpretation and action by internalising what we interpretatively recognise as normative for our current contexts. *This ongoing, never-ending interpretive task ... can inspire us with moral direction even as it fills us with epistemic humility*" ("Ethics and Christology," 503–4; my italics); also "What Makes Us Human? The Interdisciplinary Challenge to Theological Anthropology and Christology," *Toronto Journal of Theology* 26, no. 2 (2010): 143–60.

Raising a Moral Voice?

In this process of constructing moral codes reacting to real problems, language plays a key role. Again and again van Huyssteen emphasizes the importance of the development of increasingly complex forms of symbolic communication, including language, for becoming human and for being human.[20] Integral to our being moral selves is our ability to converse about being human, integral to our life together is our ability to discern, to imagine, and to communicate about our common life; integral to our construction of moral codes is our ability to find languages to talk about our moral codes.

In this van Huyssteen is obviously not alone in the world. Irrespective of whether ethicists point to the importance of political emotions, everyday practices, shared visions, common interests, personal needs, subconscious desires, modeling of virtues, cultivating of conscience, inherited prejudices, feelings of honor and shame, even the banality of everyday routine and ordinary custom, in short, the many ways in which we share in moral codes without always being consciously aware of these codes, the importance of communication, also in most of these processes, cannot be ignored or denied.[21]

---

20. He has been interested in the evolutionary development of human symbolic and communicative abilities, including art and language, for many years; see chapters 4 and especially 5 of his Gifford Lectures, *Alone in the World? Human Uniqueness in Science and Theology* (Grand Rapids: Eerdmans, 2006), also reflecting on what he calls material pointers to the presence of the symbolic human mind in early human prehistory in the cave paintings of southwest France and the Basque country; and more recently several lectures and published essays based on his involvement in a six-year interdisciplinary project at the Çatalhöyük Neolithic site in Anatolia, Turkey: "Coding the Nonvisible: Epistemic Limitations and Understanding Symbolic Behaviour at Çatalhöyük," in *Religion in the Emergence of Civilization*, ed. Ian Hodder (Cambridge: Cambridge University Press, 2010), 99–121; also "When Were We Persons? Why Hominid Evolution Holds the Key to Embodied Personhood," *Neue Zeitschrift für Systematische Theologie und Religionsphilosophie* 52 (2011): 329–49, on the evolution of music and language.

21. From the enormous literature on morality and values, see the very informative sociological studies by Hans Joas, like van Huyssteen a Research Fellow at the Stellenbosch Institute for Advanced Study (STIAS), including *The Genesis of Values* (Chicago: University of Chicago Press, 2001), in which he deals with the theories of major philosophers and sociologists of the twentieth century, as well as *The Sacredness of the Person: A New Genealogy of Human Rights* (Washington: Georgetown University Press, 2014), in which he deals, among others, with the way in which the value of human dignity has developed from negative experiences; but also his own action-theory in *The Creativity of Action* (Chicago: University of Chicago Press, 1996); his study on war and values, translated as *War and Modernity* (Cambridge: Polity, 2003); his collected essays entitled *Do We Need Religion? On the Experience of Self-Transcendence* (Boulder, CO: Paradigm, 2008) and his recently translated *Faith as an Option* (Stanford: Stanford University Press, 2014) in which he deals, among others, with the myth that secularization leads to a loss of morality and values; and also the edited volume on whether the formation

Scholarship that focuses on the formation of moral selves—whether via informal processes like discipline and self-regulation or socialization and internalization, or via formal processes like the deliberate focus on stages of moral development, the rational clarification of values, the psychological focus on emotions and morality, or attention to education and character formation—therefore also affirms the importance of communication in all these different phases and procedures.[22]

Jürgen Habermas, against the background of his development of a theory of communicative action over several decades, formulates the need very clearly, claiming that "an appropriate naturalistic conception of cultural evolution must do justice to both the intersubjective constitution of the mind and the normative character of its rule-guided operations."[23] The challenge for

---

of values needs religion, *Braucht Werterziehung Religion?* (Göttingen: Wallstein, 2007). Also instructive in this regard is the work of Kwame Appiah, *The Honor Code: How Moral Revolutions Happen* (New York: Norton, 2010), for his different views on how moral codes and practices are transformed.

22. From the enormous literature on moral formation, see the influential work by the Dutch Catholic moral philosopher Johannes A. van der Ven, *Formation of the Moral Self* (Grand Rapids: Eerdmans, 1998).

23. Jürgen Habermas, *Between Naturalism and Religion: Philosophical Essays* (Cambridge: Polity, 2010), 1. Both Habermas's work on the public square and his theory of communicative action often play a role in contemporary discussions on public theology—also in the Beyers Naudé Center for Public Theology at Stellenbosch University. Van Huyssteen understood his own work from early on as public theology and he often reflected on the nature of and challenges for his own interdisciplinary and postfoundational public theology, in fact, long before the Beyers Naudé Center was founded. See his "Pluralism and Interdisciplinarity: In Search of Theology's Public Voice," *American Journal of Theology and Philosophy* 22, no. 1 (January 2001): 65–87, but this paper had already been read as early as 1998, in Bad Boll and St. Petersburg, and again in Pretoria in 1999; later also "The Philosophical Roots of Public Theology," in *A Faithful Witness: Essays in Honour of Malan Nel*, ed. Hennie J. C. Pieterse and Christo H. Thesnaar (Wellington: Bible Media, 2008); as well as "Interdisciplinary Theology as Public Theology," *Acta Theologica* (2011): Suppl. 14, 95–111. This aspect of his work was honored by George Newlands in "Public Theology in Postfoundational Tradition," *Evolution of Rationality*, 394–417; see also Delwin Brown's response, "Public Theology, Academic Theology: J. Wentzel van Huyssteen and the Nature of Theological Rationality," *American Journal of Theology and Philosophy* 22, no. 1 (January 2001): 88–101; as well as by Gys Loubser, in his unpublished doctoral dissertation at Stellenbosch entitled "A Public Theologian: A Critical Study of J. Wentzel van Huyssteen's Postfoundationalist Facilitation of Interdisciplinarity" (2012). For an overview of different meanings of the term "public theology," including a reference to van Huyssteen's understanding, see my "The Paradigm of Public Theology—Origins and Development," in *Contextuality and Intercontextuality in Public Theology*, ed. Heinrich Bedford-Strohm, Florian Höhne, and Tobias Reitmeier, Theologie in der Öffentlichkeit 4 (Münster: Lit Verlag, 2013), 11–23.

communicative action is obviously still ongoing, combining into our ongoing intersubjective search for normativity.²⁴

Put differently, being human means that we are involved in *The Ethical Project*, in the title of Philip Kitcher's instructive study.²⁵ According to him, morality challenges us with three tasks, namely, to understand the evolutionary genealogy of our moral sensibilities, to consider the metaethical presuppositions of our moral sensibilities, and to develop a normative stance in the face of moral challenges. The naturalistic pragmatism that he proposes, Kitcher explains, accordingly "counsels societies to work hard at training their members to follow precepts they deem most important."²⁶

Finding moral language to speak about present-day real moral challenges, which includes finding ways of informing, persuading, and motivating members of our societies to actually practice the normative convictions of our moral codes (and if necessary to overcome the "forms of blindness bequeathed

---

24. Over the past years Habermas increasingly also engaged theological ethicists in discussions of morality and values, in this intersubjective search for normativity; see his widely followed conversation with then still Cardinal Ratzinger, *The Dialectics of Secularization* (San Francisco: Ignatius, 2005); as well as the ensuing consultation published as *An Awareness of What Is Missing: Faith and Reason in a Post-Secular Age* (Cambridge: Polity, 2010).

25. Philip Kitcher, *The Ethical Project* (Cambridge, MA: Harvard University Press, 2011); for a similar approach, also from a naturalistic viewpoint, but argued in a different way, that will probably also soon become widely influential, see Mark Johnson, *Morality for Humans: Ethical Understanding from the Perspective of Cognitive Science* (Chicago: University of Chicago Press, 2014). In a way that reminds one of van Huyssteen's own (early) interlocutors, Johnson also argues for an alternative approach to what he describes as "moral absolutism." "Moral absolutism is immoral, in that it shuts down precisely the kind of empirically informed ethical inquiry we most need for our lives. Moreover, moral absolutism is dramatically at odds with what we are learning about the nature of moral motivation, thinking, and appraisal. Our best alternative view—one that is supported by a large and growing body of scientific research—reveals that moral deliberation is a process of interwoven imagination, emotion, and reasoning" (26–27).

26. Kitcher, *The Ethical Project*, 102. A central part of that is actually to overcome the resistance hard-wired into us, in his words, "Human evolutionary history may have bequeathed to us forms of blindness that make reliable compliance with some prescriptions difficult." For van Huyssteen this is also an extremely important insight, and one that is based on evolutionary epistemology itself: "Evolutionary epistemology also reveals that we humans can indeed take on cognitive goals and moral ideals that cannot be explained or justified in terms of survival-promotion or reproductive advantage only . . . Capacities . . . have emerged in our biological history [that] cannot be explained only in terms of biological/evolutionary terms any more. In this sense we clearly transcend our biological origins and do have the ability to transcend what is given to us both in biology and culture" ("Ethics and Christology," 494).

to us"), is therefore central to the ongoing human ethical project[27]—although finding moral language is obviously not enough.[28]

Rendering Altruism?

One particularly difficult contextual and existential problem could serve as illustration—namely, the difficulty of living together with strangers and therefore of constructing moral codes, finding moral languages that could speak adequately to these real challenges.

Evolutionary ethicists seem to agree that the development of altruism—at least superficially—seems to present an intellectual challenge to those who claim that it all happened based on natural selection. Why would beings intent on survival seem to care for others? Would one not rather expect competition and conflict? Since Darwin himself, evolutionary thinkers accordingly felt challenged to explain the natural development of a moral sensitivity[29] and

---

27. Finding adequate ways of speaking ethically, finding suitable forms of "pro-social preaching," in the words of Christopher Boehm, *Moral Origins: The Evolution of Virtue, Altruism, and Shame* (New York: Basic Books, 2012), is in itself a complicated task. In theological ethics the church is sometimes called "a community of moral discourse," but this description raises the complex question regarding the nature of this moral discourse. The final chapter of the study on *Nature and Altering It* (Grand Rapids: Eerdmans, 2010) by Allen Verhey, the late ethicist from Duke, is called "From Narrative to Practices, Prophecy, Wisdom, Analysis, and Policy," 119-33. This is an obvious attempt to refer to several modes of moral language that all seem necessary and important—and modes addressed both to insiders and to the public. His choice of modes of moral discourse is again influenced by the earlier work of the ethicist from Chicago, James Gustafson, who already distinguished between different modes when he analyzed the ethical documents produced by the Ecumenical Movement; see also his Stob Lecture at Calvin College ("Varieties of Moral Discourse: Prophetic, Narrative, Ethical, and Policy," in *Seeking Understanding: The Stob Lectures, 1986-1998* [Grand Rapids: Eerdmans, 2001], 46-76). This typology of moral discourses has also often been used by several South African ethicists and friends of van Huyssteen, including Etienne de Villiers and Nico Koopman.

28. In an extremely important analysis of apartheid ethics, Johan Kinghorn ("Die etiek van gun-aan-ander," in *Die NG Kerk en Apartheid*, 169-75) argued that it was an ethics based on the claim that apartheid supporters "granted others" everything that they themselves enjoyed (although of course apart, separately), but that they did not actually "do unto others" that which they claimed they granted the others. One could therefore claim, as Kitcher is also doing, that the real ethical test lies not in what we say and how we speak (and believe), but in what we actually do (and omit).

29. Charles Darwin developed his ideas in *The Descent of Man* (1872); see the range of informative essays in Philip Clayton and Jeffrey Schloss, eds., *Evolution and Ethics: Human Morality in Biological and Religious Perspective* (Grand Rapids: Eerdmans, 2004), of which many deal with issues of love. See particularly the extremely helpful and comprehensive volume of

most of the time altruism was seen as the heart of morality as such, if not the only real moral sentiment.[30] Why would beings driven by the survival of the fittest care at all—for others?

Although many are still occupied by this challenge, it is today also commonly agreed that the problem is indeed only superficial since there are many convincing theoretical explanations and well-documented empirical evidence for the necessity of the development of altruism.[31] Not only do we know that and how primates show forms of altruistic love, but we can also understand the reasons why this is necessary for life together in small bands of hunter-collectors.[32]

Still, there remain difficulties regarding aspects like—for example—the *nature*, the *motive(s)*, and the so-called *range* (or *scope*) of altruism. This is true not only for evolutionary ethics attempting to explain the development of moral codes, and therefore how we—perhaps[33]—were gradually *becoming* the kind of human beings that we are, but also for any contemporary ethical project attempting to refigure moral codes in the face of challenges and crises, thereby arguing for ways of *being* human today.[34] Additional and particularly

---

essays by Stephen G. Post, Lynn G. Underwood, Jeffrey P. Schloss, and William B. Hurlbut, eds., *Altruism and Altruistic Love* (Oxford: Oxford University Press, 2002).

30. In his account on how things could have happened, Kitcher develops all social institutions (sexuality, property, war, punishment, division of labor, slavery) from attempts to deal with "altruism failures" and therefore what he calls "altruism expanded" was the result.

31. See the acclaimed but challenging proposal by David Sloan Wilson in *Darwin's Cathedral: Evolution, Religion, and the Nature of Society* (Chicago: University of Chicago Press, 2002) that religions fulfill this evolutionary function of forming communities of belonging.

32. See the clear, instructive, and entertaining account in Boehm, *Human Origins*.

33. Kitcher stresses the point that his account is not necessarily how things actually developed, but one that explains how things plausibly *could* have happened.

34. For van Huyssteen, this distinction is of key importance. He formulates that often and in different ways: "This implies a quite specific relationship between evolutionary epistemology and evolutionary ethics: evolutionary ethics . . . clearly reveals the biological reasons for the evolution of moral awareness, but this does not yet lead to an evolutionary explanation for the formulation of specific moral codes, laws, or norms. Evolutionary ethics can help us to reconstruct the preconditions for moral behaviour but says nothing about the validity of certain norms that have developed in cultural evolution and are thus constrained by sociocultural conventions. This is the reason why there are different *rationales* inherent in different sociocultural systems, and why different cultural contexts may lead to different moral codes. Evolutionary epistemology thus provocatively reveals what happens as, both epistemologically and morally, we make our way through our highly contextualized worlds. . . . What now becomes clear is that ethical behaviour is indeed a product of our biological evolution but this fact by itself does not entail any normative assertions: from the fact that morality has developed we cannot conclude that any particular trait of human behaviour is good or bad (right or wrong) in an ethical sense. Put differently, an evolutionary account of ethics does not support any specific

daunting dimensions to moral challenges today—for being human, in distinction from becoming human in pre-history—come with the complexities of living together in such large numbers.[35] What does innate altruism mean under these infinitely more complex conditions?[36]

Regarding the *nature* of altruism, many and diverse attempts to refigure moral codes by developing typologies of love or by defending specific forms of love over against others are well-known and still abounding in ethical discourses. The almost classical threefold depiction of love—*erōs, philia, agapē*—has now become controversial and outdated, but many other discourses have replaced it.[37] Well-known is the ethics of care, developed in

---

moral code, but it may help us to understand why such codes have developed" ("Ethics and Christology," 494-95). Elsewhere, he makes the same argument in different ways, agreeing with Anthony O'Hear (*Beyond Evolution* [Oxford: Clarendon, 2002]): "Precisely because of distinctive traits like consciousness, self-awareness, reflectiveness and rationality, we humans have the added ability to take on cognitive goals and ideas which cannot be justified merely in terms of survival-promotion and survival advantage. Therefore, our very typical human quest for rational knowledge, but also our moral sensibilities, our aesthetic appreciation of beauty, and our religious disposition, while all deriving in important ways from our biological nature, once having emerged cannot only be analyzed in biological or evolutionary terms. In this sense, then, we clearly transcend our biological origins, and in so doing have the ability to transcend what is given us in both biology and culture.... We are prisoners neither of our genes, nor the ideas we encounter as we each make our personal and individual way through life" ("Construction and Constraint," 324).

35. Today, human beings live in large communities, villages, cities, and the sprawling urban realities of today's world; in often changing and porous cultural communities, nations, races, countries, continents; in social communities, political entities, integrated worlds of labor, trade, and finance; in a rapidly globalizing world with an increasingly global economy; in the network-society of communication, media, electronics, and virtual reality. What makes the challenges even more daunting is the rapidly changing nature of all these dimensions. The innate moral sensitivities developed over thousands of years in small bands hardly serve as sufficient preparation for these new realities of today's world. We share the legacies of cultural and political developments of empires, ideologies, wars, and violence. We live in a world of movement and flux, of exiles and fugitives, asylum seekers, tourists and visitors, outsiders and newcomers, foreigners and migrants, immigrants and aliens, in short, a changing world of increasing strangeness and strangers, everywhere, and therefore need much more complex and in fact adaptable, fluid, and changing ways of living with others and strangers.

36. It is interesting to remember that Auguste Comte (1798-1857) was the one who coined both the terms "altruism" and "sociology"—and some describe his work as close to what today is called evolutionary ethics.

37. For some classical treatments, see Anders Nygren, *Agape and Eros* (Philadelphia: Westminster, 1953), and Gene Outka, *Agape: An Ethical Analysis* (New Haven: Yale University Press, 1972). For more recent discussions, see, for example, Stephen G. Post, *A Theory of Agape* (Lewisburg: Bucknell, 1990); Colin Grant, *Altruism and Christian Ethics* (Cambridge: Cambridge University Press, 2000); and Caroline J. Simon, *The Disciplined Heart: Love, Destiny,*

many different ways since Carol Gilligan's initial contrast with an ethics of justice.[38] One could claim that the equally popular *ubuntu* ethics—although also contested and critiqued—fulfills a similar role in some South African circles.[39] One could also remember the many discourses of solidarity,[40] of

---

and Imagination (Grand Rapids: Eerdmans, 2007). Of special importance, see the discussion from a feminist perspective by Beverly W. Harrison, "The Power of Anger in the Work of Love: Christian Ethics for Women and Other Strangers," in *Weaving the Visions: New Patterns in Feminist Spirituality*, ed. Judith Plaskow and Carol P. Christ (San Francisco: Harper & Row, 1989), 214–25.

38. Since Carol Gilligan's influential *In a Different Voice* (Cambridge, MA: Harvard University Press, 1982) and Nel Noddings's *Caring: A Feminine Approach to Ethics and Moral Education* (Berkeley: University of California Press, 1984) many other major feminist contributions have further developed this form of ethical discourse, stressing human response to others rather than traditional ethical approaches. See Joan C. Tronto, *Moral Boundaries: A Political Argument for an Ethic of Care* (New York: Routledge, 1993); Virginia Held, *The Ethics of Care* (Oxford: Oxford University Press, 2006).

39. The notion of *ubuntu*, according to many descriptions of a worldview and anthropology present in different African cultures, is often employed to call for a spirit of solidarity, inclusion, and mutual service. Its uses range from popular language to scholarly studies, from church leaders like Desmond Tutu to constitutional court judges like Yvonne Mokgoro to philosophers like Thaddeus Metz and Augustine Shutte. It is a contested notion, often because of the question how inclusively it functions in reality, especially with regard to otherness, difference, and strangers; see Mfuniselwa J. Bhengu, *Ubuntu* (Cape Town: Novalis, 1996); Augustine Shutte, *Ubuntu* (Pietermaritzburg: Cluster, 2001).

40. See Rebecca Todd Peters, *Solidarity Ethics: Transformation in a Globalized World* (Minneapolis: Fortress, 2014); also the influential work by Martha C. Nussbaum, *Political Emotions: Why Love Matters for Justice* (Cambridge, MA: Harvard University Press, 2013). She explains why it is important to cultivate public emotions. There are two reasons. "One is to engender and sustain strong commitment to worthy projects that require effort and sacrifice. . . . Most people tend toward narrowness of sympathy. They can easily become immured in narcissistic projects and forget about the needs of those outside their narrow circle. . . . The other related task for the cultivation of public emotion is to keep at bay forces that lurk in all societies and, ultimately, in all of us; tendencies to protect the fragile self by denigrating and subordinating others. . . . Disgust and envy, the desire to inflict shame upon others—all of these are present in all societies, and, very likely, in every individual human life. Unchecked they can inflict great damage . . . These forces lurk in every society and need to be counteracted energetically by an education that cultivates the ability to see full and equal humanity in another person, perhaps one of humanity's most difficult and fragile achievements" (2). For an instructive discussion on one specific emotion, see Rachel Herz, *That's Disgusting: Unraveling the Mysteries of Repulsion* (New York: Norton, 2012).

empathy,[41] of compassion,[42] of doing unto others,[43] of the golden rule,[44] of friendship,[45] even of the "objects of our desire"[46]—all attempts to emphasize

> 41. See the collection of essays by Amy Coplan and Peter Goldie, eds., *Empathy: Philosophical and Psychological Perspectives* (Oxford: Oxford University Press, 2014); in the work of the Stellenbosch ethicist Nico Koopman on so-called hybridity notions of empathy, sympathy, and inter-pathy occupy an important place. See "Towards Reconciliation and Justice in South Africa: Can Church Unity Make a Difference?" in *Peace and Reconciliation: In Search of Shared Identity*, ed. Sebastian Kim, Pauline Kollontai, and Greg Hoyland (Burlington: Ashgate, 2008), 95–108.
> 42. See Maureen H. O'Connell, *Compassion: Loving Our Neighbour in an Age of Globalization* (Maryknoll: Orbis, 2009); and the volume of critical essays by Lauren Berlant, ed., *Compassion: The Culture and Politics of an Emotion* (New York: Routledge, 2004), also with an interesting essay on Hannah Arendt by Deborah Nelson, "Suffering and Thinking: The Scandal of Tone in Eichmann in Jerusalem," 219–44. See especially the very informative collection produced after discussions between leading scientists and Tibetan Buddhists, including the Dalai Lama, Richard J. Davidson and Anne Harrington, eds., *Visions of Compassion* (Oxford: Oxford University Press, 2002). They explain: "While there is a modest research tradition in the Western behavioral sciences concerned with altruism, prosocial behaviour, the development of sympathy, empathy, and so on, the dominant note of the biobehavioral sciences in the West has been tragic-machismo: We find our origins in ancestors we call 'killer apes,' ponder our potential for violence, explore the genetic and biochemical bases of our capacity for selfishness, depression, and anxiety. In contrast, Tibetan Buddhism has long celebrated the human potential for compassion . . . sees compassion as a key to enduring happiness and, even more fundamentally, spiritual transformation" (v).
> 43. See the influential study by Elliott Sober and David S. Wilson, *Unto Others: The Evolution and Psychology of Unselfish Behavior* (Cambridge, MA: Harvard University Press, 2003).
> 44. See Jacob Neusner and Bruce Chilton, eds., *The Golden Rule: The Ethics of Reciprocity in World Religions* (New York: Continuum, 2008).
> 45. Approaching love, relationships, community, and even life in society via notions of friendship has become popular in philosophical and especially Catholic theological and ethical circles; for overviews, see Neera Kapur Badhwar, ed., *Friendship: A Philosophical Reader* (Ithaca, NY: Cornell University Press, 1993), and Leroy S. Rouner, ed., *The Changing Face of Friendship* (Notre Dame: University of Notre Dame, 1994); for constructive arguments, see David B. Burrell, *Friendship and Ways to Truth* (Notre Dame: University of Notre Dame, 2000); Paul J. Wadell, *Becoming Friends: Worship, Justice, and the Practice of Christian Friendship* (Grand Rapids: Brazos, 2002); Donald X. Burt, *Friendship and Society* (Grand Rapids: Eerdmans, 1999), and Gilbert C. Meilaender, *Friendship: A Study in Theological Ethics* (Notre Dame: University of Notre Dame, 1981), all of them Catholic; and also E. D. H. (Liz) Carmichael, *Friendship: Interpreting Christian Love* (London: T&T Clark, 2004), a study born from her South Africa experiences.
> 46. See Oliver O'Donovan, *Common Objects of Love: Moral Reflection and the Shaping of Community* (Grand Rapids: Eerdmans, 2009); also Hannah Arendt's early study on Augustine, *Love and St. Augustine* (Chicago: University of Chicago Press, 1997); also the discussion in Julia Kristeva's valuable interpretation of Arendt, *Hannah Arendt* (New York: Columbia University Press, 2001), 30–48.

different aspects of altruistic love as central to being human and therefore to our moral project.

Regarding the *motive* of these diverse forms of altruistic love, the conceptual questions become infamously difficult. Is all altruism in the last resort perhaps only forms of egoism? Are all our forms of altruistic love not perhaps motivated by our own needs, desires, and self-love? These are variations of the equally difficult questions, debated by scholars from so many different disciplines, whether gifts can truly be given, or whether gifts are not necessarily always forms of trade, negotiation, and manipulation, as well as the closely related question whether gratitude could ever be regarded as proper motivation for moral action.[47]

Similarly, it remains a contested question for morality and ethics whether *The Reasons of Love* can in the final analysis be anything else than self-love.[48] Many, including evolutionary ethicists, vehemently deny that all altruism is motivated by self-love and they construe other explanations, origins, and arguments.[49] Others argue that even if self-love is ultimately the motive behind all other forms of love, this could—and should—be regarded as completely natural, normal, and morally acceptable.[50] In apartheid South Africa, after all, this was a key argument in the ethical and theological justification of the ideology and system.[51]

Regarding the *range* of altruistic love, however, the challenges become less conceptual and far more existential and urgent, sometimes even

---

47. The literature is abundant, but see, of special theological interest, John D. Caputo and Michael J. Scanlon, eds., *God, the Gift, and Postmodernism* (Bloomington: Indiana University Press, 1999), including an essay by David Tracy; and Risto Saarinen, *God and the Gift: An Ecumenical Theology of Giving* (Collegeville: Liturgical, 2005).

48. See the acclaimed work by the Princeton philosopher Harry G. Frankfurt, *The Reasons of Love* (Princeton: Princeton University Press, 2004), and also his essays *The Importance of What We Care About* (Cambridge: Cambridge University Press, 2005), particularly the essay with the same title.

49. See the discussions in Jonathan Seglow, ed., *The Ethics of Altruism* (London: Frank Cass, 2004) as well as Stephen J. Pope's earlier *The Evolution of Altruism and the Ordering of Love* (Washington: Georgetown University Press, 1994), but also in many of the studies on morality from the perspective of evolutionary ethics.

50. See Darlene F. Weaver, *Self-love and Christian Ethics* (Cambridge: Cambridge University Press, 2002), and Neil Messer, *Selfish Genes and Christian Ethics* (London: SCM, 2007); also my "On Self-love: Impulses from Calvin and Calvinism for Life in Society?" in *Calvin Today: Reformed Theology and the Future of the Church*, ed. Michael Welker, Michael Weinrich, and Ulrich Möller (London: T&T Clark International Continuum, 2011), 158-80.

51. For the ideological role of self-love in apartheid ethics, see my "Views on Calvin's Ethics from a South African Perspective," *Reformed World* 57, no. 4 (December 2007): 306-44.

threatening and terrifying, namely, when we are faced with strangeness and strangers.[52]

Relating to Strangers?

The question about the scope of our altruism is the question whether and if indeed how far our altruism—including our ethics of compassion, care, *ubuntu*, or solidarity—extends to others, to outsiders and those who are different, or whether it remains restricted to the boundaries of our in-groups, whichever way defined, and therefore also whether our natural moral sensibilities and altruistic inclinations provide us with the necessary ethical insights and languages—whether of vision, values, virtues, norms, interests, emotions, conscience—to live together with strangers, and if indeed, *how*?[53]

In short, how do we construct our moral codes, how do we refigure our moral visions, values, and virtues, to live with strangers? How do our available moral discourses help us to talk about strangers today?[54]

It is not surprising that words like "difference," "otherness," and "strangeness" are used so widely today. In their different ways, they capture some of the most fundamental challenges of life together in an increasingly globalizing

---

52. The issue may in fact be far more complicated than this, in that loving the neighbor may already present much more of a challenge than we may suppose. In many ways we have become so accustomed to the moral codes and the ethical discourses built on love of the neighbor that we may regard this as normal and natural, forgetting how difficult and challenging the idea may in fact be. Today, some ethical discourses are increasingly reminding us of these difficulties. For a very powerful reminder of the extraordinary difficulties of loving the neighbor, often even of making sense of the notion that we should love our neighbor, see Slavoj Zizek, Erci L. Santner, and Kenneth Reinhard, *The Neighbour: Three Inquiries in Political Theology* (Chicago: University of Chicago Press, 2005). They begin with the famous arguments of Freud (in *Civilization and Its Discontents*) that the mere thought of loving the neighbor is bewildering and unthinkable, and even more so if the neighbor is a perfect stranger.

53. For an argument that standard moral theories have led us astray since they make us expect too much of ordinary human beings regarding strangers, see Judith Lichtenberg, *Distant Strangers: Ethics, Psychology, and Global Poverty* (Cambridge: Cambridge University Press, 2013). For instructive historical essays, see Francis W. Nichols, *Christianity and the Stranger* (Atlanta: Scholars, 1995).

54. In South Africa, violent outbursts of xenophobia all over the country have deeply disturbed many people in recent years; for a study of possible causes, see the work by Fellows of STIAS (like van Huyssteen), Heribert Adam and Kogila Moodley, *Imagined Liberation: Xenophobia, Citizenship and Identity in South Africa, Germany and Canada* (Stellenbosch: Sun, 2013).

world.⁵⁵ A whole litany of historical, cultural, social, economic, and cultural aspects can be offered to remind us of the tension-filled and often dangerous nature of this life together—social and economic inequalities and injustices, ideological and religious prejudices, ecological crises, not to mention wars and threats of war. It may seem that natural altruism—sometimes easily—reaches its limits and boundaries when confronted with difference and otherness. It is therefore also not surprising that someone like the British literary critic and social commentator Terry Eagleton (for example)⁵⁶ describes the whole ethical task as one of *Trouble with Strangers*.⁵⁷

This was, after all, also the question in 1983 in South Africa, and it remains the challenge today, and probably not only in South Africa. Perhaps it could therefore be helpful to be reminded—via a superficial typology based on a survey of contemporary literature—of several different ethical discourses in which living with strangers is constructed in different ways and according to different moral codes.

---

55. Many developments and figures obviously played an influential role, but among them the work of Emmanuel Levinas could perhaps be highlighted; see as introduction Adriaan Peperzak, *To the Other: An Introduction to the Philosophy of Emmanuel Levinas* (West Lafayette, IN: Purdue University Press, 1993), and for implications for contemporary political theology, J. Aaron Simmons, *God and the Other: Ethics and Politics after the Theological Turn* (Bloomington: Indiana University Press, 2011).

56. There are of course also many others who see the encounter with strangeness and strangers as of key importance; see Richard Kearney, *Strangers, Gods and Monsters* (New York: Routledge, 2003). It is the third volume in his philosophical trilogy pursuing the role of what he calls "philosophy at the limit" (together with the earlier *On Stories* and *The God Who May Be*). His ongoing wager is that "by sounding out certain borderlands separating Us from Others we may become more ready to acknowledge strangers in ourselves and ourselves in others" (20). See also the informative essay by LeRon Shults, "The Philosophical Turn to Alterity in Christology and Ethics," in *Christology and Ethics*, 179–211, especially the final section, in which he surveys diverse options.

57. Terry Eagleton, *Trouble with Strangers: A Study of Ethics* (Oxford: Blackwell, 2009). In a fascinating, comprehensive argument, he claims that most ethical theories can be assigned to one of Jacques Lacan's three psychoanalytical categories (imaginary, symbolic, Real) and that all these (three kinds) of ethical approaches fall short when contrasted with what he regards as "the richer ethics of socialism and the Judaeo-Christian tradition" (vi). The whole book is a sustained argument to support this claim. It is divided in these three parts and the enduring challenge of the stranger forms the criterion against which all these ethical theories are measured.

Recognizing Kin?

A first moral discourse about altruism, for obvious reasons often dominant in evolutionary forms of ethics,[58] including the study of primates[59] and the study of human origins[60] as well as the study of cognitive evolution[61] and psychological and emotional development,[62] builds on the crucially important task of learning to live with others in mother-child attachment and in the immediate bonds within small groups.

Recognizing kin, recognizing them as kin, and even recognizing others who may not be kin but who join and share the small group as welcome in the band are all fundamental to our moral and human development. In descriptions of *Human Origins*, living with (others as) kin therefore plays a central

---

58. Over the years the term "evolutionary ethics" referred to many different approaches; see the instructive overview of different waves until the early 1990s by Paul Lawrence Farber, *The Temptations of Evolutionary Ethics* (Berkeley: University of California, 1998). He concludes with a careful but critical appraisal of the potential for evolutionary ethics to contribute to actual moral deliberation in contemporary situations; for a much briefer overview, see Jeffrey P. Schloss, "Evolutionary Ethics," in *Encyclopedia of Science and Religion*, ed. J. Wentzel van Huyssteen (New York: Macmillan, 2003), 285-87; for a more extensive discussion by Schloss, see his introduction "Evolutionary Ethics and Christian Morality: Surveying the Issues," in *Evolution and Ethics: Human Morality in Biological and Religious Perspective*, ed. Philip Clayton and Jeffrey Schloss (Grand Rapids: Eerdmans, 2004), 1-24.

59. See the authoritative Frans de Waal's 2003 Tanner Lectures in Princeton, focusing his decades of work with primates and researching evolution on the question of the development of human morality, with responses by other well-known figures, including Philip Kitcher, as well as Robert Wright, Christine Korsgaard, and Peter Singer, in *Primates and Philosophers: How Morality Evolved*, ed. Josiah Ober and Stephen Macedo (Princeton: Princeton University Press, 2006); also his earlier *Good Natured: The Origins of Right and Wrong in Humans and Other Animals* (Cambridge, MA: Harvard University Press, 1996).

60. See the authoritative work by Christopher Boehm, *Moral Origins: The Evolution of Virtue, Altruism, and Shame* (New York: Basic Books, 2012); also the volume of essays with several well-known contributors, Warren S. Brown, Nancey Murphy, and H. Newton Malony, eds., *Whatever Happened to the Soul? Scientific and Theological Portraits of Human Nature* (Minneapolis: Fortress, 1998).

61. See the volume by Nancey Murphy and Warren S. Brown, *Did My Neurons Make Me Do It? Philosophical and Neurobiological Perspectives on Moral Responsibility and Free Will* (Oxford: Oxford University Press, 2007). For an instructive debate on the same themes—including neurological determination, free will, human agency, and the possibility of responsibility, even the justification of justice and punishment—between the neuroscientist Wolf Singer and the theological ethicist Wolfgang Huber, see *Von den Grenzen der Erkenntnis und der Unbegrenztheit des Glaubens* (Berlin: Theater der Zeit, 2009).

62. See the authoritative work by Paul Bloom, *Just Babies: The Origins of Good and Evil* (New York: Crown, 2013); also the widely acclaimed and popular study by Jonathan Haidt, *The Righteous Mind* (New York: Penguin, 2012).

Living with Strangers?

role in understanding our moral development as human beings, including "the evolution of virtue, altruism, and shame" (Boehm).

Small groups develop ways to form *Joint Commitment*.[63] In fact, it is possible, imaginable—again, plausible, not necessarily actually the prehistorical case—that the story of our becoming human could be told in such a way that learning to live with kin involved establishing the rudimentary forms of social, legal, and political institutions that we know today, in other words, that basic altruism led to increasingly complex ways of social life together. Particularly important and interesting would, for example, be the nature and role of trust.[64]

Yet, even if that was indeed the case, and even in many ways remains the case, it is still also possible to imagine that these forms of altruism excluded some others, regarded them as not belonging, as no kin, as outsiders, as strangers, perhaps even as threats and enemies. In fact, some of the mechanisms and institutions of in-group altruism and love for kin could even have depended on and resulted from threatening encounters with strangeness and strangers.

It is, accordingly, possible to imagine that these small groups were *Bound to Differ*,[65] that they needed otherness and strangers in order to establish, define, and strengthen their own identity and belonging. After all, we know that this is indeed the case and therefore the challenge today—in many forms

---

63. Margaret Gilbert, *Joint Commitment: How We Make the Social World* (Oxford: Oxford University Press, 2014); for ways of developing shared values, see also Bernard Lategan, "Developing Common Values in Situations of Plurality and Social Transformation," in *Living Theology: Essays Presented to Dirk J. Smit on His Sixtieth Birthday*, ed. Len Hansen, Nico Koopman, and Robert Vosloo (Wellington: Bible Media, 2011), 441-53. Van Huyssteen agrees that Jesus used the Sermon on the Mount "as a way of challenging the traditional Hebrew understanding of 'culture,' ancestry, and 'in-group' by turning away from notions of kin-relatedness to a new notion of relatedness based on shared values instead" ("Ethics and Christology," 504).

64. The two books on the evolution of political systems by Francis Fukuyama provide an interesting example; see *The Origins of Political Order: From Prehuman Times to the French Revolution* (New York: Farrar, Straus and Giroux, 2011), and its successor, *Political Order and Political Decay: From the Industrial Revolution to the Globalisation of Democracy* (New York: Farrar, Straus and Giroux, 2014). Together they offer a fascinating albeit controversial historical reconstruction of the cultural evolution of "life together" in these societies. One could also take his earlier study on the key role of trust in economies into account, and the claim that successful attempts to extend trust and to make it more general than just kin, the in-group, and one's own community also lead to economic progress; see his *Trust: The Social Virtues and the Creation of Prosperity* (New York: Simon & Schuster, 1996), as another illustration of cultural evolution in living together with strangers.

65. See the argument on identities depending on difference in Wesley Kort, *Bound to Differ* (University Park: Pennsylvania State University Press, 1992), to which Russel Botman returned in his work on different occasions.

of racisms, nationalisms, and diverse other essentialisms. Many forms of in-group altruism depend on simultaneous exclusion of others.

Risking Hospitality?

There are, of course, good reasons to extend our altruistic love also to strangers, to the others whom we do not know. After all, many people today share the moral sentiment that "a stranger is just a friend you do not know."[66]

In modern, liberal societies such a moral code has been internalized by many. Behind the differences, the otherness, and the strangeness of others is just another human being, someone like us, many people believe. People are basically similar, the same, with similar needs, fears, and joys. It is therefore fully possible that we can share a common world and can accept and love one another without much difficulty, many people today probably believe.

It may be an idealistic and even romantic view, yet obviously not without major value for moral life in our contemporary world — it may indeed be "a precept to deem most important" (Kitcher) in many societies today. It is therefore not surprising that so many authors, moral philosophers, and ethicists propagate this kind of language. For them, practicing hospitality is a risk worth taking. We may just reap more benefits than we would have expected. We may perhaps be surprised by experiences of reciprocity, where strangers indeed show themselves as friends we did not know.

Ethicists therefore write about strangers as gifts, about receiving strangers, about welcoming strangers, about unknowingly hosting angels through acts of hospitality. In theological circles, for example, attempts have become popular to provide biblical, traditional, ecclesiological, and even doctrinal justification and support for an ethics of hospitality toward strangers.[67]

Still, an ethics of hospitality is obviously primarily applicable on a personal level, in direct and immediate relationships of individuals with others.

---

66. In the 1960s, the American singer Jim Reeves made a song with this title popular in South Africa.

67. See John Koenig, *New Testament Hospitality: Partnership with Strangers as Promise and Mission* (Philadelphia: Fortress, 1985); Christine D. Pohl, *Making Room: Recovering Hospitality as a Christian Tradition* (Grand Rapids: Eerdmans, 1999); Patrick R. Keifert, *Welcoming the Stranger: A Public Theology of Worship and Evangelism* (Minneapolis: Fortress, 1992); Thomas W. Ogletree, *Hospitality to the Stranger: Dimensions of Moral Understanding* (Minneapolis: Fortress, 1985); and from the Stellenbosch theologian Robert Vosloo, *Engele as gaste: Oor Gasvryheid teenoor die Ander* (Wellington: Lux Verbi, 2006), which was also translated into Dutch and published in the Netherlands.

The challenges become much more problematic on social, political, economic, and structural levels.[68]

Reckoning on Reciprocity?

The structural challenge can of course be addressed by way of so-called indirect reciprocity. For complex modern societies in particular the phenomenon of indirect reciprocity is of utmost importance. Life together in our world today depends completely on indirect reciprocity.[69]

People are willing to support others, even to make sacrifices in order to support others, in the expectation that they will again benefit one day in a similar way, from the sacrifices and contributions of still others, although in most cases of course not the original recipients of our contributions. Paying taxes is a case-book example, but almost the whole of social, economic, and political life in modern societies rests on forms of indirect reciprocity. There is no direct link or personal bond between donors and recipients, and in fact neither between what we contribute and what we receive, which raises interesting challenges for accounts based on natural selection.

Still the reality is that we reckon daily on the fact that our contributions to social life and our willingness to share will be returned and rewarded. The crucial aspect is of course that these are all anonymous, impersonal, and therefore indirect ways of living with others, sharing with others, supporting others, helping others, and in turn depending on others, benefiting from others and being sustained by others. Examples are easy to multiply. It is obvious that this is an extremely important form of living with strangers today.

However, the exact way in which such indirect reciprocity should be described as moral and therefore as part of the ongoing ethical project of humanity raises many difficult and controversial issues. One obvious objection is the fact that indirect reciprocity takes place almost unconsciously; it is so

---

68. To mention one example, what does hospitality mean for a university like Stellenbosch, van Huyssteen's alma mater, to which he recently returned as extraordinary professor? The university is in a process of transformation, in order to be more inclusive. Accordingly, hospitality is one of the key institutional values today. Precisely for that reason, however, the so-called language policy is at the heart of painful public controversies about the future of this traditionally Afrikaans-speaking university.

69. Different branches of evolutionary ethics have been studying and describing the development of reciprocity in several ways. In some fields scholars pursue so-called network reciprocity and cooperation studies, in order to understand and describe the dynamics of reciprocity.

deeply woven into the fabric of contemporary life itself that we do not really experience our role as a moral task or activity, we do not feel challenged by the presence of any strangers, and we do not consciously regard our own participation as the result of ethical considerations and decisions on our part. A second objection is the fact that, whenever it no longer takes place unconsciously, but must be decided or at least carry away our approval, we often restrict our reciprocity and exclude others—which precisely raises the question of the stranger. Therefore, although reciprocity may indeed be hard-wired in us, we still decide and determine how far we will distribute it and how far we will reckon on it.[70]

Relying on Tolerance?

In this sense, the ethical discourse on tolerance is definitely different. It is also widespread, popular, and pervasive today, particularly in secular, democratic, and pluralist modern societies, and the language of tolerance most certainly makes us aware of the presence of strangeness and strangers, in fact, tolerance depends on that presence and presumes to be the most adequate response to that presence.[71]

Many people today may superficially believe that practicing tolerance is the proper—wise and pragmatic, but also moral and responsible—way of living with strangers. Tolerance may thus be one of "the moral precepts that most people today would deem important to follow" (Kitcher). Beneath the surface, however, the reality is much more complicated and contested and real problems facing our ethical project much more difficult and demanding. The truth is that ethical discourse based on tolerance has become controversial for a variety of reasons.[72]

---

70. Even "if . . . nature tells us *that* we will practice reciprocity . . . it does not necessarily tell us how we will practice reciprocity." Reciprocity may indeed be basic to our human character, but the way in which we understand and practice it across our cultures, traditions, and communities is not uniform. For example, some use it more for bridging, but others use it more for bonding—and therefore for excluding others and strangers; see William S. Green, "'Wired for Reciprocity': Some Concluding Reflections," in *The Golden Rule*, ed. Jacob Neusner and Bruce D. Chilton (New York: Continuum, 2009), 170-72.

71. For a classical defense of (American) tolerance, see the 1996 Castle Lectures in Yale's Program in Ethics, Politics, and Economics by Michael Walzer, *On Toleration* (New Haven: Yale University Press, 1997), xii: "Toleration makes difference possible, difference makes toleration necessary."

72. For an instructive debate, see Luca di Blasi and Christoph F. E. Holzhey, eds., *The Power of Tolerance: A Debate: Wendy Brown and Rainer Frost* (New York: Columbia University Press, 2014), including a helpful epilogue, 71-102.

Tolerance has been described as *An Elusive Virtue* or even as "An Impossible Virtue."[73] Some point to the *Boundaries of Toleration* and others call for moving *Beyond Tolerance*.[74] According to some, tolerance always involves "something demeaning to the beneficiaries."[75] According to some, it is possible to describe practices but not a virtue of tolerance.[76] According to others, including Paul Ricoeur, tolerance is caught somewhere "between intolerance and the intolerable."[77] According to some, tolerance expects too much—and recent human history offers several glaring examples.[78] According to others, tolerance expects too little—and the well-known South African Truth and Reconciliation Commission could serve as concrete example.[79] In short, moral discourses that would merely propose toleration toward strangers as the precept deemed most important and helpful would certainly fall short in several respects.

Respecting Dignity?

A much stronger moral suggestion for living with the many strangers in the world whom we may never personally encounter comes from those who argue

---

73. David Heyd, ed., *Tolerance: An Elusive Virtue* (Princeton: Princeton University Press, 1996); Bernard Williams, "Toleration: An Impossible Virtue?" in *Tolerance: An Elusive Virtue* (Princeton: Princeton University Press, 1996), 18–27.

74. Alfred Stepan and Charles Taylor, eds., *Boundaries of Toleration* (New York: Columbia University Press, 2014), with an extensive interview with Salman Rushdie, 7–34; Gustav Niebuhr, *Beyond Tolerance: Searching for Interfaith Tolerance in America* (New York: Viking, 2008).

75. Alfred Stepan and Charles Taylor, "Introduction," in *Boundaries of Toleration*, ed. Alfred Stepan and Charles Taylor (New York: Columbia University Press, 2014), 2.

76. See Williams, "Toleration," 18–27.

77. See Paul Ricoeur, *Tolerance Between Intolerance and the Intolerable* (Providence, RI: Berghahn, 1996).

78. Tolerance itself has therefore been severely rejected from both the left and the right; see Herbert Marcuse, "Repressive Tolerance," in *A Critique of Pure Tolerance*, ed. Robert P. Wolff, Barrington Moore Jr., and Herbert Marcuse (Boston: Beacon, 1969), 95–137; as well as Henryk Broder, *Kritik der reinen Toleranz* (Berlin: WJS, 2008).

79. Notions like forgiveness, reconciliation, truth, responsibility, justice, and restitution, which all played a crucial role in the hearings, the official report, and the public reception (and criticism) were clearly much stronger than mere toleration, and their background and rootedness in spiritual, religious, and moral traditions and communities were both significant and problematic and contested; see Elna Mouton and Dirk J. Smit, "Shared Stories for the Future? Theological Reflections on Truth and Reconciliation in South Africa," *Journal of Reformed Theology* 2, no. 1 (2008): 40–62.

for showing respect in one form or another. Again, respect can also function in different moral codes and ethical discourses. Perhaps the most dominant ethical discourse today centered on the notion of respect is the one arguing for respect for human dignity and for human rights. The genealogy of this discourse of human dignity is of course contested[80] and the nature and therefore the application of the notions of human dignity[81] and human rights[82] even more so. Still, it is fair to claim that wherever these notions are employed in moral codes they serve the purpose of guaranteeing respect for and thereby protecting the integrity of everyone, including strangers.

The very fact that "human" dignity and "human" rights are respected and protected, not the rights of citizens or of particular groups or individuals, shows the ethical intention behind this moral vision and code. It strives to be an inclusive, even called universal, vision and code, thereby orientating us on how to live with strangers, at least in borderline situations where their rights—however defined—may be under threat. One very informative and widely influential account, for example, is the defense of inherent natural rights by Nicholas Wolterstorff—an understanding of respect that developed as a direct result of his personal experiences of real-life problems in South Africa.[83]

Of course, the notion of respect can also lead to other ethical discourses and moral codes with different emphases. An instructive example is to be found in the work of the sociologist Richard Sennett in his early work entitled

---

80. See the informative and for many surprising account by John Witte, *The Reformation of Rights: Law, Religion and Human Rights in Early Modern Calvinism* (Cambridge: Cambridge University Press, 2007).

81. In the Faculty of Theology of Stellenbosch University the notion of human dignity plays an important role, also as one possible focus for research, community interaction, and teaching. To this vision, the late rector and vice-chancellor Russel Botman, who received the Abraham Kuyper Prize at Princeton Seminary in 2013, made a major contribution, through his life and work, his research, and his leadership in church, public life, and education. For his own work on human dignity and rights, see Karin Sporre and H. Russel Botman, eds., *Building a Human Rights Culture* (Falun: Dalarna, 2003); H. Russel Botman, "Covenantal Anthropology: Integrating Three Contemporary Discourses of Human Dignity," in *God and Human Dignity*, ed. R. Kendall Soulen and Linda Woodhead (Grand Rapids: Eerdmans, 2006), 72-88.

82. For an interesting argument based on the conviction that Darwinism's evolutionary ethics undermines the idea of human dignity, making it "unlikely that any other support for the idea of human dignity will be found" since human dignity is shown "to be the effluvium of a discredited metaphysics," see James Rachels, *Created from Animals: The Moral Implications of Darwinism* (New York: Oxford University Press, 1990).

83. For an intriguing autobiographical account of how his personal passion for social justice and human rights came about as well as his own summary of the argument and contents of his main works on these themes, see Nicholas P. Wolterstorff, *Journey towards Justice: Personal Encounters in the Global South* (Grand Rapids: Baker, 2013).

Living with Strangers?

Respect in a World of Inequality—again based on his personal experiences of real-life problems in an urban neighborhood[84]—but also in his recent trilogy of works on human life together, in which he movingly describes human beings today as working together to make life together possible in our cities.[85]

Another example could be found in the varied and complex ethical discourses contributing to the formation of democratic culture in general. Although they may take on many forms and moral codes, democratic cultures in general often stress some form of mutual respect for difference and otherness. Precisely for that reason it has been possible to contrast (inclusive and respectful) democratic cultures with the "myths of nationhood," as the respected Stellenbosch philosopher Johan Degenaar prophetically warned at the time of the advent of the new and democratic South Africa.[86]

These ethical discourses may stress the role of laws, even in the formation of conscience (and morality) necessary for democracy,[87] they may stress the role of education and emotional formation for democracy,[88] they may stress

---

84. Richard Sennett's *Respect in a World of Inequality* (New York: Norton, 2003) is based on his recollections of growing up in a Chicago housing project. He deals with themes such as "scarcity of respect," "what respect means," "the shame of dependence" and "compassion which wounds," "an argument about welfare," "the mutual in mutual respect," and finally "the politics of respect."

85. In *The Foreigner* (London: Notting Hill, 2011), Sennett discusses case studies of experiences of foreigners (Jews, political exiles) in major cities (Venice, Paris). Recently, he also began with a trilogy that will conclude with the third study on life together in today's urban centers. The first study, *The Craftsman* (New Haven: Yale University Press, 2008), describes human beings as workers and the second study, *Together: The Rituals, Pleasures, and Politics of Cooperation* (New Haven: Yale University Press, 2012), describes human beings as workers who work together. Van Huyssteen's love for the complex and exciting ways of living together in modern cities, particularly New York, is legendary among their friends.

86. Johan Degenaar, "The Myth of a South African Nation," *Occasional Papers* 40, Institute for a Democratic Alternative for South Africa. The main argument was again published in a much shortened form as "No Sizwe: The Myth of the Nation," *Indicator South Africa* 10, no. 3 (1993): 11–16.

87. See Lynn Stout, *Cultivating Conscience: How Good Laws Make Good People* (Princeton: Princeton University Press, 2011).

88. Discussions within educational circles about education for democracy have been continuing for more than a century and in several countries, in the United States since John Dewey's influential *Democracy and Education* (1915). For an influential recent statement about the task of education to educate for democracy, and about its failure in this respect in the United States, see Martha Nussbaum, *Not for Profit: Why Democracy Needs the Humanities* (Princeton: Princeton University Press, 2010). She argues that education for democracy should perform a threefold task: developing critical and self-critical thinking skills; developing the ability for what she calls positional thinking, that is, imagining oneself in the situation of others; and developing empathy, feelings of care for others. She has of course already addressed issues

the role of respect for fundamental equality with a view to democracy,[89] they may even stress the role of commonsense judgment in the exercise of democratic culture—yet they all very often involve notions of respect for difference and otherness.

Rejoicing in Difference?

For some, however, the notion of respect sounds too empty and formal. They would prefer more positive, enthusiastic, and affirming ways of living with strangeness and strangers. For them, strangers are not merely to be tolerated, respected, and allowed to participate in democratic culture, but also to be enjoyed and celebrated. For this kind of moral code and ethical vision, what makes living with strangers possible (in fact, enjoyable, exciting, good) is not the characteristics that strangers share with us (like dignity and rights), but rather precisely what makes them different, what distinguishes them, what makes them "strange" in our eyes in the first place.

A much-celebrated scholarly contribution from this perspective came from the work of the well-known researcher of diverse communities over several decades, the German-Jewish sociologist Norbert Elias who lived and worked in Britain and the Netherlands, but also at the Center for Interdisciplinary Research in Bielefeld. In the words of his popular haiku, still hanging as the motto in the portal of this Center, "How strange these people are/How strange I am/How strange we are."[90]

Again, this acknowledgment of the richness of diversity that we have to incorporate in our moral codes and ethical discourses for living with strangers comes in many forms. Three instructive examples from three influential scholars contributing to social ethics would be the Canadian social philosopher Charles Taylor's work on "multiculturalism and the politics of recognition,"[91]

---

of education for development in her earlier *Creating Capabilities: The Human Development Approach* (Cambridge, MA: Harvard University Press, 2011).

89. Laurie Ackermann, *Human Dignity: Lodestar for Equality in South Africa* (Cape Town: Juta, 2013).

90. From his many works, see *The Established and the Outsiders*, ed. Cas Wouters (Dublin: UCD, 2008); *The Loneliness of the Dying* (Oxford: Blackwell, 1985); and the introduction by Steven Loyal and Steven Quille, eds., *The Sociology of Norbert Elias* (Cambridge: Cambridge University Press, 2004).

91. See the well-known discussion in Amy Gutmann, ed., *Multiculturalism and "The Politics of Recognition": An Essay by Charles Taylor with Commentary by Amy Gutmann, Steven C. Rockefeller, Michael Walzer, and Susan Wolf* (Princeton: Princeton University Press, 1992).

the North American philosopher Kwame Appiah's work on *Cosmopolitanism*,[92] and the German Wolfgang Huber's work on "the dignity of the different."[93]

Restoring Justice?

However, attempts to base our living with strangers on notions like reciprocity, tolerance, respect, and rejoicing in difference may all too easily mask and try to ignore the harsh realities of tension, conflict, inequality, and injustice. Evolutionary ethicists often point to the evolutionary importance of developing conflict-solving mechanisms in groups and instruments of peace-making and reconciliation.[94] Within kinship relations and small groups peace-making may already be extremely important, but perhaps easier to achieve, than between strangers sharing a common world. The reality is that what divided people from one another is very often not merely harmless, innocent, and even interesting cultural differences, but histories of competition and conflict, relationships of inequality and oppression, realities of exclusion and alienation, experiences of violence and war.[95]

The deeper challenges, therefore, of living with strangers very often have to do with finding moral codes and ethical arguments built on restoring broken relationships, finding forgiveness, confession and awareness and demonstration of guilt, achieving reconciliation, achieving healing, and—of extreme importance—restoring justice, from punitive justice to restitution,

92. See Kwame A. Appiah, *Cosmopolitanism: Ethics in a World of Strangers* (New York: Norton, 2006), but also his earlier *The Ethics of Identity* (Princeton: Princeton University Press, 2005), as well as his discussion with Amy Gutmann in their *Color Conscious: The Political Morality of Race* (Princeton: Princeton University Press, 1996).

93. See Wolfgang Huber, "The Dignity of the Different—Towards a Christian Ethics for Pluralist Societies," in *Living Theology: Essays Presented to Dirk J. Smit on His Sixtieth Birthday*, ed. Len Hansen, Nico Koopman, and Robert Vosloo (Wellington: Bible Media, 2011), 427-40. His title deliberately slightly modifies the expression and the nature of the argument used by Rabbi Jonathan Sacks, *The Dignity of Difference: How to Avoid a Clash of Civilizations* (London: Continuum, 2011).

94. See van Huyssteen's discussion of de Waal's well-known four kinds of behavior as the basis of our sociality, namely, empathy, the ability to learn and follow social rules, reciprocity, and peace-making. "Construction and Constraint," 328-29.

95. One widely known example today in church and religious circles is of course the way in which many communities struggle to rejoice in same-sex relationships; see the study by van Huyssteen's Princeton colleague William Stacy Johnson, *A Time to Embrace: Same-Gender Relationships in Religion, Law and Politics* (Grand Rapids: Eerdmans, 2006); for South African perspectives, see Paul Germond and Steve de Gruchy, eds., *Aliens in the Household of God: Homosexuality and Christian Faith in South Africa* (Cape Town: David Philip, 1997).

from punishment to pardon to restorative justice.⁹⁶ Living with strangers in the real world is not a romantic and harmonious affair, but concrete struggles to overcome our real *Trouble with Strangers* (Eagleton).

It is for this reason that ethical discourses of unity, reconciliation, and justice were at the heart of the struggles in apartheid South Africa and remain at the heart of struggles today in a so-called "new" South Africa.⁹⁷ It is obviously also for this reason that ethical discourses addressing more global challenges today also have to deal with the realities of terrorism, violence, and war, of exclusion, marginalization, and resistance, of oppression and empire.⁹⁸

Resisting the Enemy?

It is no wonder, therefore, that many accounts of altruism come up against difficult questions of range and scope. Ethical accounts of personal outreach to strangers (like extending kinship and showing hospitality) as well as accounts

---

96. For South African reflections on costly forgiveness, see Desmond M. Tutu, *No Future Without Forgiveness* (New York: Doubleday, 1999); Allan A. Boesak and Curtiss P. DeYoung, *Radical Reconciliation: Beyond Political Pietism and Christian Quietism* (Maryknoll: Orbis, 2012); also my "Restitution," in *The Oxford Encyclopedia of the Bible and Ethics*, ed. Robert L. Brawley (Oxford: Oxford University Press, 2015).

97. For South African reflections on reconciliation, see the prose works of the respected poet and social commentator Antjie Krog: *Country of My Skull* (New York: Random, 1998); *A Change of Tongue* (Cape Town: Struik, 2003); *Begging to Be Black* (Cape Town: Struik, 2010); and *There Was This Goat* (Pietermaritzburg: UKZN, 2009), written with Nosisi Mpolweni and Kopano Ratele, investigating the TRC testimony of Notrose Nobomvu Konile. See also her collected essays on South Africa since the TRC, *Conditional Tense: Memory and Vocabulary after the South African Truth and Reconciliation Commission* (Chicago: Seagull, 2013); as well as her scholarly essays dealing specifically with the notion of reconciliation, "The Young Wind Once Was a Man," *International Journal of Public Theology* 8, no. 4 (2014): 373-92, in which she explores the work of so-called indigenous /Xam informants together with the iconic figures of Nelson Mandela and Desmond Tutu to describe a specific way-of-being (fully embodied as integral part of all nature and life) that can redefine forgiveness, reconciliation, and ultimately the self; and similarly "'This Thing Called Reconciliation . . .': Forgiveness as Part of an Interconnectedness-towards-wholeness," *South African Journal of Philosophy* 27, no. 4 (2009): 353-66.

98. For South African perspectives on economic exclusion and injustice and ecological destruction, see the joint German–South African study document edited by Allan A. Boesak, Johann Weusman, and Charles Amjad-Ali, eds., *Dreaming a Different World* (Stellenbosch: Sun, 2010); for economic inequality and injustice in South Africa, see the earlier work by the Stellenbosch economist Sampie Terreblance, *A History of Inequality in South Africa 1652-2002* (Pietermaritzburg: University of KwaZulu-Natal, 2002); for power and injustice on a global scale, see his recent *Western Empires, Christianity and the Inequalities Between the West and the Rest 1500-2010* (Parklands: Penguin, 2014).

of more impersonal and systemic inclusion (like reckoning on reciprocity, demonstrating tolerance, respecting dignity, and celebrating difference) all face similar challenges. When is hospitality no longer proper and when are tolerance and respect no longer applicable? When do we come to the boundaries of our moral codes? When is forgiveness seemingly not fair, reconciliation seemingly not possible, justice seemingly not within human reach? When do strangers become potential or real enemies?

In fact, there are those who would argue that our ethical project and our moral codes need enemies, that we should regard some strangers as enemies, at least those who seem to threaten our moral worlds.[99] With the contemporary resurgence of political theologies, we are repeatedly reminded of the importance of the enemy in the political theology of Carl Schmitt, still one of the inspiring figures behind today's attempts, albeit his influence is problematic and contested.[100] Again, these questions are not merely theoretical, abstract, and innocent, but real-life, empirical, and existential challenges for ethical discourse today.[101]

Regarding Evil?

The question of the enemy directly leads to another ethical challenge, namely, the nature, presence, and role of evil in the moral codes we construct, if at all.

---

99. See the controversial but fascinating study of apocalypticism by the Boston historian Richard Landes, *Heaven on Earth: The Varieties of the Millennial Experience* (Oxford: Oxford University Press, 2011), and the importance of images of the enemy in both former and contemporary millennial movements.

100. The controversial German jurist Carl Schmitt, whose influence is today again so dominant behind the resurgence of political theologies, is well known for the central importance that he attached to the notion of the enemy. The notion of politics itself, he argued, depends on the distinction between friend and enemy. The Jewish scholar Jacob Taubes reported a private discussion that he had with Schmitt in the latter's old age, where they discussed Paul's letter to the Romans, chapter 9, and how he explained to Schmitt that enemy is mentioned together with beloved, which means that (for Paul) the enemy is now included, and there is no longer a political enemy. Schmitt was, according to Taubes, impressed, and asked him to explain that to the people before he died, which is what he did in his famous lectures on Romans, when he was literally dying, published as *The Political Theology of Paul* (Stanford: Stanford University Press, 2004). For this incident, see the book itself, as well as the appendixes.

101. For the contemporary relevance of the Schmitt doctrine, see Francis Schüssler Fiorenza, "Prospects for Political Theology in the Face of Contemporary Challenges," in Francis Schüssler Fiorenza, Klaus Tanner, Michael Welker, Johann Baptist Metz, Jürgen Moltmann, and Elisabeth Schüssler Fiorenza, *Politische Theologie: Neuere Geschichte und Potenziale* (Neukirchen: Neukirchener Theologie, 2011), 41–63; also Paul W. Kahn, *Political Theology: Four New Chapters on the Concept of Sovereignty* (New York: Columbia University Press, 2012).

In his essay on evolutionary ethics and theological ethics, van Huyssteen also raises the problem of evil, with reference to Hannah Arendt.[102] Having followed Maxine Sheets-Johnstone's evolutionary reconstruction of the roots of morality—from our bodies (moving and being moved to move) to attachment and attunement (beyond awareness) and empathy (via cognitive processes and responsivity) to moral awareness (via trust) to a rationality of care—he also follows her evolutionary reconstruction of the roots of evil, namely, the turning away from empathy (to the exclusive concern with one's own advancement and therefore to male-male competition, aggression, violence, and war).

In the banality of evil, in the mindless and thoughtless diligence to duty that Arendt (so controversially) perceived in Eichmann, we observe the devastating ethical impact of turning away from empathy. Thus, according to Sheets-Johnstone, the eventual ethical failure was rooted in an emotional failure that led to a cognitive failure that finally led to the ethical failure. For her, this shows pan-cultural roots of evil in human nature itself (present in our evolutionary development, before all later and particular cultural expressions and elaborations of this nature of human nature). For Sheets-Johnstone (and van Huyssteen) our evolutionary roots thus show the potential for evil (or lack of empathy) in human nature. The potential for evil, however, is not yet evil; since both the capacities for good and evil are innate, we have to find our own responsible ways (facing our real-life moral challenges). Van Huyssteen often stresses the notion of responsibility, in line with his overall program of postfoundational rationality, and it is worth quoting him at length here:

> Accepting that our moral awareness has evolved also means accepting that our moral codes may not be fixed forever as unchangeable entities. As humans, therefore, we are indeed free to find our own moral goals in this world and an evolutionary approach to ethics and morality helps us to understand under which circumstances we have created the kinds of values and moral

102. In fact, he deals with evil on more than one occasion; see the "Introduction" to *In Search of Self*, 1–30, where he and Erik P. Wiebe raise the question of evil directly in relation to the mystery of selfhood: "The idea of a socially constructed self, and therefore also the increasingly popular idea of multiple selves . . . could indicate that the self is something that cannot be definitely known. . . . The idea of socially constructed, multiple selves does, however, pose significant challenges for Christian theology. One challenge of moving toward a conception of multiple selves or notions of no-self is the difficult problem of evil: if there is no self, or if there are only multiple selves, it would be easy to disregard what we might call 'the potential for evil' inherent in every person. Would not the reality of multiple selves . . . help us to avoid taking full responsibility for dangerous evil acts? For those of us who are theologians, at least, might it be that the problem of evil by itself may necessitate a stronger argument for maintaining a notion of an integrated self?" (2–3).

codes that we have.... In an evolutionary approach to ethics the status of these kinds of beliefs ("the belief that ethical norms are unchangeable and derivable from some set of eternal, divine principles") will rightly be challenged, and the creation of moral norms ... will be found to lie on a constructive, cultural level. This, of course, means that humans in principle are free to change their moral codes, but this also means that humans carry great *responsibility* for themselves and that this *responsibility* cannot and should not easily be delegated to "objective divine moral codes" (in this sense, for example, even the Ten Commandments and Jesus' love command, over time, are historically revealed as a posteriori moral laws, even as they have acquired over time the authority of biblical truth). This also frees us from the foundationalist need for an idea of absolute truth; our idea of truth is relative to our historical and social contexts and their histories, and only a coherentist, postfoundationalist approach can sufficiently explain this. What we find here, then, is as an open view of evolution: basic patterns of our behaviour depend on, and have been developed through, our evolutionary past. But this is not a deterministic view, because we humans have the *responsibility* to make our own decisions on what counts as the norms and limits to our own behaviour. We are, therefore, constrained, but not determined by our evolutionary past.[103]

From their perspective, it becomes obvious how deeply problematic it would be to deny our own involvement in evil and to locate evil outside us, perhaps also in the other and the strangers. Yet, this is what has so often happened in human history and even in our moral codes and ethical discourses. Not only the enemy, but indeed evil itself (ascribed to our enemies) becomes crucial to our own moral sensibilities and ethical systems.[104]

---

103. Van Huyssteen, "Should Theology Take Evolutionary Ethics Seriously?" 459–64 (463–64); see also "Ethics and Christology," 495–96; as well as the whole essay entitled "Construction and Constraint." It is interesting that van Huyssteen's friend and South African ethicist Etienne de Villiers has over the years increasingly developed an ethical approach that he calls an ethics of responsibility; for different ways of understanding his work as an ethics of responsibility, see my essay in his festschrift, "Etienne de Villiers as Etikus van Verantwoordelikheid," *Verbum et Ecclesia* 33, no. 2 (2012).

104. See the powerful "alternative history" of modern philosophy by Susan Neiman, who also takes Hannah Arendt's account as her point of departure, in *Evil in Modern Thought: An Alternative History of Philosophy* (Princeton: Princeton University Press, 2002), and again in the third part of her *Moral Clarity* (Princeton: Princeton University Press, 2009), 299–437; also Terry Eagleton, *On Evil* (New Haven: Yale University Press, 2010); and the human rights scholar from Yale, Paul W. Kahn, *Out of Eden: Adam and Eve and the Problem of Evil* (Princeton: Princeton University Press, 2007), with the central thesis that evil did not appear in

DIRK J. SMIT

One such fascinating yet disturbing account has been given by the literary scholar from New York, Andrew Delbanco, in his *The Death of Satan: How Americans Have Lost the Sense of Evil*. Calling his book "a kind of national spiritual biography of the American people," he uses American literature through the centuries to illustrate the growing loss of the kind of Augustinian understanding of evil (as the absence of the good in all of us) and the increasing preference for an understanding in which evil is located not in us (also), but outside, in the other, the enemy and the stranger.[105] Of course, similar accounts can be provided of many other cultural, political, and religious traditions in our world today. For many of them, notions of strangeness and notions of evil easily inform one another, with dramatic—often disastrous—effects on moral codes, ethical discourses, and everyday life.

Remembering Victims?

Perhaps against this background, the German philosopher and discourse ethicist Karl-Otto Apel made his famous comments in an interview that the fundamental moral task is that "we must not forget those who are absent." According to him, this is the precondition for the universality of ethics.[106]

---

classical thought because the Greeks lacked a conception of will, which the Judeo-Christian tradition put at the center of its idea of the human, which illustrates how fundamental categories of our views of human nature are products of our cultural traditions. "*Evil*," he argues, "is the pathology of the will; it *is love gone wrong*" (3; my italics).

105. Andrew Delbanco, in his *The Death of Satan: How Americans Have Lost the Sense of Evil* (New York: Farrar, Straus and Giroux, 1995). He shows how the society increasingly moved to "the age of blame," where evil is located in the other and denied in oneself. For this reason he describes Abraham Lincoln as "the greatest Augustinian in our history" because in his Gettysburg speech he "fostered no enmity." "He held up a vision of a world drenched in sin, but free of targetable devils. The only evil that Lincoln understood, with a singleness of purpose that is both appalling and sublime, was the evil of incompleteness" (135). Perhaps it should not be surprising that Augustinian thought (also on evil) is making such a comeback today, in ethical and political theories; see the Chicago dissertation by Charles T. Mathewes, also dealing with Arendt's views on Augustine, *Evil and the Augustinian Tradition* (Cambridge: Cambridge University Press, 2001); also Stanley Hauerwas, "Seeing Darkness, Hearing Silence: Augustine's Account of Evil," in *Working with Words: On Learning to Speak Christian* (Eugene, OR: Wipf & Stock, 2011), 8–32; as well as several essays in the collection by John D. Caputo and Michael J. Scanlon, eds., *Augustine and Postmodernism: Confessions and Circumfession* (Bloomington: Indiana University Press, 2005), including an essay by Scanlon on "Arendt's Augustine," 159–72.

106. Sander Griffioen and René van Woudenberg, "We Must Not Forget Those Who Are Absent: Interview with Karl-Otto Apel on the Universality of Ethics," in *What Right Does*

This is, of course, a reminder of all those who are not already part of our moral and public discussions (future generations, as well as those marginalized and excluded today), but therefore and primarily also a reminder to remember the victims of history and the victims in our world. Victims of injustice and violence are perhaps the ultimate strangers. If they are dead, they no longer have any opportunity to become part, to be respected, to be included—except if they are remembered.

This is again a reminder of the similar approach in the influential work on the methodology of science by the German educationalist Helmut Peukert, in which he so famously argued for "anamnetic solidarity," in other words, a solidarity of memory, in which the victims of history are remembered, in some form of hope for justice.[107]

Realizing Our Own Strangeness?

In a way, this leads to the widespread and influential discourse today reflecting on the mystery of being human and of being strangers ourselves, even strangers *to* ourselves. Our being *In Search of Self*[108]—also in *this* sense that we are continuously seeking to understand more fully the mystery of our own nature and being—demonstrates how we are struggling to live with strangeness and strangers, namely, ourselves.[109]

Many of these discourses on being strangers to ourselves are not necessarily directly ethical, but they certainly have important implications for our

---

Ethics Have? Public Philosophy in a Pluralist Culture, ed. Sander Griffioen (Amsterdam: VU Press, 1990), 11–21.

107. Peukert in turn is building on a debate between Horkheimer and Benjamin. When Benjamin said that there should always remain hope for some form of justice for the victims of history, Horkheimer disparagingly commented that Benjamin was doing theology, and Peukert is interested in asking the question what kind of theology this could have been; see Helmut Peukert, *Science, Action and Fundamental Theology: Toward a Theory of Communicative Action* (Cambridge, MA: MIT, 1984).

108. See the essays in J. Wentzel van Huyssteen and Erik P. Wiebe, eds., *In Search of Self: Interdisciplinary Perspectives on Personhood* (Grand Rapids: Eerdmans, 2011), arranged under four themes, regarding the origins of our selfhood, the multiplicity of the self, questions regarding the self and identity, and the self as an emergence. From a wide variety of disciplines and perspectives, the twenty-five collaborators reflect on "the heart of the matter: the human condition, and what it is that really makes us human" (x).

109. For another illustration, see also the work of Paul Ricoeur, in his 1986 Gifford Lectures, *Oneself as Another* (Chicago: University of Chicago Press, 1992), an argument that van Huyssteen often engages with, for example, *In Search of Self*, 2–7, and then pursuing these themes extensively in the volume itself.

ethical projects and our moral codes.¹¹⁰ Sometimes, however, these discourses are indeed directly and deliberately ethical, and *do* in fact deal with some of the most burning real-life challenges of our time. The French literary scholar and psycho-analyst Julia Kristeva's work *Strangers to Ourselves* could serve as powerful illustration.¹¹¹ When she speaks about living with strangers and about having the experience of being strangers ourselves, she is referring to the everyday experience of millions of people in our world today concerning citizenship and nationality. She focuses on France, but the issue obviously affects millions of others, almost everywhere. She reflects on the experiences of foreigners, people without rights, people who cannot understand local languages, do not share local customs, do not feel they belong or that they are accepted anywhere, who do want to be integrated and who do not want to feel excluded.

Building on Freud, she astutely remarks that he deliberately did *not* speak of foreigners; instead "he teaches us how to detect foreignness in ourselves"

---

110. In John de Gruchy's search into the mystery of being human many moral implications and ethical challenges and considerations have been implicit but they have also come to the fore, in different ways; see his successive book projects on humanism, *Being Human: Confessions of a Christian Humanist* (London: SCM, 2006); *John Calvin: Christian Humanist and Evangelical Reformer* (Wellington: LuxVerbi, 2009); his edited volume *The Humanist Imperative in South Africa* (Stellenbosch: Sun, 2011); and *Led into Mystery: Faith Seeking Answers in Life and Death* (London: SCM, 2013). Perhaps one could claim that the same is true of two other long-standing South African friends of van Huyssteen, J. J. F. (Jaap) Durand and Denise M. Ackermann, who in their latest publications all focused on mystery, even on meditation and mysticism. In a definite sense the mystery of being human was of course also the theme behind van Huyssteen's own Gifford Lectures, *Alone in the World? Human Uniqueness in Science and Theology* (Grand Rapids: Eerdmans, 2006), for which he received the Andrew Murray–Desmond Tutu Prize.

111. Julia Kristeva, *Strangers to Ourselves* (New York: Columbia University Press, 1991). Yet another illustration from de Gruchy's humanism project is extraordinarily instructive and interesting. In his essay "Neurobiological Foundations" (in *The Humanist Imperative in South Africa*, ed. John W. De Grucy [Stellenbosch: Sun, 2011], 41–55) the neuropsychologist Mark Solms gives a very informative description of "the way in which the biological system of values embodied in our instincts is communicated to each individual animal," namely, through our seven feelings of seeking, pleasure, anger, fear, panic/grief, care, and play. Then he continues to argue, however, that the uniquely human aspect of our brains is a matter of the volume of the prefrontal lobes in relation to the rest of the brain, and their task is to inhibit, thereby permitting choice and allowing thinking and language. Precisely because of these abilities, however, he concludes, "we humans are uniquely ignorant of our own motivations. We do not know why we do what we do. Our actions are so far removed from the instincts that motivated them (and unconsciously guide them) that we no longer know what we are trying to achieve." For that reason we "*deny the mystery and make up a story about it,* we confabulate and we believe our own confabulations" (my italics), he says, concluding, "the human capacity for opaque motivation, self-deception and hypocrisy is *truly* unique" (his italics).

because "that is perhaps the only way not to hound it outside of us."[112] The "fundamental question," she concludes, belongs to the "metaphysical realm" since, "for the first time in history, we are confronted with the following situation: we must live with different people while relying on our personal moral codes, without the assistance of a set that would include our particularities while transcending them." A "paradoxical community" is therefore emerging, she says, "made up of foreigners who are reconciled with themselves to the extent that they recognize themselves as foreigners." We all only have and share our weakness, she concludes, "a weakness whose other name is our radical strangeness."[113]

Redeeming Kenosis?

This again leads to a final dimension to the talk about living with strangeness. Although he does not use the term "stranger," the South African cosmologist George Ellis[114] does focus on notions of enmity and evil in his own account of altruism as kenosis.[115] For him, kenosis is of fundamental importance, both metaphysically and cosmologically, since it describes for him the structure (or "deep nature") of creation and all reality, as well as ethically, since it describes for him both the nature of human nature as well as the aims of our ethical project (or "our way of action").

Ellis defines "kenosis" as "a joyous, kind, and loving attitude that is willing to give up selfish desires and to make sacrifices on behalf of others for the common good and the glory of God, doing this in a generous and creative

---

112. *Strangers to Ourselves*, 191. She continues: "Freud brings us the courage to call ourselves disintegrated in order not to integrate foreigners and even less so to hunt them down, but rather to welcome them to that uncanny strangeness which is as much theirs as it is ours" (191–92).

113. *Strangers to Ourselves*, 191.

114. George F. R. Ellis is Emeritus Distinguished Professor of Complex Systems in the Department of Mathematics and Applied Mathematics at the University of Cape Town and renowned for his contributions to theoretical physics and cosmology, for which he received the Templeton Prize in 2004. Together with Nancey Murphey, he published *On the Nature of the Universe* (Minneapolis: Fortress, 1997).

115. Ellis, "Kenosis as a Unifying Theme for Life and Cosmology," in *The Work of Love: Creation as Kenosis*, ed. John Polkinghorne (Grand Rapids: Eerdmans, 2001), 107–26. For other essays on kenosis, see the contributions by among others Ian Barbour, Arthur Peacocke, Holmes Ralston III, Malcolm Jeeves, Michael Welker, Jürgen Moltmann, Keith Ward, Paul Fiddes, and Sarah Coakley in the same volume, as well as Sir John Templeton's own *Agape Love* (West Conshohocken, PA: Templeton Foundation Press, 1999).

way, avoiding the pitfall of pride, and guided and inspired by the love of God and the gift of grace."[116] Kenosis, for him, involves a choice for generosity and forgiveness. In that way, it creates hope for reconciliation, in that "anybody can be redeemed." It means loving our enemy "rather than giving in to hate," it is the "refusal to give in to the hatred embodied in the enemy image," it applies — and "here is the hardest part" — also to the oppressors, as they too are human.[117]

It is precisely this element of kenosis which, for Ellis, is missing in many of the accounts given by proponents of socio-biology of the processes of giving up individual desires in favor of the common good, thereby creating communities and societies out of individuals with diverse interests and wishes. These descriptions, for him, often do "not encompass the full depth of the kenotic idea, for (they do) not extend to one's enemies" and do not necessarily involve "the moral power of forgiving and sacrifice."[118] In fact, he concludes — true to his own Quaker tradition — by defending a very strong notion of "the kenotic spirit," involving a refusal to go onto the "slippery slope" responding to evil with evil, which "is the dangerous road easily leading to the 'untermensch,' torture, and retaliatory genocide."[119] Over against "the standing model of the social sciences in most fields," which observes "that people in many cases act in self-interest in the political, social, and economic spheres" and from that imputes "that they ought to do so,"[120] he rather argues that kenosis is the nat-

---

116. "Unifying Theme," 108, with every phrase in this description very carefully formulated in order to prevent misunderstandings, provide motivations, and explain aspects. In the process, he argues that alternative suggestions, like notions of "enlightened self-interest" or "altruism," are not sufficient since they are not "deep" enough because they miss the "hard edge" that kenosis provides. Of special importance, for him, is the fact that kenosis depends on the nature of God (as known to us in the self-giving life of Jesus Christ). For the challenging question what the notion of the love of God could mean, see also the collected essays in Kevin J. Vanhoozer, ed., *Nothing Greater, Nothing Better: Theological Essays on the Love of God* (Grand Rapids: Eerdmans, 2001).

117. "Unifying Theme," 112.

118. "Unifying Theme," 119. In this regard, he refers to the South African experience, to Desmond Tutu's work on forgiveness, and to the movements for restorative justice that developed out of this experience. The theme of forgiveness is of course so central that it could have been mentioned as a separate ethical discourse on living with the stranger — including the challenges both of forgiving and of being forgiven.

119. "Unifying Theme," 123. For insightful discussions of the temptation to give in to practices of torture, see also the important work of van Huyssteen's immediate Princeton colleague George Hunsinger, as in his edited volume, *Torture Is a Moral Issue: Christians, Jews, Muslims, and People of Conscience Speak Out* (Grand Rapids: Eerdmans, 2008).

120. "Unifying Theme," 113. This reminds one of the — also pacifist — ethical position developed and defended by Stanley Hauerwas in his 2001 Gifford Lectures, *With the Grain of the Universe: The Church's Witness and Natural Theology* (Grand Rapids: Brazos, 2001). Both his

ural way—integral to the nature of God, to the nature of the universe, and to human nature, and therefore of our moral codes as well.

One final illustration of the same mystery, albeit a very different argument (and using incarnation rather than kenosis), is found in the work of another of van Huyssteen's collaborators, the 2010 Gifford Lectures by Roger Scruton, *The Face of God*. He closes his final lecture with a discussion of Wagner—also of such existential importance for van Huyssteen—and argues that we encounter the face of God everywhere, "in all that suffers and renounces for another's sake." He continues,

> When someone enters the moment of sacrifice, throwing away what is most precious, even life itself, *for the sake of another*, then we encounter the moment of supreme gift.... In the moment of sacrifice people come face to face with God.... We should not be surprised, therefore, if God is so rarely encountered now. The consumer culture is one without sacrifices; easy entertainment distracts us from our metaphysical loneliness. The rearranging of the world as an object of appetite obscures its meaning as a gift. The defacing of *eros* and the loss of rites of passage eliminate *the old conception of human life as an adventure within the community and an offering to others*. It is inevitable, therefore, that moments of sacred awe should be so rare among us.... You may think that this does not matter—that mankind has had enough of sacred mysteries and their well-known dangers. But ... by remaking human beings and their habitat as objects to consume rather than subjects to revere we invite the degradation of both.[121]

Being Human?

Looking back at such a (superficial) survey of contemporary ethical literature and such an (arbitrary) typology of ethical discourses on the challenges and

---

title and his motto came from the Mennonite ethicist Howard Yoder, who also claimed that this way of life is living with the grain of the universe.

121. Roger Scruton, *The Face of God* (London: Continuum, 2012), 177-78 (my italics). In his even more recent Stanton Lectures at the University of Cambridge, published as *The Soul of the World* (Princeton: Princeton University, 2014), Scruton again offers an extensive discussion of "Facing Each Other" in the broader context of his argument on naturalism and religion (96-114). For van Huyssteen's interpretation of the religious motives in Wagner, see "Building Effective Bridges to Culture: God and Redemption in the Work of Richard Wagner," in *The God of Love and Human Dignity: Essays in Honour of George M. Newlands*, ed. Paul Middleton (London: T&T Clark, 2007), 85-106.

possibilities of living with strangers, some concluding observations suggest themselves.

Many of the presuppositions of apartheid ethics at the time are in fact still alive and well today, albeit in different forms.[122] From a specifically theological and Christian perspective one could perhaps also add other contested presuppositions, all still around in other forms.[123] Regarding some of these presuppositions, specific forms of evolutionary ethics could perhaps have helped us in seeing the dangers more clearly. However, specific forms of evolutionary ethics might also have been used to strengthen the ethical arguments supporting apartheid.[124]

One only has to read the moving, sometimes terrifying historical account by Jonathan Glover with the painfully ironic title and subtitle *Humanity: A Moral History of the Twentieth Century* to realize with sadness how far we have jointly come with the ethical project.[125] Much the same could be said of present-day South Africa. Since 1983, much has changed, yet much has stayed painfully the same. Although the fall of apartheid fulfilled many hopes and alleviated many fears, one could argue that new hopes have been increasingly lost and new disappointments and fears have grown. Many of our continuing

---

122. One could mention the is-ought fallacy of ethical thought; the confusion between facts and values; the confusion between an ethics of (merely) granting others and an ethics of (really) doing unto others.

123. One could for mention the tension between ethics based on creation and ethics based on re-creation; the misuse of the medieval motto *gratia non tollit naturam sed perficit*; the misuse of natural theology traditions and natural law arguments.

124. One could mention the lack of respect for human dignity, the disregard for individual human rights, the inclination of many not to care for the weak, the regard for the group's survival more than the needs of the individual, the lack of understanding for values, the stress on instincts and natural urges, the history of eugenics—many of these convictions and arguments were indeed at work in the early days of apartheid ideology, when scientific and sociological theories at the time played an important part in what took place. On more than one occasion, van Huyssteen therefore also warns against a normative misuse of evolutionary ethics: "We should therefore be careful to always distinguish between the *evolution of moral awareness*, and the *evolutionary justification of moral codes*. Evolutionary ethics in the second sense has a bad history and has resulted in ideologies like Social Darwinism" ("Ethics and Christology," 495; again, "Construction and Constraint," 326–27).

125. Jonathan Glover, *Humanity: A Moral History of the Twentieth Century* (New Haven: Yale University Press, 2000). His seven parts successively deal with "ethics without the moral law" (in which he deals with the challenges since Nietzsche), "the moral psychology of waging war," "tribalism," "war as a trap," "belief and terror" (in which he deals with Stalin and his heirs), "the will to create mankind anew" (in which he deals with what he calls "the Nazi experiment"), and "on the recent moral history of humanity." He describes the purpose of the book as "an attempt to give ethics an empirical dimension," but it is in truth a book about "recent human barbarism" (x).

challenges and crises still have to do with our difficulties in practicing altruism and living with strangers.[126] The notion of moral progress may therefore indeed be much more complicated, controversial, and even contested than is sometimes allowed and acknowledged.[127]

Over the years, however, the important implications for ethical theory in van Huyssteen's life project became increasingly clearer. Because he takes the insight of evolutionary theories regarding our *becoming* human so seriously, it allows him to demonstrate the nature of our moral roots and the crucial importance of altruism in our search for our human selves very clearly. Because he is convinced that we cannot simply deduce our *being* human and our contemporary moral codes merely from our evolutionary roots, it allows him to very helpfully show both *that* and *how* we continuously construct our own moral codes, in the face of real-life, contextual, and existential, problems. Because this task is an ongoing and constructive ethical project he correctly stresses the fact that we cannot simply claim insight into timeless and eternal ethical truth-claims and moral values.

For those of us who work from within the Reformed tradition of Christian theology—known for its slogan *ecclesia reformata semper reformanda* and for its radically contextual and historical understanding of its own confessional tradition—van Huyssteen's stress on the ongoing, self-critical, and constructive task sounds very appealing and convincing.[128] The ongoing challenge to

---

126. As South Africans we need to recover our empathy. This was the main argument of psychologist and member of the Truth and Reconciliation Commission Pumla Gobodo-Madikizela, in her *A Human Being Died That Night: A South African Woman Confronts the Legacy of Apartheid* (New York: Houghton Mifflin, 2003), a decade ago. Today, many more observers would agree with this kind of depiction when describing the state of the nation after two decades of democracy.

127. Van Huyssteen himself of course does not understand progress in a positivistic sense as convergence to truth, but in his postfoundationalist sense as effectively answering real problems posed in a particular context and across contextual boundaries, but, when applied to morality, even such an understanding could raise skeptical questions, depending on how one reads the context with its problems. Of course, the notion of "evolution"—of humanity, of rationality, of morality—almost undeniably suggests progress. For a discussion of the notion of moral progress, see the controversial work of the Princeton philosopher Peter Singer, *The Expanding Circle: Ethics, Evolution, and Moral Progress* (Princeton: Princeton University Press, 2011).

128. He obviously must have had different experiences of the Reformed tradition and theology because, especially in his earlier work, he often took what he called Reformed theology as the prime example of the kind of eternal, unchanging, and authoritative systems against which he wanted to develop an alternative way of doing theology, but I could never recognize his experience of being Reformed in the Reformed theologians whom my generation encountered—Jonker, Durand, Bosch, Boesak, Botman—and the Reformed tradition in which

understand and practice altruism, also for those evolutionary ethicists who are of the opinion that altruism forms the basis of our moral sense and all its resulting social institutions, illustrates the nature of the ethical project. The challenge to find ways of living with strangers—as one of the ultimate tests of our altruism—very specifically serves to illustrate the nature of the ethical project.[129]

This chapter is a deliberate attempt to acknowledge, recognize, and listen to voices of many of van Huyssteen's friends and colleagues over many years—from many contexts and many experiences.[130] It has always been a

---

we worked, and this impression would only be strengthened during ongoing encounters with other theological and confessional traditions in the ecumenical church; for my experience of being Reformed, see *Essays on Being Reformed: Collected Essays 3*, ed. Robert R. Vosloo (Stellenbosch: Sun, 2009); *Opstelle oor Gereformeerd-wees vandag: Versamelde Opstelle 4*, ed. Len D. Hansen (Stellenbosch: Sun, 2009); or more recent essays, "Reformed Ethics," in *Dictionary of Scripture and Ethics*, ed, Joel B. Green and Jacqueline E. Lapsley (Grand Rapids: Baker, 2011), 661-64; "Trends and Directions in Reformed Theology," *The Expository Times 7*, no. 122 (April 2011): 1-14; "'No Polycarps Among Us'? Questions for Reformed Political Theology Today," *Studies in Christian Ethics: Critical Directions and Developments in Reformed Theological Ethics* 28, no. 2 (2015).

129. In July 2014, we were privileged to discuss several of these issues in Princeton, when the van Huyssteens had already left their Seminary house of twenty-five years and were staying for a few days like visitors in Payne Hall, waiting to return to South Africa after twenty-five years, after visiting children and grandchildren in California. In their own lives, the van Huyssteen family experienced many of these challenges of living with strangers and being strangers over many decades—up to the very practical and painful experiences that Kristeva deals with, including residence permits, passports, visas, the right to vote, always having family in different places, and always leaving someone behind. Van Huyssteen never wrote about these practical moral problems and ethical considerations in his own academic work. For their friends, however, there was never any doubt about their shared commitment to moral visions and values related to life with the other and the stranger, both in South Africa and abroad. Over many years, Hester van Huyssteen's passion and personal engagement for moral causes was always deeply appreciated by many of their friends—acceptance and inclusion of outsiders; bridging divides and reconciliation; care for the poor; defending the rights of minorities, including language rights; opposing war and violence; a strong sense of fairness and justice and a willingness to speak out, when necessary.

130. In a way, it was therefore an attempt to practice the narrative extension of human self-awareness and consciousness that Ricoeur argued for in many different ways (in *Oneself as Another*; in *Time and Narrative*; in *The Course of Recognition*; and in *Memory, History, Forgetting*), and which van Huyssteen has been taking increasingly seriously in his recent work, also at STIAS. Sharing our stories, our recollections, and our memories enables us "to deeply empathize and identify with others . . . it propels us through empathy, beyond self-reference to relationships with others. . . . It is this extension of the 'circle of selfhood' that . . . ultimately liberates us from an all-consuming narcissistic interest without liquidating ourselves as selves. Narrative understanding thus generates a basic act of empathy whereby the self flows from

privilege and great joy to have him as friend and conversation partner over several decades. In different ways all these friends were struggling with the same issues—being human and not being alone in our world. Contemporary ethical discourses attempt different ways of finding adequate language to talk about strangers in order to develop moral codes and find concrete ways to live together. Some of these discourses may sound abstract and innocent; in reality they are about life and death.

---

itself toward the other in a free variation of imagination. Thus narrative imagination transforms self-regarding into a self-for-another" (*In Search of Self*, 4); again in his still unpublished Dawid de Villiers Lectures, Stellenbosch, November 2014, "Theology and the Archaeology of Personhood." For a similar interest, see the recent work of the Stellenbosch systematic theologian Robert R. Vosloo, "Memory, History, and Justice: In Search of Conceptual Clarity," *Nederduitse Gereformeerde Teologiese Tydskrif* 53 (2012), Supplementum 3:215–27; and "The Writing of History as Remedy or Poison? Some Remarks on Paul Ricoeur's Reflections on Memory, Identity and 'the Historiographical Operation,'" in *Texts, Contexts and Methods: Reflections on Historiography and Identity in the Persian Period Jehud*, ed. Louis Jonker (Munich: Mohr Siebeck), 11–28. Perhaps one could therefore claim that these friends of many years were all doing in their different places and in diverse ways what van Huyssteen has been justifying in his own academic project, namely, pursuing ethical discourses and constructing moral codes with a view to living together with strangers in a challenging real world.

Contributors

M. Craig Barnes is president of Princeton Theological Seminary.

Justin L. Barrett is professor of psychology at Fuller Theological Seminary's Graduate School of Psychology and chief project developer at the Office for Science, Theology, and Religion Initiatives.

John Hedley Brooke was the first Andreas Idreos Professor of Science and Religion at Oxford University, where he is an emeritus fellow of Harris Manchester College. He is the author of many books and articles, including *Science and Religion: Some Historical Perspectives* (1991).

D. Etienne de Villiers is emeritus professor in the faculty of theology of the University of Pretoria, South Africa. He taught Christian ethics and professional ethics for engineers and is currently working on a monograph on the contemporary relevancy of Max Weber's ethic of responsibility.

Celia Deane-Drummond is professor of theology and director of the Center for Theology, Science and Human Flourishing at the University of Notre Dame. She is the author of *Wonder and Wisdom: Conversations in Science, Spirituality and Theology* (2006), *Christ and Evolution* (2009), and *The Wisdom of the Liminal: Evolution and Other Animals in Human Becoming* (2014).

David Fergusson is professor of divinity and principal of New College at the University of Edinburgh. He is the author of *Creation* (2014) and coeditor (with Paul T. Nimmo) of *The Cambridge Companion to Reformed Theology* (2016).

Agustín Fuentes is professor and chair of the department of anthropology at the University of Notre Dame. He is the author of *Evolution of Human Behavior* (2008) and *Biological Anthropology: Concepts and Connections* (2011).

Tyler S. Greenway is a research fellow and doctoral candidate at Fuller Theological Seminary's Graduate School of Psychology.

Niels Henrik Gregersen is professor of systematic theology at the University of Copenhagen. He is the coeditor of *Information and the Nature of Reality: From Physics to Metaphysics* (2010) and the author of *Incarnation: On the Scope and Depth of Christology* (2014).

Ian Hodder is the Dunlevie Family Professor in the department of anthropology at Stanford University. He is the author of *Reading the Past: Current Approaches to Interpretation in Archaeology* (2003) and *Entangled: An Archaeology of the Relationships between Humans and Things* (2012).

Christopher Lilley is a teaching fellow and PhD candidate in systematic theology and philosophy at Marquette University.

Daniel J. Pedersen holds a PhD in theology from Princeton Theological Seminary.

Richard Potts is director of the Human Origins Program at the US National Museum of Natural History. He is also curator of the Smithsonian's Hall of Human Origins and is the author of the companion book *What Does It Mean to Be Human?* (2010).

Michael Ruse is director of the Program in History and Philosophy of Science at Florida State University. He is the founding editor of the journal *Biology and Philosophy* and edits a series in the philosophy of biology for Cambridge University Press.

Dirk J. Smit is distinguished professor of systematic theology at Stellenbosch University and honorary professor at the Humboldt University in Berlin. He has published extensively in Reformed theology, public theology, and ethical theory.

CONTRIBUTORS

Ian Tattersall is curator emeritus in the Division of Anthropology at the American Museum of Natural History. He is the author of *Masters of the Planet: The Search for Our Human Origins* (2012) and *The Rickety Cossack and Other Cautionary Tales from Human Evolution* (2015).

Keith Ward is Emeritus Regius Professor of Divinity at the University of Oxford and professorial research fellow at Heythrop College. He is the author of *God: A Guide for the Perplexed* (2013) and *Christ and the Cosmos* (2016).

Michael Welker is professor and director of the Research Center for International and Interdisciplinary Theology at the University of Heidelberg. He is the author of many books, including *Gottes Geist: Theologie des Heiligen Geistes* (2015) and *Gottes Offenbarung: Christologie* (2016); he is the coeditor of *The Depth of the Human Person* (2014).

Wesley J. Wildman is professor of philosophy, theology, and ethics at Boston University School of Theology. He is the author of *Religious and Spiritual Experiences* (2011) and *Science and Religious Anthropology* (2016).

Index of Authors

Appiah, Kwame, 299
Aquinas, Thomas, 120, 123, 215, 223, 246
Arendt, Hannah, 3, 211, 255
Aristotle, 138, 215, 217, 220, 143–44, 148
Armstrong, James, 192–93
Asad, T., 48
Assmann, J., 229
Audi, Robert, 221
Augustine, 159, 217
Ayer, A. J., 118

Balswick, Jack O., 70
Barbour, Ian, 185–86
Barr, James, 3
Barrett, Justin L., 64–68, 71–72
Barth, Karl, 19–20, 133
Bayertz, Kurt, 260
Bellah, R., 50, 54
Bentham, Jeremy, 264
Berger, Peter L., 141
Beyer, Peter, 261
Bloch, M., 46, 85
Bolhuis, J. J., 36
Botha, Rudolf, 244
Boyer, Pascal, 17, 48, 49, 237
Breiner, Peter, 259
Brooks, A. S., 100
Brown, Delwin, 10

Brown, Harold, 11
Bultmann, Rudolf, 248

Calvin, John, 19
Camus, Albert, 134
Cantor, Geoffrey, 182, 190
Clayton, Philip, 9
Clough, David, 220, 239, 240–41
Coakley, Sarah, 202, 203, 206, 208, 209, 210, 213

Darwin, Charles, 28, 161, 214, 247
Davidson, Donald, 8
Dawkins, Richard, 99–100, 133, 169–70, 206, 216
Deacon, Terrence, 92
Deane-Drummond, Celia, 82–83
Degenaar, Johan, 297
De Gruchy, John, 275
Deleuze, Gilles, 146–47
Dennett, Daniel, 133
De Villiers, D. Etienne, 260, 265
De Waal, Frans, 217–22
Dewey, John, 138, 142–43, 264
Diamond, Jared, 136
Dilthey, Wilhelm, 264

Eagleton, Terry, 289, 300

INDEX OF AUTHORS

Edelman, Gerald, 139
Edwards, Jonathan, 160–61
Eldredge, Niles, 135
Elias, Norbert, 298
Ellis, George, 307, 308

Feldman, Marcus, 86
Feuerbach, Ludwig, 133
Frankfurt, Harry, 287
Fuentes, Agustín, 207, 212, 219, 223

Gell, A., 50
Gibson, James J., 138–39, 142
Gilbert, Margaret, 291
Gilligan, Carol, 285
Gironi, Fabio, 8
Glover, Jonathan, 310
Gould, Stephen J., 135, 167, 169
Gray, Asa, 164, 247–48
Gregersen, Niels Henrik, 1, 9

Haidt, Jonathan, 74
Haldane, J. B. S., 157
Halfwassen, J., 228
Hamm, B., 233
Harris, Mark, 236
Harris, Sam, 154
Hartshorne, Charles, 153
Hawking, Stephen, 114
Heidegger, Martin, 44, 134, 185
Henshilwood, C., 34
Hitchens, Christopher, 154
Hodder, Ian, 18
Hodge, Charles, 247
Huber, Wolfgang, 299

Ingold, T., 44

Jablonka, Eva, 87
James, William, 138, 143, 264
Jarvinen, Matthew J., 66–68, 71–72
Jenson, Robert W., 18
Johnson, Dominic, 210
Jonas, Hans, 250

Kant, Immanuel, 12, 153–54, 264

Kelemen, Deborah, 77
Keller, Evelyn Fox, 195–97
Kendall, Jeremy, 86
King, Pamela E., 70
Kitcher, Philip, 281, 292, 294
Klein, R., 32, 33
Kloppenberg, James, 264
Knight, Chris, 244
Kort, Wesley, 291
Kuhn, Thomas, 5

Lahti, David, 256
Lakatos, Imre, 5–6, 8
Laland, Kevin N., 86
Lamb, Marion, 87
LaPlace, P., 127
Latour, Bruno, 20
Laudan, Larry, 5, 11
Lindbeck, George, 7
Lloyd, Geoffrey, 175–76
Loubser, Gys, 1
Luckmann, Thomas, 141
Luther, Martin, 194, 226

Magnus, Albertus, 215
Maximus the Confessor, 239, 245–46
McBrearty, S., 100
McFarland, Ian, 245
McKie, Robin, 240
McMullin, Ernan, 8
Merleau-Ponty, Maurice, 2, 16
Merton, Robert, 180
Meskell, L., 49, 54
Meyer, B., 48, 53
Mithen, Steven, 15, 17
Moritz, Joshua, 239
Morris, Simon Conway, 242
Müller, Hans-Peter, 257
Munch, Edvard, 134
Münch, Richard, 261
Murphy, Nancey, 8

Neville, Robert Cummings, 142, 153
Nietzsche, Friedrich, 135, 149
Nowak, Martin, 202, 205, 209

Odling-Smee, F. John, 86

Index of Authors

Pacey, Arnold, 178, 191–92, 194
Pannenberg, Wolfhart, 5–6, 20
Pattison, George, 177–78, 185
Peirce, Charles Saunders, 138
Pelagius, 217
Peterson, Gregory, 214
Pinker, Steven, 161
Plato, 126
Polkinghorne, John, 183
Popper, Karl, 5–6
Putman, Hilary, 260
Pythagoras, 145

Rahner, Karl, 154
Rawls, John, 254
Reeves, Josh, 10
Reid, Thomas, 249
Reimer, Kevin S., 70
Rescher, Nicholas, 9, 11, 15, 252, 254
Reynhout, Kenneth A., 1
Ricoeur, Paul, 3
Robinson, J. T., 29
Rosaldo, R., 44
Russell, Robert J., 7

Sandel, Michael, 257–58
Sartre, Jean-Paul, 12, 135
Schleiermacher, Friedrich, 152
Schmitt, Carl, 301
Schrag, Calvin, 11–12, 252–53
Scruton, Roger, 309
Sennett, Richard, 296
Sheets-Johnstone, Maxine, 2–3, 211, 255, 302
Shults, F. LeRon, 1, 70
Sidgwick, William, 264

Smail, Daniel Lord, 17
Smit, Dirk, 270
Smith, Christian, 214
Sosis, Richard, 84
Stapleton, T. J., 12
Sterelny, Kim, 89
Stringer, Chris, 240

Tattersall, Ian, 18, 27, 32, 33, 36, 37, 38, 236, 240, 244
Taylor, Charles, 6–7, 298
Templeton, A. R., 35
Thompson, John B., 3
Tillich, Paul, 133, 143
Tödt, Heinz-Eduard, 270

Van Huyssteen, J. Wentzel, 25, 64–65, 132–34, 151–52, 155, 174–77, 197, 208–15, 225, 250–56, 262–70, 273, 275, 276, 278, 302, 311
Varela, Francisco, 139, 142

Wake, David, 86
Walzer, Michael, 261
Weber, Max, 57, 250, 257–62, 263–66
Weinberg, Steven, 115, 116
West-Eberhard, Mary Jane, 87
Wheeler, P., 9
Whitehead, Alfred North, 138–39, 142–44, 147, 151–53
Wildman, Wesley J., 151–52
Wilkinson, David, 242
Wolterstorff, Nicholas, 67, 296
Wrangham, R., 31
Wuketits, Frank, 16

Index of Subjects

Adam and Eve, 129, 157–59
Adaptability, 103–5, 108
Aesthetic judgment, 179–97
Altruism, 282, 283, 284, 287, 288, 289, 290, 291, 292, 312
Angels, 72
Anthropocentrism, 238–41, 244, 246–47
Anthropology, 236
Anthropomorphism, 132–33, 152–53
Apartheid, 274
Architecture, 185, 190–92
Art, 176–78, 189, 191, 194
Australopithecines, 65
Australopithecus, 30
Axiology, 132–55

Beauty: in architecture, 193; in science, 181–84; in scientific instruments, 193; in technology, 193–94
Belhar Confession, 273
Biblical literalism, 3
Bipedality, 28–30
Body phenomenology, 2, 16
Bull horns, 45, 51, 53

Canon, 229
Cartesian dualism, 114
Çatalhöyük, 43, 64–65

Chain of being, 220
Chance and free will, 126
Chimpanzees, 69–70
Christian ethics, 251, 255
Christianity, 53, 56
Christology, 14, 19–20, 244, 246
Clockwork universe, 187–88
Cognition, 132–44, 152–53
Cognitive fluidity, 175, 178, 197
Cognitive pluralism, 13
Cognitive science, 68; of religion, 76
Commitments: religious, 5, 7
Community niche, 91
Complex systems, 135–44
Continuity/discontinuity, 19
Cosmos: as open and emergent, 127, 128
Creation, 238, 247
Creative explosion, 100
Culture: unity-diversity, 102, 109

Darwinian evolution, 158, 163, 164, 211, 212, 213
Denisovan, 66
Differentiation, 261–62
Dinka, 49
Disease, 186, 196
Dogmatic loci, 230
Dogmatics: legal and theological, 227

Index of Subjects

Dogs, 74–77
Domestication, 64–65, 72, 74–79
Dominion, 72–75, 78–79

Embodiment, 137–40, 143–44; of human beings, 5, 14, 17, 19
Empirical/subjective reasons, 13
Empiricism, 118
Engagement, 137, 139–49
Enlightenment, 224
Entanglement, 44, 47, 50, 52
Epigenetics, 128, 129; inheritance, 87
Epistemic responsibility, 252–53
Epistemology, 5, 10, 13, 14–16, 21; evolutionary, 13–17
Eschatology, 245–49
Ethics, 275, 281, 297; normative, 255–56; of responsibility, 250, 257–70
Eugenics, 195
Evolution, 120, 123, 124, 277, 282, 291; mode of, 26, 38; theistic, 164–66
Existential situations, 233
Explanation: causal/semantic, 4, 8; *explanans/explanandum*, 6
Extinction, 105–7
Extra-terrestrial life, 241–42

First-/second-order statements, 5, 7
Foundationalism/nonfoundationalism, 10
Free agency, 119
Free will, 40

Genesis, 65, 72–75, 79, 238, 243
Gifford Lectures, 236–49
Göbekli Tepe, 43
God: concept of, 226–28; nature of, 117
Grace, 130

Hermeneutics, 3–4, 8, 10, 12
Homo floresiensis, 156
Homo habilis, 65
Homo sapiens, 31, 65, 156, 203, 212, 238, 244, 247; origin and evolution of, 96, 100–105, 108
Homo sapiens sapiens, 88
Homo species, 30–33

INDEX OF SUBJECTS

Professional ethos, 232
Providence, 245–49
Psychology, 70; cognitive, 65, 77; developmental, 68, 77; evolutionary, 65–66; social, 73
Purpose, 104–8; in evolution, 125, 128

Quantum vacuum, 113

Rationality, 252–54, 276; dimensions of, 11–12; and faith, 5, 8, 11
Realism: critical, 1, 4–5, 7, 8; scientific, 8
Redescription, 4, 8
Reformation: four *sola*s, 233
Relativism, 3
Religion, 64–65, 71
Resurrection, 248

Scripture: authority of, 228–30; fourfold weight of, 228–30
Sedentism, 75–76
Semiotic species, 92
Sisters of Charity, 205
Skulls, 51, 60
Smithsonian Institution, 97–98
Soul, 120–23
Spiritual body, 124
Stone tools, 31–33

Strangers, 288, 291, 292, 293
Subjectivist faith, 234
Suffering, 49
Supernaturalism, 8, 21
Symbolic: awareness, 15, 17–20; behavior, 101–3, 109; inheritance, 87; thought, 34–35

Teresa, Mother, 204, 205
Theology, 225–35; academic, 230; institutionalized, 232; interdisciplinary, 1–2, 9–10, 19; postliberal, 7; practical, 232
Theory of mind (ToM), 68–74, 79; higher-order (HO-ToM), 65–71, 73, 78–79; representational, 69
Theōsis, 125
Tolerance, 294, 295
Tool, 73, 76–77
Transcendence, 50
Transdisciplinarity, 95
Transversality, 12
Truth, 226, 234

Umwelt, 88, 93
Unknowns, 18

Value: intrinsic, 116–17

www.ingramcontent.com/pod-product-compliance
Lightning Source LLC
Chambersburg PA
CBHW031250230426
43670CB00005B/116